APPROVING SOFTWARE PRODUCTS

M. Ghiassi

APPROVING SOFTWARE PRODUCTS

Proceedings of the IFIP WG 5.4 Working Conference on Approving Software Products (ASP-90)
Garmisch-Partenkirchen, F.R.G., 17–19 September, 1990

Edited by

WOLFGANG EHRENBERGER
Gesellschaft für Reaktorsicherheit Forschungsgelände
Garching, F.R.G.

1990

NORTH-HOLLAND
AMSTERDAM · NEW YORK · OXFORD · TOKYO

ELSEVIER SCIENCE PUBLISHERS B.V.
Sara Burgerhartstraat 25
P.O. Box 211, 1000 AE Amsterdam, The Netherlands

Distributors for the United States and Canada:
ELSEVIER SCIENCE PUBLISHING COMPANY INC.
655 Avenue of the Americas
New York, N.Y. 10010, U.S.A.

Library of Congress Cataloging-in-Publication Data

IFIP WG 5.4 Working Conferences on Approving Software Products (1990 : Garmisch-Partenkirchen, Germany)
Approving software products : proceedings of the IFIP WG 5.4 Working Conference on Approving Software Products (ASP-90), Garmisch-Partenkirchen, F.R.G., 17-19 September, 1990 / edited by Wolfgang Ehrenberger.
p. cm.
Includes bibliographical references.
ISBN 0-444-88843-8
1. Computer software--Evaluation--Congresses. 2. Computer software--Quality control--Congresses. I. Ehrenberger, W. D. II. Title.
QA76.76.E93I35 1990
005.3'028'7--dc20 90-7802
CIP

ISBN: 0 444 88843 8

Printed in The Netherlands.

FOREWORD

The need for **high quality software products** increases as software gets involved in wider application areas and as it is used more and more by the broad public. The problems of software quality have been known for a long time; it is only until recently, however, that the idea of protection of the **"normal" user** against poor product quality came up. This has lead to the concept of a software **quality sign** or software quality seal.

This concept was supported by **juridical** aspects of software quality: **liability** and **guarantee** of certain services. The quality sign should make visible to the user that he gets a good product and that its services can be insured, as other products' services can.

The aspects of **software licensing** have had their first roots in the qualification of software for safety or security purposes and their second ones in the formal **certification** of compilers and of software for telecomunications. In such areas standards for the requirements of the software products exist. This is not so for general purpose software at present. In this case it is the **product description** that tells the potential buyer what he may expect. If a certain quality is being claimed that description shall not mislead the customer and it shall provide a firm basis in the legal sense.

So, open points are among others:

- **protection of the broad public against poor software quality,**
- **issuing quality signs,**
- **liability and guarantee of service,**
- **proper information of the customer.**

These aspects can not be treated exhaustively by individual companies or countries. They are as international as the distribution of software products is. I am grateful that the **Commission of the European Communities** has recognized that challange; it has created the **project SCOPE** for investigating the related areas and proposing solutions. This conference presents preliminary results. The **International Federation for Information Processing** and the **TC7 of the European Workshop of Industrial Computer Systems** have also taken up the issue of software certification as an important one and have therefore decided to sponsor this event. IFIP Working Group 2.3 has cooperated in the International Programme Committee. The Gütegemeinschaft Software, the Gesellschaft für Informatik and the Gesellschaft für Meß- und Automatisierungstechnik have given their help. It is my pleasure to thank all of them.
This conference and the contributions to this volume are meant as a forum for discussion of the above mentioned questions. May they form a step towards the International Standards that we are needing in this area.

To my knowedge this is the first time that the item of approving general purpose software and its certification is the only topic of an international conference. I would like to **thank all authors** of this volume for their contributions to this new and important area and hope that the readers find the necessary guidance for their problems in this challenging field of informatics and law.

Wolfgang Ehrenberger
Garching, Germany

Sponsors

IFIP	International Federation for Information Processing WG 5.4
EWICS	European Workshop on Industrial Computer Systems, TC 7 "Systems Reliability, Safety and Security"
VDI/VDE/ GMA	Gesellschaft für Meß- und Auto- matisierungstechnik des Vereins Deutscher Ingenieure und des Verbands Deutscher Elektrotechniker
GGS	Gütegemeinschaft Software
GI	Gesellschaft für Informatik

International Programme Committee

N. Abu al Ata	(F)	
S. Bologna	(I)	
F. Copigneaux	(F)	
B.K. Daniels	(UK)	
W. Ehrenberger	(D)	(Chairman)
R. Galego	(E)	
M. Lehmann	(UK)	
S. Lindskov Hansen	(DK)	
G. Knorr	(D)	
R. Konakowski	(D)	
J.C. Lauture	(CEC)	
B. Littlewood	(UK)	
T. Moynihan	(IRL)	
M. Maiocchi	(I)	
D.L. Parnas	(CND)	
J.M.A. Rata	(F)	
G. Schildt	(A)	
I.C. Smith	(UK)	
J. Zalewski	(PL)	

National Organizing Committee

W. Ehrenberger
H.L. Hausen
G. Knorr

TABLE OF CONTENTS

SESSION 1

STANDARDS AND CERTIFICATION 1

Approving Software Products
W. Ehrenberger (Editor)
Elsevier Science Publishers B.V. (North-Holland)
IFIP, 1990

IT SYSTEMS, SOFTWARE QUALITY STANDARDS, CERTIFICATION AND LEGAL ASPECTS WITHIN ESPRIT

CEC/DGXIII-ESPRIT Programme

I. FROM QUALITY TO CERTIFICATION

The ESPRIT programme (started in 1984) is pursuing its efforts in reliability, testing, safety and security. After a progressive launch of projects, the following topics are now covered:

- i Quality, Dependability, Reliability models and tools (REQUEST, TRUST, MUSE, PDCS).
- ii European data base on quality metric (REQUEST, SCOPE).
- iii Fault Tolerance (SMART, DELTA4, REQUEST, PDCS).
- iv Productivity assessments (evaluation of quality impact on productivity, and cost estimation) (COSMOS, MERMAID, SPEM).
- v Quality of management, clerical and safety critical systems (MUSE).
- vi Testing and software reliability (TRUST, REQUEST, DESCARTES).
- vii Software Maintenance (MACS, REDO).
- viii Accuracy of Numerical Data Processing (DIAMOND).
- ix Software CertificatiOn Programme in Europe (SCOPE).
- x Secure Office systems (MARS).
- xi Demonstration of Reliability for Safety Computer Systems (DARTS).
- xii Development of methodologies for non-functional requirement specification (dependability, usability,...)(ORDIT).
- xiii KBS validation (methods and tools) (VALID).
- xiv Metrics Education Toolkit (METKIT).

These, and future actions coming within the new workprogramme are intended to contribute to improving the quality of European software and systems. Consequently further actions related to safety systems, standards consensus, and technology-transfer needs may follow. Project SCOPE is a major player, taking into account past ESPRIT results, and ensuring the link with official bodies.

II FROM CERTIFICATION TO THE USE OF FORMAL METHODS

THE ESPRIT ROLE AND SUPPORT

Formal methods are a natural science, giving the chance to designers, testers and maintainers to perform their respective task in a non-empiric way.
Mis-used or inappropriate formal methods have led to some reluctance from a part of the system engineering community. It may appear that there is only a small gain in using FM, in particular if the use of FM for safety purpose, is not requested, or if the productivity gain is not proved.
However, quality requirements are becoming more and more precise, drastic, and necessary, and this implies directly (e.g. formal proofs) or indirectly (e.g. the functional description languages) the use of formal methods. We may also situate the areas of application of formal methods against the present major key problems of system development, which are the following ones:

1 - loss of creativeness, by lack of rigour
2 - loss of trace of past actions
3 - heterogenity of developments
4 - reliability and safety not specified and not proved
5 - productivity minimum
6 - lack of quality

Formal Methods aims to address these issues, and this will have an impact on many aspects of human activities. For instance we have FM for CAD VLSI, for management, etc, and we can imagine the benefits we may gain form the use of Formal Methods, and of their genericity.

The ESPRIT role is to answer to the above requirements by encouraging, standards, methods support tools and environment for the use of Formal Methods. This explains why we have globally, at this moments, more than 100 universities and 50 companies which are involved in Formal Methods through the ESPRIT programme.

The ESPRIT actions have been divided in three steps:

1. First call '84: Launch of seven projects (around 100 man years), supporting main streams of different life cycle views:

    RAISE (RLS VDM based);
    SEDOS (Lotos, Estelle);
    PROSPECTRA (Pannda, Ada/Anna based);
    METEOR (Erae, Cold);
    TOOL-USE (Deva);
    GRASPIN (Segras language for incremental graphical specifications);
    GIPE (Centaur system, generation of environments).

2. Second and third call ('86-'87): Launch of complementary B-type projects, either development, or application oriented.

   Development:
   DRAGON, REPLAY, KNOSOS (Methods for reusability);
   FORMAST (Development of asynchronous systems);
   GENESIS (Environment for proof applications).

   Applications:
   VIP (VDM spec of the PCTE interface);
   SEDOS-DEMO (Estelle environment);
   FORFUN (Analog/Digital circuits);
   ATES (Environment and proofs for scientific applications).

3. The first ESPRIT II call ('88) which was oriented on integration of past results and industrialisation

   ICARUS (requirement capture)
   LOTOSPHERE (Lotos environment)
   COSMOS (Cos Management with metrics of Specification)
   REDO (proving concept for maintenance applications)

DIRECTIONS FOR THE FUTURE FOR USE OF FORMAL METHODS

At this stage a new generation of tools and environments are making the use and the re-use of formal methods, very manageable and in a productive way. We also are observing an integration and a convergence of the initial streams. This is concretised by:

i) many ongoing industrial applications,

ii) environments to go on the market (e.g. from projects RAISE, GIPE (Centaur), GENESIS, ESTELLE DEMO (EWS), PROSPECTRA, etc... (SYN 89), and

iii) European or ISO standards for key languages such as ESTELLE, LOTOS, VDM, RSL.

After a five-year period of maturation, a more industrial use of formal methods, by means of these new tools, and the number of teams which have been trained, should be imminent.

A new set of projects are going to be launched, covering these three areas:

1. Integration and demonstration of generic technologies for system integration.

2. The use of FM in producing large scale industrial systems.

3. Formal methods for KB design.

Moreover the specific area of system verification and validation, is also a key topic to be covered in future calls. All this will hopefully contribute to a new level of use of formalisms, that is to say, to integrate FM ion new support developments systems, to us FM for large scale system quality, and to implement FM for AI systems.

III CERTIFICATION CONFORMANCE TESTING AND STANDARDS

A EUROPEAN SCENE MORE STRUCTURED AND MORE TRANSPARENT

EC policy has been to support European umbrella organisations for active standard and certification bodies, inside the CEN-CENELEC (MoU89). Through CEN-CENELEC two main actions are currently under way to focus national activities at a European level:

1. EC quality label: With the 1992 market objective, new structures for certification are being set up by CEN-CENELEC. These new structures or global coordinating bodies for certification are inside the EOTC (European Organisation for Testing and Certification), the ECITC (European Sectorial Committee for IT Testing and Certification - vertical), and the EQS (European Quality Specialised Committee -horizontal).

2. EC standards (EN): CEN-CENELEC is also sponsoring European panel groups, for standardisation which aims:

i) to obtain harmonised standards;
ii to expand national markets to European markets;
iii) to be in a better position for ISO standards.

In order to speed-up the take-off of this mechanism and to make it more efficient, cooperation between the European organisations, is a key topic. This implies that everybody concerned with certification and standard procedures:

i) should know the national representatives of the official bodies (CEN, ECMA, ISO,...);

ii) should implement liaisons with the right contact points, synchronised with other country initiatives if possible;

iii) to chose an order of standardisation procedures, which reinforce the European position (e.g.: firstly CEN-CENELEC, secondly ISO);

iv) to make sure that all body representatives are aware of what is happening at different places, in order to avoid duplication of work, and increase the efficiency of the successive procedures.

IT CONFORMANCE AND STANDARDS

The EC is actively supporting improvements of homogeneity, productivity and quality of the IT industry, the support for European standards, and European conformance testing services.

This explains the strategy of ESPRIT and CTS programmes which have respectively sponsored:

- The PCTE interface standard, language standards (PROLOG, LISP, VDM...), support of existing language standards such as ADA, and the project SCOPE.

- The provision of independent third party testing and assessment service of the technical conformance to OSI, ISO and EN standards.

IV. LEGAL ASPECTS FOR IT SYSTEMS

The need for legal assessments, harmonisation, and evaluations in EC is quite important for the two following reasons:

1. IT systems involve new technologies, which are still not well perceived. This may explain why we have such assessments as "Software is unmaterial" which prevents to consider software as a product.

2. As for norms and certification, a significant range of IT legal aspects has to be covered and harmonised between the different EC countries.

Consequently there is an important need to cover all legal aspects related to:

- property rights;
- safety, security, quality, certification;
- tax (VAT or customs rights).

However, for the first two points there is a start for legal bases and regulations:

* Proposal for a council directive on the legal protection of computer programs (COM (88) 816 final-SYN 183, 17 March 1989).
* Council directive concerning general product safety (COM (89) 162 final SYN 192, 7 June 1989: Official Journal).

V. CONCLUSION

Through the different European actions which are under way (EOQC, EWICS, CTS, ESPRIT, CEN-EOTC, etc.), and the coming results, the Quality Challenge is taken seriously, but everybody has to deal with the fact that coordination must be increased. Indeed, from the quality of development to reciprocal recognition or to the delivery of an EC seal, all procedures, tools and services have to be ready, accepted and available to the largest industrial audience, in a coherent and transparent way.

To comply to these requirements for success, it is necessary that major efforts are made between all existing bodies:

i) avoiding duplication of panels, tasks, standards;

ii) ensuring complementarity of panels, tasks, standards;

iii) ensuring transparency and information between all national body representatives. A map of all contact points in Europe and all ongoing work should always be available and updated.

Finally, the European software market could be better defined if software is considered as a real product. This remains a major improvement to be legally implemented. This will allow the European IT and software industries to work under a clear economic situation.

<u>*REFERENCE*</u>

SYN89: For further information, project synopses can be obtained from the CEC, ESPRIT INFORMATION OFFICE, DGXIII/A2, BRE 10/178, Rue de la Loi 200, B-1049 Brussels.

Approving Software Products
W. Ehrenberger (Editor)
Elsevier Science Publishers B.V. (North-Holland)

The SCOPE Project: an Overview

Philippe Robert and Alain Roan
VERILOG
150 rue Nicolas Vauquelin - 31081 TOULOUSE Cedex - France
Phone: (33) 61.40.38.88 - Fax: (33) 61.40.84.52
e-mail: Philippe_Robert_VERILOG@eurokom.ie

1 - INTRODUCTION

The aim of this paper is to present the SCOPE project which is supported by the Commission of European Communities under the second phase of the ESPRIT programme (P 2151). SCOPE started at the beginning of March 1989 and is to last 4 years. Now, after one year, the first results are available and are presented below.

SCOPE is an acronym for Software CertificatiOn Programme in Europe. SCOPE's aims are to develop and to put into practice technology for Software Certification before it can be standardized and finally implemented.

1.1 - Objectives of the Project

More precisely, SCOPE's main objective is to propose a general scheme allowing the certification of software against a specification. The scheme should apply to all type of software, from commercial packages to embedded software for safety critical systems; however, critical software in areas already covered by existing certification regulations (for example civil aviation or nuclear industry) are not addressed by SCOPE.

This scheme defines the limits of the certification to be performed and the characteristics of software including the relevant aspects of functionalities, performance constraints, and non-functional attributes.

A second objective is to demonstrate the applicability of the scheme with regard to cost-effectiveness, legal considerations and acceptability by the parties concerned.

Finally, the scheme will be promoted within the existing European IT standardisation and certification bodies.

The certification scheme must:

- be flexible to cope with the evolution of assessment technology and new software development practices; procedures and mechanisms must exist to extend the certification scheme to cover new application areas or new technical developments as they arise; it must provide mechanisms to monitor the practice of certification performed within the scheme, implying self-regulation and self-improvement capabilities;

- make use of existing and already accepted technologies, taking into account and contributing to existing standards and current certification practices and profiting from them; SCOPE develops new techniques for demonstration purposes and does not aim at developing and validating specific techniques.

1.2 - The Definition of Certification

Certification is the process of evaluation by an independent third party of the conformance between the actual service provided by a software product and a common reference.

This common reference defines the characteristics to be assessed by the certifier and allows the user to check whether the certified product fits its intended use.

When certification is not mandatory it is up to the producer to decide whether submit the product for certification against this common reference.

As with certification in other industries, the common reference must be defined independently of any particular use of the product.

However, unlike other areas of industries, the common reference for software certification cannot merely rely on a set of standards defining the required characteristics for each product category. Some clearly-identified software products categories (compilers, protocols, etc...) are being certified using this approach. Unfortunately, the extreme diversity of software products makes generalisation of category standards unpractical.

SCOPE proposes to define the common reference in each case as an agreement between the producer and the certifier within a standard framework that enforces fairness, repeatability and understandability of the resulting certificate. Of course, to be of value, this agreement must reflect the public's expectation of quality

1.3 - Rationales for the Project

In mature areas of industry, certification schemes already exist and are widely used; the existence of certification is indicative of this maturity. Information Technology is a recent field of industry and very few certification initiatives have been set up so far. This state of affairs can be seen as a limitation to trade in the software industry. It is difficult for non-specialist clients to select in confidence the right product. This situation is further complicated by the fact that no largely accepted reference or measurement system exists for software in general. Moreover, the building of the European Market in 1993 raises much concern in the field of Information Technology. The setting-up, on a European level, of a certification scheme valid for a wide range of software would not only encourage software trade between the EC countries, it would also help to clarify relationships between the parties concerned with respect to legal or insurance matters.

In addition, the Software Engineering community has been active for a long time and there are claims that there is enough R&D and experimentation in metrics and assessment techniques to identify the kernel which can be applied in industrial projects for quality evaluation. A part of this knowledge and techniques is now ready to be transferred to industry for the implementation of Software Certification. The success of this transfer will be the source of new experience and data which will surely open new perspectives for research.

1.4 - Organisation of the Paper

This thus concludes the first Section of this Paper.

In the second Section, several certification approaches, currently in use in the IT field, are presented.

The third Section gives an overview of the organisation of the SCOPE project and its workplan.

Early achievements after one year of activity are presented in Section 4.

The future plans of the project conclude this paper.

2 - EXISTING APPROACHES TO SOFTWARE CERTIFICATION

The Software Industry is very young compared to other areas of industry and the concept of certification is thus not widespread. However, a few areas of software industry are already covered by certification practices:

- civil aviation, railways and nuclear industry, for which certification of software is a result of statutory requirements for systems safety (aircraft, signalling, power plants); the recent introduction of software in critical parts of these systems has led to the development of certification schemes for software;

- some product categories, such as compiler or communication components, can be validated, thanks to the existence of standards describing the required functionalities.

These two examples are very different, in respect to levels of criticity and approach: in aeronautics for example, the concept of "process certification" is used while in the other case a "product certification" approach is considered.

It is worth discussing these concepts of "process certification" and "product certification" for a better understanding of the state of the art. The distinction is briefly outlined in the following Section and dealt with more fully in [1].

We go on to present the certification of software for the Civil Aviation and the validation of compilers. Among other certification schemes recently developed, the certification of Software Quality Assurance systems and the German GGS are of particular interest and are presented in further sections. Other approaches are described in [2].

To conclude, three different levels can be considered in order to certify software:

. the product itself,
. the project which leads to the product,
. the organisation which hosts the project.

Of course, we consider that combining these approaches could be of interest.

2.1 - Organisation Process or Product Certification

The very nature of software is of importance for certification. Until recently, software was only considered as immaterial, i.e. merely a service. Historically, the natural way was to assess the development process of the software rather than the software itself.

It is reasonable to consider a correlation exists between the application of state of the art software development methodologies and the final quality of the software product. However, even if this correlation does exist, it seems difficult to rely entirely on the causal link between the quality of the development process and that of the resulting product.

Another point of view is to consider that pieces of software are in fact industrial products. The basic principle is then to directly assess the compliance of the service provided by the software product with that which is specified or required. This involves several steps: describing and quantifying the specified service, measuring the actual service, and assessing the level of conformity.

In cases where the specified service is determined by a standard, this approach can be adopted, provided that assessment and measurement techniques can be devised.

2.2 – Civil Aviation

Airworthiness certification has been mandatory for aircraft for a long time now. The implementation of safety critical systems using computers in recent aircraft programmes has led the airworthiness authorities to develop a specific standard for software. Its latest version, Do 178–A [3], was used for the certification of the Airbus A320 aircraft, for example.

In this context, the method that leads to certification is a good example of the "process certification" approach:

- certifier and manufacturer agree on the criticality of the software depending on the potential consequences of a software failure;
- they then agree on a software development methodology and certification plan, since no single development methodology is recommended by Do 178–A;
- the software is developed, tested and validated according to the methodology; each of the corresponding activities must produce documentary evidence of their application and exhibit traceability;
- this evidence is analyzed by the certifier who grants the certificate.

The limitation of this approach is the lack of proof of final product quality and, for larger scale application, the cost of producing certifiable products.

2.3 – Compiler Validation

Compiler validation is an example of the other approach: the scheme does not refer to the process of compiler development.

Such a scheme exists for several languages for which there is a standard definition (for example, Fortran or Ada). This standard definition specifies the functionalities expected of a compiler for syntactic and semantic aspects, error detection and generated code.

The approach used by the certification scheme relies on the design of test suites which are submitted to the compiler under validation, resulting in compiling errors with diagnostics or production of executable code. This method is thus purely product–oriented.

Several of these certification schemes have been set up in Europe under the Conformance Testing Services (CTS) programme.

The advantages of this approach to software certification are its relatively limited cost and its good acceptance and understanding by producers and customers alike.

However, this approach has two major limitations. Firstly, the validated correctness of the compiler is limited to the cases that appear in the test suite and no other quality attributes, such as performance, are assessed. The second limitation is the lack of generality; to set up such a scheme, there is a need for standard a-priori definition of the certifiable characteristics (mainly functionalities) of the product. Several types of product, such as communication components or graphical packages, have a similar validation scheme. However, this approach cannot be extended to the majority of software products, due to their diversity.

2.4 - Software Quality Assurance Certification

Another way of ensuring that software meets its requirements is to implement and apply a good quality management system for its production. Assessing an organisation's quality system should give confidence in the quality of the products that come out of that organisation. This approach is a generalisation of the "process certification" described above. A third-party assessment of software quality systems, based on the EN 29000 series of standards, has been developed under the Conformance Testing Services programme (CTS) of the CEC [4].

The main issues for assessment are:

- quality policy and organisation;
- the design method;
- tests and reviews;
- the configuration management system.

The result of a successful third-party assessment is the delivery to the organisation of a label which can be used for a specific category of software products. After that, the producer must undergo regular third-party controls in order to keep its certificate.

Though very similar in principle to the "process certification" described above, this approach does not suffer the same drawbacks concerning the costs involved. This is due to the fact that individual developments are controlled by in-house quality management, which is itself third-party controlled. However, the same remarks apply concerning the quality of a given product which cannot be guaranteed by the quality of its development process.

2.5 - The German GGS Initiative

In Germany, software quality labels are awarded by Gütegemeinschaft Software (GGS), which is mainly dedicated to software packages without safety relevance. The approach used is purely product-oriented and the label is granted on the basis of:

- the software product description (which must clearly define what the product should and should not do),

- the software product itself (limited to the executable code and its documentation), which must satisfy the description.

The test procedure is defined by a standard [5] giving the requirements for product description and specifying the use of "black-box testing" techniques to ensure the consistency of the product with its description.

The GGS scheme is interesting for SCOPE, since it addresses a wide range of software and uses the "product" approach. However, some limitations are of importance, namely that only correctness and documentation quality are assessed and that embedded software is not addressed.

3 - ORGANISATION OF THE SCOPE PROJECT

To meet SCOPE objectives, the project organisation consists of three main topics:

- technical definition: oriented towards practical development and demonstration of techniques on real industrial projects;
- technology transfer: to prepare the implementation of certification on the following levels:
  - liaison with national and European standardization bodies,
  - participation of future users,
  - explicit information dissemination;
- legal and administrative acceptance: it must be sure that the proposed procedures are legally acceptable and that they fit within the existing European certification context: this objective will be met by coordination with standardization bodies and by a legal study undertaken within the project by professional lawyers.

These tasks are implemented by the consortium of the project and its workplan.

3.1 - Partnership

The success of a project like SCOPE resides in the technical expertise of its consortium, in the fields of Software Engineering and software assessment. This expertise comes from both academic and industrial areas. The extend of SCOPE partnership is relatively large for an ESPRIT project, in order to give more weight to the consensus to be found and demonstrated by the project. Moreover, several partners have longstanding experience with standardisation bodies.

The project currently comprises 11 partners representing 7 EC countries:

- AEA Technology (UK) is the British atomic energy authority; it has strong experience of Software Engineering R&D projects and in the certification of nuclear systems; in addition, AEA provides certification-related services to industry;
- Dublin City University (IRL) interests reside in Software Engineering and industrial links; more precisely, it aims at being a center of expertise for software certification.
- Elektronikcentralen (DK) is a test laboratory with experience in software assessment and metrication and close relationship with industry; moreover, it is active in many international standardization committees.
- ERIA (SP) one of the largest Spanish software-houses: is active in Quality Assurance consultancy and has a wide experience in software development;

- Etnoteam (I) is a reference company in Italy for Software Quality; Etnoteam actively promotes the spread of software quality technology in industry.

- Glasgow College (UK) interest lies in the mathematical and statistical modelling of quantitative measurement of software quality; the College is also interested in the academic/industrial interface and technology transfer;

- GMD (FRG) is a German R&D institute specialised in Information Technology; software metrication, validation and testing are important working topics; moreover GMD is active in the field of IT standardisation;

- GRS (FRG) is a non-profit organisation specialised in safety assessment for nuclear systems; GRS also has strong ties with German and international standardisation and certification bodies;

- Strathclyde University (UK) is located in Glasgow; its Computer Science Department has a long standing interest in research and teaching in Software Engineering; its Law School has interests in computer-related law as well as in European Community law;

- The City University London (UK) has two poles of interest: quantitative reliability assessment and the development of software metrics. The City University has been involved in many R&D projects in the field of software engineering;

- VERILOG (F) is the prime contractor of the project; it is the leading French company developing Software Engineering technology; VERILOG is the producer and vendor of CASE tools, such as the quality diagnosis tool "Logiscope".

3.2 - Workplan of the Project

The SCOPE project is planned to last 4 years. This timescale and the ambition of the project, led the workplan to be divided into two sequential work-packages. The first, a definition phase and a limited feasibility demonstration of software certification, was planned to last 18 months. The second work-package is the main phase. It was not completely planned out at the beginning of the project and its definition has been refined during the first workpackage.

The workplan of the first work-package is presented below, while that of the second phase is outlined in the Conclusion. The overall organisation for the work within this project was based upon a loop involving technology definition, experimentation and evaluation (see figure 1). These activities are supported by a Data Base service. This process is expected to converge and lead to the public release of validated Certification Technology.

The workplan of the first work-package is organised into four main tasks:

- a technology survey and definition task with the role of:

  . identifying the state of the art of Software Certification,
  . defining the Certification Model,
  . preparing the first set of experiments,
  . evaluating the results of those experiments,
  . coordinating with national and international standardisation bodies,
  . covering the legal aspects,
  . planning the second phase of the project;

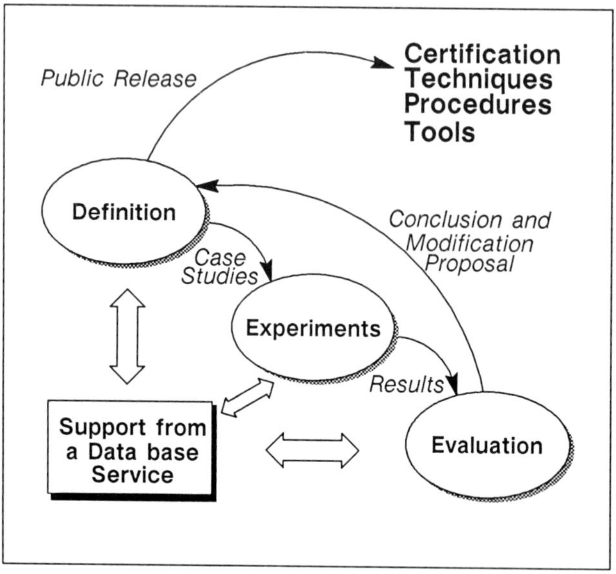

Figure 1: Technology Validation Mechanism

- an experimentation task in which specific partners independently carry on six case–studies; the case–studies are based either on partners' in–house projects or on projects provided by organisations external to SCOPE;

- a Data–Base task which covers the adaptation and improvement of REQUEST results (REQUEST is a now completed ESPRIT I project), the development of data transfer tools, the collection of case–studies data, and support to case study evaluation;

- a management task.

4 – EARLY ACHIEVEMENTS

SCOPE has been active for one year and the definition work performed so far has proved fruitful. Although the definition tasks are not all completed, their achievements can already be foreseen. The presentation of these achievements has been subdivised into four areas: the setting–up of a certification technology, coordination with organisation external to the project, legal matters, and the first set of experiments.

4.1 – Technology

SCOPE is based on the assumption that the technology of software quality and assessment developed by the research community is ready for use in Software Certification. In consequence, SCOPE strategy is to use existing techniques to build a consistent framework and to rationalise their application.

To implement this strategy, SCOPE has made significant efforts to establish the state of the art in Software Certification. The first part of this work was to concentrate on current practice, a sample of which is presented in Section 2. Then followed a survey of various cooperative R&D projects (mainly Esprit) related to software assessment. Finally, major Software Engineering techniques were reviewed and classified depending on whether they concur to build software quality or whether they can be used to assess it; their potential use for Certification was evaluated. The results of this activity are presented in a report available to the public [2].

Since then, work has focused on the setting up the necessary framework. Up until, the objective for the first phase has been to obtain a sufficient basis to drive the second phase. So far, the architecture of the framework has been defined and progressive enhancements are expected in the future.

The Certification Framework is composed of two parts: the Certification Model that precisely defines the notions used, and the Certification Method that describes the various steps leading to the certification of a software product. These two parts are intimately related as shown in figure 2.

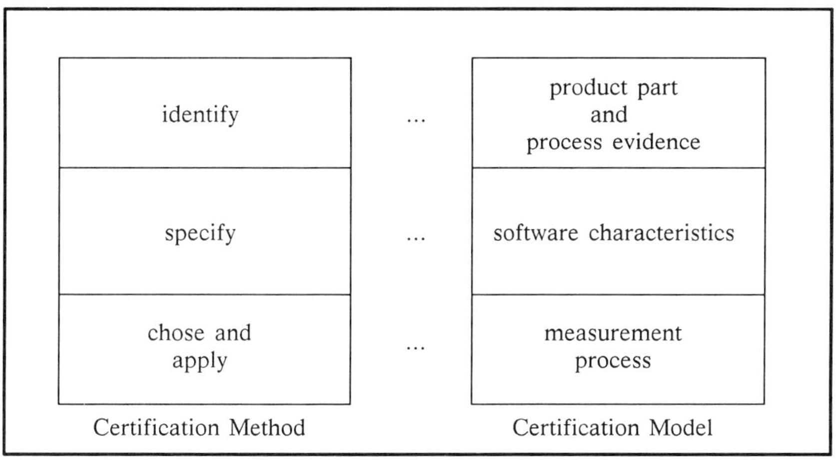

Figure 2: SCOPE Certification Framework

The Certification Method is composed of the following steps:

- identification, in the software product submitted to certification, of the recognised product parts and element of development and process evidence; (for example, source code, user's manual or Software Quality Assurance Plan used for the development of the product);

- specification of the software characteristics to be assessed; for example, an appropriate level of correctness and reliability; this is based on an examination of the descriptive product parts (user's manual or requirement specification);

- choice and application of measurement and assessment techniques; the choice depends on the characteristics to be assessed, the available product parts or process evidence and the applicable techniques.

The Certification Model is composed of four sub–models that define the notions introduced by the Certification Method: a Software Product Model, a Software Development Process Model, a Software Characteristics Model and a Measurement Model. These models are subsets of the state of the art and at the current stage of the project are minimal, simple but sufficient to proceed to the second phase of the project.

The Software Product Model is basically a list of product parts defined with precision. In its current state, it is only a subset of all the possible parts of a product. The aim is not to identify all the elements present in a product but only those that may be useful in the Certification Process.

The Software Development Process Model identifies items of process evidence that may be useful to facilitate product measurements. In a sense, this approach tries to reconcile the two ideas of "process" certification and "product" certification.

The Software Characteristics Model is the kernel of the Certification Model. It defines what, in a software product, can be assessed. As such, it will affect the relevance of any label based on SCOPE results. To be of any value, the characteristics that compose this model must correspond to the public notion of software quality. For the moment this model consists of definitions of "correctness" and "reliability" and refinements to the notion of "workmanship". The major issue in producing this model is to be able to define the characteristics without ambiguity.

The Measurement Model is more complex. The problem is to deal with the complexity of the state of the art measurement and assessment techniques. The number of applicable metrics proposed in the literature is extremely large and their conditions of application vary enormously. The approach taken by the Measurement Model is modular; a small set of metrics and assessment techniques, that can be mastered by a specialist, is encapsulated in what is called a "Certification Brick". This encapsulation lets the "brick" behave as a single assessment technique and gathers all the relevant information:

. software characteristics,
. necessary product parts or item of process evidence,
. conditions for its application (for example, programming language for static analysis),
. applicable tools,
. the predictable cost of its application.

The knowledge enclosed in a Certification Brick is expected to be transmissible and standardisable. In this way, we plan to implement the necessary flexibility of our framework: the set of bricks in use can evolve, which means validating new ones and discarding old ones as new technologies appear.

An example of Certification Bricks that are being developed at the moment deals with static complexity assessment of source code; this brick can be used to assess various aspects of maintainability, it needs the source code for its application, and is limited to certain programming languages. The aim is to have it implemented on several static analysis tools. The results of this work are at present being used to produce the Certification Model report [6].

4.2 - Connection with Standardisation Bodies

One important activity of the project is to establish good relations with national and international standardisation and certification bodies. The rationale for this activity is to have early feedback from the people involved these areas, to avoid proposing a scheme that would go against current practices and, finally, to prepare the implementation of the project results.

This activity has led to extended contacts in Germany, France and other partners' countries as well as on a European level with CEN-CENELEC, the CTS programme and the European Workshop on Industrial Computer Systems (EWICS). Moreover, SCOPE has actively participated in the organisation of the IFIP Working Conference on Approving Software Products.

The achievements of this activity are provided in [7, 8].

4.3 - Legal Study

The first activity of the SCOPE legal study was to produce an overview of legal issues related to software liability and certification [9, 10].

Then, the legal situation in France and the UK was analyzed with specific reference to:

. product standards,
. the certification of products,
. the liability of the parties involved in certification,
. the relationship between certification and software liability.

This analysis is partly dealt with in [11]. The overall aim of this task is to define a legal framework (contracts) for certification that is consistent with various European regulations.

4.4 - Case-Studies and Data Base

The preliminary experiments on Software Certification performed during the first part of SCOPE concerned six industrial projects. The goals were to contribute to the building of a pragmatic certification technology by producing Certification Bricks, to set up an adequate data collection strategy in connection with the data base activity, and to prepare the larger scale experiments.

The six experiments are:

- case-study TANGO: a medical data-base system developed in a fourth-generation language; correctness was the main attribute assessed by deriving a formalised description of the functionalities from the user documentation [12];

- case-study VICTOR: a business software mainly written in SQL; the approach was to analyze both the code and the requirement specification [13];

- case-study WHISKY: an operator information system developed in Fortran; emphasis was put on static and dynamic analysis;

- case-study X-RAYS: a plant performance monitoring system; the effort was oriented toward process metrics and static analysis [14];

- case–study YANKEE: a document management system; special interest was put on data collection and comparability of data [15];

- case–study ZULU: the front–end of a Software Engineering tool; emphasis was on correctness using a standard test suite and on maintainability using complexity measurements.

Due to the fact that the initial definition of the case–studies was performed in parallel with the beginning of work on the Certification Model, they could not be considered a validation of the SCOPE approach. The direction that was taken was to use these experiments as a bottom–up approach to the definition of the Certification Technology. For each of them, the software attributes to be assessed were informally identified; then an assessment plan was set up taking into account these attributes as well as the specific experience of the partner responsible for each case–study. The diversity of approaches is being evaluated at the time of writing, and it has already produced enough material for around twenty Certification Bricks.

The other important issue of this experiment activity was data collection. The objective was to demonstrate the practicality of collecting assessment data for the long–term validation and improvement of assessment techniques. The achievements in this area were:

- the identification and standardisation of a kernel set of metrics,

- the definition and implementation of a data–base storing this kernel set [16],

- the development of forms and transfer tools to collect the corresponding data.

The main SCOPE data base is centralised. PC copies are available on each case study site in order to collect the data locally and to filter it for confidentiality reasons. The filtered data can be transfered to the central data base by means of ASCII files.

5 - CONCLUSION - FUTURE PLANS

The goal of this paper has been to give an overview of the ESPRIT project SCOPE after one year of activity. The project is at the key phase of defining its second work–package, the basis of which has just been defined and is outlined in the present document.

SCOPE is of great importance for three reasons. Firstly, its technical goal is to produce a synthesis of a large branch of Software Engineering (metrication and software assessment techniques) in order to transfer it for practical application in industry. The second point is the strategic importance of Software Certification; on one hand, it is a way the software industry can become mature and, on the other hand, certification will be a powerful means of further integrating Europe's software industry. Finally, the increasing use of software embedded in systems that need to be certified for safety reasons, will demonstrate the necessity for software certification.

The achievements of SCOPE so far, have been to define a general Certification Framework that incorporates a subset of today's state of the art. A first investigation of the legal issues of Certification has been carried out. Good connections with national and international standardisation bodies have been set up. Finally, experiments with industrial software products have provided the project with valuable experience in data collection, transfer and storage issues.

As a consequence of these results, the project is ready to start its second work–package. Emphasis will be put on demonstrating the feasibility of Software Certification by means of a larger number of case–studies to experiment the proposed Certification Framework. These case–studies will be supported by an enhanced data base and the development of specific tools. In addition, the requirements specification of a "certifier workbench" will be developed.

A second direction will prepare the implementation of the project results: a synthesis of the technical results will be made, material for standardisation work will be drafted, and relations with involved bodies (standardisation, certification, industry, and users) will be consolidated. The legal investigations will be extended to several other EC countries.

Finally, work will proceed throughout the rest of the project to enlarge on the results already obtained in Certification Technology.

REFERENCES

[1] F. Copigneaux,
Software Process and Product Certification,
in B. de Neuman edt., CSR Conference: Software Certification, pp 23–42, Sept. 88, Elsevier.

[2] SCOPE Consortium,
Software Certification: State of the Art,
SCOPE/SCOPE/R 1.1.1.1//RL/01, SC.89/066, Sept. 1989.

[3] Radio Technical Commission for Aeronautics
Software Considerations in Airborne Systems and Equipment Certification,
RTCA/DO–178A, 1984.

[4] F. Rienstra,
Software Quality Assurance,
in The CTS Technical Days, CEC, Oct. 1987.

[5] Deutsches Institut für Normung
Anwendungssoftware, Prüfgrundsätze,
DIN V 66 285, October 1985

[6] SCOPE Consortium
Report on the Certification Model,
SC.90//SCOPE/T1.1.1.1/RP/01, August 1990 (to be produced)

[7] W. Ehrenberger
Report on the Connection to Standardisation Bodies from March 89 to August 89,
SCOPE/GRS.we/T 1.1.4//DL/00, SC.89/070, Sept. 1989.

[8] W. Ehrenberger
Report on the Connection to Standardisation Bodies from Sept. 89 to Feb. 90,
SC.90/002/GRS.we/T 1.1.4/RP/01, Feb. 1990.

[9] R. Wilson and I. Lloyd,
First Report on the Legal Aspects of SCOPE,
SCOPE/STH/T 1.1.5/REPORT/DL/00, August 89.

[10] I. Lloyd and R.I. Wilson
Software Quality – Some Legal Issues,
To appear in proc. of Approving Software Products (ASP'90), September 90, Elsevier.

[11] R. Wilson and I. Lloyd
Second Report on the Legal Aspects of SCOPE,
SC.90/012/STH.rw.il/T 1.1.5/RP/01, February 90.

[12] T. Moynihan and N. O'Connor,
Towards a Method to Assessing the Quality of User–Oriented Functional Specifications,
To appear in proc. of Approving Software Products (ASP'90), September 90, Elsevier.

[13] G. Agostoni and P. Caliman
Assessing Quality for Business Oriented Software: An Experience on an Application Supported by Relational Data Bases,
To appear in proc. of Approving Software Products (ASP'90), September 90, Elsevier.

[14] M. Neil and R. Bache
Validating Technologies for Certifying Software Products,
To appear in proc. of Approving Software Products (ASP'90), September 90, Elsevier.

[15] R.B. Hunter, K.B. Kirkwood and A.K. Rae
Automate Data Collection from Software Development Projects,
To appear in proc. of Approving Software Products (ASP'90), September 90, Elsevier.

[16] AEA Technology and Strathclyde University,
Database Definition: Data & Database Issues Report,
SC.90/009/AEA.STH/T 1.3.1/RP/02, Feb. 1990.

Approving Software Products
W. Ehrenberger (Editor)
Elsevier Science Publishers B.V. (North-Holland)

A new approach to software certification

Martin Davies

Principle Software Engineer

BSI Quality Assurance

15 May 1990

1 Introduction

In my opinion, software standards have three major failings. Firstly they are nearly always outdated by the time they are produced, secondly they frequently invent rather than codify current practice and finally that they are not usually developed in conjunction with a method for test. Software products rarely conform with standards, except in a generic way, and therefore the traditional certification model cannot be used for most software products[1].

Traditional certification relies on the ability to define and judge the fitness for purpose of a product for a specific application. In computing, the applications domain is too varied to allow standardisers to specify it, and without a specification it is impossible to test fitness for purpose. Computing is not alone in suffering from these problems, in many other areas it is also difficult to define the performance characteristics of an object. For example, although condoms are certified to a standard, no one would pretend that the cannot fail as a means of contraception. The fact that fitness for purpose is impossible to fully define does not preclude certification, where there is a clear need for improved quality and a method can be found for measuring and improving the quality of a product.

Software needs certification. A large number of companies are critically dependent on software for their continued existence. Software is traditionally of poor quality, and the quality of a package cannot be determined before purchase. The difference between a poor quality product and a high quality product is determinable - the issue that is not determinable is when and with what effect a product will fail.

1. Traditional certification as defined in ISO/IEC Guide 2: *General Terms and their definitions concerning standardisation and related activities.*

BSI QA has recognised the requirement for software certification for some time, and as well as developing methods for test for a number of specific markets covered by standards (e.g. language standards) we are also involved in assessment of software for safety critical applications. However, the time appears right for a more general system which will allow the certification of applications programs, at a commercially viable cost. This has encouraged BSI to design the Software Product Approval Service, which requires the software supplier to conform to the best of current practice.

2 Objective

The objective of software certification, as we see it, is to provide a noticeably higher level of assurance to the customer that a product purchased will be of high quality. We considered a variety of traditional methods for trying to ensure high quality.

2.1 Metrics

There are well known models for the development of software and some of these provide a figure for the reliability expected from the software. Our experience of these systems is that while they may have some validity when viewing programs in general, their reliance on purely statistical analysis mean that for a specific program their usefulness is severely restricted.

2.2 Program Proving

Program proving is a relatively immature, but extrememly poverful technique. Unfortunately program proving must be discounted for all, but the most critical applications, for the following reasons:

- o There is a limit to the size of program which can be practically proved
- o The tools available to support this type of activity are immature
- o Most commercial programs lack a mathematical specification
- o There are problems with modeling concurrency

My belief is that, in the future, program proving will form the basis of certification, particularly for critical applications.

2.3 Black box testing

The problem with using a black box testing strategy is that the tests are unlikely to cover all the possible uses made of the system. This is particularly true when the program operates in real time.

2.4 White Box testing

White box testing is an important part of testing a system, and offers some advantages over black box testing. For certification purposes it has some disadvantages:

- o It may be difficult to access all the source code (as some of the routines used may be part of other proprietary systems)
- o It is prone to error (as assessment of the necessary tests has to be done by hand)
- o It is time consuming and therefore expensive
- o The specification may not be formal enough to allow the assessor to understand the possible inputs.

2.5 Conclusion

We concluded that none of the above methodologies offered the correct balance of commercial flexibility and user satisfaction. It was therefore decided that an amalgam of the above could be created which relied on some parts of each and offered an effective and responsive system.

3 The approach

Our proposed system of software certification is based upon assuring the customer that the product is of reasonable quality, stable, supported and maintained by the supplier.

3.1 Quality

As with the traditional Kitemark and Safetymark[1] certification schemes, an assessment is made of the supplier's quality management system to the relevant parts of the ISO 9000 series. This is traditionally supplemented by a type test based on a method of test prescribed in a standard. For software there are no functional standards (e.g. none for word processing) and therefore a requirements specification must be produced for the product and agreed with the users. We plan to assess the testing performed by the supplier to ensure that all the features listed in the specification are tested.

3.2 Stability

We plan to make an assessment of the stability of the product. The issues examined include: the number of releases produced per year, the number of outstanding complaints about the software, the number of years the product has existed and an analysis of the complexity of the task. Although in absolute terms none of these measures will ensure stability - they will imply it. The stability evaluation corresponds to the use of metrics.

3.3 Support and Maintenance

There is a saying in the software industry about testing being what the users are for. There is some truth in this. For no matter how well a product is tested, users will find the real bugs, and that even a bug free product requires a manual which will allow the user to understand its functionality. User feedback and the user manual are therefore crucial parts of our proposed system.

We plan to use user feedback as a method of ensuring product enhancement. The supplier company will have to produce a release plan for the product, and before a product can be released all bugs reported before the cut off date have to be either fixed or documented.

---

1. The Kitemark and Safetymark are BSI QA's traditional family of certification marks used to assure the quality of products ranging from Crash helmets to Cookers.

4. In action

BSI QA has produced a Product Approval Specification[1] which illustrates in greater detail the requirements a supplier will have to meet in order to carry a certification mark on their software product, and although this system gets us no closer to bug free software it is a step on the road towards higher quality software.

1. A document PAS-SED1: *Generic software scheme* is available from Software Engineering, BSI QA, Box 375, Milton Keynes, MK14 6LL, United Kingdom.

SESSION 2

TESTING

Approving Software Products
W. Ehrenberger (Editor)
Elsevier Science Publishers B.V. (North-Holland)
IFIP, 1990

ON THE EFFICIENCY OF STATISTICAL TESTING WRT SOFTWARE STRUCTURAL TEST CRITERIA *

Pascale THÉVENOD-FOSSE

Laboratoire d'Automatique et d'Analyse des Systèmes du C.N.R.S.
7, Avenue du Colonel Roche
31077 Toulouse Cedex - FRANCE

ABSTRACT

Statistical testing consists in stimulating a program by test samples randomly selected according to a defined probability distribution on the input domain. First, we propose a framework to evaluate the efficiency of statistical testing as a verification tool. Many structural or functional test criteria exist in the literature, which are often used nowadays to select deterministic test inputs. The notion of statistical testing quality wrt test criteria is then defined, which allows to quantify the random test input hardness according to such criteria. A subsumption relation between two criteria, called R-subsumption, is deduced and a partial ordering of fifteen structural criteria using this relation is shown. The theoretical study is illustrated with some numerical results obtained for a small program. Finally, we discuss the intrinsic limits of structural testing, whether the input test data are deterministic or randomly generated.

1. INTRODUCTION

The paper concerns software fault removal problem. More precisely we restrict our attention to the first step of fault removal, called verification [Lap 89]. The two next steps, i.e. diagnosis and correction, are not addressed here. Verification is the process of checking whether the system adheres to properties called verification conditions, and the related techniques are dependent on two main principles: 1) static verification involving no actual execution of the software, and 2) dynamic verification which consists in exercizing the software by supplying to it either symbolic inputs in the case of symbolic execution, or valued inputs in the case of testing. Substantial work which has already been done in both verification types [DeM 87] shows their complementary roles in a fault removal process. The study presented below focuses on testing methods.

Since exhaustive testing is generally not possible, one must choose a subset of the whole input domain. The test efficiency wrt fault exposure depends on the adequacy of the selected test inputs. In [Lap 90], the methods for the determination of the test data are classified according to two viewpoints:

* This work was supported in part by the CEC under ESPRIT BRA Project 3092 "Predictably Dependable Computing Systems (PDCS)".

- criteria for selecting the test inputs, which may relate to either the function or the structure of the system, leading respectively to functional (or black box) and structural (or white box) testing;
- generation of the test inputs, which may be either deterministic or probabilistic; in the first case, called deterministic testing, test inputs are predetermined by a selective choice according to the adopted criteria; in the second case, called random or statistical testing, test inputs are selected according to a defined probability distribution on the input domain, and both the distribution and the number of input data are determined according to the adopted criteria.

This classification encompasses hardware and software testing methods. By setting up four main classes of test data (structural deterministic, functional deterministic, structural statistical, functional statistical), it removes the usually preconceived idea that random testing is by essence a black box testing method. The present paper is an attempt to clarify the notion of **structural statistical testing of software**.

Many structural criteria have been defined and compared in the literature on deterministic testing [Rap 85, Gir 86, Nta 88, Fra 88, Zei 88, Cla 89, Bie 89, Wey 90], and this class of testing methods is probably the most widely used. Based on the analysis of the program control or data flow, these criteria try to fill the gap between branch testing and path testing. Our main goal is to propose a framework to quantify the efficiency of statistical testing as a verification tool, and to utilize it (as a first step) in the case of structural criteria. **Section 2** provides the framework, with basic definitions related to statistical testing quality from which a subsumption relation between two criteria, called R-subsumption, is naturally derived. **Section 3** focuses on structural criteria and a partial ordering of fifteen current criteria according to the R-subsumption relation is shown. This ordering is in accordance with the one induced by the subsumption relation defined in deterministic approaches [Rap 85, Nta 88]. Some results related to a small program illustrate the theoretical work. In **section 4**, a brief discussion on the strengths and weaknesses of structural testing confirms the hopeful complementary features of deterministic and random test inputs wrt fault removal [Mor 78, Dur 84, Nta 84, The 89, Ham 89].

2. BASIC DEFINITIONS

2.1. Statistical testing quality

During a statistical testing experiment, N executions of the program under test are performed with random input data selected according to a defined probability distribution on the input domain. N is called the test size.

DEFINITION 1. The *statistical testing quality* is the probability that a faulty program fails at least once during an experiment. It is noted Q_N for a test size N. ❑

In other words, Q_N is the probability that N random test cases detect at least one error in a faulty program. Inversely, $(1-Q_N)$ is the probability that a faulty program does not fail during a test of size N, i.e. that an experiment states a faulty program is correct. Obviously, Q_N depends on 1) the actual faults and errors they can create, 2) the chosen probability distribution on the input domain, and 3) the test size N. Let p be the average probability that the program fails on one random input data from the chosen distribution. Theorem 1 gives a basic relation [Gir 73, The 89], whose proof is obvious since (1-p) is the probability of no failure per execution.

THEOREM 1. For a presumed value p of the failure probability, the test quality Q_N and the test size N are linked by the relation: $(1-p)^N = 1-Q_N$.

❑

Hence equation (1a) gives the test quality associated with a fixed test size, and equation (2a) gives the minimum test size required to reach a target test quality.

$Q_N = 1 - (1-p)^N$ equation (1a)

$N = \log(1-Q_N) / \log(1-p)$ equation (2a)

Let us consider two programs S1 and S2 the failure probabilities of which, noted p1 and p2 respectively, are such that $p1 \geq p2$. Equation (1a) shows that for a fixed N, the test quality for S1 is better than the one for S2. That is to say, from equation (2a), the lowest is the failure probability, the largest is the test size required to reach a target test quality. Roughly speaking, "the more data the better" as said in [Gou 83]. Corollary 1 is then deduced from theorem 1.

COROLLARY 1. For a given input probability distribution, if a test size N is required to reach a test quality Q_N for a presumed failure probability p, then any fault f involving a failure probability at least p has a probability at least Q_N to be revealed during N executions with random data.

❑

The problem arising from theorem 1 is a suitable assessment of the parameter p. For hardware, there are fault models for physical changes (stuck-at faults, couplings, pattern sensitive faults, etc.), and several methods have been stated to evaluate the failure probabilities associated with these faults and deduce a relevant value of p. Unfortunately, in the present state of the art it does not seem feasible to define an accurate software design fault model, so that the failure probabilities related to actual faults cannot be evaluated a priori and other directions must be investigated to approximate the value of p. Different approaches have already been proposed: in [Gir 73] the author suggests to determine p from the frequency of use of each instruction, or through simulation by seeding faults in the program; Hamlet's approach is to relate p to the program textual space instead of the input domain [Ham 86]; ... More generally, an a priori value p could be connected to any test criterion, which leads us to the notion of statistical testing coverage wrt test criteria.

2.2. Statistical testing coverage wrt test criteria

A large amount of testing criteria have already been defined in previous work on deterministic methods [DeM 87]. They refer either to the program structure, or to the program functions, or both. Each criterion specifies a set of elements to be exercised during testing, where "elements" and "exercised" can take different meanings depending on the criterion. For example: branch testing means that each "program branch" has to be "executed"; mutation testing requires that each "mutant" is "killed" (or in other words, each "seeded fault" is "revealed"); etc. Let S_{Ai} be the set of elements to be exercised from a test criterion A_i.

DEFINITION 2. A *test criterion A_i is covered with probability q_N* if:

a) each element $\in S_{Ai}$ has a probability at least q_N to be exercised during a statistical test of size N,

and b) there is one (or several) element(s) $\in S_{Ai}$ whose the probability to be exercised is not higher than q_N.

q_N is called the test quality wrt A_i.

❑

Let p_k be the probability that a random test input exercises an element $k \in S_{Ai}$. The probability to exercise k with N random test inputs is then: $1 - (1-p_k)^N$.

THEOREM 2. The test quality q_N wrt a criterion A_i and the test size N_{Ai} are linked by the relation: $(1-P_i)^{N_{Ai}} = 1-q_N$ with $P_i = \min \{p_k, k \in S_{Ai}\}$.

❑

Proof. Definition 2 means that :

a) $\forall k \in S_{Ai}$, $q_N \le 1 - (1-p_k)^{N_{Ai}} \Leftrightarrow (1-p_k)^{N_{Ai}} \le 1-q_N$

and b) $\exists k \in S_{Ai}$ such that $q_N = 1 - (1-p_k)^{N_{Ai}} \Leftrightarrow (1-p_k)^{N_{Ai}} = 1-q_N$

$\Rightarrow$ $1 - q_N = (1-\min \{p_k\})^{N_{Ai}} = (1-P_i)^{N_{Ai}}$

❑

Hence equation (1b) gives q_N for a given N_{Ai}, and equation (2b) gives the minimum test size required to reach a target test quality wrt A_i.

$q_N = 1 - (1-P_i)^{N_{Ai}}$ equation (1b)

$N_{Ai} = \log (1-q_N) / \log (1-P_i)$ equation (2b)

Theorem 2 implies corollary 2 (in the same way as theorem 1 implies corollary 1).

COROLLARY 2. For a given input probability distribution:

1) if a test size N_{Ai} is required to reach q_N wrt a criterion A_i, then any criterion A_x such that $P_x = \min \{p_k, k \in S_{Ax}\} \ge P_i$ is covered with a probability at least q_N during N_{Ai} executions with random data (i.e. the test quality wrt A_x is at least q_N);
2) for a target test quality q_N: $P_x \ge P_i \Leftrightarrow N_{Ax} \le N_{Ai}$, $\forall A_i, A_x$.

❑

Definition 2 and theorem 2 can be generalized to deal with a set of several criteria.

DEFINITION 3. Let $A = \{A_1, \ldots, A_k\}$ be a set of k criteria. The *set A is covered with probability q_N* if:

a) each of the k test criteria $\in$ A has a probability at least q_N to be covered during a statistical test of size N,

and b) there is one (or several) criterion(a) $\in$ A whose the coverage probability is not higher than q_N.

q_N is called the test quality wrt the set A.

❑

THEOREM 3. The test quality q_N wrt a criteria set $A = \{A_1, \ldots, A_k\}$ and the test size N_A are linked by the relation: $(1-P)^{N_A} = 1-q_N$ with $P = \min \{P_i, i = 1, \ldots, k\}$.

❑

Hence equation (1c) gives q_N for a given N_A, and equation (2c) gives the minimum test size required to reach a target test quality wrt the criteria set A.

$q_N = 1 - (1-P)^{N_A}$ equation (1c)

$N_A = \log (1-q_N) / \log (1-P)$ equation (2c)

In other words, to cover a set $A = \{A_1, \ldots, A_k\}$ one has only to cover a single criterion A_x such that $P_x = \min \{P_i, i = 1, \ldots, k\}$.

Remark.

The similarity between theorem 1 and theorem 2 (or 3) shows that a test size N_{Ai} (or N_A) provides a test quality $Q_N \ge q_N$ if the actual software failure probability p is equal to or greater than P_i (or P). Hence, the problem of test criteria adequacy wrt actual faults could be less acute in case of statistical testing than in case of deterministic testing. This point will be discussed in section 4.

2.3. R-subsumption relation

In [Rap 85, Nta 88, Fra 88, Cla 89], the term "subsumes" (or "includes") is used with the following sense : "A_i subsumes A_k if any test set which satisfies A_i for a given program also satisfies A_k". With regards to statistical testing, and from the definitions in § 2.2, the natural meaning of the subsumption relation is: "A_i subsumes A_k if any test set which covers A_i with probability q_N for a given program also covers A_k with a probability at least q_N ($\forall$ q_N)". This is equivalent to definition 4 below, in which the relation is called R-subsumption ("R-" for Random inputs).

DEFINITION 4. With regards to statistical testing and for any test data criteria A_i and A_k, we say that:

- *A_i R-subsumes A_k* if $P_i \leq P_k$ for any program and whatever be the input probability distribution ;
- *A_i strictly R-subsumes A_k,* denoted $A_i \rightarrow A_k$, if A_i R-subsumes A_k and $P_i < P_k$ for some program and some input probability distribution;
- *A_i and A_k are incomparable* if neither $A_i \rightarrow A_k$ nor $A_k \rightarrow A_i$.

❑

The R-subsumption relation, whose transitivity is obvious, induces a partial ordering of test criteria.

3. COMPARISON OF FIFTEEN PATH SELECTION CRITERIA

Path selection criteria are a subset of structural test criteria. Based on the program control flow graph or data flow graph, each of them selects a finite subset of paths to be executed during testing. We briefly recall some flow graph theoretic concepts and notations [Rap 85]. Then fifteen criteria are compared according to the R-subsumption relation. The study leads to a partial ordering which is identical to the one induced by the subsumption relation, under the same hypotheses on the program structure [Rap 85, Nta 88].

3.1. Program flow graph concepts

A program can be decomposed into disjoint blocks b_i, where a block is a maximal set of ordered statements always sequentially executed, the first statement in a block being the only one which can be executed after a statement from another block. Figure 1a shows a program Q with four blocks. In b_1, "X := 1+Random(R)" means that the variable X is an integer number randomly selected from a uniform distribution in the range [1—R], where R is a constant. In the **control flow graph** G of a program (Fig. 1b), each block b_i is represented by a node n_i, and there is a directed edge from n_i to n_k, denoted (i,k), if and only if the first statement of b_k can be executed after the last statement of b_i. If (i,k) exists, n_k is called a successor of n_i, and n_i a predecessor of n_k. n_i is a start node if the first statement of b_i is the program start statement (no predecessor). It is an exit node if b_i ends with a halt statement (no successor). Ω and E denote the set of all nodes and the set of all edges in G, respectively. A path in G is a finite sequence of nodes (n_1, ..., n_j), $j \geq 2$, such that there is an edge (i,i+1) for i = 1, ..., j-1. A path is complete when n_1 is a start node and n_j an exit node.

In **data flow graphs**, further informations on interactions involving variable definitions and affected references are added to the control flow. An example of such a data flow graph is the Definition Use graph (def/use) proposed in [Rap 85].

```
b1    START
      X := 1 + Random (R)
      Y := 2

b2    [A]  if X ≥ 500 then goto B

b3    X := X * Y
      Y := Y + 1
      goto A

b4    [B]  print (X)
      END
```

(a) Program Q

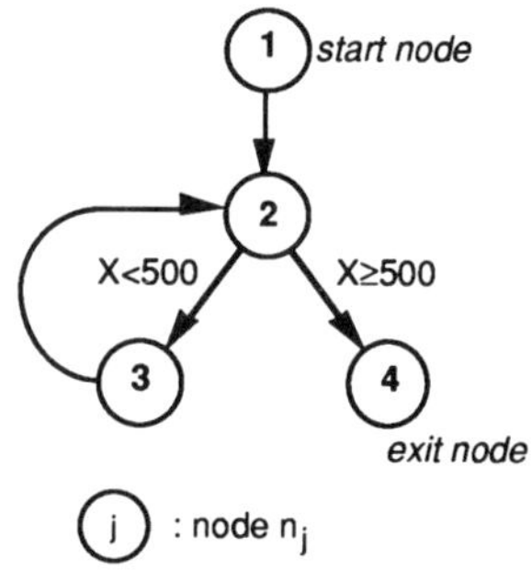

(b) Control flow graph

$\Omega = \{n_j\}$	def(j)	c-use(j)	dcu(v,j)	$E = \{(i,k)\}$	p-use(i,k)	dpu(v,j)
n_1	X, Y	ø	dcu(X,1) = $\{n_3, n_4\}$	(1,2)	ø	dpu(X,1) = dpu(X,3)
n_2	ø	ø	dcu(Y,1) = $\{n_3\}$	(2,3)	X	= {(2,3), (2,4)}
n_3	X, Y	X, Y	dcu(X,3) = $\{n_3, n_4\}$	(2,4)	X	dpu(Y,1) = dpu(Y,3)
n_4	ø	X	dcu(Y,3) = $\{n_3\}$	(3,2)	ø	= ø

(c) Sets related to the def-use graph

FIGURE 1. Example of control and data flow graph: program Q.

def(j) = $\{v \in V$ / v has a def in node n_j which can be used outside $n_j\}$

c-use(j) = $\{v \in V$ / v has a c-use in n_j with no def of v within n_j before the c-use$\}$

p-use(j,k) = $\{v \in V$ / v has a p-use in edge (j,k)$\}$

For each $v \in$ def(j):

dcu(v,j) = $\{n_k \in \Omega$ / $v \in$ c-use(k) and there is a def-clear path wrt v from n_j to $n_k\}$

dpu(v,j) = $\{(i,k) \in E$ / $v \in$ p-use(i,k) and there is a def-clear path wrt v from n_j to (i,k)$\}$

FIGURE 2. Some sets related to the def/use graph. V is the variable set.

Here, each variable occurrence is classified as being either a definition (def), or a reference in a computation (c-use), or a reference in a predicate (p-use). Let V = {v} be the set of variables. A variable v has a def (resp. a c-use) in a node n_j if there is a statement in b_j containing a def (resp. a c-use) of v. If b_j ends with a conditional transfer statement, then each variable involved in the branch predicate has a p-use in every edge (j,k), $\forall\, n_k$ successor of n_j. For Q (Fig. 1), it means that: X and Y have a def in n_1; in n_3, X and Y have first a c-use, then X has a def, then Y has another c-use followed by a def; X has a c-use in n_4, and a p-use in both edges (2,3) and (2,4). The def/use graph is created by associating two sets of variables with each node n_j noted def(j) and c-use(j), and one set of variables with each edge (j,k), noted p-use(j,k). Figure 2 outlines the definitions of these sets and Fig. 1c gives the sets obtained for Q. A def-clear path wrt a variable v from node n_j to node n_k is a path (n_j, n_1, ..., n_m, n_k) with no def of v in n_1, ..., n_m ($m \geq 0$). A def-clear path wrt a variable v from node n_j to edge (i,k), is a path (n_j, n_1, ..., n_m, n_i, n_k) with no def of v in n_1, ..., n_m, n_i ($m \geq 0$). For example, as n_2 contains no def in Fig. 1, (n_1, n_2, n_3) is a def-clear path wrt X and wrt Y, from n_1 to n_3 and from n_1 to (2,3). Two sets are related to each pair (variable v, node n_j) such that v has a def in n_j (Fig. 2 and Fig. 1c): a node set dcu(v,j), and an edge set dpu(v,j). Based on the def/use graph, a family of criteria has been derived [Rap 85]. Depending on the criterion, it is asked that for each variable definition, *all* or *some* def-clear paths wrt the variable from the node containing the def to *all* or *some* of the nodes and edges containing *uses* or *c-uses* or *p-uses* of the variable reachable by some such path be executed.

3.2. Partial ordering according to the R-subsumption relation

Five of the studied criteria are connected to the control flow graph: Instructions (each statement has to be executed), Branchs (every edge has to be exercised), Boundary-Interior Paths [How 75], Structured Paths [How 77], and All-Paths (each complete path must be executed). The other ones are based on data flow graphs: 2-DR Interactions [Her 76], Required Pairs and Required k-Tuples [Nta 84], and the seven criteria based on the def/use graph [Rap 85, Fra 88]. All these criteria are described for example in [Nta 88]. Those taken as examples in the proof of the partial ordering (§ 3.2.2) are briefly recalled in § 3.2.1. Our assumptions on the program structure are the "classical" ones found in [Rap 85, Nta 88] for instance. The problem of unexecutable paths is tackled in section 4.

3.2.1. Some path selection criteria

If a program contains no loop, ***Boundary-Interior Paths*** is equivalent to All-Paths. In presence of loop(s), it restricts the number of complete paths to be executed by requiring only two different ways of exercising each loop: the first one enters the loop but does not iterate it, while the second one iterates it at least once. A ***2-DR Interaction*** involves a definition to a variable v in a node n_j and a reference to v in another n_k such that there is a def-clear path wrt v from n_j to n_k, and the corresponding criterion amounts to testing each 2-DR interaction. ***Required Pairs*** are an extension of 2-DR Interactions which includes the following additional required pairs to be exercised: a) for each 2-DR interaction involving a reference in a branch predicate, a required pair is produced for each outcome of the predicate, and b) if the definition or the reference occurs in a loop, two iteration counts are considered, one specifying that the loop be exited at the first opportunity and the other one that the loop be iterated a larger number of times. ***Required k-Tuples*** are extensions of Required Pairs which ask that each sequence of k-1 (or less) related 2-DR interactions be exercised (Required 2-Tuples means Required Pairs). From the family of criteria based on the def/use graph, ***All-Defs*** [respectively: 1) ***All-C-Uses***, and 2) ***All-P-Uses***] requires that for every node n_j and every variable v $\in$ def(j), one executes a def-clear path wrt v from n_j to some element of dcu(v,j) or dpu(v,j) [respectively: 1) to each node of dcu(v,j), and 2) to each edge of dpu(v,j)]. ***All-C-Uses/Some-P-Uses*** [resp. ***All-P-Uses/Some-C-Uses***] asks that for every node n_j and every variable v $\in$ def(j), one executes a def-clear path wrt v from n_j to each element of dcu(v,j) [resp. dpu(v,j)], and if dcu(v,j) [resp. dpu(v,j)] is empty a def-clear path wrt v from n_j to some element of dpu(v,j) [resp. dcu(v,j)].

3.2.2. Partial ordering induced by the R-subsumption

THEOREM 4. Figure 3 shows the partial ordering of fifteen path selection criteria according to the strict R-subsumption relation. Criterion A_i strictly R-subsumes criterion A_k if it is specified in Figure 3 or if it results from the transitivity of the relation.

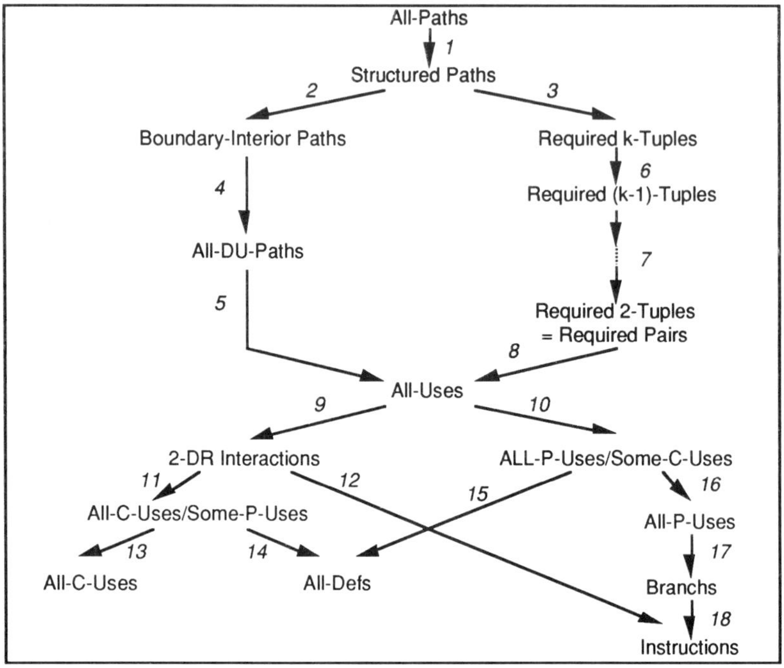

FIGURE 3. A partial ordering of fifteen structural test criteria according to the strict R-subsumption relation.

Proof.

To demonstrate a strict R-subsumption $A_i \rightarrow A_k$ between two criteria, two types of reasoning are performed depending on whether the corresponding sets of elements to be exercised, S_{Ai} and S_{Ak} respectively, cannot be compared or are such that $S_{Ai} \supseteq S_{Ak}$ from the criteria definition. Here, we give the principle of each of the two proof types, with one example and the list of the relations whose demonstrations are similar. Then, three examples of programs are used to show that criteria which are not ordered in Figure 3 are incomparable.

1) $A_i \rightarrow A_k$ with S_{Ai} and S_{Ak} not comparable.

- Principle.
  - One first prove that A_i R-subsumes A_k (i.e. $P_i \leq P_k$) by showing that:
    $\forall\, x \in S_{Ak}, \exists\, y \in S_{Ai}$ such that $p_x \geq p_y$.
    Hence, $\min \{p_x, x \in S_{Ak}\} \geq \min \{p_y, y \in S_{Ai}\} \Leftrightarrow P_i \leq P_k$.
  - Then one gives a program example for which the relation is strict ($P_i < P_k$) for some input probability distribution. Hence $A_i \rightarrow A_k$.
- Example: Branchs $\rightarrow$ Instructions *(18)*.
  The sets associated with A_i = "Branchs" and A_k = "Instructions" are:
  $S_{Ai} = E = \{\text{edges } (q, j)\}$; $S_{Ak} = \Omega = \{\text{nodes } n_j\}$.
  - Let Prob[x] denote p_x, $\forall\, x \in S_{Ak}, S_{Ai}$.
    $\forall\, n_j \neq$ start node, if n_j has: a single predecessor n_q, Prob[n_j] = Prob[(q, j)];
    several predecessors n_q, Prob[n_j]$\geq$Prob[(q, j)] $\forall\, n_q$.
    If n_j is the start node, Prob[n_j] = 1. Hence, $P_i \leq P_k$.

- For the program R in Figure 4a, the relation is strict:
  $P_i = \text{Prob}[(2,3)] = 1/8$, and $P_k = \text{Prob}[n_4] = 3/8 \Leftrightarrow P_i < P_k$.
- Other relations: *2, 3, 4, 8, 9, 11, 12, 17.*

2) *$A_i \rightarrow A_k$ with $S_{Ai} \supseteq S_{Ak}$.*

- Principle.
  As $S_{Ak} \subseteq S_{Ai}$ implies that $P_i \le P_k$, one only gives an example of program for which the relation is strict.
- Example: All-C-Uses/Some-P-Uses ➜ All-C-Uses *(13).*
  In Fig. 4a: dcu(X,1) = $\{n_3\}$ with two def-clear paths wrt X from n_1 to n_3, (n_1, n_3) and (n_1, n_2, n_3); dcu(Y,1) = ø and dpu(Y,1) = {(2,3), (2,4)}. Hence,
  for All-C-Uses/Some-P-Uses:
  $S_{Ai} = \{[(n_1, n_3) \text{ or } (n_1, n_2, n_3)], [(n_1, n_2, n_3) \text{ or } (n_1, n_2, n_4)]\}$
  $\Rightarrow P_i = \min\{1/2 + 1/8, 1/8 + 3/8\} = 1/2$;
  for All-C-Uses: $S_{Ak} = \{[(n_1, n_3) \text{ or } (n_1, n_2, n_3)]\} \Rightarrow P_k = 1/2+1/8 = 5/8 \Leftrightarrow P_i < P_k$.
- Other relations: *1, 5, 6, 7, 10, 14, 15, 16.*

3) *Criteria A_i and A_k which are incomparable using the R-subsumption relation.*
The fact that A_i does not strictly R-subsume A_k will be denoted $A_i \neg A_k$. To show that two criteria are incomparable, it is sufficient to find two programs such that in one of them $P_i < P_k$ (i.e. $A_k \neg A_i$) while $P_k < P_i$ (i.e. $A_i \neg A_k$) in the other one. From the R-subsumption transitivity, it results:

$(A_i \neg A_k) \Rightarrow (A_i \neg A_j)$, $\forall A_j$ such that $A_j \rightarrow A_k$;
and $(A_i \neg A_k) \Rightarrow (A_j \neg A_k)$, $\forall A_j$ such that $A_i \rightarrow A_j$.

Hence, examples are not required for each of the twenty non-ordered couples of criteria, and one has only to prove the eight relations $A_i \neg A_k$ specified below. Three programs are used in the demonstration: Q (Fig. 1), R and S (Fig. 4a, b).

a) *"2-DR Interactions" ¬ "Branchs" (program R).*
There are two 2-DR interactions in R: X defined in n_1 and referenced in n_3; Y defined in n_1 and referenced in n_2. Hence,
for 2-DR Interactions: $S_{Ai} = \{(n_1, n_3), (n_1, n_2)\} \Rightarrow P_i = 1/2$;
for Branchs: S_{Ak} = {four edges} $\Rightarrow P_k = 1/8$ i.e. $P_i > P_k$.

b) *"All-C-Uses/Some-P-Uses" ¬ "Instructions" (program R).*
For All-C-Uses/Some-P-Uses: $P_i = 1/2$ (see *§2* of the proof).
For Instructions: $P_k = 3/8$ (see *§1* of the proof) i.e. $P_i > P_k$.

c) *"All-C-Uses" ¬ "All-Defs" (program R).*
For All-C-Uses: $P_i = 5/8$ (see *§2* of the proof).
As each complete path in R is a def-clear path wrt X from n_1 to some edge of dpu(X,1) = {(1,2), (1,3)}, one obtains for All-Defs:
$S_{Ak} = \{[\text{any path}], [(n_1, n_2, n_3) \text{ or } (n_1, n_2, n_4)]\} \Rightarrow P_k = \min\{1, 1/8 + 3/8\} = 1/2$,
i.e. $P_i > P_k$.

d) *"All-Defs" ¬ "All-C-Uses" (program S).*
From the data flow graph of S, one obtains five non-empty sets:
dpu(X,1) = {(1,2), (1,3), (4,5), (4,6)} = E;
dcu(Y,1) = $\{n_3, n_5\}$; dcu(Y,2) = $\{n_5\}$; dcu(Z,1) = $\{n_2, n_6\}$; dcu(Z,3) = $\{n_6\}$. Hence,
for All-defs: S_{Ai} = {[any path, for X ∈ def(1)], [(n_1, n_3), for Y ∈ def(1)], [(n_2, n_4, n_5), for Y ∈ def(2)], [(n_1, n_2), for Z ∈ def(1)], [(n_3, n_4, n_6), for Z ∈ def(3)]}
$\Rightarrow P_i = \min\{1, 1/2, 3/8, 1/2, 3/8\} = 3/8$;

for All-C-Uses: S_{Ak} = {4 complete paths}
$\Rightarrow$ $P_k = \min\{\text{Prob[each path]}\} = 1/8$ i.e. $P_i > P_k$

e) *"All-P-Uses/Some-C-Uses"* $\neg$ *"All-C-Uses" (program S).*
All-P-Uses/Some-C-Uses applied to S leads to the same value P_i as the criterion All-defs in *d)*, i.e. $P_i = 3/8$. Hence $P_i > P_k$, with $P_k = 1/8$ from *d)*.

f) *"All-P-Uses"* $\neg$ *"All-Defs" (program S).*
Only the variable X is referenced in the predicates. As X is used in every branch and is never redefined after the start node, one obtains for All-P-Uses: $P_i = \min\{\text{Prob[each edge]}\} = 1/2$. For All-Defs $P_k = 3/8$ from *d)*. Hence $P_i > P_k$.

g) *"Boundary-Interior Paths"* $\neg$ *"Required Pairs" (program Q).*
Let path(q) denote the path in Q with q iterations of the loop (n_2, n_3, n_2). For example: path(0) = (n_1, n_2, n_3, n_2, n_4), path(1) = (n_1, n_2, n_3, n_2, n_3, n_2, n_4), etc.
For Boundary-Interior Paths: S_{Ai} = {(n_1, n_2, n_4), path(0), any path(q) $\forall\, q \geq 1$},
with Prob[any path(q) $\forall\, q \geq \alpha$] = Σ Prob[path(q)], $\forall\, q \geq \alpha$ equation (3)
For Required Pairs:
S_{Ak} = {(n_1, n_2, n_4), path(0), path(1), any path(q) $\forall\, q \geq 2$}.
Equation (3) implies that for any α, β such that $\alpha > \beta$:
Prob[any path(q) $\forall\, q \geq \alpha$] $\leq$ Prob[any path(q) $\forall\, q \geq \beta$] $\Rightarrow P_i \geq P_k$,
and any value $R \geq 583$ gives $P_i > P_k$ (see numerical results in § 3.3 and Fig. 5).

h) *"Required k-Tuples"* $\neg$ *"All-DU-Paths" (program S).*
In S, there is no sequence of more than two related 2-DR interactions, and the sequences of two related 2-DR interactions are:

- "Y defined in n_1, then referred in n_3" followed by "Z defined from Y in n_3, then referred in n_6";
- "Z defined in n_1, then referred in n_2" followed by "Y defined from Z in n_2, then referred in n_5".

Hence, Required k-Tuples ($\forall\, k \geq 3$) gives:
S_{Ai} = {(n_1, n_3, n_4, n_6), (n_1, n_2, n_4, n_5)} $\Rightarrow$ $P_i = 3/8$.
As All-C-Uses requires the execution of each complete path in S from *d)*, and All-DU-Paths R-subsumes All-C-Uses from Fig. 3,
for All-DU-Paths: S_{Ak} = {4 complete paths} $\Rightarrow$ $P_k = 1/8$ i.e. $P_i > P_k$.
❑

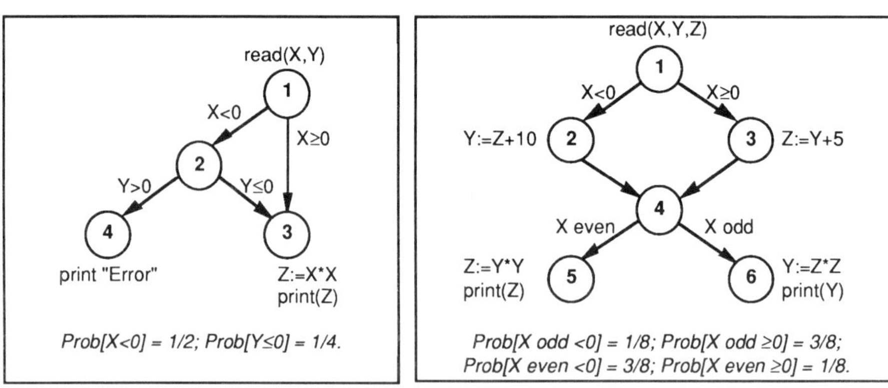

(a) Program R **(b) Program S**

FIGURE 4. Programs R and S with given input probability distributions.

3.3. Numerical results

The empirical study reported in [Gad 89] encompasses ten small Pascal programs. For each criterion A_i in Fig. 3, two kinds of numerical results confirm and illustrate the R-subsumption relations set above.

1) *Theoretical computation:* for different input probability distributions, assessment of the probabilities p_k of exercising each element $k \in S_{Ai}$; hence, evaluation of the theoretical coverage probability P_i related to A_i and, from equation (2b), of the test size N_i required to reach a test quality $q_N = .999$.
2) *Experimental results:* statistical test runs of size N = 5000 have been performed to get experimental estimates e_k of the probabilities p_k, with $e_k = t_k / 5000$ if k is exercised t_k times during a test run; hence an experimental assessment of P_i, $E_i = \min \{e_k, k \in S_{Ai}\}$, and the associated test size from equation (2b) with $P_i = E_i$.

In each studied case, theoretical computation and experimental results were in accordance, and they verify the partial ordering shown in Fig. 3. Due to the lack of place, we can only introduce here few results related to the program Q (Fig. 1).

Figure 5a shows the ordering induced by the relation "$P_i \leq P_k$ whatever be the input probability distribution", i.e. "for Q, A_i R-subsumes A_k". Each of the six squares contains criteria leading to the same expression $P_i = \min \{p_k, k \in S_{Ai}\}$ which is given to the right of it. The notation path(q) represents the path in Q with q iterations of the loop (see *§3.g* in the proof of theorem 4). The input X is an integer number randomly selected from a uniform distribution in the range [1—R], and formula have been derived to evaluate the values P_i (i = 1, ..., 5) as functions of R (see Fig. 5a for $R \geq 500$). Figure 5b gives the results for R = 500, 600, 700, ..., 1 500. Figure 5c shows the test sizes required to reach a test quality $q_N = .999$, from equation (2b). From theorem 3, N1 executions of Q with random inputs provide a test quality .999 wrt the set of twelve criteria (All-Paths is not considered as it leads to an infinite test size). The numerical results confirm the significant influence of the input probability distribution on the test size required to reach a target test quality wrt a criterion, or equivalently on the test quality reached for a given test size [The 89]. For example, $R = 500 \Rightarrow N1 = 3451$ executions to reach $q_N = .999$ wrt the criteria set, while only 47 executions are required with R = 600. Inversely, 47 executions with R = 500 provide a test quality $q_N = .09$ instead of .999 with R = 600. Experiments provide good assessments E_i of the P_i. For example, from twelve test runs with R = 600, 700 and 1000, the mean (resp. maximum) values of the relative errors $|E_i - P_i|/P_i$ are 0.9% (4.5%) for $P_2 = P_3$ and 0.4 % (0.9%) for P_5. Each test run leads to an observed value E_5 such that the associated required test size is equal to the theoretical size N_5 related to P_5. From the values E_2, the discrepancies between experimental and theoretical evaluations of test sizes are negligible ($\leq$?)

4. DISCUSSION

The well known weakness of current structural and functional test criteria is the lack of connection with **actual fault exposure** [Ham 89]. From our definitions, it means that there is no direct relation between the program failure probability p and the coverage probability P_i of any criterion A_i. By using a P_i value as an a priori value of p to determine the test size, there is no guarantee that the statistical testing quality Q_N (definition 1) reaches the target one. All what we know is that $Q_N \geq q_N$ if and only if $p \geq P_i$ (see remark in § 2.2). In the case of deterministic testing, a fault is

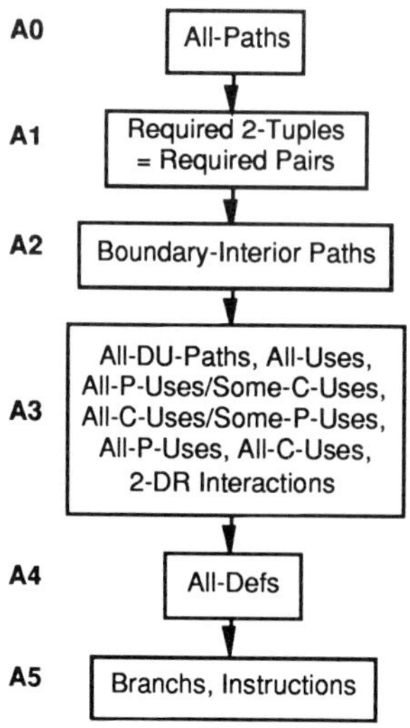

$P0 \approx 0$ due to the infinite number of complete paths in Q.

$P1 = \min\{$ Prob[(n_1, n_2, n_4)]; Prob[path(0)]; Prob[path(1)]; Prob[any path(q), $\forall q \geq 2$] $\}$.
$= \min\{ (R - 499) / R; 250 / R; 166 / R; 83 / R \}$.

$P2 = \min\{$ Prob[(n_1, n_2, n_4)]; Prob[path(0)]; Prob[any path(q), $\forall q \geq 1$] $\}$.
$= \min\{ (R - 499) / R; 250 / R; 249 / R \}$.

$P3 = \min\{$ Prob[(n_1, n_2, n_4)]; Prob[any path(q), $\forall q \geq 1$] $\}$.
$= \min\{ (R - 499) / R; 249 / R \}$.

$P4 =$ Prob[$(n_1, n_2, n_3, n_2, n_3)$] = Prob[any path(q), $\forall q \geq 1$].
$= 249 / R$.

$P5 =$ Prob[(n_1, n_2, n_3)] = Prob[any path(q), $\forall q \geq 0$].
$= 499 / R$.

The numerical expressions given here are those for $R \geq 500$.

(a) Criteria ordering and coverage probabilities P_i, i = 0, ..., 5.

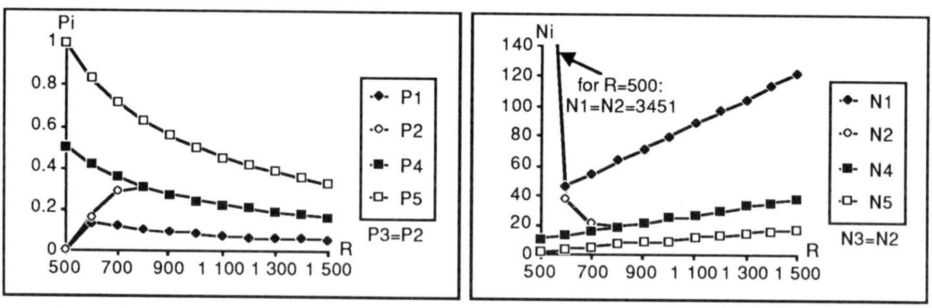

(b) P_i (i = 1, ..., 5) with the input X uniformly distributed in [1—R].

(c) Test sizes N_i required for q_N =.999, with X uniformly distributed in [1—R].

FIGURE 5. Some results for the program Q.

revealed if and only if at least one of the test inputs selectively chosen according to the adopted criterion exposes the fault. Hence, one can expect that errors due to faulty behaviors related to the criterion are most probably detected by deterministic inputs, while the probability of revealing the other faults is higher in the case of random inputs. This is one of the main complementary features of deterministic and statistical testing listed in [The 89].

Concerning **path selection criteria**, the theoretical evaluation of coverage probabilities P_i as functions of the input probability distribution involves an analysis of the program which is useful to determine appropriate input probabilities, i.e. such that the associated test size, and then test time, are reasonably large. In practice, whether the test inputs are deterministic or randomly selected, structural criteria can be applied only to programs whose control and data flow graph complexity remains tractable. For large programs, different criteria must be investigated. In spite of the intrinsic limits of the structural criteria, theoretical orderings using the subsumption or the R-subsumption relations are needed to guide numerous users which adopt these criteria nowadays. It is well obvious that more stringent is the criterion, more efficient is the associated test input set. Hence, as each criterion involves a proper testing size (see [Bie 89, Wey 90] for deterministic testing, and equation (2b) for statistical testing), the criterion choice can result from an objective compromise between test efficiency and cost constraints.

An **unexecutable path** is a path the execution probability of which is null whatever be the input distribution. The existence of such paths sets a problem wrt path selection criteria as no test set can satisfy a criterion involving an unexecutable path (for statistical testing, $P_i = 0 \Rightarrow N_i \rightarrow \infty$). The program analysis performed to evaluate P_i should point out unexecutable paths, although there is no general algorithm to decide whether a path is executable or not. To cope with this problem, a family of feasible criteria, derived from the one based on the def/use graph [Rap 85], is proposed in [Fra 88]. Roughly speaking, the feasible criteria restrict the sets of elements to be exercised by excluding unexecutable paths. A partial ordering of these criteria using the subsumption relation is also shown in [Fra 88], which differs slightly from the one related to the previous def/use criteria [Rap 85]. One can also demonstrate that the partial ordering of the feasible criteria induced by the R-subsumption relation is identical to the one given in [Fra 88].

5. CONCLUSION

The definitions proposed in section 2 allows to **quantify the efficiency of statistical testing wrt any criterion**. The ideal criterion asks that every residual fault in a software be revealed. Unfortunately, it does not seem feasible to refer to an accurate software design fault model in the present state of the art. Hence, the ideal criterion cannot be used to select test inputs and other criteria must be studied. This paper mainly concentrates on **structural criteria** which are often used in practice. It does not meant that such criteria are the best ones in our mind, but they are possible approaches to determine both an input probability distribution and a test size such that the program structure is properly scanned during a statistical testing experiment. Other criteria are under investigation, for example the one involved in the modeling tool outlined in [The 89] which is based on the program functions. An **experimental work** is currently performed on a piece of **industrial software** from the nuclear power field, to study the fault exposure power of statistical testing runs determined from various criteria. Finally, let us recall that software validation involves both fault removal and **fault forecasting** [Lap 89], and that statistical testing performed with an input probability distribution representative of user profile allows a quantitative assessment of the software reliability [Cur 86]. Our current work also concentrates on this second facet, which is not addressed in the present paper.

ACKNOWLEDGMENT

I thank Alain Costes, Jean-Claude Laprie, Yves Crouzet and Hélène Waeselynck at LAAS for their constructive comments and suggestions during the preparation of this paper. I am grateful to Jean-Yves Gadeau for the experimental work he performed in our research group within the scope of a student project.

REFERENCES

[Bie 89] J. M. Bieman, J. L. Schultz: "Estimating the number of test cases required to satisfy the All-du-paths testing criterion", *3rd IEEE Symposium on Software Testing, Analysis and Verification*, Key West, USA, December 1989, pp. 179-186.

[Cla 89] L. A. Clarke et al.: "A formal evaluation of data flow path selection", *IEEE Transactions on Software Engineering*, Vol. SE-15, No. 11, November 1989, pp. 1318-1331.

[Cur 86] P. A. Currit, M. Dyer, H. D. Mills: "Certifying the reliability of software", *IEEE Transactions on Software Engineering*, Vol. SE-12, No. 1, January 1986, pp. 3-11.

[DeM 87] R. A. DeMillo et al.: "Software testing and evaluation", *The Benjamin/Cummings Publishing Company, Inc.*, Menlo Park (CA), USA, 1987.

[Dur 84] J. W. Duran, S. C. Ntafos: "An evaluation of random testing", *IEEE Transactions on Software Engineering*, Vol. SE-10, No. 4, July 1984, pp. 438-444.

[Fra 88] P. G. Frankl, E. J. Weyuker: "An applicable family of data flow testing criteria", *IEEE Transactions on Software Engineering*, Vol. SE-14, No. 10, October 1988, pp. 1483-1498.

[Gad 89] J-Y. Gadeau: "Analyse des performances du test statistique de logiciel", *Student Project*, Laboratoire d'Automatique et d'Analyse des Systèmes, Toulouse, France, June 1989.

[Gir 73] E. Girard, J-C. Rault: "A programming technique for software reliability", *1st IEEE Symposium on Computer Software Reliability*, New York, USA, 1973, pp. 44-50..

[Gir 86] M. R. Girgis, M. R. Woodward: "An experimental comparison of the error exposing ability of program testing criteria", *1st Workshop Soft.Testing*, Banff, Canada, July 1986, pp. 64-73.

[Gou 83] J. S. Gourlay: "A mathematical framework for the investigation of testing", *IEEE Transactions on Software Engineering*, Vol. SE-9, No. 6, November 1983, pp. 686-709.

[Ham 86] D. Hamlet: "Testing for probable correctness", *1st IEEE Workshop on Software Testing*, Banff, Canada, July 1986, pp. 92-97.

[Ham 89] R. Hamlet: "Theoretical comparison of testing methods", *3rd IEEE Symposium on Software Testing, Analysis and Verification*, Key West, USA, December 1989, pp. 28-37.

[Her 76] P. M. Herman: "A data flow analysis approach to program testing", *Australian Comput. Journal*, Vol. 8, No. 3, November 1976, pp. 92-96.

[How 75] W. E. Howden: "Methodology for the generation of program test data", *IEEE Transactions on Computers*, Vol. C-24, No. 5, May 1975, pp. 554-559.

[How 77] W. E. Howden: "Symbolic testing-design techniques, costs and effectiveness", *NTIS PB-268518*, May 1977.

[Lap 89] J-C. Laprie: "Dependability: a unifying concept for reliable computing and fault tolerance", Chapter 1 in "Dependability of resilient computers" (Ed. T. Anderson), *BSP Professional Books*, UK, 1989, pp. 1-28.

[Lap 90] J-C. Laprie: "Dependability: basic concepts and associated terminology", *PDCS Project First Year Report (ESPRIT Project 3092)*, Volume 1, Chapter 1, May 1990.

[Mor 78] P. B. Moranda: "Limits to program testing with random number inputs", *COMPSAC'78*, Chicago, USA, November 1978, pp. 521-526.

[Nta 84] S. C. Ntafos: "On required element testing", *IEEE Transactions on Software Engineering*, Vol. SE-10, No. 6, November 1984, pp. 795-803.

[Nta 88] S. C. Ntafos: "A comparison of some structural testing strategies", *IEEE Transactions on Software Engineering*, Vol. SE-14, No. 6, June 1988, pp. 868-874.

[Rap 85] S. Rapps, E. J. Weyuker: "Selecting software test data using data flow information", *IEEE Transactions on Software Engineering*, Vol. SE-11, No. 4, April 1985, pp. 367-375.

[The 89] P. Thévenod-Fosse: "Software validation by means of statistical testing: retrospect and future direction", *Int. Working Conference on Dependable Computing For Critical Applications*, Santa Barbara, USA, August 1989, pp. 15-22.

[Wey 90] E. J. Weyuker: "The cost of data flow testing: an empirical study", *IEEE Transactions on Software Engineering*, Vol. SE-16, No. 2, February 1990, pp. 121-128.

[Zei 88] S. J. Zeil: "Selectivity of data-flow and control-flow path criteria", *2nd IEEE Workshop on Software Testing, Verification and Analysis*, Banff, Canada, July 1988, pp. 216-222.

Approving Software Products
W. Ehrenberger (Editor)
Elsevier Science Publishers B.V. (North-Holland)

A Bayes Sequential Statistical Procedure for Approving Products in Mutation-Based Software Testing

Mehmet Şahinoğlu *
Department of Statistics
Mathematical Sciences Building
Purdue University
West Lafayette, Indiana 47907
xnse@vm.cc.purdue.edu

Eugene H. Spafford
Software Engineering Research Center
Department of Computer Science
Purdue University
West Lafayette, Indiana 47907
spaf@cs.purdue.edu

Abstract

Mutation analysis is a well-studied method of measuring test-case adequacy. Mutation analysis involves the *mutation* of a program by introduction of a small syntactic change in the software. Existing test data sets are then executed against all these *mutant programs.* If the test data set is adequate for testing the original program, it will distinguish all of the incorrect mutant programs from the original program. As an ad-hoc procedure, a stopping criterion is conventionally based on a given "Y% of the mutants to be distinguished" with a certain "confidence level of X%" over a multiplicity of random test cases.

Alternatively, we propose a Bayes sequential procedure for testing $H_0 : p = p_1$ (acceptable fraction of live mutants to demonstrate good quality) vs. $H_A : p = p_2$ (unacceptable fraction of live mutants to demonstrate bad quality). This derives a sequential probability ratio testing (SPRT) that is the most economical sampling scheme with given prior probabilities, decision and sampling cost functions. The implementation of our proposed method on a sample program shows the cost effectiveness of the new technique as compared to the current, deterministic approach, which was not structured by statistical hypothesis testing.

---

* Currently visiting Purdue University from Middle East Technical University (METU), Ankara, Turkey on a Fulbright Scholarship, support which is gratefully acknowledged.

1 Introduction

Software testing is a critical phase of the software development life cycle. However, software testing can be an expensive proposition. One desires to obtain an adequate measure of the reliability of a software system while minimizing the expenditure of resources. Testing is always a trade-off between increased confidence in the correctness of the software under examination, and constraints on the amount of time and effort that can be spent testing that software.

For over a decade, researchers have been working with *program mutation* as a method of developing test cases to test software.[1] A basic goal of program mutation is to provide the user with a measure of test set *adequacy*, by executing that test set against a collection of program *mutations*. Mutations are simple changes introduced one at a time into the code being tested. These changes are derived empirically from studies of errors commonly made by programmers when translating requirements into code, although theoretical justification also can be found for their selection[13].

A mutant is *killed* if the execution of the mutated code against the test set distinguishes the behavior or output of the mutation from the unmutated code. The more mutants killed by a test set, the better the measured adequacy of the test set. By proper choice of mutant operators, comprehensive testing can be performed, [5] including path coverage [16] and domain analysis. [26] By examination of unkilled mutants, testers can add new test cases to better the adequacy score of the entire test set.

Mutation analysis is designed to substantiate the correctness of a program Φ. Mutation analysis strives to develop test data that, when applied to the program Φ, illustrates the equality of the *intended* and *observed* behaviors of Φ. This methodology is normally embedded in a test environment that enables a tester to test his program interactively.

Somewhat more formally, the mutation approach is to induce syntactically correct changes into a program Φ, thereby creating a set of *mutant programs*. Each mutant represents a possible error in Φ, and the goal of the tester is to construct a set of test data τ that distinguishes the output or behavior of $\Phi(\tau)$ from that of all mutant programs. Test data sensitive enough to distinguish all mutant programs is deemed adequate to infer the probable correctness of Φ.

The mutation analysis methodology is as follows: submit a program Φ and a set of test data τ whose adequacy is to be determined. The mutation system first executes Φ with respect to τ. If the results are incorrect, then certainly Φ is in error. However, if the results appear correct, it may still be that Φ is in error, for the test data set τ may not be adequate to distinguish this inherent incorrectness. In this case, a set of *mutant programs* are created, call them $\Phi_1, \ldots, \Phi_m$. Each mutant program differs from the original program Φ by one single-point, syntactically correct change. Such *mutant transformations* are statically defined for a language Λ and designed to expose errors frequently committed by programmers using Λ.

For each execution of a mutant against the test set, $\Phi_i(\tau)$, exactly one of two things happens:

[1] The mutant $\Phi_i(\tau)$ yields different results than $\Phi(\tau)$, or

[1] Program mutation has been well documented in the literature and will only be summarized here. The reader unfamiliar with mutation testing is directed to recent references on mutation for detailed descriptions and further references, e.g. [8, 24, 17, 6, 27, 19].

[2] The mutant $\Phi_i(\tau)$ yield the same results as $\Phi(\tau)$.

In the first case, the mutant is said to be *dead* since the mutant difference between Φ_i and Φ has been distinguished by τ. In the second case, either:

[a] τ is not adequate to distinguish the mutant that gave rise to Φ_i, or

[b] Φ and Φ_i are *equivalent programs* and no test data τ can distinguish their behavior (the "error" that gave rise to Φ_i was not an error at all, but an alternate encoding of Φ). Such a Φ_i is called an *equivalent mutant.*

Test data that leaves no live mutants or only equivalent mutants is said to be of adequate sensitivity to infer the probable correctness of Φ. Moreover, the ratio of dead mutants to the total number of nonequivalent mutants yields a relative measure of the adequacy of the test data τ in testing Φ. The test set τ may be augmented with additional test cases and the process repeated until an appropriate level of test case adequacy or threshold level in the cost of the test (in terms of dollars, resources, etc.) has been reached. The test set τ can then be carried into the maintenance stage of the software life cycle.

2 On MOTHRA and the Stopping Rule

The MOTHRA software testing environment [10, 9, 8, 15] is an integrated set of tools and interfaces that support the planning, definition, preparation, execution, analysis, and evaluation of mutation-based tests of software systems. MOTHRA is designed to be used starting at the earliest stages of software development and continuing through the progressively later stages of system integration, acceptance testing, operation, and maintenance. It has been in use at Purdue and other locations for the last few years as a testbed for experimental work in software engineering.

One of the drawbacks to full mutation testing with a system such as MOTHRA involves the number of mutations that must be executed. Each mutation is equal to the size and complexity of the original program, and the number of mutants is proportional to the square of the number of lines of source code present in the original software. Each mutant may need to be run against many test cases before being distinguished from the original code. For routines in the hundreds of lines of code, this may result in millions of separate executions.

It would be beneficial to test only a small statistically random sampling of mutants against the given test cases to determine, at some arbitrary level of confidence, that the program is correct. This would be of great utility in situations where full mutation testing would be too expensive, too time consuming, or simply beyond the capabilities of the available testing software.

Conventionally, a typical mutation system user must specify test requirements of the following form: [15] "I must be X% sure that Y% of the mutants of type Z are killed in unit A." Here, X% is the degree of assurance MOTHRA will use to perform the random selection of mutants of type Z in unit A. The user must still monitor the status information to determine whether or not the stopping criteria Y% for the test of mutants of type Z in unit A has been achieved. Hence, one defines a stopping criterion based on a given "Y% of the mutants to be killed" with a certain confidence level X% over a multiplicity of test-cases.

This approach may be defined as a deterministic stopping rule-of-thumb, since the entire experiment is of a random nature and is not structured by statistical hypothesis testing. The customary ad hoc approach, although straightforward and easy, may result in a waste of testing time and resources due to lack of a statistical risk analysis. The only definitive statement that can be made from such testing involves achieving a 100% level of mutant distinction.

3 Sequential Statistical Procedures

The usual statistical hypothesis-testing procedures ordinarily have fixed sample size. In particular, the statistical testing procedures have only answered the question, "Do we have sufficient evidence to declare a particular hypothesis false?" Other models address the question, "When have we corrected an 'optimum' number of errors? That is, should we now release the software?" [2] However, if we allow the sample size to increase without limit, we can obtain a test for any prespecified probability of occurrence of Type I and Type II errors.[2] Thus, if testing for $H_0 : p = p_1$ vs $H_A : p = p_2$, we can assure ourselves of our choice given the probability of a wrong decision. We can thus test software to any prespecified level of confidence and criticality, rather than to some single, theoretical "optimum" point. [11, 14]

Our approach will be to sample $X_1 = x_1, \ldots, X_k = x_k$ and after each observation $X_k = x_k$, make a decision based on $x_1, \ldots, x_k$ whether or not to continue sampling. If we stop, we want to choose between H_0 and H_A. [23]

4 The Sequential Probability Ratio Test (SPRT)

Let $x_1, x_2, \ldots$ be i.i.d r.v.'s with p.d.f. f(x;p) $p \in \Omega = \{p_1, p_2\}$. Let $f_1(x) = f(x; p_1); f_2(x) = f(x; p_2)$. We want to test $H_0 : p = p_1$ vs $H_A : p = p_2$ without fixing the sample size in advance. [23, 25]

For a fixed sample size k, the NP (Neyman Pearson) Lemma tells us to reject for large values of the ratio

$$\lambda_k = \frac{f_2(x_1)f_2(x_2)\ldots f_2(x_k)}{f_1(x_1)f_1(x_2)\ldots f_1(x_k)} \tag{1}$$

Wald [23] tells us to consider the sequence of ratios $\lambda_1(x_1), \lambda_2(x_1, x_2), \ldots, \lambda(x_1, \ldots, x_k)$, i.e. consider the sequence:

$$\frac{f_2(x_1)}{f_1(x_1)}, \frac{f_2(x_1)f_2(x_2)}{f_1(x_1)f_1(x_2)}, \frac{f_2(x_1)\ldots f_2(x_k)}{f_1(x_1)\ldots f_1(x_k)} \tag{2}$$

Definition: The SPRT [25, 23, 12] (Test) for testing $H_0 : p = p_1$ versus $H_A : p = p_2$ is a rule that states:

1. if $\lambda_k(x) >= \mathcal{A}$, stop sampling and reject H_0 (accept H_A).
2. if $\lambda_k(x) <= \mathcal{B}$, stop sampling and reject H_A (accept H_0).

[2] In this context, a Type II error is mistakenly accepting a faulty program. A Type I error is mistakenly rejecting a good program as faulty.

3. if $\mathcal{B} < \lambda_k(x) < \mathcal{A}$, continue sampling and take another observation x_{k+1}.

Here $\mathcal{A}$ and $\mathcal{B}$ are constants determined so that α = P{Type I error} = P{Reject $H_0 \,|\, p_1$}, i.e. probability of rejecting H_0 when $H_0 : p = p_1$ is true. β = P{Type II error} = P{Fail to Reject $H_0 \,|\, p_2$}, i.e. probability of accepting H_0 when H_A is true.

Namely, if N is the stopping time for this procedure,

$$\alpha = P_{p_1}(\lambda_N(x) >= \mathcal{A}) \tag{3}$$

$$\beta = P_{p_2}(\lambda_N(x) <= \mathcal{B}) \tag{4}$$

5 Binomial SPRT

Let $x_1, x_2, \ldots$ be i.i.d. Bernoulli r.v.'s with p.d.f. f(x;p) = $p^x(1-p)^{1-x}$ x=0,1.
We now wish to test for $H_0 : p = p_1$ vs $H_A : p = p_2$. [20, 23]

$$z_i = \log(\frac{f(x_i;p_2)}{f(x_i;p_1)}) = \begin{cases} \log(\frac{p_2}{p_1}) & \text{if } x_i = 1 \\ \log(\frac{1-p_2}{1-p_1}) & \text{if } x_i = 0 \end{cases}$$

Then

$$S_k = \sum_{i=1}^{k} Z_i = r_k \log(\frac{p_2}{p_1}) + (k - r_k)\log(\frac{1-p_2}{1-p_1}) \tag{5}$$

where r_k = number of 1's in $x_1, \ldots, x_k = \sum_{i=1}^{k} x_i$. We observe $S_k = s_k$ and continue sampling if $b < s_k < a$ i.e.

$$b < r_k \log(\frac{p_2}{p_1}) + (k - r_k)\log(\frac{1-p_2}{1-p_1}) < a, \tag{6}$$

$$b < r_k(\log(\frac{p_2}{p_1}) - \log(\frac{1-p_2}{1-p_1})) + k\log(\frac{1-p_2}{1-p_1}) < a \tag{7}$$

Solving the inequality for r_k, we obtain, as illustrated in figure 1:

$$\frac{b - k\log((1-p_2)/(1-p_1))}{\log((p_2)/(p_1)) - \log((1-p_2)/(1-p_1))} < r_k < \frac{a - k\log((1-p_2)/(1-p_1))}{\log((p_2)/(p_1)) - \log((1-p_2)/(1-p_1))} \quad \text{if } p_2 < p_1 \tag{8}$$

6 An Economical Bayesian SPRT in Mutation-Based Testing

We now propose a Bayes sequential procedure for testing $H_0 : p = p_1$ (acceptable fraction of live mutants to demonstrate good quality) vs. $H_A : p = p_2$ (unacceptable fraction of live mutants to demonstrate bad quality), where the prior distribution is given as $P(p = p_1) = a_1, P(p = p_2) = a_2; a_1 + a_2 = 1, p_1 < p_2$.

This derives a sequential probability ratio test (SPRT) that is the most economical sampling scheme with given prior probabilities, and decision and sampling cost functions. The implementation of our proposed method on a sample program shows the cost effectiveness of the new technique as compared to the current, deterministic approach, which

$\alpha = \beta = 0.100,\ p_1 = \frac{1}{4},\ p_2 = \frac{3}{4}$

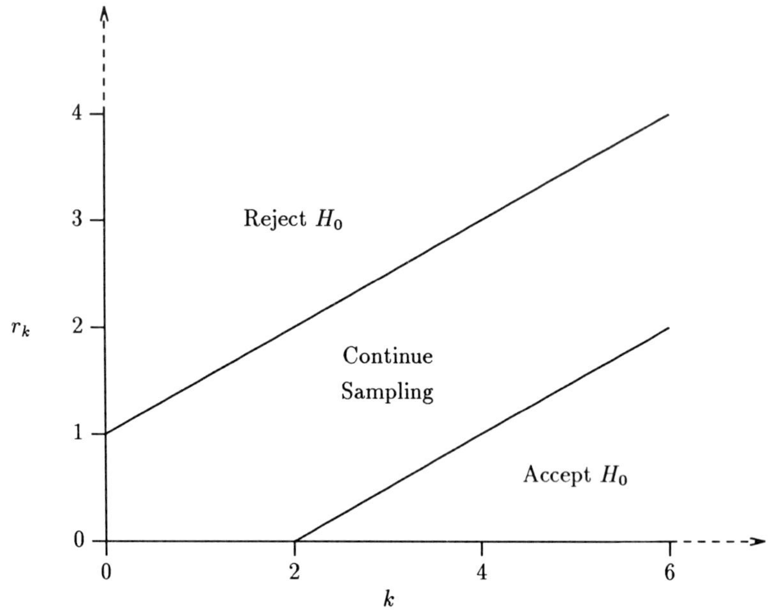

Figure 1: $r_k = \sum_{i=1}^{k} x_i$ vs. k

was not structured by statistical hypothesis testing. We note here that Bayesian Sequential testing also defaults to the simple sequential procedure with no priors; or, if used with priors, when the sample size increases the a effect eventually becomes negligible. [12]

In a mutation-based testing environment, a sample (batch) of mutants (items) is inspected (executed against a test data set) and the mutants are classified as either dead (effective) or live (defective). Let p denote the fraction of live mutants within a selected sample of nonequivalent mutants. We assume that:

- a critical fraction of live mutants, p_0, is known to exist;
- that a sample with a fraction of live mutants $p < p_0$ is accepted as a good sample (the program is judged correct); and
- others with $p > p_0$ are programs not yet judged correct, and are returned for further testing or rejected.

Let $P(p)$ denote the prior distribution function based on apriori subjective software engineering judgment. Within the sample for the software product submitted for inspection, we have the following: $P(p = p_1) = a_1, P(p = p_2) = a_2$ where $a_1 + a_2 = 1$ and $p_1 < p_0 < p_2$.

Also, let W_{21} denote the decision cost incurred if a software product with fraction live-mutants p_1 is rejected, analogous to the type-I probability of α in rejecting a good product mistakenly. Similarly, let W_{12} denote the decision cost incurred if a software product with a fraction live-mutants p_2 is accepted, analogous to the type-II probability of β in accepting a bad product mistakenly. Let c denote the cost of inspecting a single mutant. Now, the problem is to determine the most economical sampling inspection plan. We want to structure our problem of product acceptance sampling to that of testing two simple hypotheses $H_0 : p = p_1$ vs. $H_A : p = p_2$. Namely, we decide to accept a software product if H_0 holds true, and to reject it if H_A holds true. Otherwise, we continue sampling.

In a sequential sampling inspection plan, one mutant (item) is inspected at a time and the inspection is stopped as soon as sufficient evidence is observed in favor of either of the hypotheses. Hence, as long as the cost of inspection depends merely on the total number of mutants inspected and no extra overhead cost is involved, a sequential sampling inspection plan will be the most economical one. Wald and Wolfowitz [22] proved that when testing two simple hypotheses, the sequential probability ratio test requires, on average, the fewest observations among all tests with the same power.

Thus, this means that of all the sampling plans with the same or lower decision costs, a plan based on the SPRT will have the minimum cost of inspection. For mutation testing, where each test involves potentially expensive execution of mutated programs against large test sets, this finding is especially important.

Following is the method of arriving at the optimum SPRT procedure based on the basic theory given by Barnard [3]:

The optimum test procedure will be given as:

- Continue inspection as long as $\lambda_2 < \lambda = (a_1/a_2)l(x,y) < \lambda_1$
- Stop inspection and accept the batch as soon as $\lambda > \lambda_1$
- Stop inspection and reject the batch as soon as $\lambda < \lambda_2$

where x and y denote, respectively, the number of dead mutants and live mutants obtained at any stage, and $l(x,y)$ is the likelihood ratio. This ration is equal to: $l(x,y) = (p_1/p_2)^y(q_1/q_2)^x$ where $q_1 = 1 - p_1$ and $q_2 = 1 - p_2$.

It is more convenient to write the inequality in step 1 of the above as follows:

$$L = \frac{a_2\lambda_2}{a_1} < l(x,y) < U = \frac{a_2\lambda_1}{a_1} \tag{9}$$

in which similar rules for acceptance and rejection apply.

Let $A(U, L, p)$ be the probability that a sample with fraction live-mutants p will be accepted. Let $R(U, L; p) = 1 - A(U, L; p)$ be defined as the rejection probability. Let $S(U, L; p)$ denote the average number of mutants required to be inspected.

To obtain equations for the optimum boundaries, we proceed in the manner indicated in equation (9). [21] The decision boundary is the locus of points such that the expected cost of taking an immediate decision is equal to the expected cost of taking at least one more observation and continuing the test. For instance, when $\lambda = \lambda_1$, we calculate the expected cost of acceptance as a function of the prior probabilities and decision costs. If we take another observation, then a dead mutant leads to accepting the sample, incurring a decision cost (W_{12}), and a live mutant will take us to a point where we either continue the test or reject immediately, incurring a decision cost (W_{21}). We determine λ_1 to be that value for which these two costs of accepting immediately and of taking one more observation to continue the test, if necessary, are equal. It is noted, in general, that the difference between the expected cost of an immediate decision and expected cost of continuing the test should decrease as the sample (mutant) size increases considerably.

As a result of the optimization procedure, [21] i.e., equating the expected cost of an immediate decision to the expected cost of at least one more mutant inspected, we have the following equations as a result:

For $\rho = (\lambda_2/\lambda_1) < (p_1/p_2)$,

$$\lambda_1 = \frac{W_{12}p_2R(p_2/p_1,(\lambda_2p_2)/(\lambda_1p_1);p_2) - c - p_2cS(p_2/p_1,(\lambda_2p_2)/(\lambda_1p_1);p_2)}{W_{21}p_1R(p_2/p_1,(\lambda_2p_2)/(\lambda_1p_1);p_1) + c + p_1cS(p_2/p_1,(\lambda_2p_2)/(\lambda_1p_1);p_1)}; \tag{10}$$

$$\text{and for } \rho = \frac{\lambda_2}{\lambda_1} > \frac{p_1}{p_2},\ \lambda_1 = \frac{W_{12}p_2 - c}{W_{21} + c} \tag{11}$$

Similary,

$$\rho = \frac{\lambda_2}{\lambda_1} < \frac{q_1}{q_2},\ \lambda_1 = \frac{W_{12}q_2A(q_2/(\rho q_1),q_2/q_1;p_2) + c + q_2cS(q_2/(\rho q_1),q_2/q_1;p_2)}{W_{21}q_1A(q_2/(\rho q_1),q_2/q_1;q_1) - c - q_1cS(q_2/(\rho q_1),q_2/q_1;p_1)} \tag{12}$$

7 Barnard's Score Notation for a Binomial SPRT

The following derivation is from [21]:

According to Barnard [3], any sequential probability ratio test procedure for a binomial population can be reduced (without much loss in accuracy) to a scoring procedure as follows: Take the logarithms on both sides of (9) and divide throughout by $\log(q_1/q_2)$:

$$\frac{\log L}{\log(q_1q_2)} < X - Y\frac{\log(p_2/p_1)}{\log(q_1/q_2)} < \frac{\log U}{log(q_1/q_2)} \tag{13}$$

and then define:

$$H_1 = \frac{\log U}{\log(q_1/q_2)} \tag{14}$$

$$H_2 = \frac{\log L}{\log(q_1/q_2)} \tag{15}$$

If we round off b, H_1 and H_2 to the nearest integers, the sequential likelihood ratio test procedure reduces to the following scoring scheme: Start with a score H_2, and add one to the score for each dead mutant observed, and subtract b for each live mutant found. Reject the sample (assume the test data is not strong enough) if the score falls to zero or less, and accept the sample if the score reaches $2H = H_1 + H_2$.

As a procedure for calculation, in practice, we shall first have to fix values for a_1, a_2, p_1, p_2, W_{12}, W_{21}, and c. The quantity b can then be calculated by

$$b = \frac{\log(p_2/p_1)}{\log(q_1/q_2)} \tag{16}$$

Then calculate

$$2H = \frac{-\log(\rho)}{\log(q_1/q_2)} \tag{17}$$

Where ρ can be estimated by calculating the interval given by:

$$\frac{c^2}{[w_{12}(q_1 - q_2) - c][W_{21}(q_1 - q_2) - c]} < \rho < 1 \tag{18}$$

From experience, it appears that the lower limit, or any number a little higher than the lower limit, can serve as a good first guess for ρ in order to start the iteration. Formulae for the average sample size and acceptance probability of such a scheme have been given by Burman [7] and Anscombe [1]. They are exact if b, H_1 and H_2 are integers. The error involved in rounding off is small if b is greater than 10, and this is often the case in practice. If we replace $A(U, L; p)$ etc., as defined earlier, by $A(H_1, H_2; p)$ etc., in score notation, we get, if $\rho < p_1/p_2$:

$$\rho = F(\rho) = \frac{W_{12}q_2A(2H-1,1;p_2) + c + q_2cS(2H-1,1;p_2)}{W_{21}q_1A(2H-1,1;p_1) - c - q_1cS(2H-1,1;p_2)} \tag{19}$$
$$* \frac{W_{21}p_1R(b,2H-b;p_1) + c + p_1cS(b,2H-b;p_1)}{W_{12}p_2R(b,2H-b;p_2) - c - p_2cS(b,2H-b;p_2)}$$

If $\rho > (p_1)/(p_2)$, we get

$$\rho = F_1(\rho) = \frac{[W_{12}q_2A(2H-1,1;p_2) + c + q_2cS(2H-1,1;p_2)][W_{21}p_1 + c]}{[W_{21}q_1A(2H-1,1;p_1) - c - q_1cS(2H-1,1;p_1)][W_{12}p_2 - c]} \tag{20}$$

In both cases, b and $2H$ are as denoted in (16) and (17).

To solve equations (19) and (20), we start with some guessed values for ρ and proceed with the iteration until we get the same value of ρ. Hence, when we get a value that gives rise to the same value of $2H$ as was used in the previous iteration, we stop and take that as our solution. Once ρ is obtained, we calculate λ_1 and λ_2 from equations (10) and (12) or (11) and (12).

Wald, Barnard and Bartlett [23, 3, 4] have given simple asymptotic formulae for the chance of acceptance and average sample size of an open scheme. Setting $X = p(b+1)$ we consider the limit $p \to 0$ with X constant. Wald's formula for the chance of acceptance then becomes

$$A = \frac{\exp(R_2T) - 1}{\exp(R_2T) - \exp(-R_1T)} \tag{21}$$

where

$$X = \frac{T}{(\exp(T) - 1)}, \quad R_1 = \frac{H_1}{(b+1)}, \quad \text{and } R_2 = \frac{H_2}{(b+2)}$$

Barnard and Bartlett's formula lead to the same result except that X is replaced by $X = 2/(T+2)$, which is equivalent to the earlier X formula when X is near 1. Wald and Bartlett [4, 22] give a formula for the average sample size S as defined by:

$$\frac{S}{b+1} = \frac{R_1P - R_2(1-P)}{1-X} \tag{22}$$

provided $X \neq 1$, while for $X = 1$

$$\frac{S}{b+1} = R_1R_2 \tag{23}$$

as $p \to 0$, S and $(b+1) \to \infty$, and their ratio tends to the limit shown.

8 Illustrative Examples as Applied to Mutation

To illustrate this method, we applied it to the *trityp* program, first presented in [18]. This program takes as input three integers representing the length of the sides of a triangle, and then determines whether sides define scalene, isosceles, equilateral, or illegal. This program was chosen because of its widespread use in the testing literature, and because of our familiarity with it in other work (e.g., [15] and [19]).

The routine contains 30 lines of Fortran-77 code. The MOTHRA mutation environment generates 951 mutants for this program, 107 of which are equivalent (leaving 844 non-equivalent). The smallest test set we know of that can kill 100% of non-equivalent mutants has 27 test cases.

Our proposed most economical sequential test method is as follows:

1. Initialization. Set $Sum = H_2$. Set $\mathcal{T} = \emptyset$, where $\mathcal{T}$ is the set of test cases generated so far. Generate the non-equivalent mutants, $\mathcal{M}$, for the program. Set $\mathcal{H} = \emptyset$, where $\mathcal{H}$ is a holding set for mutants. Go to step 2.

2. Select a mutant $m \in \mathcal{M}$ at random. $\mathcal{M} = \mathcal{M} - m$. Go to step 3.

3. Execute m against $t, \forall t \in \mathcal{T}$. If m is killed, remove it from $\mathcal{M}$ and go to step 4, else $\mathcal{H} \leftarrow \mathcal{H} + m$ and go to step 5.

4. $Sum = Sum + 1$ If $Sum >= 2H$ accept the test set and stop, else go to step 2.

5. $Sum = Sum - b$. If $Sum > 0$ go to step 2, else go to step 6.

6. Develop a new test case, τ that kills the current mutant, m. Set $\mathcal{T} \leftarrow \mathcal{T} + \tau$. Go to step 7.

7. $\forall m \in \mathcal{H}$ execute m against τ. If m is killed, set $\mathcal{H} \leftarrow \mathcal{H} - m$, set $Sum = Sum + b + 1$. If $Sum >= 2H$, accept the test set and stop. Otherwise, go to step 2.

In short, we are adding test cases to $\mathcal{T}$ until we are able to kill a total of H_1 mutants, selected at random, when executed against the cases in $\mathcal{T}$. After this is accomplished, we stop, and then use $\mathcal{T}$ to test the original, non-mutated code.

For our tests, we used the prior probabilities and costs developed for the examples in [21]. The following tables illustrate our results. The first column in each table indicates the number of mutants selected in step 2 before it was necessary to generate a new testcase. The second column indicates the number of live mutants after executing **all** mutants against the test cases accumulated in $\mathcal{T}$ to that point.

In each of the following tables, the first column represents the number of test cases that are in the set $\mathcal{T}$ at that point in the test. The second column represents the number of mutants executed (as in step 3) before we stop to accept the test set or generate a new test case to add to $\mathcal{T}$. The third column indicates the number of non-equivalent mutants that would still be considered live if they **all** were executed against the test set $\mathcal{T}$, as would be done in the deterministic method of mutation testing.

8.1 Example 1

In this example,

$$a_1 = \frac{5}{9}, a_2 = \frac{4}{9}, p_1 = 0.01, p_2 = 0.10, W_{21} = 400, W_{12} = 500, \ and \ c = 1$$

The necessary calculations result in values of

$$H_2 = 34, 2H = H_1 + H_2 = 68, b = 24$$

Cases in T	Mutants Examined	Total Live Mutants
0	1	844
1	3	692
2	5	627
3	6	538
4	7	510
5	8	453
6	11	433
7	27	345
8	32	282
9	35	199
10	60	106
11	90	93
12	108	71
13	116	61
14	accept	53

Thus, the test set was accepted after generating 14 test cases when *Sum*, as described in section 8, reached $2H = 68$, or exceeded it. These 14 test cases form a test set that kills over 93% of the live mutants using the deterministic approach, and that is acceptable at the level of 99% (i.e., $100(1 - p_1)\%$) with our proposed testing approach.

Note that in the worst case, the number of mutant executions required is given by:

$$0 * 1 + 1 * 3 + 2 * 5 + 3 * 6 + \ldots + 13 * 16 + 1 = 1116$$

as compared to the deterministic case requiring

$$0 * 844 + 1 * 692 + \ldots + 13 * 61 = 5361$$

8.2 Example 2

In this example,

$$a_1 = 0.5981, a_2 = 0.4019, p_1 = 0.008663, p_2 = 0.041856, W_{21} = 143.6, W_{12} = 266, c = 1$$

The necessary calculations result in values of

$$H_2 = 12, \ 2H = H_1 + H_2 = 44, \ \text{and}\ b = 46$$

In this case, we accept the test set after generating 11 test cases that kill 88.4% of the live mutants using the deterministic approach, and is acceptable at the level of 99.13% with our suggested approach.

Cases in $\mathcal{T}$	Mutants Examined	Total Live Mutants
0	1	844
1	2	692
2	3	575
3	5	538
4	6	451
5	7	423
6	8	369
7	20	351
8	24	337
9	27	243
10	32	217
11	accept	98

9 Summary Discussion and Conclusions

As Barnard [3] has remarked, Wald's sequential procedure for testing the fraction defective of a batch of articles can be conveniently expressed in terms of a scoring system, as follows: [21]

> Sample the batch by drawing articles randomly from it one by one. Add 1 for a non-defective article, $-b$ for a defective. With starting score zero, accept the batch if the score reaches or exceeds H_1, reject it if the score falls to or below H_2. Continue sampling until one or another decision is reached. Or, identically, sample the batch, count +1 for a non-defective item, $-b$ for a defective. With starting score H_2, accept the batch if the score reaches $2H$, reject it if the score falls to zero or less.

In our mutation-oriented testing, the acceptance and rejection is of a test data set necessary to thoroughly test a piece of software. Once we accept a test set, we execute the original program against it to see if the software is correct. If we reject a test data set, we continue to augment the test data set until it is accepted.

When compared with the traditional method of mutation testing, this approach results in a great reduction in the number of executions required to judge a test set as adequate. Using the deterministic method may result in literally millions of executions as each mutant is executed against each test case, as the number of mutants is on order of the number of lines in the program, squared. However, our method may result in only a few hundred or thousand mutant executions to achieve a test set that can be used to test the software to the same level of confidence.

For instance, in our first example, the statistical sequential method we have described required no more than 1116 mutant executions, where the deterministic method required 5361 executions. Furthermore, our proposed SPRT resulted in a test data set with a statistically-determined probability of 99% adequacy, while the deterministic method resulted in a measure of only 93% of the mutants killed. Similarly, in example 2, our method required no more than 218 mutant executions compared to the 4196 executions required on the same test data for the deterministic case. Our method provided a test set 99.13% accurate (assuming correct priors and cost factors), while the deterministic method applied to the same test set only provides a measure of 88.4% adequacy.

We believe that the efficiency of our sequential approach, coupled with power of mutation testing, provides a cost-effective form of generating reliable test sets. Our proposed statistical sequential method requires only that we be able to establish costs of faulty acceptance, rejection, and sampling (mutant selection and test case generation), and prior testing probabilities—all of which are possible to do in most production environments.

References

[1] F. J. Anscombe. Tables of sequential inspection schemes to control fraction defective. *Journal of the Royal Statistical Society*, CXII(Part II):180–206, 1949.

[2] S. Bai and Y. Yun. Optimum number of errors corrected before releasing a software system. *IEEE Transactions on Reliability*, 37(1):41–44, April 1988.

[3] G. A. Barnard. Sequential tests in industrial statistics. *Journal of the Royal Statistical Society*, Suppl. 8:1–27, 1946.

[4] M. S. Bartlett. The large-sample theory of sequential tests. *Proceedings of the Cambridge Philosophy Society*, 42, 1946.

[5] Timothy A. Budd. *Mutation Analysis of Program Test Data.* PhD thesis, Yale University, 1980.

[6] Cathy Bullard and Eugene H. Spafford. Testing experience with MOTHRA. In *Proceedings of 25th Southeast ACM Conference*, Birmingham AL, April 1987.

[7] J. P. Burman. Sequential sampling formulae for a binomial population. *Journal of the Royal Statistical Society*, Suppl. 8:98–103, 1946.

[8] B. J. Choi, Richard A. DeMillo, Edward W. Krauser, R. J. Martin, Aditya Mathur, A. Jefferson Offutt, Hsin Pan, and Eugene H. Spafford. The MOTHRA tool set. In *Proceedings of the Hawaii International Conference on System Sciences*, Jan 1989.

[9] Richard A. DeMillo, Dany S. Guindi, K. N. King, W. M. McCracken, and A. Jefferson Offutt. An Extended Overview of the MOTHRA Mutation System. In *Proceedings of the Second Workshop on Software Testing, Verification and Analysis*, July 1988.

[10] Richard A. DeMillo and Eugene H. Spafford. The MOTHRA software testing environment. In *Proceedings of the 11th NASA Software Engineering Laboratory Workshop*, Dec 1986.

[11] Mehmet Şahinoğlu and Eugene H. Spafford. A sequential statistical procedure in mutation-based testing. In *Procedings of the 28th Reliability Spring Seminar*, pages 127–148, Boston, MA, April 1990. Central New England Reliability Chapter of the IEEE.

[12] R. Govindarajalu. *Sequential Statistical Procedures.* Academic Press, 1975.

[13] William E. Howden. *Functional Program Testing.* Prentice Hall, Englewood Cliffs, NJ, 1988.

[14] William Hsu, Mehmet Şahinoğlu, and Eugene H. Spafford. An experimental approach to statistical mutation-based testing. Technical Report SERC-TR-63, Software Engineering Research Center, Purdue University, February 1990.

[15] R. J. Martin. Using the MOTHRA software testing environment to ensure software quality. In *Proceedings of the IEEE National Aerospace and Electronics Conference*, May 1989.

[16] G. Myers. *The Art of Software Testing.* John Wiley and Sons, New York, NY, 1979.

[17] A. Jefferson Offutt and K. N. King. A fortran 77 interpreter for mutation analysis. In *Symposium on Interpreters and Interpretive Techniques*, pages 177–188, St. Paul, MN, June 1987. ACM SIGPLAN.

[18] C. V. Ramamoorthy, S. F. Ho, and W. T. Chen. On the automated generation of program test data. *IEEE Transactions on Software Engineering*, SE-2(4), 1976.

[19] Eugene H. Spafford. Extending mutation testing to find environmental bugs. *Software Practice and Experience*, 20(2), February 1990.

[20] Statistics Research Group. *Sequential Analysis of Statistical Data: Applications.* Columbia University Press, 1945.

[21] M. K. Vagholkar and G. B. Wetherill. The most economical binomial sequential probability ratio test. *Biometrika*, 47(1 and 2):103–109, 1960.

[22] A. Wald and J. Wolfowitz. Optimim character of the sequential probability ratio test. *Annals of Mathematical Statistics*, 19:326–339, 1948.

[23] Abraham Wald. *Selected Papers in Statistics and Probability.* McGraw Hill, 1945.

[24] P. J. Walsh. *A Measure of Test Case Completeness.* PhD thesis, State University of New York at Binghamton, 1985.

[25] G. B. Wetherill and K. D. Glazebrook. *Sequential Methods in Statistics.* Chapman and Hall, 1986. Third edition.

[26] Lee J. White and E. K. Cohen. A domain strategy for computer program testing. *IEEE Transactions on Software Engineering*, 6(3):247–257, May 1980.

[27] M. R. Woodward and K. Halewood. From weak to strong: Dead or alive? an analysis of some mutation testing issues. In *Proceedings of the Second Workshop on Software Testing, Verification and Analysis*, July 1988.

Approving Software Products
W. Ehrenberger (Editor)
Elsevier Science Publishers B.V. (North-Holland)

Functional Testing of Optimizing C Compilers

M. Ghiassi, Ph.D.

Department of Decision and Information Sciences
Santa Clara University

Abstract

Most programmers today use a high-level programming language for application development. The C programming language, in particular, is one such language whose increasing popularity has indirectly resulted in some new C compilers. These compilers support native and cross developments for an ever increasing number of general purpose and dedicated microprocessors. In order for these compilers to be accepted, they must be correct, reliable, and efficient. This paper introduces a hybrid approach for testing and validating optimizing C compilers that will satisfy these goals.

Keywords: Software testing, compiler validation, software quality

Introduction

In current programming environments, most programmers implement their programs using a high-level programming language. The popularity of high-level languages is due in part to increased productivity with these languages as opposed to low-level languages and program portability. The C programming language, in particular, has seen an enormous growth in programming applications ranging from UNIX-based system programming to robotics, graphics, and embedded applications.

The introduction of new microprocessors has also contributed to a growing interest in high-level languages. These new microprocessors address different market needs and are used in workstations, graphics devices, industrial and embedded applications. To support these microprocessors, software tools are developed that allow the programmer to design and develop programs using high-level programming languages. This paper will focus specifically on one such software tool — the optimizing C compiler.

The widespread popularity of the C programming language in the 1980's, the emerging ANSI C standard [ANSI 1989], and the portablility features of C compilers have all resulted in new and complex C compilers. Regardless of whether the compiler is a native or cross one, some compilers emit assembly code that will be assembled with a compatible assembler while other compilers emit direct object code. Some cross compilers also are designed to support a class of applications such as the embedded segment that requires features not generally available in the native versions.

New optimizing C compilers are also most often target and application-specific. They offer options that let the programmer choose several levels of code optimization. In general, these optimizing compilers are partitioned into four components. They are:

1. The driver
2. The front end
3. The optimizer
4. The code generator

Most optimizing compilers are constructed as two-pass compilers. During the first pass, the driver parses the command line and automates the compilation process by invoking each component of the compiler and the supporting language tools (assembler and linker). Parameters are also passed to each component. The front end then reads in the source program, verifies the code for syntactical and semantical correctness and, if successful, translates the source code into an intermediate language. During the second pass, the compiler takes the intermediate representation as input to the optimizer, performs local and global optimizations and, through the code generator, produces assembly language or object code.

In order for these compilers to be widely accepted, they must be correct, reliable, and efficient. Compilers are large and complex software systems that exceed 100K lines of code. Although it is impossible to prove compiler correctness or any software system of this size, one can demonstrate it. This paper describes a hybrid approach for testing and validating optimizing C compilers to ensure their correctness.

Compiler Testing

Testing is defined as "the process of exercising or evaluating a system by manual or automatic means to verify that it satisfies specified requirements or to identify differences between expected and actual results" [IEEE 1983]. The testing activities, in general, include unit testing, integration testing, and production or acceptance testing. These activities are described in more detail later in this paper.

The methodology used to implement these activities include white-box and black-box testing [Basili 1987, Hamlet 1989, Omar 1989]. In white-box testing, test cases are developed to ensure that every statement in the program is executed at least once. Tools are available that will measure the extent of the coverage of the test suites based on the application of this method. But achieving even 100% coverage in white-box testing does not imply completeness of the testing process since white-box testing does not address the "logic testing" of the programs. Further testing is necessary to ensure the correctness of the logic of the program. Black-box testing is a complement to the white-box testing approach. In black-box testing, the focus is to ensure that the program module conforms to its requirements. In this approach, no knowledge of the internals of the module is assumed. Test cases are developed that test the functionality of the module by examining the correctness and efficiency of the input to and output from each module. This approach is also known as glass-box or functional testing [Howden 1987, Myers 1979].

A hybrid approach utilizing concepts from both white-box and black-box testing is recommended. This approach requires the test process to start early in the design phase of the compiler development and includes testing by the development team, the software quality assurance (SQA) team, and teams of independent testers both from within the development organization and from outside users of the compiler.

Validation Goals

The first step in testing is to define a set of goals for the test process. The goals used for C compiler validation are:

1. Correctness
2. Conformance
3. Accuracy
4. Efficiency
5. Coverage
6. Acceptance

The hybrid approach achieves these goals through a set of commercially available compiler validation tools and by contributions from all the participating teams throughout the test and validation process. This process includes steps to achieve unit, module, and system-level testing with the responsibilities divided among the participating groups.

Test Process

The test process is an on-going activity that begins at the design stage. The first phase of this process begins with unit testing.

Unit Testing

Unit testing examines the correctness of the individual constructs of the language. The base line used for unit testing is the ANSI standard for C programming language [ANSI 1989, Kernighan 1978].

Several test suites are commercially available that will perform unit testing. These test suites are a collection of small and medium size test cases that were designed using the C standard as their bases and are normally annotated by specifying the section or sections of the standard that they cover. The Plum Hall Validation Suite for C and the Perennial C Validation suite are two examples of such test suites. These suites automatically perform unit testing and are normally self-checking.

Some test suites also provide a test generator that will produce self-checking test cases covering many combination of language constructs. Although these suites are large (around 50 Megabytes) and time consuming, they have the advantage of being automated. For example, these test suites can be configured to be used as a whole or by sections. They can be set up to run overnight and in a self-checking, self-reporting mode. Although they do not test for every possible combination of language construct, these suites are relatively complete in their unit testing mode.

While these suites comprehensively test the correctness of the individual constructs of the language, they still do not address extensions and exceptions to the language that a vendor's compiler may have introduced. Additional unit tests need to be developed that will specifically address such cases. These additional tests and the test suites are then used during the development process to ensure correctness and conformance to program specification. These tests are the primary tools used during the development process. Successful execution of these test suites will satisfy the correctness and conformance goals. Once the compiler passes these test suites, it is ready for the next phase of the validation process.

Integration Testing

Once unit testing has been completed, the code is frozen again and the compiler is prepared for integration testing. The first stage in this process is to establish the unit under test (UUT). Self-booting of C compilers is one approach used to accomplish this task. The source code to the compiler is compiled by a production-level host compiler to produce the first generation binaries. These binaries are then used to compile the source code again. The resulting second generation binaries are used to compile the source code once more. If the last two generation binaries are identical, the self-booting process has completed successfully and the UUT has been established. The source for this version of the compiler is then frozen, and copies of the executables are distributed to the test team for further test and validation.

The next phase of this integration process tests the compatibility of the compiler with other components of the language tool. These components are the assembler, the linker, and the debugger. The UUT and these tools should be used to execute some application programs to ensure their compatibility with each other.

Module Testing

During the module testing of the compiler, test cases are developed to validate the correct behavior of each module or component of the compiler. The front-end and the back-end or code generator are adequately tested during the unit testing by the standard test suites. The driver and the optimizer, however, are not specifically tested during these phases. In particular, the drivers have many switches that are unique to that compiler. Test cases that examine the correct behavior of every switch must be designed and developed to ensure correctness. These test cases should test for the functionality of individual switches and the use of multiple switches on the command lines.

Testing the optimizer is a more difficult task than testing the other components [Ghiassi 1987]. This difficulty is due to the architecture-specific nature of the optimizers and the lack of adequate test tools. Most optimizers are designed to take full advantage of the underlying hardware architecture that the compiler uses. Because of this characteristic, optimizer test suites are generally not portable and, as a result, it is difficult to use commercially available test suites. The second difficulty for testing optimizers is the lack of test tools that will allow examination of intermediate representations used internal to the compilers. Examining the intermediate representations will require access to the source code and, thus, a change from a functional testing approach to a white-box testing one. In practice, small test cases are generally too trivial for the optimizers and the large test cases are hard to analyze, thereby making it a challenge to test optimizers.

The ANSI standard for C programming language has included libraries as part of the compiler. The libraries and run-time support are generally tested by the standard C test suites. These suites, however, are not adequate to test every aspect of the libraries. The accuracy of the floating-point operations, for example, is one aspect of library testing that needs additional tests. Testing the accuracy of the floating-point operation requires establishing accuracy goals that will be compatible with the industry and IEEE standards. A set of test programs are available that validates conformance to the ANSI/IEEE standard and provides a measure of the degree of accuracy a compiler is providing [ANSI 1985]. Execution of these test programs to successful completion will achieve the accuracy goal of compiler validation.

Architecture- and Application-Specific Testing

As stated previously, new C compilers are developed that address different applications and architectures. The cross compilers, in particular, support features that are both architecture- and application-specific. Test cases need to be developed that address such cases.

Architecture-specific testing requires that the uniqueness of individual microprocessors be considered. For example, the Intel 8086 family of microprocessors uses segmentation schemes to control memory addressing. In this architecture, addresses are calculated using a segment register and a 16-bit offset. The CPU provides four different segment registers. These segment registers are used for the various types of memory access which are unique to the 8086 family of compilers. In C, the keywords near (offset only) and far (segment:offset) express the mode of addressing to be used. Different memory models are also available with most 8086 C compilers. Test cases that examine memory addressing and different memory models need to be developed to ensure the correctness of the 8086 family of C compilers.

Application-specific testing requires the development of test programs that include features unique to specific applications such as graphics, embedded systems, robotics, etc. For example, cross compilers targeted toward embedded applications have additional capabilities. These compilers are designed to support code ROMability, code reentrancy, position independent code, and in-line assembly code.

Consider code ROMability. When targeting code for a firmware environment, one must look at code and data locatability. Firmware applications depend on proper code and data location. In such environments, some sections of code must reside in ROM while other sections should be placed in RAM. In most applications, "strings", "literals", and "const" sections can reside in either ROM or RAM. The data section presents a problem unique to embedded applications development. Since the variables located in this section have compile-time initializers, they must be included in ROM. However, because they are modifiable variables, they can only be used from a RAM location. Compilers and linkers designed for embedded development usually support a feature that copies the initialized data from ROM to RAM at program startup. Without such a feature, initialized data could not be changed at run time. Test cases should be developed that will not only examine these features but also validate the ROMability of the code for embedded applications.

Consider also code reentrancy. Reentrancy is required because many embedded applications work with real-time, task switching executives and interrupt drivers written in C. Writing reentrant applications require compiler libraries to also be reentrant in order to allow recursive function calls in such environments. Compilers supporting such developments are almost always reentrant. To make a compiler reentrant, all local variables must be placed on the stack. A reentrant library function, therefore, cannot use any global variable. To validate reentrancy, tests are required that use recursive functions, or programs need to be developed that use the interrupt capability of the compiler.

Regression Testing

The next step in the functional testing of compilers is to examine the behavior of the compiler against the regression library of test programs. In general, regression testing is performed when a change to the source code occurs. A subset of test programs from the regression library is then selected and run to ensure that these modifications have not introduced new defects in the software system. A good candidate from the library is a collection of field-reported problems that have been fixed in the current or previous releases of this or similar compilers. Since the source of these test programs is diverse, they are usually compiled and executed manually and the output is examined for correctness. These problems must be resolved since they reflect a customer-reported problem requiring a definite resolution.

System Testing

Previous testing efforts have concentrated on unit and module testings. In this phase of testing known as system testing, large and complex programs will be compiled using the new compiler under real-life circumstances. Large and complex test cases will also be used to push the compiler to its limits and to allow us to identify the boundary conditions.

System testing takes advantage of existing, UNIX-based software tools. The Emacs editor and Rogue are two examples of such tools. They are considered to have complex C constructs not typically found in most C programs and will help to exercise the compiler.

The UNIX operating system itself is also an excellent candidate for the system testing of C compilers. Although a time consuming effort, it provides several additional advantages. To ensure the correctness of the UNIX build and execution, the process must include the validation of the UNIX operating system itself. The process should begin with an already built UNIX reference system. A UNIX validation suite, such as System V Validation Suite (SVVS) and/or the AIM's benchmark, should first be run and the results saved for future comparison. The entire UNIX source can then be compiled. Portions of the kernel code which deals with volatile variables should be compiled without optimization to ensure correctness. Once a successful build is accomplished, the same UNIX validation suites should be run and the results compared against the old ones for both correctness and efficiency. Finally, the C compiler can be tested for UNIX compatibility. In particular, the System V Interface Definition (SVID) compatibility can be measured during this process.

A final step in system testing should include the compilation of different programs representing a variety of applications such as graphics, CAD, and robotics.

Performance Evaluation

Once the correctness of the C compiler has been established, efficiency goals become the focus of the validation process. The efficiency of compilers is measured in terms of the compile rate, the size of the generated code, and the speed of the executables.

The compile rate defines how fast a compiler compiles a programs. It measures the number of lines of code compiled per second. Because the compile rate decreases significantly when a compiler is invoked with the optimization switch on, the measurements should be taken both with and without optimization. In practice, programs are first compiled without optimization until all syntax errors are removed. The program is then re-compiled with optimization for better (faster/denser) code generation. Note that optimization levels provided today range from code execution optimization to code density optimization. Test cases should be developed that examine and measure both ends of the spectrum.

Benchmark tools are also available that will measure the performance of C compilers. This performance is measured in terms of the size and the speed of the generated code. These benchmarks can be grouped into two categories. The small benchmarks are available in the computer literature and include Ackerman, Dhrystone, Linpack, Livermore Loops, Puzzle, Sieve, Stanford, and Whetstone. These benchmarks are used to measure compiler performance and are also used for compiler tuning. Recently, a new set of large and complex benchmarks has been developed by the System Performance Evaluation Cooperative (SPEC). These benchmarks include software from different application areas and measure the compiler's behavior as a system. A set of reference values is also provided that will allow for easy comparison with similar compilers.

Production Testing

The last phase is the production-level testing of a C compiler both for testing and information purposes. The C compiler up to this stage has been tested both by development and independent teams. Development team testing examined the behavior of the compiler with respect to the validation goals while external testing by independent users of the C compiler tested compiler usage under real-life circumstances. Additional testing of the compiler includes production and acceptance testing. The first step in production testing is to address the defects reported by the beta sites. The defects reported by these groups are, depending on the nature of the defects, either fixed or documented.

Additional testing performed at this stage are multi-user tests and stress testing to identify the lower bounds of compilation limits for ANSI-conforming C compilers. With multi-user testing, several users are assigned to use the compiler over some time period. This testing examines how the C compiler utilizes the underlying operating system including the number of temporary files opened, the scratch and swap space requirements, and the memory requirements with or without optimization. Also examined is how the performance of the compiler is affected when several users use it simultaneously.

Stress testing is performed to find the limits of the compiler and to ensure that the ANSI-defined lower bounds are met. The lower bounds that need to be identified for the user include parameters such as conditional constructs and nesting levels for include files. Other parameter values such as the number of allowable cases in a switch statement, number of external names in one source file, number of local variables per block, number of macros per source file at any time, number of characters in a "logical" source line, and the number of characters per string constant are determined. Additional parameters unique to the compiler under test must also be identified and documented.

Test coverage and analysis tools should be used throughout the testing process to provide informative metrics that will measure the confidence level achieved as a result of the test process. The coverage goal is examined; if the goal is reached, testing is considered to be adequate. Otherwise, additional test cases are developed to test those areas of the compiler that were identified as "not tested" by such test coverage and analysis tools.

Finally, the release goals set earlier are examined to ensure that all goals are achieved before the final release of the compiler. If this release is not the first one, then a migration document should also be prepared that will guide the users through a smooth transition to the new release of the compiler. The management of the development process should also select the maintenance team for this release and make sure that maintenance tools are available for them. A tentative update and maintenance release of the compiler should also be set to ensure that any defect found during the actual use of the compiler can be duly addressed.

Conclusion

This paper presented a hybrid approach for C compiler validation. The steps required to test and validate native and cross C compilers were introduced, and the software tools available for testing a general purpose C compiler were identified. Also addressed were the specific needs of C compilers targeting different application areas. Proper implementation of the methods recommended in this paper along with on-time use and execution of the test tools should result in correct, reliable, and efficient production-level C compilers.

Acknowledgment

The author would like to thank Lucille Ching for her comments and Microtec Research, Inc. for their support of this research.

References

1. ANSI/X3.159-1989, "ANSI Standard for the Programming Language C."
2. ANSI/IEEE std. 754-1985, "IEEE standard for Binary Floating-Point Arithmetic."
3. Basili, V. R. and R. W. Selby, "Comparing the Effectiveness of Software Testing Strategies," IEEE Transaction on Software Engineering, Dec. 1987, pp. 1287-1296.
4. Ghiassi, M., "Software Quality: Design it in from the Start," Computer Design, Vol. 23, No. 9, July 1985, pp. 91-97.
5. Ghiassi, M., "Validating Optimizing Compilers," Proceedings of the 1987 IEEE-WESCON Conference, Vol. 31, No. 2, pp. 1-13.
6. Ghiassi, M. and M. S. Arratoon, "Developing a C Compiler Validation Suite," Proceedings of the 1985 IEEE-WESCON Conference, Vol. 29, No. 37, pp 1-7.
7. Hamlet, R., "Theoretical Comparison of Testing Methods," Proceedings of the ACM SIGsoft, 1989.
8. Howden, W. E., "Functional Program Testing & Analysis," McGraw-Hill, New York, 1987.
9. Howden, W. E., "The Theory and Practice of Functional Testing," IEEE Software, Sept. 1985, pp. 6-17.
10. IEEE std. 729-1983, "IEEE Standard Glossary of Software Engineering Terms."
11. Kernighan, B. W. and D. M. Rtichie, "The C Programming Language," Prentice-Hall, 1978.
12. Myers, G. J., "The Art of Software Testing," New York, Wiley, 1979.
13. Omar, A. A. and F. A. Mohammed, "Structural Testing of Programs: A Survey," ACM SIGsoft, Software Engineering Notes, Vol. 14, No. 2, April 1989, pp. 62-70.
14. Pressman, R. S., "Software Engineering," 2nd Edition, New York, McGraw-Hill, 1987.
15. Seyfer, H. K., "Tailoring Testing to a Specific Compiler — Experiences," ACM Proc. SIGPLAN Symposium on Compiler Construction, 1982.

Manoochehr Ghiassi: is currently an associate professor in the Department of Decision and Information Sciences at Santa Clara University. He received a B.S. from Tehran University, IRAN, in 1970 and an M.S. in economics from Southern Illinois University at Carbondale, Illinois, in 1974. He also received an M.S. in Computer Science in 1979 and a Ph.D. in Industrial Engineering in 1980 both from the University of Illinois at Urbana-Champaign. His current research interests involve software engineering and simulation modeling. He is a member of IEEE, ACM, and a senior member of AIIE.

Above author may be reached at: M. Ghiassi, 213 Kenna Hall, Santa Clara University, Santa Clara, CA 95053, USA

SESSION 3

VALIDATION AND CONFORMANCE TESTING

Approving Software Products
W. Ehrenberger (Editor)
Elsevier Science Publishers B.V. (North-Holland)

Software certification by demand: an experience from a third-party laboratory

A. Bertolino, C. Carlesi, M. Fusani

Istituto di Elaborazione dell'Informazione, CNR, Pisa, Italy

Abstract:

There is still a sort of ambiguity about the expression "software certification". The dated, common-sense based IEEE definition "... a written guarantee that a system or computer program complies with its specified requirements [IEEE Standard no. 729]" does not provide useful guidance for organizing an effective certification service. Besides, a certificate issued according to this interpretation is inevitably mistaken for a "guarantee" of product adequacy, that which cannot be definitely risked on at the state of the art.

As an independent laboratory which has been offering this kind of service for some years, by request by Public Administrations, users and producers, we have been getting more and more aware of that. So, we have conceived and applied a process in which a defined set of characteristics of both software product and developing project are submitted to a defined Validation Suite. This process ends with a formal declaration showing the actions performed and their results.

This is what we mean by software certification.

The Validation Suite must be designed for a class of product criticity and may be adjusted for each application field.

In practice, our laboratory had to perform both the tasks of putting together Validation Suites for a number of cases and of carrying out the certification processes. If we would refer our work to some proposed certification schemes (like the European Community's), this would not be exactly the role of a *certification body*, which is not supposed to work directly in definition of standards. However, lack of established, commonly agreed rules, along with urges from the demand side, convinced the laboratory to take on both aspects of the job.

The paper describes some critical aspects faced by the laboratory during the preparation and application of the Validation Suite to actual software products certification.

In particular, the concept of certifiability (that determines the feasibility of applying a Validation Suite leading to a positive certificate) is added to the yet conspicuous set of -ilities qualifying a product.

Techniques used in the Validation Suite are picked up from defined standards and recommendations for designing "good" software, and provide a way to deal with imperfect user specifications. Such techniques include inspection, testing and tracing specifications to code and vice-versa.

Problems rising from the peculiar experience of independent certification, such as dealing with manufacturer's privacy and interfacing software products to external inspectors, are also presented and a trace for their solution is proposed.

Approving Software Products
W. Ehrenberger (Editor)
Elsevier Science Publishers B.V. (North-Holland)
IFIP, 1990

Approving Real-Time Software: Current Practice and Trends

Rajko Milovanovic (1), Adnan Kulenovic (1)
Miodrag Askrabic (2), Dragan Vujadin (2)
Gojko Babic (3), Zoran Salcic (3), Andreja Markovic (3)

(1) ETF, University of Sarajevo, Sarajevo, Yugoslavia
(2) Energoinvest Iris, Sarajevo, Yugoslavia
(3) Energoinvest Kibernetika, Sarajevo, Yugoslavia

ABSTRACT

Embedded real-time software systems often exhibit two specific features: (1) dedicated hardware, used as a platform exlusively for real-time software package, and (2) hard isolation of system software and system hardware aspects from the approval / validation / verification standpoint. Typical examples are industrial control and supervisory systems, embedded military systems, communication systems, etc. Approval process is significantly influenced by these factors. The first factor frequently precludes, due to performance possible performance degradation, addition of software modules needed within approval process. The second one tends to make software approval process - by the end user - hard to formalize, due to his typical tendency to give approval only on the system (i.e. hardware and software combined). The paper presents recent experiences related to these factors, for software projects in each of cited application areas. Current, sometimes manadatory, practice within these is compared with practice related to other classes of software; it is also contrasted with emerging trends in software engineering.

Approving Software Products
W. Ehrenberger (Editor)
Elsevier Science Publishers B.V. (North-Holland)

Conformance Testing of Implementations of Graphics Standards

Rolf Ziegler, Martin Göbel

Fraunhofer - Arbeitsgruppe für Graphische Datenverarbeitung (FhG-AGD)
Wilhelminenstraße 7, D-6100 Darmstadt, West Germany
Tel. ++49 6151 1000 31, Fax ++49 6151 1000 99
e-mail: goebel@agd.fhg.de

The widespread acceptance of Graphics Standards like GKS, GKS-3D, CGM, and PHIGS as international standards for computer graphics leads to a software market offering a lot of implementations of these standards, even before it becomes official.
This paper describes conformance testing of computer graphics standards. The first testing service was established for GKS. The development of this service was finished 1989. The testing service for CGI is still under development and a prototype is now available. The testing services for both standards rely very highly on the visual checks of a human tester. Furthermore an important consideration is whether the human judgement of the correctness of pictures can be replaced, at least in part, by automatic processes.

1. INTRODUCTION

People who buy an implementation of a graphics standard like GKS, GKS-3D, CGM, and PHIGS require a guarantee of the correct functioning and its compliance with the standard. Test suites that test implementations to determine conformance to standards are needed. It is desirable to have the test suite available at the time the standardization process of the certain graphics standard are finished. This means that both, standard and test suite, have to be developed in parallel.
The foundations for the certification of graphics standard software are layed at a workshop held at Rixensart near Brussels in 1981 [1]. Experts on graphics, and experts on certification of software systems discussed the issue of how to apply

certifications to graphics software. In 1985, the first phase of the conformance testing service programme (CTS1) was launched by the Commission of the European Communities. Within CTS1 the testing service for the Graphical Kernel System (GKS) was developed. Testing laboratories are GMD (Germany F.R.), NCC (United Kingdom) and AFNOR (France).
Two years later the second phase of the CTS-programme (CTS2) started. Within CTS2 a project is now underway to develop testing tools for the emerging Computer Graphics Interface (CGI) standard.
The testing service will lead to a certificate of conformity. This is an important characteristic for quality for clients of computer graphics software. The conformance testing service enables the users of the graphics standard software as well as the implementers to test the conformity of the certain implementation to the standard (pre-test). In order to obtain a certificate the implementation has to be tested by an official testing labority. NCC (United Kingdom) and AFNOR (France) are currently discussing the establishing of these laboratories.

2. TESTING OF GKS IMPLEMENTATIONS

The Graphical Kernel System (GKS) [2] is the first international standard for programming computer graphics applications. GKS defines a standardized interface between application programs and a graphical system. Moreover it is a unified methodology for defining graphical systems and their concepts. GKS supports graphics output, interactive operator input, picture segmentation and segment manipulation. The graphical standard GKS covers a wide field of 2D-applications in interactive computer graphics.
The first testing service for graphics software was developed for testing implementations of GKS. The GKS document is essentially an informal specification written in a natural language. Interpreting the specification in terms of a computer program requires human intellectual effort. Errors can occur. The testers take the complete GKS implementation, subject it to an intensive test suite, and hope to discover errors. The test suite is a sequence of test programs and is based on a simple model which involves two interfaces: the application interface between GKS and an application program, and the human interface where GKS output is observed and input devices are operated.

The testing strategy for GKS involves five distinct test series [3]:

- data consistency,
- data structure,
- error handling,
- input/output, and
- metafile.

The data consistency test series examine the GKS description tables which describe the configuration and certain properties of the GKS implementation. The tests check the values in the description tables for consistency and conformity with the GKS standard.
The data structure test series ensure that the values in the GKS state lists are manipulated correctly. This is done by setting, modifying and inquiring the values.
The error handling test series produce error situations and then checks that an error mechanism in line with the GKS standard is supported by the implementation.
The input/output test series provide a check of the GKS Implementation as a whole. This is done through a comprehensive set of tests which cover all the input and output capabilities of GKS. The graphical output is produced by the tests and checked against a set of reference pictures. The Evaluator's Manual gives a list of items to be checked for each picture. The input is tested by a set of defined operator actions which should produce specific results on a display.
The metafile test series check that the GKS metafile is used correctly. Metafiles are created and checkpoints are used to enable visual comparison between screen output and reference pictures. The metafiles are then interpreted and the sessions are interrupted at exactly the same checkpoints so that the output from metafile interpretation can be checked against the reference pictures. The GKS state list entries from the generating and interpreting sessions are also checked to ensure that they are identical.
The test programs in each serie are grouped into sets, each of which contains the cumulative test programs for a specific level of GKS. The five test series are testing different areas of the GKS standard. They are of different complexity. Each test series assumes that the previous test series ran without major errors. If the description tables that are examined in the first test series cannot be inquired it would not make sense to run the data structure test series as this test series gets its information about the workstation under test from the workstation description table. Therefore the test programs should be executed in the order listed above.
The GKS testing service is offered by several european testing laboratories.

3. TESTING OF CGI IMPLEMENTATIONS

The Computer Graphics Interface (CGI) [4] defines the interface from a graphics system to a graphical device. A CGI virtual device may be a hardware device or a software implementation. A specific implementation is bound to an environment (like hardware, operating system, control software) and may be influenced by other controlling interfaces in the environment. These dependencies have to be taken into account and increase the complexity of the tests.
CGI defines control, output, segment, input, and raster functions. This set of functions covers the whole GKS functionality (CGI as GKS workstation) and in addition provides raster functionality. It is expected that CGI will become International Standard at the beginning of 1991.
A project is now underway to develop testing tools for the emerging Computer Graphics Interface (CGI) standard in parallel to the standardization process. The development team aims to build on the experience gained in constructing and using the GKS tools.

3.1. Test System Structure

The definition of the CGI standard covers several parts. Beside the functional description there exist additional standards for encodings (binary, character, clear text) and language bindings (FORTRAN, Pascal, Ada, C). The CGI testing service aims to build testing tools which cover all these requirements. CGI implementations with different language bindings as well as implementations with different encodings. The evaluation of the requirements lead to the illustrated CGI test system structure. The main components are the description of the implementation under test, the test case database and the test suite interpreter (TSI).

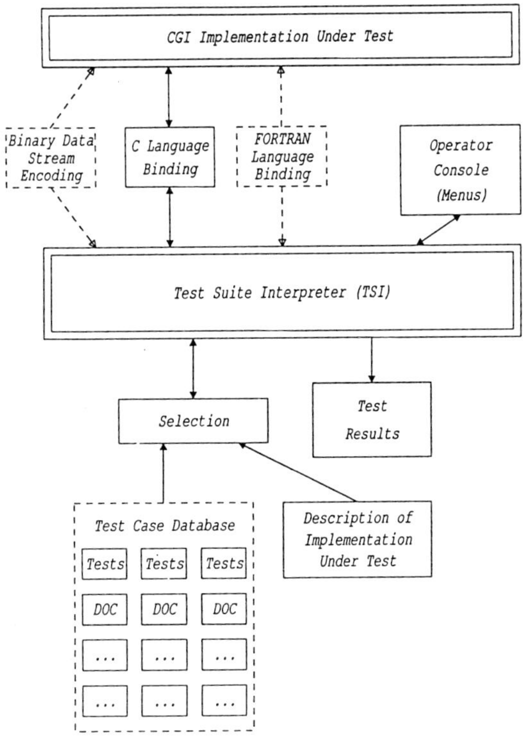

CGI Test System Structure

Valid CGI implementations (which conform to the standard) can differ in the functionality (profiles) and in the capabilities of the virtual device. Therefore the CGI standard defines description tables which describe the certain implementation. The test system component 'description of the implementation under test' reflects all description tables defined within the CGI standard. Furthermore certain state list entries which are noted as implementation dependent (e.g., the bundle representations) are included. This description must be set independently from the test. A program called inquiry tool will call the necessary inquiry functions to gain the information. If necessary the entries will be set manually. This effort is needed to have the information available in a file in a unique and well defined format. Dependent on the description of the CGI implementation under test the test cases are selected ('selection').

The 'test case database' contains all implemented test cases. The structure of the database is a directory structure subdivided according to the functional parts of the

CGI standard (control, output, input, segments, raster). During runtime the complete test set for a specific implementation under test will be selected. Each selected test case contains additional documentation (help utility) which describes and documents the test.

Example:

Following is the help text for Test Case 'Polymarker Geometry - Type and Position'

> TARGET:
> Type and Position of the Polymarker primitive are checked here.
>
> DISPLAY:
> This is done by drawing several marker. All markers are centred horizontal and their position is marked by annotation lines. They are drawn within one box and the type is described by annotation text.
>
> CHECKS:
> Please check, that 5 markers are visible. The 5 markers should be centred to the position annotated by lines and a surrounding box.
> The marker types should be (from top to bottom) described by annotation text:
> Plus Sign, Star, Circle, X, Dot.

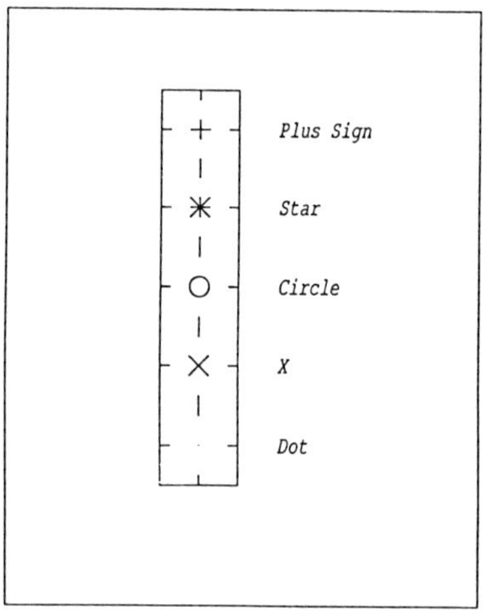

Test of Polymarker

The test cases are implemented in a C-like pseudo code. Selected test cases are interpreted by a test suite interpreter (TSI) which interprets the pseudo code according to the language binding or data stream encoding of the implementation under test. Thus the tests are portable to different environments. The available prototype can interpret pseudo code to an implementation realized as a procedural C language binding. Until the end of the project (mid of 1991) additionally the TSI will be able to interpret to FORTRAN, binary and character encoding. The standards for the Pascal and Ada language binding and the clear text encoding won't be considered, because up to now their standardization process has not been started. The selection of the test cases depends on the description of the implementation under test. The 'test results' are collected within a file and contain pass/fail answers and additional remarks.

3.2. Test picture design

The testing strategy is similar to the GKS testing strategy (no metafile tests) but the design of the test software were changed in some major parts [5].
The CGI test suite includes automatic testing and visual checking. Data consistency/structure and error handling tests can be tested automatically, the main test will be done by visual checking of output by a human tester. The decision of the test suite developers was to cover as many aspects as possible of the CGI implementation under test. But the test software must be designed in a way that the tester won't become bored or tired. Therefore the requirements for the designer of the required test software were to keep the tests interesting, simple, and uncluttered. Visual cues (self-annotating test pictures) have to be included to aid the judgement of the tester. Finally, redundant tests have to be avoided.
The specification of the CGI test suite does not rely on the concept of reference pictures (such as was used in GKS). The wide range of functionality of CGI in addition to diverse hardware capabilities makes the selection of appropriate reference pictures impossible. Test cases interpreted by the TSI generate visual output. The human tester has to examine whether the result corresponds to the required behaviour, defined within the standard.
The CGI test system satisfies all requirements according to the design and specification criteria. The test pictures are very simple with self-annotating visual cues. The annotation utilities use the POLYLINE, POLYMARKER and TEXT function and certain attribute functions. A possibility for using cues is boxing i.e. POLYLINE drawn round the primitives to be checked. Each test case is documented explicitly. The human tester can get additional help by this documentation which is available either on a separate screen (on-line documentation) or within a comprehensive manual. The TSI interprets the test case. Furthermore the TSI manages the reporting of the test results and the on-line test

documentation (if feasible). Thus a user interface was designed to handle interaction with the tester and to access the test documents, so as to present information to the tester. Finally, information is passed to the automatic report generator, concerning the tester's assessment of whether a test has been passed or failed.
As mentioned above the CGI test system is available as a prototype. This first version will be capable to test CGI devices covering the GKS level 0A functionality realized as 'C' language binding implementations.

3.3. Automatic Testing - the future ?

The realized CGI test system includes visual checking and automatic testing. The output/input test which is the main part of the test is done by visual checking. Automatic tests are performed for checking whether a certain profile is implemented, whether the inquiry functions deliver correct information and the error handling mechanism behaves correctly. These tests concentrate on checking consistency of description table entries and default/current setting of state list entries, but not on output visible on the screen.
The described scheme as used in the GKS and CGI validation service relies strongly on human checking: it is thus subjective and limited by the accuracy of the human eye and brain. An important consideration is whether the human judgement of the correctness of pictures within the CGI test system can be replaced, at least in part, by some automatic processes. The need is certainly great: CGI defines a much richer set of primitives and attributes, compared to GKS, and the demands on the human tester will be severe. Thus we evaluated whether automatic testing of visual output could be applied and integrated within the CGI test system.
How can the test program 'see' the generated visual output? The first approach [6] we made was to examine the raster image - we call this testing at the raster interface. CGI includes a function (GET PIXEL ARRAY) that returns the colour of each pixel within a specified rectangle. The raster interface is thus a practical point at which to examine graphical data.
Our preferred approach is to analyse the raster data generated by the implementation in response to a test program. We define a number of conditions that must be satisfied, and analyse raster data to verify whether this is indeed the case. For example we develop a number of conditions that characterise a line. These conditions will include a set of pixels that must not be illuminated, a set of pixels that must be illuminated, and relationships between remaining pixels. We have looked in detail at the issue of whether a sequence of pixels adequately represents a given line, and have derived a characterisation based on human visual assessment. Furthermore we developed similar characterisations of other primitives (line primitives, polymarker, polygon primitives, cell array) and have defined certain test methods.

Similarly, we developed conditions that must be satisfied in certain graphical operations. We have looked at the attribute binding mechanism (bundle representations), the clipping mechanism, all segment mechanisms (creation, deletion, display, transformation, copy, detection, inheritance) and all raster functions. Generally these conditions relate to the raster data before and after the operation. A trivial example is segment (in)visibility. The condition for segment invisibility is that the raster data should be identically zero after the operation. Furthermore clipping is well suited to automatic testing of pixel maps. We draw a picture using a set of output primitives and attributes, with clipping set to 'off'. The pixel map is stored, and the screen cleared. We repeat the process exactly, but with clipping this time set to 'on'. The pixel map is again retrieved. The area outside the clipping rectangle must be cleared to the background colour, and the interior must match on a pixel-by-pixel basis with the interior of the original.

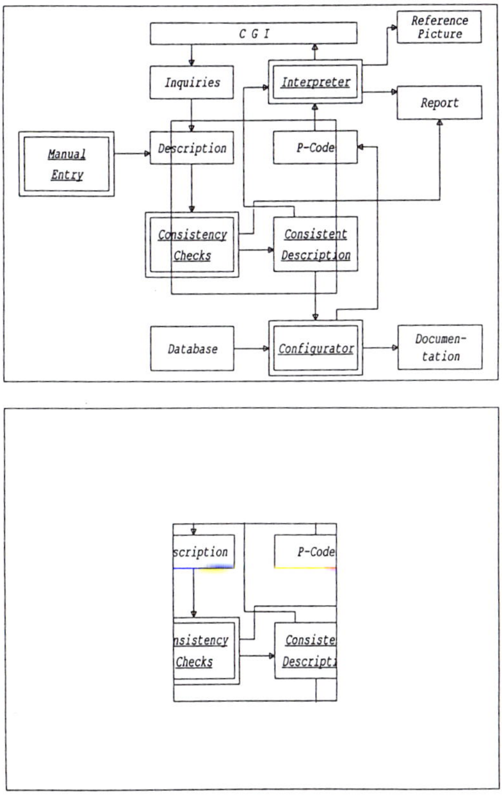

Clipping Test

We have seen that many graphical operations such as segment visibility, have a very simple effect on the pixel map of a raster device and so can be checked by automatic means. Our work has shown, however, that care is needed in this comparison process to allow for rounding errors - particularly in the discretisation step. The automatic testing of output primitives is not evaluated completely. The attributes (e.g., line type) have no precise definition within the standard. Thus the definition of evaluation conditions can be very subjective. Additional work must be done to solve this problem.
In the case of CGI devices which do not provide the function GET PIXEL ARRAY (allowed in CGI) we have to find an additional way of pixel readback, e.g., picture capture by a camera (camera input). To decide whether camera input can be used as pixel readback depends upon the question 'Can we predict the camera frame buffer by a given graphical output generated by CGI?'. To answer this question we made some experiments with different sets of graphical output on a monochrome screen. The camera 'sees' the physical reality. In fact the pixels on a certain screen were not square. The x-size was smaller than the y-size. Therefore the horizontal lines seemed to be thicker than the vertical lines. The camera 'sees' this thicker line. This is also true for the visual tester. We did not investigate on the acceptance of users to these deficiencies. Unfortunately there arose an additional problem. As mentioned above the CGI output was limited to colour indices 0 and 1. In contrast the camera device provided a range of 256 grey levels (0..255). The experiments showed that dependent on the adjusting of the camera one pixel is 'lighter' than another pixel. That means if one pixel will hit exactly one camera pixel, the edge of two camera pixels or the corner of four camera pixels the camera 'sees' different light intensity. These are the kinds of problems which still have to be resolved.
One major problem is to find out the definition of the function which defines the mapping from one CGI device pixel to the camera pixels (different light intensities). The second major problem is the calibration of the camera (calibration phase). We have to analyse how the physical capabilities of the device under test (pixel aperture and size) have to be fed into our camera input pipeline. All in all if we find feasible solutions (which can be implemented) we can apply the same automatic test methods described above (testing at the raster interface). Than conformance testing by automatic means will become more and more important and indeed will be included within the test suite of CGI testing.

4. CONCLUSIONS

This paper has described the test systems for testing of GKS and CGI implementations. The GKS testing service is the first testing service in the area of graphics standards. The developers of the CGI testing tools aimed to build on the experience gained in building and using the GKS testing tools. The available prototype still relies on visual testing.

Finally we described the issues and possible solution of automatic testing. The use of camera for accessing the pictures of an implementation under test requires a larger set of verification strategies, including image processing capabilities.

REFERENCES

[1] Thompson, K., Graphics certification at the European Community level, Computer Graphics & Applications, Vol. 8, Nr.1, pp. 59-61, 1984

[2] ISO/DIS 7942 - Graphical Kernel System (GKS), Functional Description, 1985

[3] Kirsch, B., Pflueger, C., Conformance Testing for Computer Graphics Standards, Internal Project Report (CTS2-CGI-072), 1990

[4] ISO/DIS 9636 - Computer Graphics Interface (CGI), Functional Specification, 1989

[5] Brodlie, K.W., Roberts, A., Visual Testing of CGI, Internal Report, School of Computer Science, University of Leeds, 1989

[6] Brodlie, K.W., Goebel, M., Roberts, A., Ziegler,R., When is a Line a Line?, Eurographics '89, Participants Edition, 1989, pp. 427-438

SESSION 4

STANDARDS AND CERTIFICATION 2

Approving Software Products
W. Ehrenberger (Editor)
Elsevier Science Publishers B.V. (North-Holland)

THE LIFE CYCLE METHODOLOGY FOR SOFTWARE PRODUCTION AND THE RELATED EXPERIENCE

Helmut Hummel

IABG, Dept. ITE
D–8012 Ottobrunn

This paper gives an overview of the Life Cycle Methodology (LCM) for software production, which will soon become a standard for the German defense area. Following a summary on background and goals, the concepts realised within the LCM are discussed and the submodels of the LCM are presented. Finally, status, further plans and experiences so far are given.

1 BACKGROUND

The German defense area is planning to re-organize its DP-standards. The currently applicable standards are to be completed and/or replaced in a form which complies with the current requirements for system technology. Especially with regard to software, the standards should take into consideration global goals of the Armed Forces, such as

- to improve and to assure software quality,
- to reduce software cost across the life-cycle,
- to improve communication between those involved in a project,
- to reduce dependencies between customer and contractor.

In this context, work for a Life Cycle Methodology (LCM) as a component within the revised standards was initiated by the German Ministry of Defense.

2 GOALS

It was the goal, that the LCM should be a *technical standard*, which controls the entire *software development process* by uniform and binding rules, and that this standard has to fulfill the following characteristics.

- *Completeness*
  All areas of the software development process have to be covered, i. e. including quality assurance, configuration management and technical project management.

- *Adaptability*
  The LCM should be generic in the sense, that it can be adapted to an individual project by a special, controlled procedure (tailoring).

- *Independence from methods and tools*
  The activities, by which the software development process will be described in the LCM, have to be functional and make no reference to a special method or tool. In principle, the LCM should not restrict the freedom to carry out an activity in a real project by applying different methods.

- *Compatibility with existing standards*
  The LCM should be compatible with US-DoD-STD-2167A/2168 and AQAP13, and, where possible, their merits should be included.

- *Maturity*
  The LCM has to be oriented to common practice. This has to be achieved by consulting industry, Federal Offices and Services from the very beginning.

- *No limitation*
  The LCM should be usable during software development as well as deployment (i. e. maintenance phase).

- *Consideration of embedded systems*
  The LCM should include precautions for dealing with real-time aspects. Especially the interdependence of hardware and software has to be taken into consideration.

- *Usability*
  The LCM should not only contain abstract rules, but also instructions, hints, check lists and recommendations, to support the application of the LCM for practical use.

Users of the LCM should be Federal Offices as well as industry. The LCM should be taken into account for requests for proposals and contract negotiations, and should be applied for project supervision, software development and maintenance.

3 CONCEPTS REALIZED WITHIN THE LCM

The following gives an overview of the concepts, which constitute the LCM and contribute to the goals mentioned in the chapter above.

3.1 Elements of the LCM

The basic elements of the LCM are *activities* and *products*, which are to be carried out or generated, respectively, during the software development process.

Activities are worksteps in the software development process, whose results and implementation can be described exactly. Activities may consist of sub-activities, under the condition, that each of these sub-activities provides defined intermediate results.

An item which is processed by or result of an activity, is called a *product*. Analogous to the decomposition of activities into sub-activities, products may be decomposed into sub-products (e. g. a single chapter of a document).

Activities are working on products, i. e. an activity may generate a product, change the state of a product or modify the contents of a product. For each (sub-) activity this behaviour is described as a matrix, called product flow (see figure 1).

from		Product	to		QA	CM
Activity	State		Activity	State		
SWD 2.4	accepted	DP Design	—	—		
SWD 3.5	accepted	SW Requirements	—	—		
SWD 4.5	accepted	Model Documents	—	—		
SWD 5.1	being processed	SW Architecture. *Process Design*	—	—		
—	—	SW Architecture. *Modularization*	SWD 5.2	being processed		
—	—	SW Architecture	SWD 5.3–5.4 SWD 6.1–6.2	submitted	✓	✓

Figure 1 Example of a product flow

3.2 LCM submodells

The LCM controls the activities and results (products) of the software development process. Thereby, not only the development process in the narrow sense is covered, but also *quality assurance*, *configuration management* and *technical project management* are considered as integral parts.

As a consequence, the LCM is structured into functional parts, so-called submodells. They comprise software development (SWD), quality assurance (QA), configuration management (CM) and technical project management (PM). These four submodels are closely interconnected and interrelated (see figure 2) and fulfill the following tasks.

- PM *plans, monitors and informs* the submodels SWD, QA and CM, respectively.
- SWD *develops and tests* according to the inputs from QA and PM, respectively.
- QA *submits quality requirements* to the submodels SWD, CM and PM, and *checks*, if they are complied with.
- CM *administers the products* generated in other submodels and *handles change requests*.

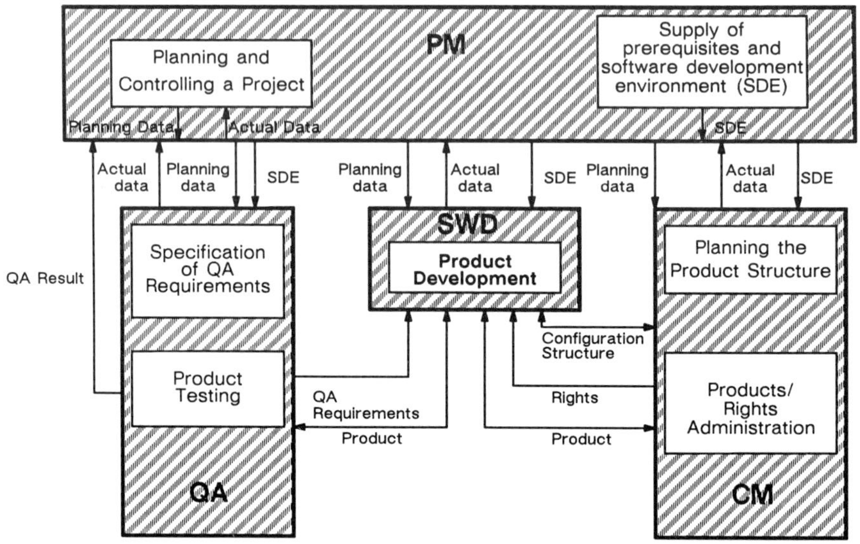

Figure 2 Cooperation of the Sub-Models SWD, QA, CM and PM

3.3 Adaptation of the LCM

The LCM is universal in the sense, that it describes the software development process from a *functional view only*, and does not imply or assume any special project characteristics or forms of organisations. This allows to use the LCM for different projects in different institutions or companies.

This implies that the LCM has to be adapted before use for a concrete project in a given environment.

3.3.1 Tailoring

The adaption to a specific project is called *tailoring*. Tailoring is the deletion of activities and products, which are not relevant for the project. This deletion is achieved by applying a set of predefined conditions. The resulting subset of the LCM becomes part of the *Project Manual*.

This leads to two steps of tailoring (see figure 3).

- *Contract-relevant tailoring* selects activities and products, which are required for the project from a global point of view. This has to be arranged by the customer before contract completion.
- *Technical tailoring* determines, whether instances of activities and products or parts thereof can be omitted in a local context. This is carried out by the contractor with customer agreement, accompanying the project.

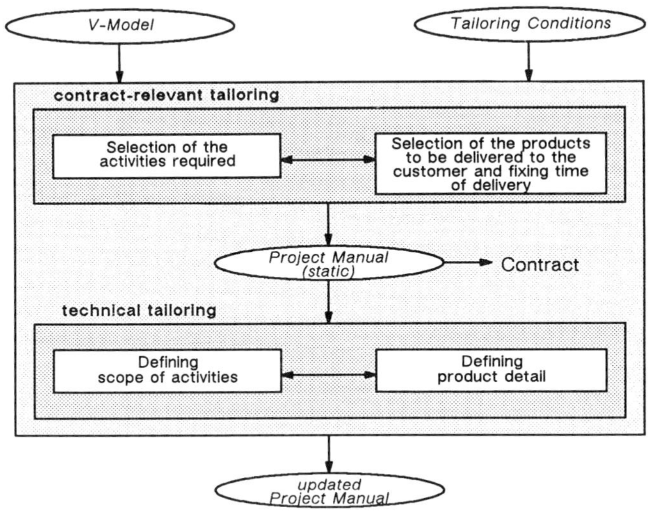

Figure 3 Steps of Tailoring

3.3.2 Organisational embedment

The independence of the LCM from organisational and project specific conditions is achieved by introducing the *concept of roles* (see figure 4). The LCM specifies different roles which are defined only with respect to experience, knowledge and qualifications necessary to carry out a (sub-) activity. The mapping of roles to activities is described by a matrix for each of the submodels SWD, QA, CM and PM, whereby an activity can be associated with several roles.

Thus, at the beginning of a project, an association of roles to organisational units or persons has to take place. This process is regulated by the Implementation Procedures for the LCM.

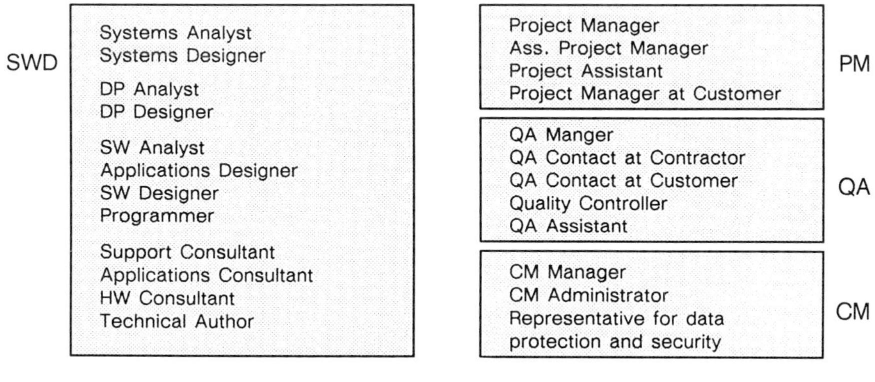

Figure 4 Roles in the LCM

3.4 Independence issues

The LCM does not prescribe any methods or tools to be used during the software development process. This is envisaged to happen in separate steps of standardisation. Thus, the LCM will not become absolete, if new and more appropriate methods and tools will evolve in the future.

The LCM also does not include a fixed interface between customer and contractor, because of the strong dependency on the given organisations on both sides. But it points out the necessity of the definition of such an interface and requires its establishment in the contract.

3.5 Underlying system structure

The LCM describes, how software – considered as part of a system – has to be developed. The meaning of "*system*" used within the LCM is in coherence with DoD-STD-2167A, and, seen from the LCM, it is a functional unit of the highest level.

A system is structured as follows (see figure 5).

- A system of high complexity normally is partitioned into *sub-systems*. Systems and sub-systems are not treated differently by the LCM.
- A system/sub-system consists of *segments with DP-portions* (DP segment) and *without DP-portion* (non-DP segment).
- DP segments are further structured into *software configuration items* (SWCI), *hardware configuration items* (HWCI) and *non-DP portions*.
- SWCIs are made up of *components* whereby the components themselves can be composed of components of a lower level, of *modules* and/or *databases*. Components are isolated software units of higher order, modules are the smallest software units of a SWCI, and databases serve for description, storage and retrieval of data in multi user mode.

3.6 User participation

In the development of the LCM the potential users have been heavily involved. Two *experts groups* have supervised and influenced the LCM.

- An *industrial experts group* with official representatives from the German industrial associations BDLI, BDV, VDMA and ZVEI took care, that the LCM reflects practical experience from real projects.
- An *agencies experts group* with official representatives from the German Federal Offices and Services made sure, that their needs are covered by the LCM.

These experts groups also took decisions on change requests and will do so in the future.

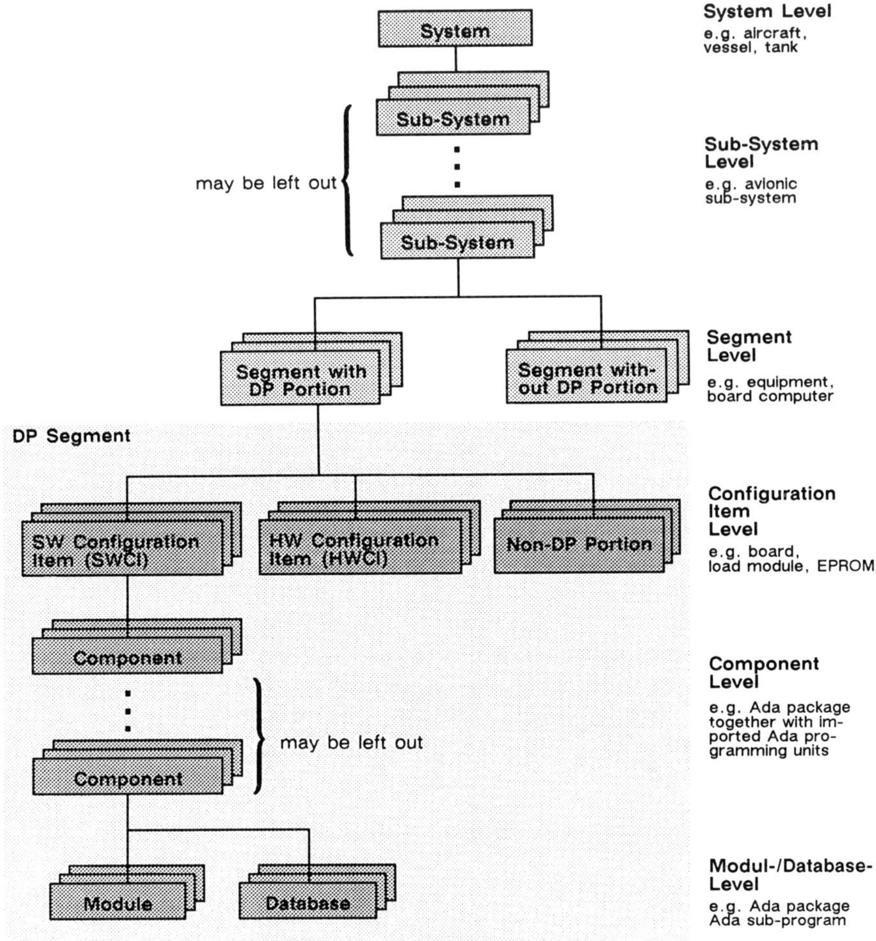

Figure 5 Systems Structure

3.7 Handling of maintenance

The LCM not only covers the software development process, but also the *deployment*. To achieve this, the LCM contains some extra (sub-) activities, and special rules and recommendations for software maintenance and modification (SWMM), which are necessary for preparation and performance of SWMM.

As far as preparation of SWMM is concerned, among others, the LCM requires the existence of a maintenance concept, supports the know-how transfer from development to maintenance and prescribes the change management. The performance of SWMM is initiated by PM, based on the results of the change management. Performance has to be done in accordance with the LCM, i. e. for maintenance and modifications the LCM has to be applied, starting from an entry point which is dependent from the kind of modification.

In this context is should be mentioned that the LCM also covers the handling of *non-developmental software*, i. e. a functional unit available on the market or from a similar project, which could be of use in the project under consideration.

3.8 Considering hardware

The LCM takes into account the features of *critical realtime software*, which is of relevance especially for embedded computer systems (ECS). In this context criticality is understood as the significance which has been assigned to possible malfunctions of the software. The LCM thus considers the level of criticality as a root for additional quality requirements.

The software development process for ECS has to be seen in close relation with the hardware development or with the chosen hardware and its characteristics. Only then the required functionality can be guaranteed. Therefore the LCM covers all those aspects and parts of a system under development, which may influence the software development.

4 THE SUBMODELS OF THE LCM

Following the four submodels of the LCM will be presented in more detail by showing their main activities and products.

4.1 The Submodel SWD

The submodel SWD regulates, which activities have to be carried out during software development, and which products (documents, software) have to be produced when.

The submodel SWD comprises the following main activities (see figure 6).

SWD 1: System Requirements Analysis and Design
Describe the requirements for the system and environment, and partition the system into DP and non-DP segments.

SWD 2: DP Requirements Analysis and Design
Describe the requirements for a DP segment and its environment, and partition the segment into SW- and HW-configuration items.

SWD 3: SW Requirements Analysis
Describe the requirements for a SWCI and its environment.

SWD 4: Modelling
Structure and describe the interaction of all functions and data with respect to purpose, criticality and structure, contents and relations.

SWD 5: Preliminary Design
Structure the SWCIs with respect to necessary/possible parallelism, subdivide into SW components and modules, and specify the interaction/interfaces of components and modules.

SWD 6: Detailed Design
Describe the components and modules with respect to the concrete implementation of their functions, the data administration and the error handling.

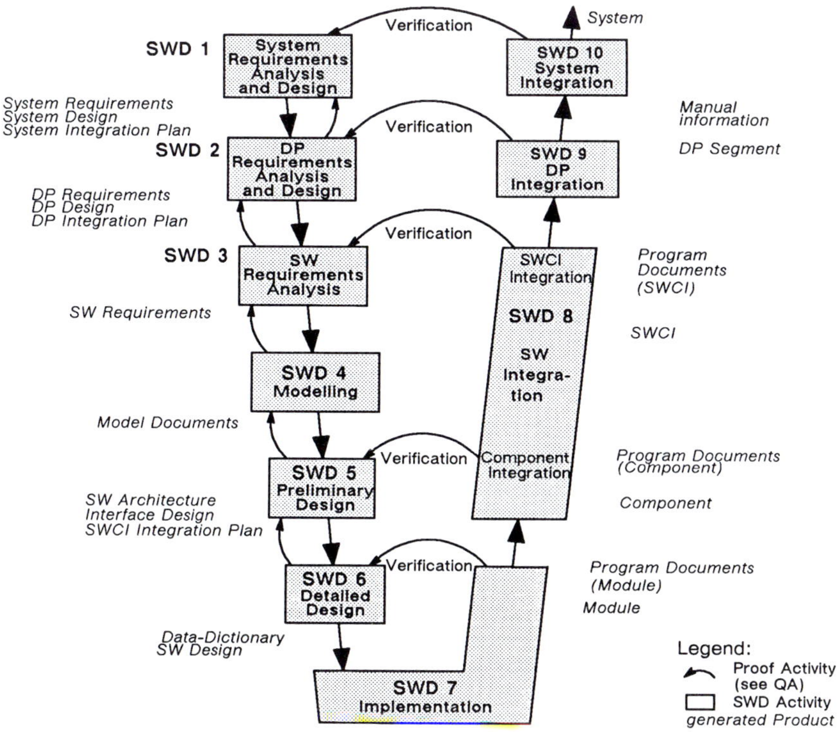

Figure 6 Acitivities and Products in the Submodel SWD

SWD 7: Implementation
Convert the output from SWD 6 to statements of the (chosen) programming language and perform informal tests of the code.

SWD 8: SW Integration
Integrate modules and components to SWCIs according to the SWCI integration plan, and perform informal tests of the integration results.

SWD 9: DP Integration
Integrate SW- and HW configuration items to DP segments according to the DP integration plan, and perform informal tests of the segment.

SWD 10: System Integration
Integrate the system from its segments according to the system integration plan, and perform informal tests.

4.2 The submodel QA

The submodel QA regulates the tasks and functions of the quality assurance within the software development process. These regulations in no way rely on or prescribe organisational structures.

The procedures established in the submodel QA ensure the fulfillment of the quality requirements, which are specified in the documents system-, DP- and SW-requirements, resulting from SWD activities.

The submodel QA comprises the following main activities (see figure 7).

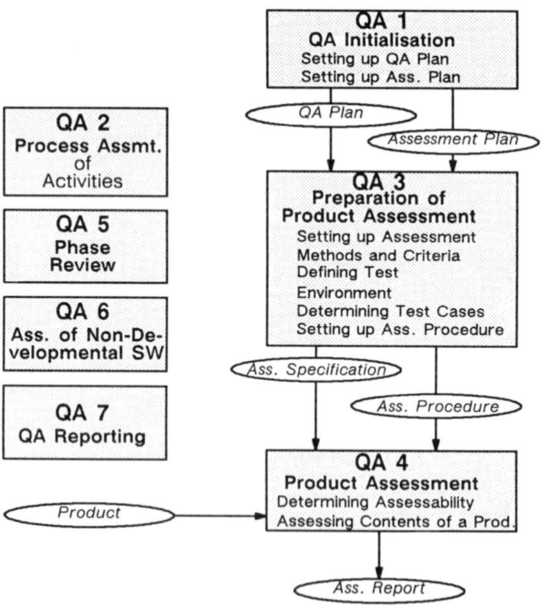

Figure 7 Activities and Products in the Submodel QA

QA 1: QA Initialisation
Define the organisational and procedural framework for QA and produce QA plan and assessment plans.

QA 2: Process Assessment of Activities
Check, whether prescribed procedures are complied with during the performance of specific activities within SWD, CM and PM.

QA 3: Preparation of Product Assessment
Set up assessment specification and -procedure, and complete the assessment plan by determination of the assessment environment. Define assessment criteria such, that an assessment can be subsequently be evaluated with respect to sufficient and successful performance.

QA 4: Product Assessment
Assess the product with respect to formal criteria and to the contents, according to assessment specification and -procedure. Record the result in an assessment record.

QA 5: Phase Review
Decide, whether the next SWD main activity can be started. Determine for that purpose, whether all planned products are available in the form required, costs and schedules have been complied with, and following activities are planned properly.

QA 6: Assessment of Non-Developmental Product
Assess the fulfillment of the quality requirement by a non-developmental product.

QA 7: QA Reporting
Evaluate the assessment records in regular intervals according to specified criteria and submit results to PM.

4.3 The Submodel CM

The submodel CM ensures, that all products are uniquely identifiable, that interrelations and deviations of different versions and variants of a configuration remain evident, and that any product changes can be made only in a controlled manner.

The submodel comprises the following main activities (see figure 8).

CM 1: CM Initialisation
Regulate the organisational and procedural framework within the CM plan and provide the resources (product library, tools).

CM 2: CM Administration
Administer products, configurations and rights. Handle configuration via the configuration identification document (CID).

CM 3. Change Management
Record and administer error reports, problem reports, proposals for improvement, etc., submit them as change requests and monitor the change procedure. (The implementation for a change itself is carried out according to the regulations of the LCM, i.e. involving all four submodels SWD, QA, CM and PM.)

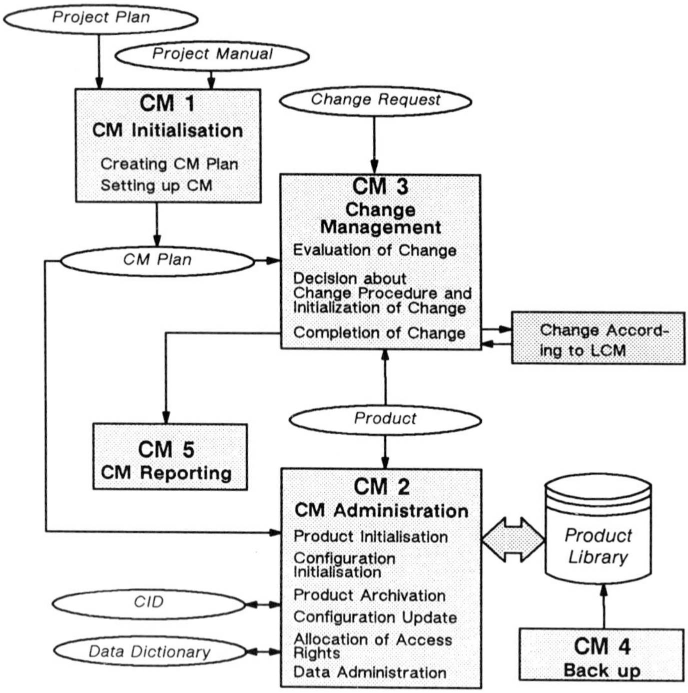

Figure 8 Activities and Products in the Submodel CM

CM 4: Back up
Make back ups, which are due to fixed times and/or scope.

CM 5: CM Reporting
Generate relevant reports for preparations of phase reviews and for information of the project management.

4.4 The Submodel PM

The submodel PM regulates the tasks and functions of the project management within the software development process. These regulations in no way rely on or prescribe organisational structures.

The tasks determined in the submodel PM comprise the planning, control and monitoring of project-internal activities. PM further is the interface to project-external units, acts as project representative and is the project information center.

The submodel PM takes into account the hierarchy of project-, activity- and subactivity-levels by requiring the PM activities "initialisation", "supervision" and "completion" for each level.

The submodel PM comprises the following main activities (see figure 9).

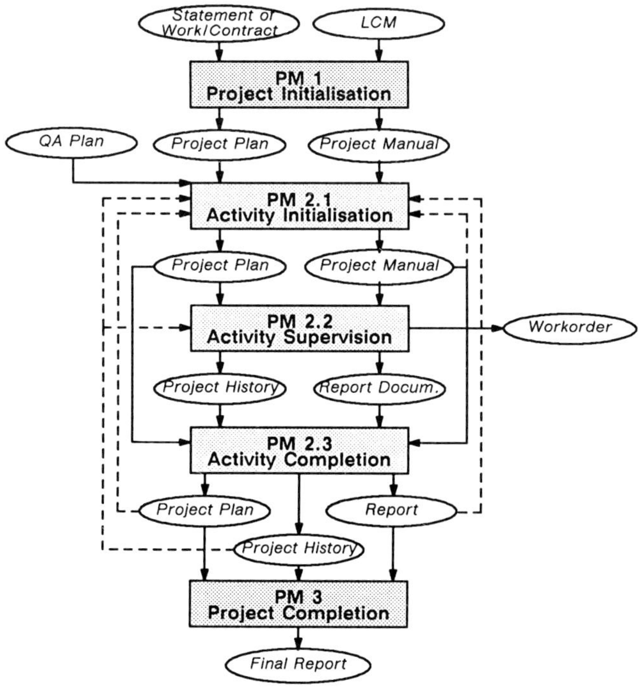

Figure 9 Activities and Products in the Submodel PM

PM 1: Project Initialisation
Define the organisational and procedural framework for PM and produce project plan and project manual, fix the modalities of project-internal cooperation as well as the interfaces to customer and subcontractor. For the project manual determine specific goals and limiting conditions as basis for the tailoring process. For the project plan include preliminary planning with respect to project organisation, cost, baselines, milestones, scheduling and personal planning. Also select and provide a development environment, especially tailored to the project.

PM 2: Project Supervision
Take means for detailed planning, monitoring and control as well as information service on the activity- and subactivity level. (These means are forming a framework about the individual (sub-) activities of a project, including the segments of initialisation, supervision and completion.)

PM 3: Project Completion
At the end of the project submit a final report, which includes a summary of the course of the project, an explanation on the results achieved, and a comparison between actual status and project plan.

5 STATUS AND PLANS

The LCM has now reached a state, which allows its release as a directive for the German defense area. This release is expected to happen in spring or summer 1990. From then on, all projects within the defense area have to be developed in accordance with the LCM. This will affect both Federal Offices and industry.

Besides national efforts, the German Ministry of Defense has already started negotiations with other nations with the goal to use the LCM also in multi-national projects.

For the next release of the LCM some improvements are planned. The LCM will be enhanced with respect to DP-security, to allow the development to trustworth software. This will be achieved by adding and/or modifying activities and products, based upon requirements, which will be derived from the "IT-Security Criteria" issued by the German Information Security Agency. The second improvement is concerned with the tailoring process. Tailoring will be presented in more detail, to make it more precise and user friendly. Moreover, consideration is also given for a tool to support the use of the LCM, specially with respect to tailoring.

6 EXPERIENCES

Because the LCM has not been released as a directive and no ongoing project volunteered, to switch to the LCM, no overall experiences are available until now.

But there are some in-house and pilot projects, which used the LCM at different stages of a project and for different purposes. Experiences from those projects showed a positive acceptance of the LCM, because the procedures, required by the LCM, are very close to common practice and the hints, recommendations and checklists, given in the LCM, proved to be of help for developers. The LCM also has been used successfully as a basis for discussions between customers and contractors.

Problems have been encountered with the tailoring process. It showed up, that the LCM is not enough elaborate and supportive in this area. As already mentioned, the next version of the LCM will contain an enhanced description of the tailoring process, which will be based on the experiences gained in the pilot projects.

SESSION 5

REQUIREMENTS, DEVELOPMENT AND LIABILITY

Approving Software Products
W. Ehrenberger (Editor)
Elsevier Science Publishers B.V. (North-Holland)

Towards a method for evaluating the quality of a user-oriented functional specification

Tony Moynihan and Noel O'Connor

School of Computer Applications
Dublin City University
Glasnevin
Dublin 9
Ireland.

In this paper we describe a method for critically evaluating a user-oriented functional specification. The method involves 'reverse-engineering' a rigorous model of the system's functionality from the documentation. The process of building the model helps expose the structure of the system and gives clues about possible defects in the documentation. We apply the method to a real instance of documentation and find a number of significant flaws which would probably have been missed by a traditional document review.

We conclude that the method is robust and its results reproducible for a system of low or moderate complexity.

INTRODUCTION

The decision to purchase a software product, or to approve the development of bespoke software, is usually made on the basis of documentation describing the product's claimed or intended functionality. Examples of documentation would range from a glossy brochure used to promote a product to a substantial, detailed functional specification. The documentation on which the 'purchaser' will make his/her decision may suffer from a number of flaws. These flaws can be at a syntactic or semantic level. There are a number of methods for assessing the quality of a document at a syntactic level. For example, the Flesch-Kincaid Readability Index is a United States Department of Defence Standard (DOD MIL-M-38748B). The DOD requires its use by contractors producing manuals for the armed services. At the semantic level perhaps the most widely used method is the CLOZE procedure (Guillemette[1]). CLOZE measures the level of 'understandability' of computer documentation but does not assess its substantive content.

Our paper describes a method for evaluating the substantive content of documentation describing the functionality of a software product. A 'rigorous model' of the product's functionality is built from the documentation. The process of building the model requires detailed, systematic analysis of the documentation and thus helps expose semantic flaws. The flaws identified may then be corrected by the developer and an improved document produced.

The notion of 'reverse engineering' a rigorous description of the functionality of a piece of software from its documentation is not new. For example, Sufrin[2] describes the use of Z to construct a model of the functionality of the UNIX utility MAKE from its SUN provided documentation. The act of building the rigorous model helped solve a number of 'enigmas' which the model-builders found in the documentation.

In this paper, we describe the process of building the rigorous model in some detail and illustrate the approach by applying it to an early draft of a piece of real user-documentation. The documentation describes the functionality of a PC-based package which we will call 'TANGO'. TANGO supports the operations and management of a health-screening clinic. The product helps with patient appointment scheduling, medical test data storage, medical report generation, patient billing and other functions. The product is now installed at a number of user-sites and is performing very successfully. The draft documentation consists of 30 pages of text and a number of diagrams. We found it to be well written and presented. The Flesch-Kincaid Readability Index is well within the acceptable range for the target readership (medical doctors, nurses and administrators).

Our modelling approach is object-oriented. In particular, we draw on the ideas of Booch[3], Coad and Yourdon[4] and Meyers[5]. We also draw on some ideas from the field of formal specification (Jones[6], Woodcock[7]).

Step 1 : *Identify candidate objects*

Our first step was to identify the application-domain objects and object-classes which are referenced in the documentation. We excluded objects, even those clearly playing an important part in the application environment, which were not explicitly recognised by the software.

Each author independently read the user documentation and drew up a list of candidate objects. The two lists were compared and found to be virtually identical. We gave each object a unique name, generally the name by which it was most frequently referred to in the documentation. We also noted any apparent synonyms for the same object. We judged nouns to be possible synonyms if they appeared to be used interchangably in the documentation or if they 'sounded' the same at a common-sense level. Further confirmation that two or more nouns were really synonyms for the one object was obtained if the same user-operations seemed to be applicable to each and if they appeared to share the same attributes.

The task took about three hours. The candidate objects we identified are shown in figure 1. The high frequency of apparent synonyms made the task quite difficult and represented a serious flaw in the document.

Object	Synonym(s)
ADMISSION	
ADMISSION NOTIFICATION	
ADMISSIONS LIST	RECORD BOOK
APPOINTMENT SCHEDULE LIST	DAY-SHEET
BIOCHEMISTRY RESULT	
BIOCHEMISTRY TEST	
BLOOD DATA RESULT	

Figure 1 - The candidate objects found

Object	Synonym(s)
BLOOD DATA TEST	
BLOOD PRESSURE RESULT	
BLOOD PRESSURE TEST	
CHEST X-RAY RESULT	
CHEST X-RAY TEST	
CONFIGURATION PARAMETER	
CONSTANT	
CROWN CRISP TEST	
CROWN CRISP TEST RESULT	
CYTOLOGY RESULT	
CYTOLOGY TEST	
CYTOLOGY TEXT	
DOCTOR EXAMINATION	PHYSICAL EXAMINATION
DOCTOR EXAMINATION CODE	
DOCTOR EXAMINATION RESULT	
DOCTOR EXAMINATION TEXT	
DOCTORS TEST	
DOCTORS TEST RESULTS	
ECG TEST	
ECG TEST RESULT	
ECG TEXT	
FAMILY HISTORY TEST	
FAMILY HISTORY TEST RESULT	
GP LETTER	DOCTORS LETTER
HAEMOCULT TEST	
HAEMOCULT TEST RESULT	
HAEMOTOLOGY RESULT	
HAEMOTOLOGY TEST	
HAEMOTOLOGY TEXT	
HEARING TEST	AUDIOMETRY TEST
HEARING TEST RESULT	
HEIGHT AND WEIGHT RESULT	
HEIGHT AND WEIGHT TEST	
INVOICE	
LABEL	
LABORATORY TEST	
LABORATORY TEST RESULTS	
LETTER	
LUNG FUNCTION RESULT	
LUNG FUNCTION TEST	
MAMMOGRAM RESULT	
MAMMOGRAM TEST	
MAMMOGRAM TEXT	

Figure 1 - The candidate objects found (continued)

Object	Synonym(s)
NEW PATIENT	
NEW PATIENT APPOINTMENT	
NURSES TEST RESULTS	
NURSES TEST	
OUTPUT	
PAST HISTORY TEST	
PAST HISTORY TEST RESULT	
PATHOLOGY RESULT	
PATHOLOGY TEST	ADDITIONAL PATHOLOGY
PATHOLOGY TEXT	
PATIENT	
PATIENT ADDRESS LABEL	
PATIENT APPOINTMENT	VISIT
PATIENT CONFIRMATION LETTER	CONFIRMATION LETTER
PATIENT FOLLOW-UP REPORT	
PATIENT LETTER	
PATIENT MEDICAL REPORT	MEDICAL REPORT
PATIENT RECALL LABEL	
PATIENT RECALL LETTER	RECALL LETTER
PATIENT TEST RESULTS	
PERSONAL DETAILS RESULT	
PERSONAL DETAILS TEST	
PHYSICAL EXAMINATION DEFAULT TEXT	STANDARD TEXT
PREVIOUS VISIT SUMMARY MEDICAL REPORT	PATIENT SUMMARY MEDICAL REPORT
PRINTER PARAMETER	
REPORT	
REPORT PARAMETER	
RETURNING PATIENT	
RETURNING PATIENT APPOINTMENT	
SAMPLE IDENTIFICATION LABEL	
SCREENING DOCTOR	DOCTOR
SCREENING NURSE	NURSE
SCREENING TYPE	
SOCIAL HABITS TEST	
SOCIAL HABITS TEST RESULT	
TEST	
TEST RESULT CODE	
TEST RESULT IDEAL RANGE	
URINALAYSIS RESULT	
URINALAYSIS TEST	
VISION RESULT	
VISION TEST	
X-RAY TEXT	

Figure 1 - The candidate objects found (continued)

Step 2 : *Identify object-class and assembly-structure hierarchies*

The object-types shown in figure 1 are highly interrelated. Some object-types denote a super-class or sub-class of other object-types. For example, TEST is a super-class which includes DOCTORS TEST, NURSES TEST and LABORATORY TEST as sub-classes.Some object-types are assembly structures built from two or more other object-types.For example, PATIENT TEST RESULTS is the aggregate of DOCTORS TEST RESULTS, NURSES TEST RESULTS and LABORATORY TEST RESULTS. Figure 1 also includes 'objects' which are actually individual instances of an object-class. For example CROWN CRISP TEST is an instance of DOCTORS TEST.

We tried to find such object structures in the documentation.We had considerable difficulty in doing this. Only one hierarchy was explicitly identified. Other hierarchies were implicit and were pieced-together only with painstaking study of the document. The task took about three hours. Figure 2 shows the provisional object structures we found.The notation used to represent the structures is drawn from Coad[4]. The 'consists of' relationship in an assembly-structure is represented with a triangle pointing to the aggregate object.

The exercise was very valuable. It greatly added to our understanding of the scope and static structure of TANGO. A nice example of abstraction in action!

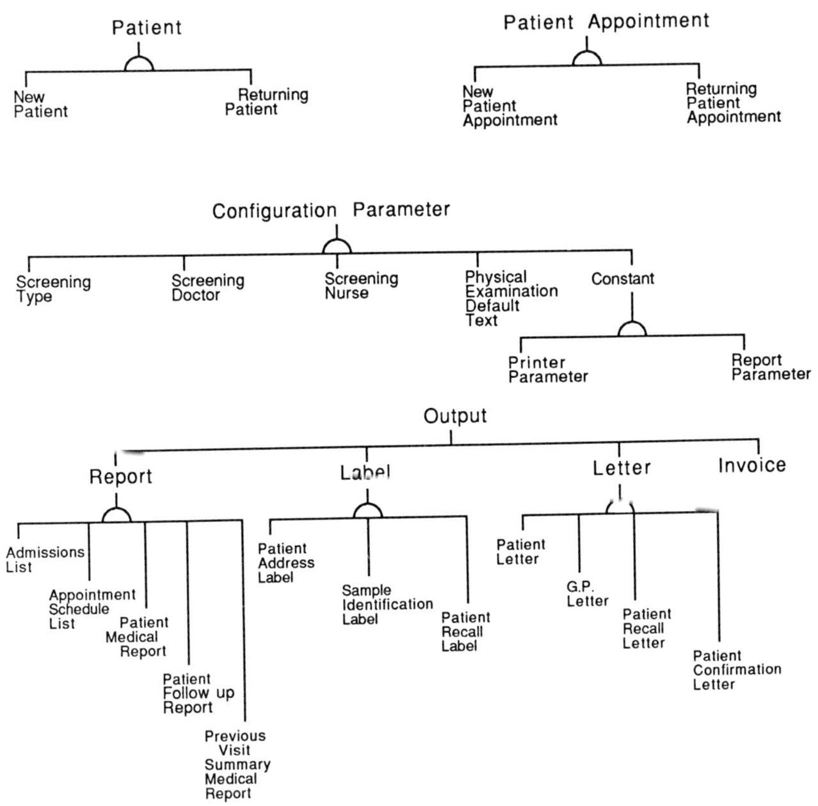

Figure 2 : The Object Class Hierarchies

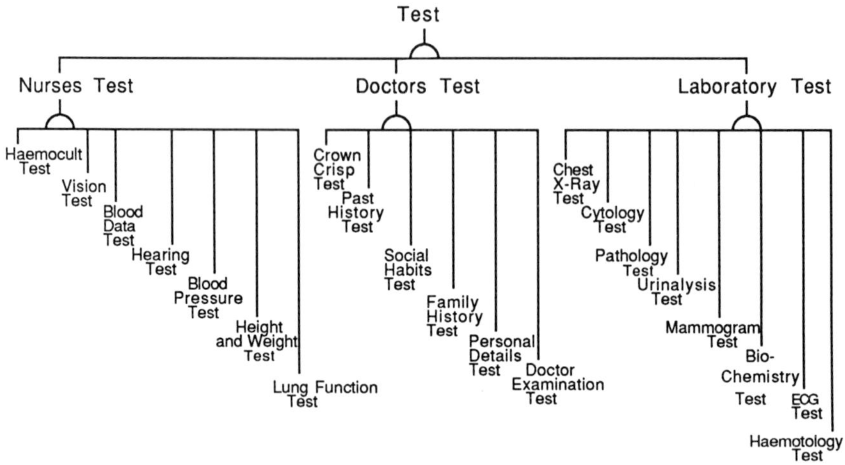

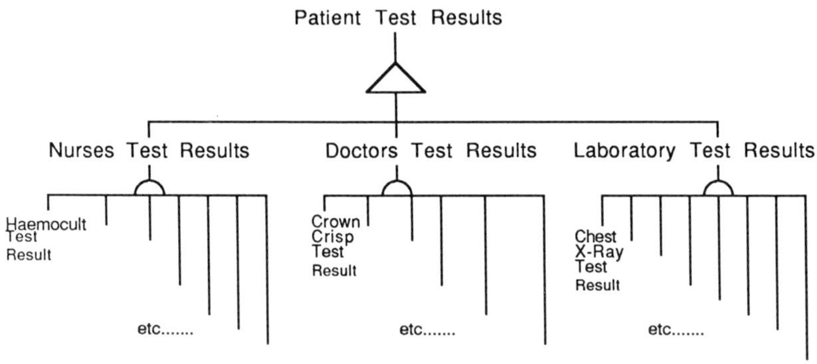

Figure 2 : The Object Class Hierarchies (continued)

Step 3 : *Identify attributes and user-operations for each object*

Our next step was to identify the attributes of each candidate object and the user-operations which could be applied to the object. We found that a number of user-operations automatically triggered-off a series of 'side-effect' operations on other objects. For example, the user-documentation states that when the user attempts to add an appointment for a new patient, the personal details of the new patient are automatically requested, and a record for that patient automatically added to the patient details file, before the appointment is processed. Some of these automatically invoked operations may also be invoked directly by the user whilst others may not.We developed a simple notation to capture this behaviour. We restricted our analysis to operations explicitly described in the user-documentation. We did NOT surmise about 'invisible' operations internal to the software.

We had difficulty gathering the attributes and operations for many of the objects because these were not explicitly recorded in an 'easy to get at way' in the document. The presence of apparent synonyms for some attributes and operations added to the difficulty of the task.

Typically, it took about 30 minutes to document a 'straightforward' object but it took up to 90 minutes to piece together the attributes and operations for a less explicitly described or 'scattered' object.

The process threw up a number of apparent anomalies in the documentation (or in our interpretation of the documentation!). For many 'objects' we could find no attributes and no operations. Could it be that these 'empty' objects were not really objects in their own right ? Could it be that they were really attributes of other objects,were unrecognised synonyms, or were intended to play some other role in the system ? These problematic objects are listed in figure 3.

ADMISSION	MEDICAL FORMULA
ADMISSION NOTIFICATION	DOCTOR EXAMINATION CODE
MAMMOGRAM TEXT	ECG TEXT
TEST RESULT IDEAL RANGE	HAEMOTOLOGY TEXT
TEST RESULT CODE	PATHOLOGY TEXT
DOCTOR EXAMINATION RESULT	X-RAY TEXT
DOCTOR EXAMINATION	CYTOLOGY TEXT
PHYSICAL EXAMINATION DEFAULT TEXT	DOCTOR EXAMINATION TEXT

Figure 3 - Candidate Objects for which no operations and no attributes could be found

In figure 4 we show some of the attributes and all of the user-operations we identified for each 'non-empty' object. For economy and clarity of presentation, we have made full use of 'inheritance' in that we have located each attribute and user-operation in the most general object-class to which it appears to apply. Members of sub-classes inherit these attributes and operations from their super-classes. Figure 4 gives a very good overview of the structure and functionality of TANGO. This is a good example of the descriptive power of abstraction and inheritance when used in combination!

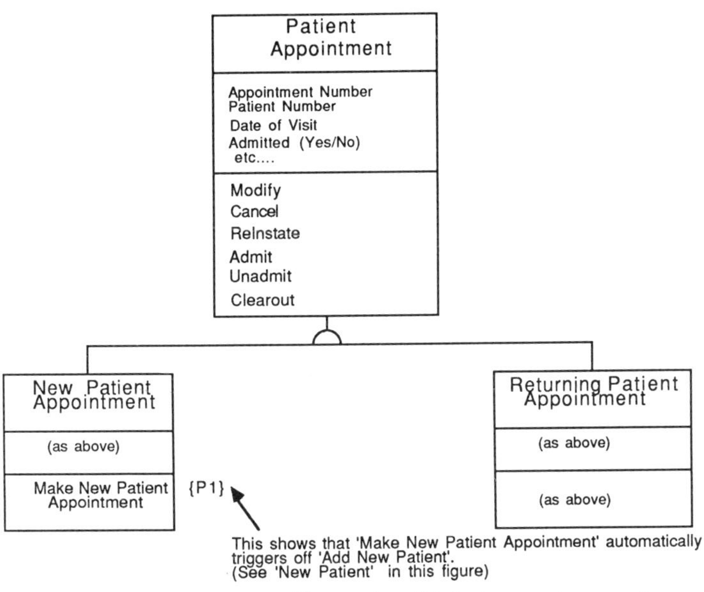

Figure 4 : Attributes and operations

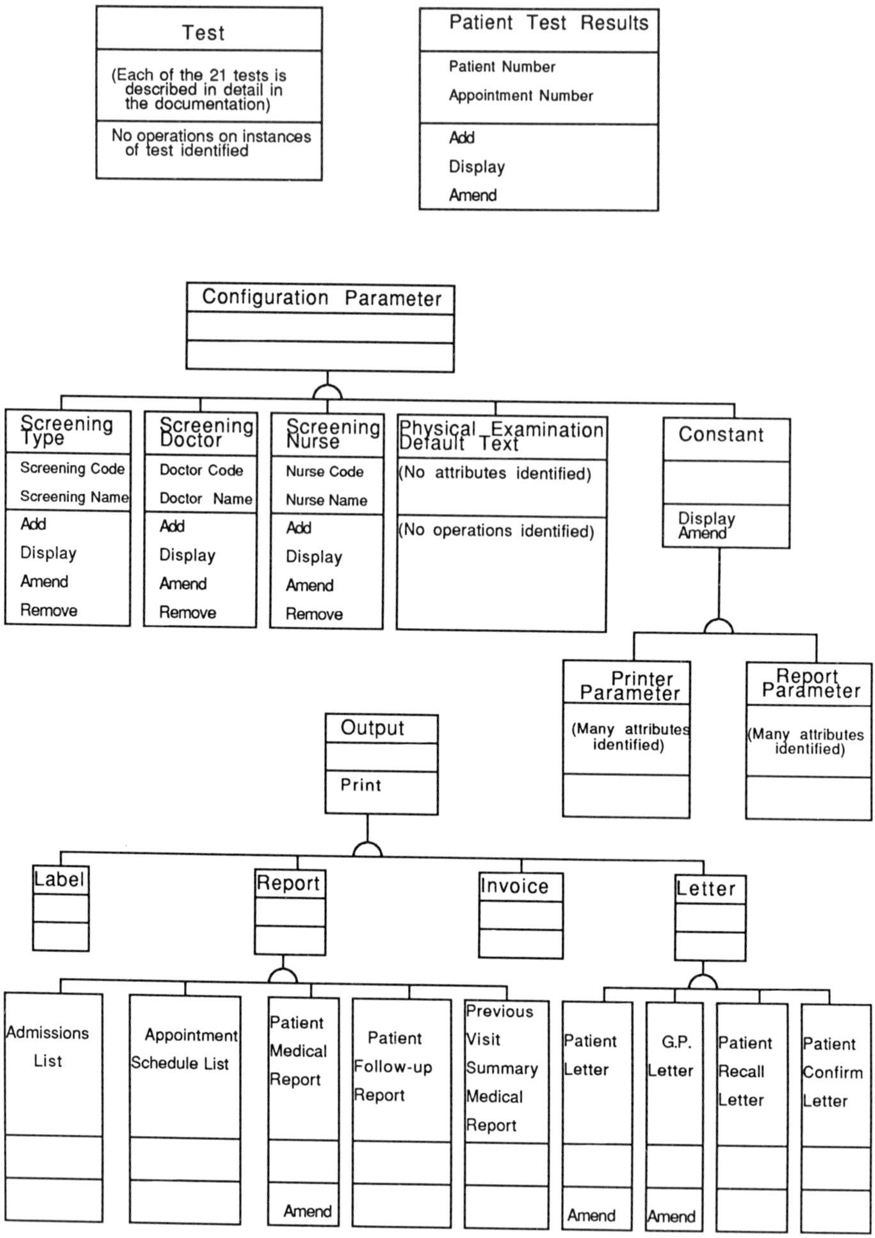

Figure 4 : Attributes and operations (continued)

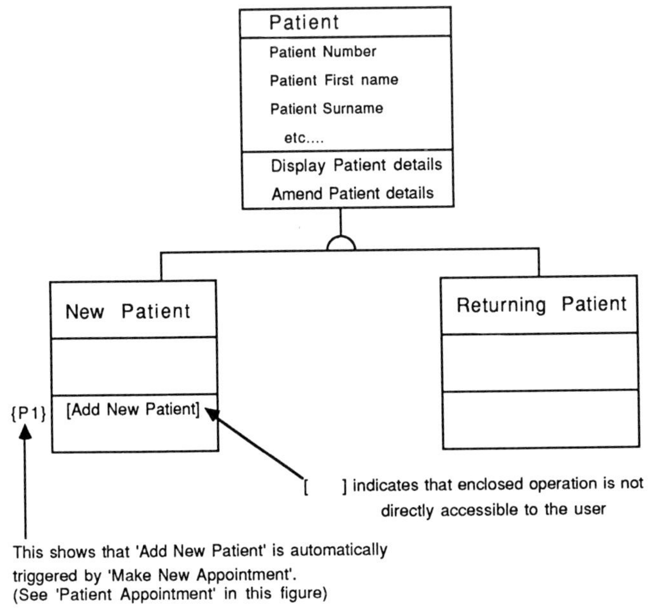

Figure 4 : Attributes and operations (continued)

Step 4 : *Identify instance connections between candidate objects*

An instance connection is a constraint on the existence of an instance of an object-class. For example, a set of test results for a patient (ie. PATIENT TEST RESULTS) can exist only if there is a corresponding instance of a PATIENT APPOINTMENT. Instance connections are an important component in the description of any system.

Figure 5 shows the instance connections we could identify from TANGO documentation. The instance connections are drawn at the highest level of generalisation at which they appear to apply. Thus lower level object-classes are shown in figure 5 only if they participate in instance connections in which the more general or aggregate object does not participate. The cardinality of each connection is also shown. Where cardinality could not be determined from the documentation, a '?' appears. We have used our own notation to express the cardinality of an instance connection. For example, APPLE<1:2--------1:1>ORANGE shows that each instance of APPLE must be associated with exactly one instance of ORANGE and that each instance of ORANGE must be associated with one or two instances of APPLE. The task of constructing figure 5 from the user-documentation was quite difficult and took about four hours to complete. Few instance connections were explicitly identified.

A number of apparent anomalies were identified. These fall into two categories :

(i) The existence of seemingly 'disconnected' objects

Despite our best efforts, we failed to identify any instance connections for 16 candidate objects (see figure 6). Maybe connections exist but they could not be deduced from the documentation. These sixteen 'disconnected' objects happen to be the same sixteen'objects' for which no attributes and operations were found (see figure 3).

(ii) The existence of instance connections of unspecified cardinality

The cardinality of four instance connections could not be established from the user-documentation:

PATIENT <1:1-------0:?> PATIENT APPOINTMENT
NURSES TEST RESULTS <?:1-----?:7> NURSES TEST
DOCTORS TEST RESULTS <?:1-----?:6> DOCTORS TEST
LABORATORY TEST RESULTS <?:1-----?:8> LABORATORY TEST

These unspecified cardinalities raise a number of questions which could be of great importance to potential users of TANGO. For example, can only one future scheduled appointment exist at any given time for a patient ? Or is it possible to stack-up a number of future appointments for a patient? If some of the nurses', doctors' or laboratory tests are not administered to a patient, do the test results for the tests which ARE administered constitute a valid set of patient test results ?

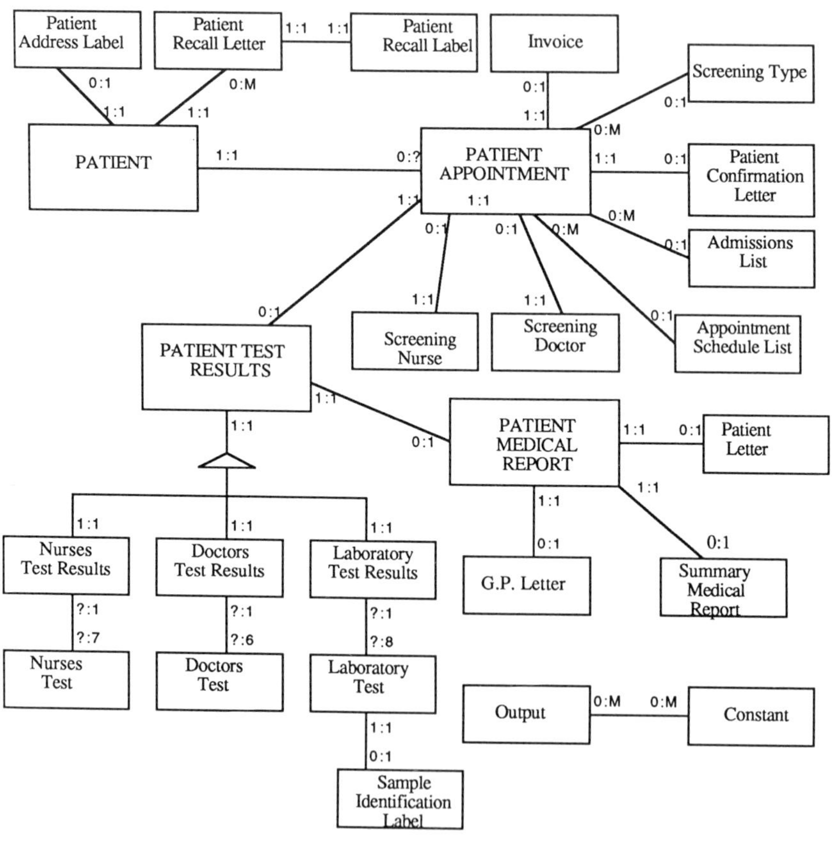

Figure 5 : Instance Connections

ADMISSION	MEDICAL FORMULA
ADMISSION NOTIFICATION	DOCTOR EXAMINATION CODE
MAMMOGRAM TEXT	ECG TEXT
TEST RESULT IDEAL RANGE	HAEMOTOLOGY TEXT
TEST RESULT CODE	PATHOLOGY TEXT
DOCTOR EXAMINATION RESULT	X-RAY TEXT
DOCTOR EXAMINATION	CYTOLOGY TEXT
PHYSICAL EXAMINATION DEFAULT TEXT	DOCTOR EXAMINATION TEXT

Figure 6 - Candidate Objects apparently participating in no instance connections.

Step 5 : *First document review session with developer*

In steps 1 through 4 we identified a number of 'puzzles' with TANGO's user-documentation. Before proceeding any further with our analysis of the document, we held a document review session with the developer to confirm the validity of our analysis and to sort out the 'puzzles'. The review session took about one hour to complete.

We first reviewed figure 1. We confirmed that all but one of the candidate synonyms really are synonyms. VISIT is not a synonym for PATIENT APPOINTMENT as we had thought, but is a synonym for ADMISSION.

We next reviewed figures 3 and 6 which list, respectively, objects that are apparently 'empty' (ie. have no attributes and no operations) and objects that do not seem to participate in any instance connections. We learnt that DOCTOR EXAMINATION actually consists of nineteen different tests,called PHYSICAL EXAMINATION TESTs, which involve examining some physical attribute of the patient (for example,his/her eyes). Each of these tests is identified with a unique code (DOCTOR EXAMINATION CODE synonym for which is TEST RESULT CODE) which is an attribute of the test rather than an object in its own right. The result for a test is DOCTOR EXAMINATION RESULT. Associated with each test is a paragraph of standard text (PHYSICAL EXAMINATION DEFAULT TEXT). The doctor may include this paragraph of text in the PATIENT MEDICAL REPORT if the result of the test is 'normal'. If the result is 'abnormal', the doctor may generate his/her own text (DOCTOR EXAMINATION TEXT).

We learnt that MEDICAL FORMULAs and TEST RESULT IDEAL RANGEs are algorithms and constants respectively used by the software when computing PATIENT TEST RESULTS. These object types appear to be 'hard-coded' into the system. The term ADMISSION NOTIFICATION was used in error in the documentation. It should have read APPOINTMENT NOTIFICATION and is a further synonym for PATIENT CONFIRMATION LETTER. The term ADMISSION refers to a PATIENT APPOINTMENT for which the PATIENT has attended and undergone tests. MAMMOGRAM TEXT, ECG TEXT, HAEMOTOLOGY TEXT, PATHOLOGY TEXT, X-RAY TEXT and CYTOLOGY TEXT refer to free text paragraphs which may be generated by clinic staff for inclusion in the PATIENT MEDICAL REPORT if, for example, the results of any of these tests are abnormal.

We next reviewed figure 5 (Instance Connections). We confirmed that our analysis was correct. We looked in particular at the four instance connections for which we could not find cardinalities. We established that the system will allow only one future, scheduled PATIENT APPOINTMENT to exist for any PATIENT (ie. future appointments can't be 'stacked up' for a patient). We also learnt that a partial set of test results does constitute a valid set PATIENT TEST RESULTS (ie. not all tests must be administered to a patient).

Following on the review we amended the various diagrams as necessary. The revised diagrams are not shown in this paper. Having resolved all the puzzles, we proceeded to the next step in the analysis.

Step 6 : *Extract the pre- and post-conditions for each operation*

We next tried to construct the pre- and post-conditions for each user-operation. We found this to be moderately difficult. Very few of the conditions were made explicit in the documentation. This forced us to rely heavily on our limited application domain knowledge and on our intuition. As a result,we were not very confident that our analysis was accurate and complete. Figure 7 shows our 'best shot' at making the pre- and post-conditions explicit. As in earlier figures, we have attached each operation to the most general object-class to which it applies. Where the pre- or post-conditions differ for a sub-class, we make this explicit in the diagram. This use of abstraction greatly simplifies the presentation.

The notation we used for recording the conditions is fairly informal, but was adequate for our purpose. Had the complexity of the application been greater, we would have been compelled to adopt a more formal and elaborate notation such as that used in VDM (Jones[6] or Z Woodcock[7]). In some of the conditions, we introduced a 'state-indicator' (Skidmore[8]). The use of the state-indicator helped us express constraints on the sequences of operations which may be validly applied to an instance of an object-class, and helped us express alternative post-conditions where the effect of an operation is contingent on the internal state of the object.

In addition to a general feeling of unease about the accuracy and completeness of figure 7, we identified a number of specific ambiguities in the documentation. For example, can we modify the details of a PATIENT APPOINTMENT after the PATIENT has been admitted ? Can we cancel a PATIENT APPOINTMENT which has not resulted in an ADMISSION but which is less than three months old (and thus not removable by 'clearout')? To make a RETURNING PATIENT APPOINTMENT must there exist an instance of a previous ,admitted PATIENT APPOINTMENT for this PATIENT ? Perhaps the answers to these questions are unimportant to users-but maybe they are!

Object	Operation	Pre-Condition	Post-Condition
Patient	Display Patient details	Patient present	(self evident)
	Amend Patient details	Patient present	(self evident)
Patient Appointment	Modify	state indicator = 1 or ?	state indicator unchanged
	Cancel	state indicator = 1 or ?	state indicator = 2
	Reinstate	state indicator = 2	state indicator = 1
	Admit	state indicator = 1	state indicator = 3
	Unadmit	state indicator = 3	state indicator = 1
	Clearout	date of visit earlier than 3 months ago and	
		if state indicator = 3	Patient Appointment moved to archive table
		if state indicator ≠ 3	Patient Appointment deleted from system
Sub-Types:			
New Patient Appoinment	Make new Patient Appointment	Patient not present	Patient present and Patient Appointment present with state-indicator = 1
Returning Patient Appointment	Make Returning Patient Appointment	Patient present and no Patient Appointment present for this Patient with state-indicator = 1 and Patient Appointment present for this patient with state-indicator = 3	Patient Appointment present with state-indicator = 1

Figure 7 : Pre and Post conditions for user operations

Object	Operation	Pre-Condition	Post-Condition
Output	Print	(self evident)	(self evident)
Sub-Types:			
Patient Medical Report	Amend	(self evident)	(self evident)
Patient Letter	Amend	(self evident)	(self evident)
G.P. Letter	Amend	(self evident)	(self evident)
Configuration Parameter			
Sub-Types:			
Screening Type	Add Display Amend Remove	(self evident)	(self evident)
Screening Nurse	Add Display Amend Remove	(self evident)	(self evident)
Screening Doctor	Add Display Amend Remove	(self evident)	(self evident)
Physical Examination Default Text	(None)		

Figure 7 : Pre and Post conditions for user operations(continued)

Object	Operation	Pre-Condition	Post-Condition
Patient Test Results	Add Display Amend	Patient Appointment with state-indicator = 3 present for this Patient	(self evident)
Constants	Display Amend	(self evident) (self evident)	(self evident) (self evident)
Medical Formula	(None)		
Test Result Ideal Range	(None)		
Doctor Examination Text	Create Display Amend	(self evident) (self evident) (self evident)	(self evident) (self evident) (self evident)
Test	(None)		

Figure 7 : Pre and Post conditions for user operations(continued)

Step 7 : *Confirm the existence of operations to add, modify, and remove instances of each object type*

By its nature, one would expect any information system to provide user-operations to add and delete instances of persistent objects and operations to modify the values of the attributes. An exception to this generalisation would be an object, such as a table of 'hardwired' constants, which by design the user is not allowed to change. In step 7, we 'walked' an instance of each object-class through its life-cycle and confirmed, or otherwise, the presence of these basic operations. If these operations are missing from the documentation, it may signal an inadvertent omission from the documentation or a deliberate design decision which may have important implications for the user. Figure 8 shows those object-classes for which one or more of the basic operations could not be found. Once again, we have made full use of abstraction in presenting the results.

Figure 8 presents a number of puzzles. While a new instance of PATIENT is automatically created when a NEW PATIENT APPOINTMENT is made, there appears to be no operation which allows the user to directly create a new instance of PATIENT.Can a new patient be added only in the context of that patient making his/her first appointment?

It appears that instances of the following objects are 'hard-wired' into the system and may not be added, changed or removed by the user : TEST, MEDICAL FORMULA, TEST RESULT IDEAL RANGE and PHYSICAL EXAMINATION DEFAULT TEXT. The first three of these object-classes specify the various tests to be applied to patients and contain parameters and algorithms for processing test results. Thus they are very central to the operation of the system. Perhaps user operations for their maintenance exist in the software, but they do not appear in the documentation.

Object	Create Operations	Amend Operations	Remove Operations
Patient	No	Yes	No
Test	No	No	No
Medical Formula	No	No	No
Test Result Ideal Range	No	No	No
Physical Examination Default Text	No	No	No

Figure 8 : Persistent objects for which no Create, Amend or Remove user-operations could be found.

Step 8 : *Final document review session with the developer*

The purpose of this final step was to confirm the validity of the analysis in steps 6 and 7 and to feed back the new 'puzzles' we had found in the documentation. The review meeting lasted about 30 minutes and the objectives were achieved.

CONCLUSIONS

In this paper we have described an approach to the task of critically examining the content of a piece of draft user-documentation. We are confident that the process of constructing the 'rigorous model' uncovered problems which a more traditional document review would have missed. Both authors of this paper independently applied the procedures to the document and our findings were virtually identical. So it looks like the procedure is robust and reproducible.

The notation we used is relatively informal but was adequate for the task. The notation would need elaboration and an increase in level of formality to cope with more complex systems. Also, tool support would be required to analyse documents describing larger or more complex systems. For very complex systems, our procedure would probably become unwieldy and the model incomprehensible-but this would be true of any static representation of a very complex system.

We have learnt that a good knowledge of the application domain is very important. The more the model builder knows about the application domain, the speedier and more thorough the analysis. Maybe the best person to build the model is a potential user!

For the future, we want to explore the idea of re-writing a user-document so that its structure and content are isomorphic with that of the rigorous model. One can even visualise a tool which would take the model as input and automatically produce a 'skeleton' of the restructured document for completion by a human author. The new 'de-bugged' document would have a 'logical' structure which users might find easier to comprehend than a document structured in any other way. The degree of benefit in such restructuring would probably depend on the extent to which the constructs in the model reflect the user's 'mental model' of the application domain (Carroll[9]).This question can only be answered by empirical research.

We also want to explore the potential of the model building process to yield new document quality metrics. For example, the proportion of operations for which pre- or post-conditions are not made explicit might constitute one useful metric of document quality.

Finally, on a different theme, we want to test the possibility of automatically generating test-cases from the rigorous model. The model can be viewed as a 'path expression' which can generate all possible legal sequences of operations on the objects in the model. In other words, the objects, attributes, operations and the pre- and post-conditions taken together constitute a grammar from which valid sentences (ie. allowable sequences of operations) may be constructed. This idea is closely related to the idea of automatic test-case generation from a formal specification Gehani[10].

ACKNOWLEDGEMENTS

This work is partially supported by the EC through ESPRIT 2 Project 'SCOPE'

REFERENCES

[1] Guillemette,R.A. 'The CLOZE Procedure:An Assessment of the Understandability of Data Processing Texts,' Information and Management,Volume 17,1989,pp.143-155.

[2] Sufrin,B. Effective Industrial Application of Formal Methods,in Ritter,G.X.,(editor),Information Processing 89-Proceedings of IFIP 11th.World Computer Congress (North-Holland,Amsterdam,1989) pp.61-69.

[3] Booch,G. 'Object-Oriented Development,' IEEE Transactions on Software Engineering,Volume SE-12 (Number 2),1986,pp.211-221.

[4] Coad,P. and Yourdon,E., Object-Oriented Analysis (Yourdon Press,New Jersey,1990).

[5] Meyer,B.,Object-Oriented Software Construction (Prentice Hall,New Jersey,1988).

[6] Jones,C.B.,Systematic Software Development using VDM (Prentice Hall,New Jersey,1990).

[7] Woodcock,J. and Loomes,M., Software Engineering Mathematics (Pitman,London,1988).

[8] Skidmore,S.,Farmer,R. and Mill,G.,SSADM Models and Methods (National Computing Centre of Great Britain,Manchester,1990).

[9] Carroll,J.M. and Olson,J.R. Mental Models in Human-Computer Interaction,in Helander,M.,(editor), Handbook of Human-Computer Interaction (Elsevier Science Publishers,Amsterdam,1988) pp.45-65.

[10] Gehani,N. and McGettrick,A.D.,Software Specification Techniques(Addison-Wesley,New York,1986) pp. 20-21.

Approving Software Products
W. Ehrenberger (Editor)
Elsevier Science Publishers B.V. (North-Holland)
IFIP, 1990

Agricultural Computing: On the Farm in 1990

The paper will look at problems of developing suitable commercial software in the field of agriculture. In this area, the gulf between the user and the writer of the software is potentially very great - with the practical farmer usually having no background in information technology and the systems designers and programmers typically unclear about what the users need and what level of IT background can be assumed. The main emphasis of the paper will be the possibilities of overcoming this gulf by participation of users in the decision making, as to what software needs to be developed, and the actual design process.

This theme will be developed both from the standpoint of the farmer and the commercial software firm. A survey of a sample of farmers, who are currently using farming software packages, will seek to establish:

a) What the farmers' history with manual systems has been. For example, what manual records they kept, why they decided to switch to a computerised system etc.

b) What the most important objectives are that farmers wish to attain from the use of a system. Farmers' needs will be analysed within the framework of twelve computer design objectives.

c) Their assessment of the software they are familiar with; its costs in terms of time and money; the difficulties and shortcomings encountered with the software; their views on the manual and documentation; training and support received from the software sellers.

Looking at the problem from the sellers' point of view, the paper will study the process of software development inside a firm producing wellknown farming packages. How much user participation is there in this process? Are prototype systems used to get an idea of user reaction? How are the manuals produced?

The paper will hope to establish to what extent the farmers' objectives are different to those of the software house and, if there is any contradiction, and how far user participation can be increased in this area.

Approving Software Products
W. Ehrenberger (Editor)
Elsevier Science Publishers B.V. (North-Holland)

EXPERIENCES IN SYSTEM MODELLING USING CASE

M. Grimmer, R. Kurpicz and J. Röhrle

Department of Informatics
ASCOM Hasler Ltd.
CH - 3000 Berne

Structured Analysis is a method for the description of systems using data flow diagrams at different levels of abstraction. Practical experience with the method has shown some disturbing deficiencies, which we aim to discuss in this paper. We would also like to present some pragmatic solutions which improve the descriptive abilities of Structured Analysis.

1. INTRODUCTION

1.1. Overview

Nowadays, CASE (computer aided software engineering) is often strongly promoted as a means of solving existing problems in the software development process. In general terms, the principle of CASE is quite simple: CASE encompasses all computer-assisted tools which support the software development process. Therefore, the available tools vary in accordance with their intended applications. There are program generators, data dictionaries and drawing tools as well as so-called integrated software engineering systems [1], which attempt to cover all phases of the software lifecycle [2]. In the following we will describe our experiences with one particular integrated system.

Irrespective of the existing theoretical problems concerning the transition from the analysis phase to the design phase, most tools try to use highly integrated methods which clearly have the advantage of being able to use stored data as well as to check consistency. The methods used in these tools are often based on classic concepts or extensions of such concepts. Depending on their flexibility, some tools may be adapted to the user's requirements.

1.2. Current status

Given the fact their CASE tools are in the initial phases of development, it is difficult to give a definitive summary of the experiences acquired in larger projects. On the one hand, some publications closely associated with the producers of case tools promise to revolutionize the software development process using CASE tools with graphic facilities. On a less optimistic note, some publications concede the possibility of increased productivity, albeit depending on certain assumptions (e.g. knowledge of methods, qualifications of staff, etc.).

Less frequent but equally interesting is the question of whether CASE tools actually assist in mastering current practical problems [3]. Here, CASE is regarded as a consequence of software engineering environment systems (SEES), which exist to support the software development process by engineering methods. Scientific studies have shown that approaches of this type definitely have less influence on the success of a project than, for example, the qualifications of the staff involved. As software development projects become more and more complex, this will continue to be true in the future.

The basic trends in data processing are :

1. The use of computers in network systems, the distribution of mainframes and workstations leads to decentralized applications.

2. The use of front-office systems, e.g. decision support systems, with a high rate of embedded dynamic structures, acquires more and more importance in comparison in traditional back-office systems, e.g. financial bookkeeping.

3. The participation of endusers software development process is of increasing importance.

4. The use of standard software, often with embedded CASE components, is increasing not only for small and medium-sized enterprises but also for larger concerns.

1.3. Application environment

Despite these serious objections, in 1988/89 the Department of Informatics of ASCOM Hasler Ltd. started using CASE. To gain experience in the development of software using CASE, the 'User Services' subdepartment was selected. The main tasks of this group are the support of database applications on PC and host as well as advice on data processing.

The Department of Informatics supports all the areas of ASCOM Hasler cooperation as shown in Fig. 1. The COPICS PPS System is installed on the IBM 3090-400 mainframe under the MVS operating system. The current database applications in SQL/DS are based on VM. About 1200 terminals are connected via the SNA network. In addition there exists a company-wide Ethernet, to which several DEC/VAX computers and some Apollo-, VAX- and SUN-Workstations are linked. Finally, we have about 800 PCs connected via PC-SA or Novell network.

2. THE USE OF STRUCTURED ANALYSIS IN A SOFTWARE DEVELOPMENT PROJECT

2.1. General information on the CASE tool used

We used STP (Software Through Pictures, IDE) instead of IEW (James Martin Corporation), because of version control, better documentation features and network facilities. All outputs such as information objects, description of processes etc. are stored and checked in a central data dictionary.

STP supports the phases of the software lifecycle using the following methods :

1 - Analysis phase
Use of Structured Analysis [4] based on data flow diagrams, to describe a system from the viewpoint of data flows.

2 - Design phase
Use of Structured Design [5] based on Structure Charts to show the interfaces of the module hierarchy.

3 - Coding phase
Enables generation of data definition statements and program code for the algorithms inherent in the process specifications.

To show the data structures, Jackson diagrams or Chen's entity relationship diagrams can be used.

It is immediately apparent that the system lacks tools to support the test phase. Because of this deficiency, a comprehensive quality control cannot be conceived.

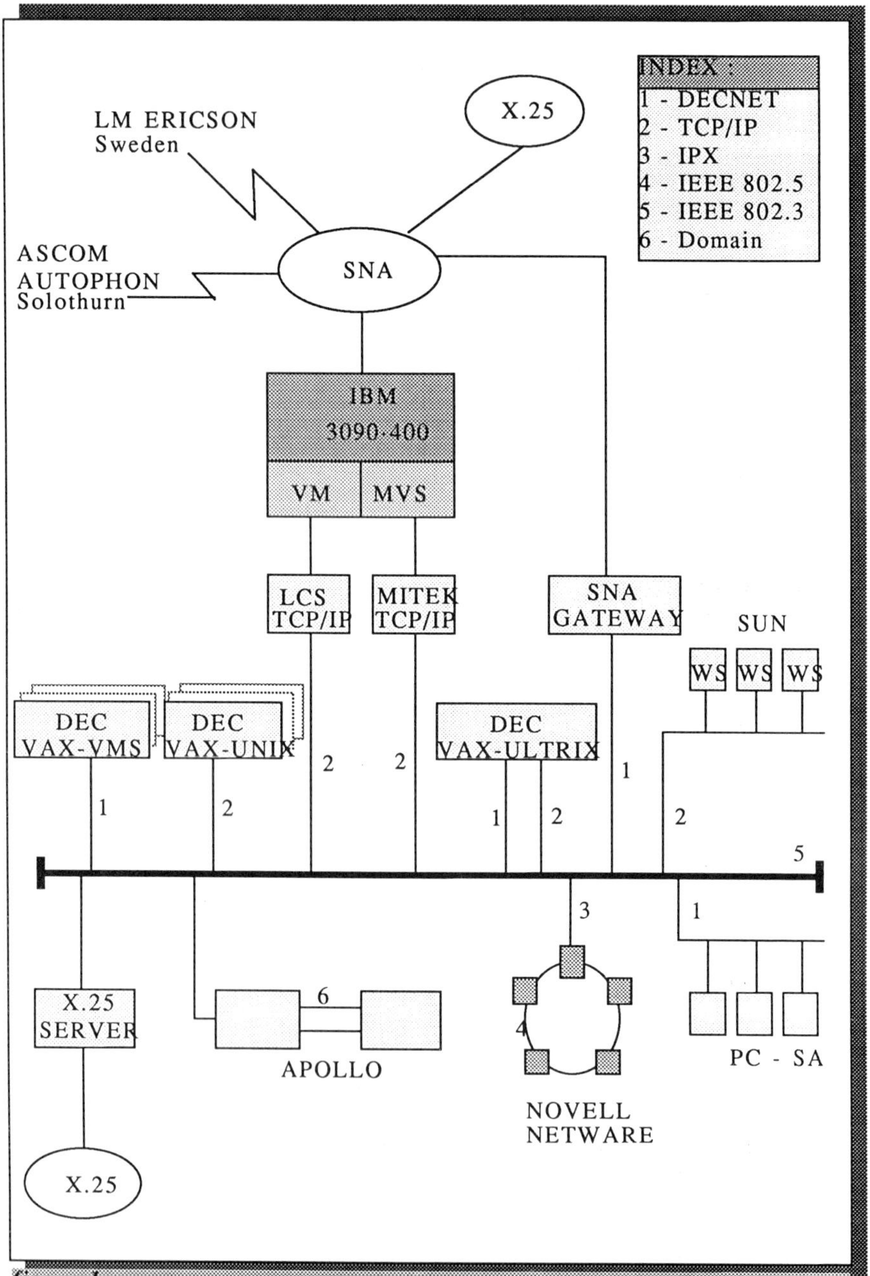

figure 1 :
ASCOM Konzernbereich Netzwerke - infrastructure

2.2. Methodology of Structured Analysis

Data flow diagrams describe a system from the viewpoint of data. The method is based on the use of a few simple symbols, and subdivision into several levels of abstraction. This reduces the amount of components and leads to a better understanding of the global context and its effects. With each decomposition of a process, the internal structures become more and more concrete. This finally leads to an elementary process which can be formulated in Structured English, a formal notation for the description of algorithms.

The use of SA for all phases of the software life cycle [6] is no longer discussed as an alternative to traditional methodologies such as project management models. It is obvious to us, that SA can only be used in the analysis phase. As a result, the specification document forms the basis for the module design.

The activities in SA are :

a) Study of the current physical data flow

Studying the environment from the viewpoint of data with the following check list :

- determination of the application's environment
- determination of user groups
- interviewing all participants
- drawing data flow diagrams
- collecting sample data types, files and forms to represent the system to be built
- review of the results and presentation to all participants

As a result, the system is described by data flow diagrams representing the current physical situation.

b) Derivation of the logical context

Substitution of milestones of the physical data flow diagram by logical equivalents.

The logical data flow diagram is developed by abstracting from the physical situation, forming information objects and non-redundant processes.

c) Modelling the new logical schema

The logical data flow diagrams are studied from an implementation feasibility point of view, to produce a system description. This logical view, consisting of a conceptual data model and redesigned data flow diagrams, forms the basis for the design phase.

For each activity in the analysis phase, there is a choice between a process-oriented and a data-oriented methodology. The data-oriented method describes a system from the viewpoint of static data, which are then processed stepwise. In general, both approaches lead to the same results. In practice, however, the process-oriented approach is better for describing the physical situation, since endusers are used to thinking in a more procedural manner, due to their experiences in a hierarchically organized world. The data-oriented method is more convenient from the logical viewpoint, since the latter has to abstract from the physical situation and an application-independant data model can be derived by methods of normalization.

3. EXPERIENCES WITH STRUCTURED ANALYSIS

3.1. Situation at the beginning of the project

The reason for using a CASE tool and its methods is the directive to improve the situation for planning and producing digital telephone systems. To achieve this, an intensive study of the existing structures was necessary, in order to simplify organizational flows. The primary goal, however, was the replacement of three enduser programs by one or more integrated database applications.

The advantages of the existing enduser programs were an adequate definition of the problems they solved and the adaptation to company-specific requirements. Nevertheless, these tools exhibited several deficiencies, which impede usage: on the one hand the transfer of data between the systems was almost always realized by 'human interfaces'; on the other hand, the applications did not satisfy the requirements of multi-user access.

The know how which the enduser acquires by training himself to write his own applications, often facilitates the working out of data processing concepts.

Prototypes are usually used to evaluate the endusers requirements if there are no definitive ideas. In our case the existing applications could be looked upon as prototypes from which we were able to learn details relating to the daily work of all relevant departments. We believe that this situation is not uncommon and is comparable to the circumstances in other companies who are attempting to detach existing applications without having to start from scratch. The increased use of standard software also reflects this trend in the software development process.

3.2. Study of the physical situation with SA

SA is based on a few simple symbols which represent data flow, data store, process and external. A model described by data flow diagrams shows a given system from the static viewpoint of the data. The different levels of the data flow diagrams show different levels of abstraction. The top level shows only the interfaces to existing applications. The next levels describe the system in detail, becoming more and more concrete the further down they go, until elementary processes are reached. These processes can then be described in a formal language like Structured English.

The initial activities of SA are very similar to conventional specification methods. Interviews with all participants show the interfaces to other areas of application or the man-machine-interface. Using this as a basis, the first diagrams can be drawn in an attempt to cover all details. For this, the different levels of the dataflow diagram permit concentration on specific application aspects and force the enduser to map each of his activities to exactly one processing unit.

By iteratively presenting the diagrams to all involved participants, the stepwise refinement leads to more and more concrete levels of abstraction. Finally, we get the elementary processes and information units, often in form of data types. By each decomposition of a process, the incoming and outgoing data flows have to be described in the next deeper level. This is usually done by Jackson diagrams, as decomposed data flows are of hierarchic nature.

The endusers often like to think in a more procedural way, which seems to be more natural than thinking in an application-independent and therefore data-oriented way. Because of this, we studied the physical situation and described the current situation of the system in a process-oriented manner. For the documentation of data structures, we prefer Jackson notation rather then Chen's entity relationship diagrams. This representation only works in the case of normalized data structures. The data structures used in the physical data flow diagrams are definitely not normalized.

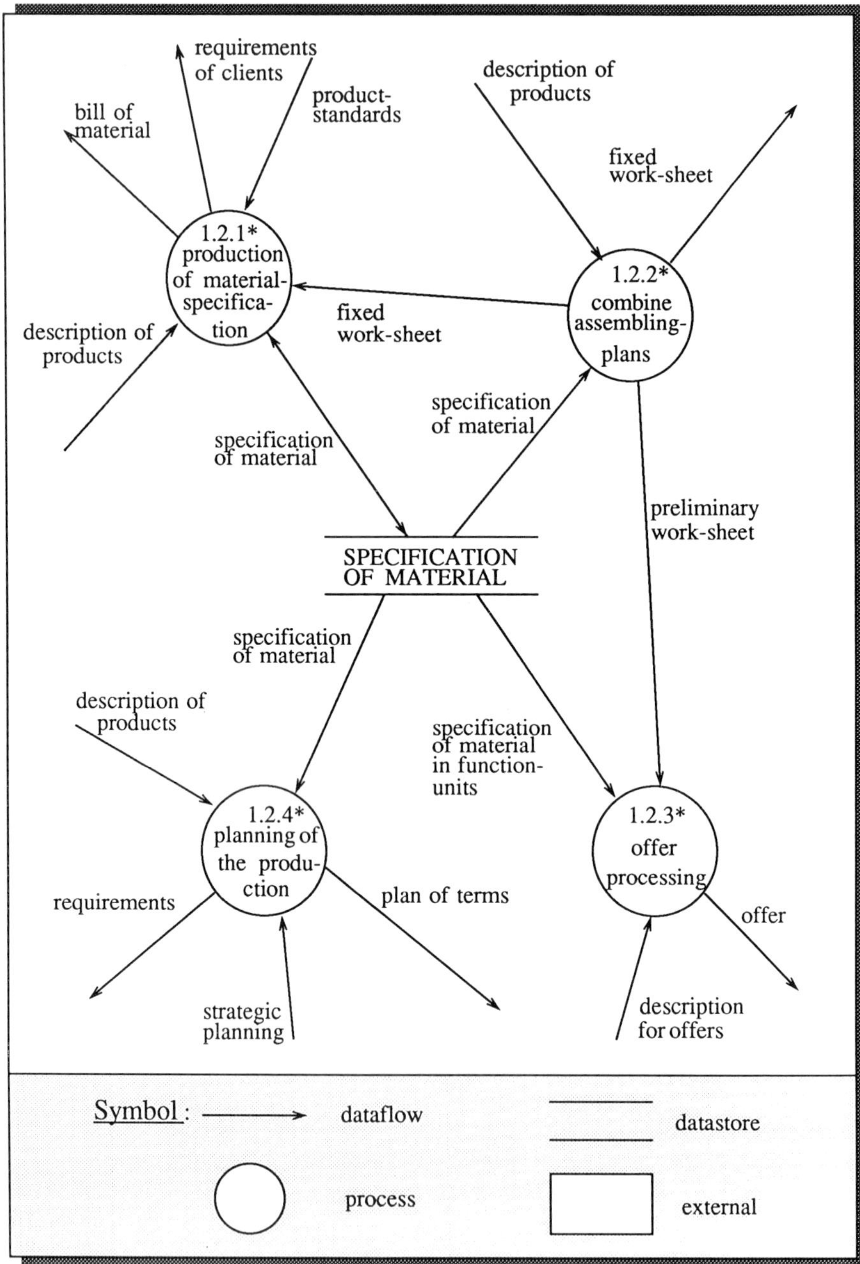

figure 2 :
decomposition 2nd level of the project

3.3. Derivation of the logical concept

After studying the current physical situation, the conceptual work began. First, all information contained in the data flow diagrams, the data structures and additional explanatory text has to be classified according to appropriate criteria. The abstraction is then effected for both processes and data structures. The process of abstracting fuzzy information to normalized information objects is often called 'data modelling'. Nevertheless, the development of an application-independent data model is done in parallel by reorganizing the different levels of the data flow diagrams, resulting in 'normalized' processes.

The 'normalization' of processes is steered by related activities in a bottom-up process. This normally leads to a different levelling. Fig. 2 shows the first level below the top level of the logical concept.

On the basis of this diagram, some basic reorganizations were made. This has facilitated the whole process of planning and producing telephone systems. A reorganization always has to take place before further applications are designed or even implemented. If this cannot be done, transitional implementations only set the existing organizational structures.

By working out application-independent data structures, one enters the area of classical data modelling, deriving information objects from unsorted data. For these normalized data structures we now use entity relationship diagrams rather than Jackson's notation.

3.4. Summary of the use of SA in a software development project

SA proved good in a medium-sized software development project. Nevertheless we had several difficulties in using both a new method and a new tool. The method was well accepted by all participants due to the use of simple symbols and the levelling of the data flow diagrams. We also found that the quality of our documents has improved, as the results could better be evaluated and controlled.

This improvement is worth spending more time on in the initial phases compared to other projects. In this project, the analysis phase took about 20% of the total effort. However, the results led to a reorganization process as well as to the design of an integrated data model.

On the other hand, we identified the following deficiencies :

a) The methods used in our CASE tool STP were not embedded into a project management methodology. Controlling a project's progress by milestones had therefore to be done using a traditional concept. The results we worked out with the CASE tool had therefore been embedded into a conventional documentation method.

b) Details showing the frequency of the involved process or the amount of activities per time unit, can only be documented in additional text. While SA describes the system from the static viewpoint of data, information of this type can certainly have greatly influence of the working out of a feasibility document, showing the advantages and disadvantages of all proposed solutions.

c) To describe sequences of processes, STP offers the overlaying of data flow diagrams by state-event-diagrams.

From the logical view, this is correct. In practice, however, we had significant problems with user acceptance. To evaluate documents of this type, it is necessary for all involved participants to have more knowledge and more experience.

3.5. Some pragmatic enhancements for SA

The deficiencies we identified in the preceding chapter could be corrected by some rather pragmatic enhancements. Fig. 3 shows that a procedural description of a sequential series of processes can also be shown by snapshots. This means that the activities to be done at one time unit are collected into one data flow diagram where snap shots only show the relevant data flows and data stores needed to activate the involved processes.

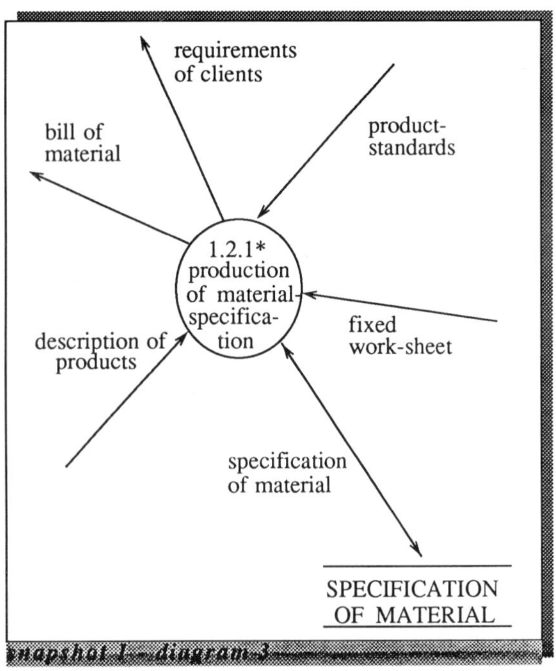

Our experience shows that snapshots can be

evaluated by all participants, including the endusers.

Information regarding the number of instances per activity or the frequency of process activation, can only be documented in extra text. With the definition of additional data types, it is possible to characterize a process also by its occurence.

As the information is stored in the data dictionary, this information can be retrieved and evaluated in the desired form.

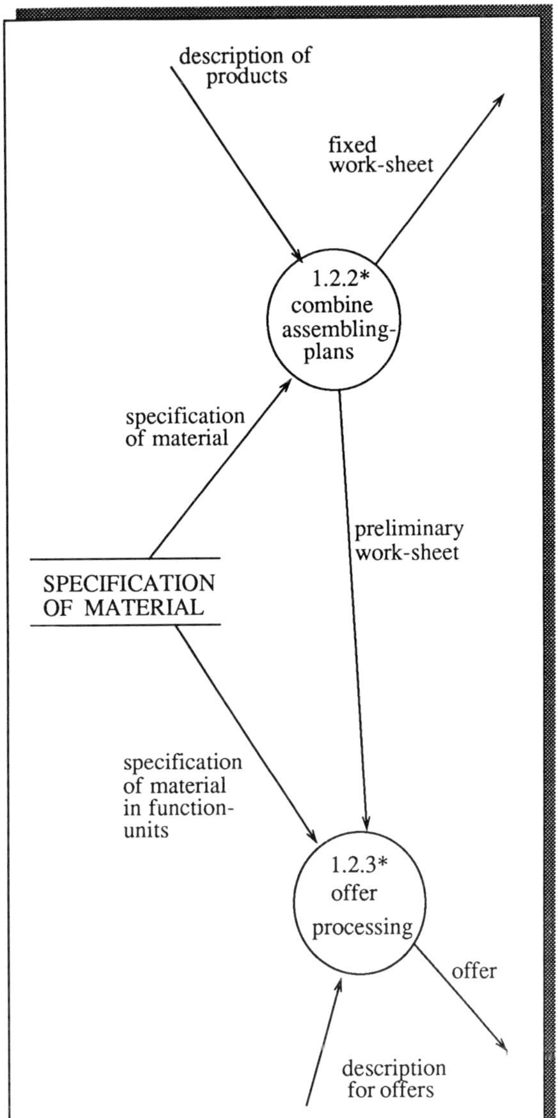

snapshot 2 - diagram 3

4. SUMMARY

On termination of the project, which took us about one year, we were able to make a summary of the experiences we made. Almost all available CASE tools are more than simple drawing tools. Nevertheless, some restrictions detract from the early euphoria. The following remarks summarize the most important findings :

a) The quality of our documents has improved since the results are better to evaluate and control. The extra amount of time we spent is therefore acceptable.

b) The use of a CASE tool is recommended since the consistency checks help to produce good results. Nevertheless, the quality of a specification document stands or falls in relation to the qualification of the analysts.

c) In general we feel the lack of some components to control quality, especially in the test phase. The facilities for generating data definition statements or program routines are almost always overrated . The actual problems lay not in the implementation phase, but in the understanding of complex facts as well as the transformation into data processing concepts.

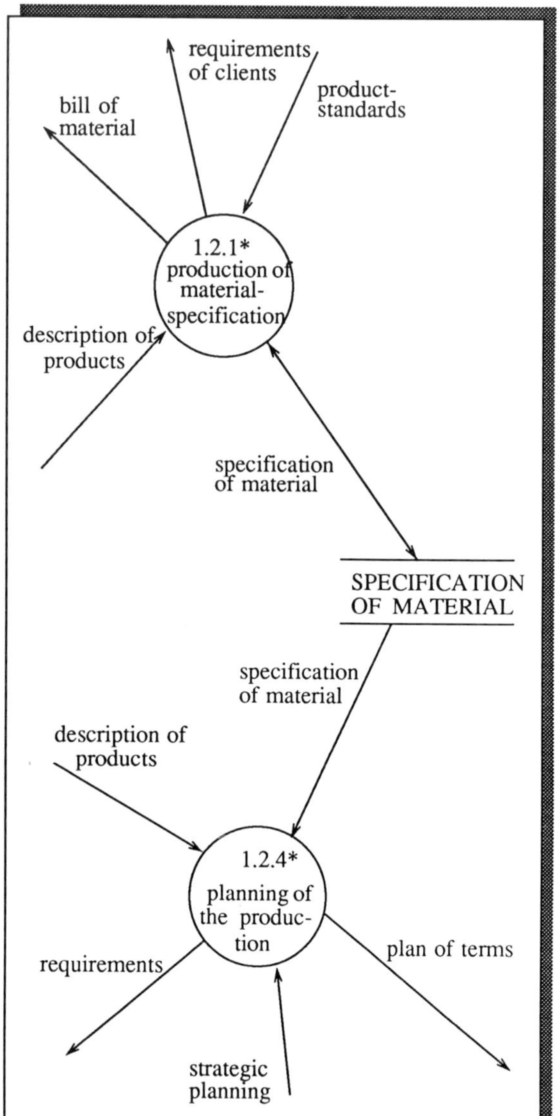

snapshot 3 - diagram 3

d) The lack of integration of the methods available with CASE tools is not really critical in practice. Nevertheless, an integrated environment should have a prototyping interface providing the possibility of implementing small systems at acceptable levels of effort. Therefore, CASE tools should incorporate the methods being developed in the prototyping environments of today.

e) As CASE tools would increasingly put the emphasis on providing facilities for enduser computing, the analyst as well as the enduser would use the same methods on the same media. Some modern tools, e.g. ORACLE-CASE, offer the integration of CASE and a 4.-GL-language. Using tools of this kind, new forms of cooperation between the enduser and the analyst are possible. This may lead to solutions to some of the actual problems we experience in the software development process.

Finally, in consideration of our overall findings, we recommend the use of CASE tools under certain circumstances. Miracles, however, cannot be expected in practice. CASE tools are a further means of mapping complex facts in a structured manner. Those looking for complete automation will be disappointed in the short or long term.

Bibliography :

[1] Oesterle, H.: Auf dem Weg zum Computer Integrated Software-Engineering. In Oesterle, H. (ed.): Anleitung zu einer praxisorientierten Software-Entwicklungsumgebung, Bd. 1, pp. 9, Halbermoos: Angewandte Informationstechnik, 1988.

[2] Xephon Buyer's Guide, Case Systems, Xephon Technology Transfer Ltd., GB 1988

[3] Diebold Management Report, Nr. 11, 1988

[4] Griese, J.: 4.-Generationssprachen und Software-Entwicklungs-Systeme. In Oesterle, H. (ed.): Anleitung zu einer praxisorientierten Software-Entwicklungsumgebung, Bd. 1, pp. 53, Halbermoos: Angewandte Informationstechnik, 1988.

[5] DeMarco, T.: Structured Analysis and System Specification. Englewood Cliffs, NY, 1978.

[6] Yourdon, E. und Constantine, L. L.: Structured Design. Fundamentals of a Discipline of Computer Program and System Design. 2. Auflage, New York: Yourdon Press, 1978.

Approving Software Products
W. Ehrenberger (Editor)
Elsevier Science Publishers B.V. (North-Holland)
IFIP, 1990

The Gütegemeinschaft Software - A Major Concept in the Certification of Software quality.

DR. GÜNTER KNORR
Rechtsanwalt
PLUTA & KNORR
Geschäftsführer
Gütegemeinschaft Software
Ulm, Germany

1. INTRODUCTION

In preparing for the single European Market starting January, 1993, a good tool for any type of product is a widely accepted standard for quality - a standard, that can be used in the whole of Europe and compliance with which can be certified in a way that is accepted everywhere.

For Software, standards are rare. Certification that a software meets the requirements of such a standard therefore gives a good piece of help in the approval of a software product for anybody involved. Speaking in terms of software quality, there is a major achievement coming from Germany: The standard created and developed by the Gütegemeinschaft Software, Frankfurt.

2. THE CERTIFICATION SYSTEM

2.1. What is the "Gütegemeinschaft Software"?

The Gütegemeinschaft Software is an association that was founded in the mid eighties to define quality criteria for software products and find a way and an organization to issue certifications for that standard. Major software and hardware manufactures participated in the initiation of the group; so did testing laboratories like the renowned "Technische Überwachungsvereine" or TÜV's in Federal Germany and big software users. Big accounting firms became members as well and scientific institutions. The first version of the Quality Requirements an Testing Directives was created in March 1985 and became a German prestandard, the DIN 66 285. Compliance with these rules gave the manufacturer a possibility to obtain from the association a quality seal under the system of the German "RAL". Since then, about 50 certificates have been issued under the rules.

2.2. The Certification Procedures

The system is as follows: A software manufacturer hires the services of an testing laboratory authorized by the Gütegemeinschaft (mainly Technische Überwachungsvereine, but specialized companies as well) to execute proper testing of compliance of its product with the rules. The testing laboratory then makes a report on the testing results and the manufacturer submits this report to the so-called "Güteausschuß". This "Güteausschuß" then decides whether the quality seal might be issued and the label "DIN-Geprüft" might be used by the manufacturer for his product. In the Güteausschuß qualified pexperts from different origins work together under the hat of the association.

Testing houses have to be authorized by the association. For such an acknowledgement exists a set of rules that intends to secure the expertise, independence and stability of such a testing laboratory. The German federal research institution GMD (Gesellschaft für Mathematik und Datenverarbeitung) makes an initial audit in a testing house applying for approval and then reports to the association. An abbreviated audit is repeated in a certain time frame by the GMD to insure that the criteria for the authorization are still met by the testing laboratory.

By some chemistry, this model organization reflects the models that have been created by the EEC later for certification and testing.

3. THE REVISED STANDARD

3.1. The German DIN Standard

Since its foundation, the Gütegemeinschaft Software has, effected by its experts in the scientific board and in the Güteausschuß redrafted, improved and expanded the quality criteria that got started in 1985. Those redefinitions lead to a second draft of the "Quality Requirements and Testing Directives" that have been approved by the general assembly of the association in 1990 and in the spring of 1990 was accepted as well by the DIN Organization as a definite German standard (DIN 66285) for quality of application software. As far as we know, there is no other standard in that specific field that has achieved such a record of practical testing and in-depth discussion in theory.

3.2. The International Expansion

In 1989, the Gütegemeinschaft therefore initiated a process of internationalization of this standard. An English version of the then available draft of the improved standard has been submitted to the respective committee of the ISO and was proposed as a new work item. In the ballot of this proposal nobody opposed and many approved acceptance of this project. Therefore, chances are good that by initiative of the Gütegemeinschaft Software an international standard for software quality will emerge in the forseeable future. The work in progress here is in its origins consistent to quality criteria already defined by ISO in the past.

4. THE SUBSTANCE OF TESTING

What is now the substance behind all this? The principle is easy: It is mainly a black-box-test executed on three levels. There is the so-called product description, the user manual and the program.

The basis of all is the product description. The content of this description is standardized by the Gütegemeinschaft. There is a minimal set of statements that are mandatory. There is of course, the possiblity for statements going beyond this. Statements that are mandatory contain positions like:

Indentification of the Product
Work Task of the Product
Functional Scope
Boundary Values
Required Configuration
Required Knowledge for Product Use

Statements must be factual and no statement may be presented as possible subject to an objective test if the correctness of such a statement could not be tested.

The test then establishes, whether the product is consistent to the product description and as well to the users manual. There are certain criteria that must be fullfilled regardless whether they are mentioned in the product sheet or not. Examples for those criteria are

Correctness of Execution
Consistency
Absence of any loss of data

The principle given may sound easy to fullfill but the experience of the Gütegemeinschaft Software is different. Though no report is submitted to the Gütegemeinschaft it a product fails to pass already in the testing stage, testing laboratories unanimously tell us that the majority of products have difficulties with compliance. This of course, is related to the fact that you need to know the standard and its criteria already in the stage of developing the product. It is not possible to generate quality in a product by testing.

5. THE FUTURE

What will be the future of the standard? If the Gütegemeinschaft achieves its goals, the standard or a internationally accepted derivation of it will define future software quality in the field of application software. As the organization structure of the Gütegemeinschaft Software does fit into the scheme of the EEC Commission for certification and testing, the Gütegemeinschaft is confident to expand in the European Surrounding.

A contract is negotiated between the Gütegemeinschaft Software and the DEKITS, the organization that coordinates the certification activities of the EEC in the Federal Republic of Germany for information technology. This will lead to acknowledgement of the Gütegemeinschaft Software as the certification body for applications software quality in Germany.

A certification board needs a standard, and as mentioned above, the standard is on its way and might become a European Standard. Interested testing houses, another requirement for EEC certification, are available in Europe. The Gütegemeinschaft is not limited to its quality seal or issuing certifications of compliance which the standard. It encourages manufacturers as well to give a declaration of compliance by themselves though it is recommanded that such a declaration (which might have legal implications) should be given only after a proper test.

Quality still is a term not widespread in the applications software market. The Gütegemeinschaft was created to change that.

SESSION 6

LIABILITY

Approving Software Products
W. Ehrenberger (Editor)
Elsevier Science Publishers B.V. (North-Holland)

Product Liability for Validation and Testing Procedures

Frank A. Koch

Summary

The paper discusses first whether software as such can be subject to product liability. The affirmative answer to this question leads to the next question to what extent principles of developing and testing software and particularly standards of validating software can be the basis - and the subject as well - of separate product liability. Comparable problems may arise by editing certifying "quality seals".

After product liability has been caused by some defect in the testing or validation procedure or inherent to the software itself the examining agency or the software producer has to examine carefully whether and to what extent a "state-of-the-art"-defense is possible in the domain of software-engineering.

1. Software as a product

Software is to be regarded as product whose defects may establish strict product liability depending only on such defects, not on fault. But even if under certain circumstances software may not be judged as product there is in any case a legal duty to maintain safety of this software. Liability in the latter case depends on the proof of fault.

The argument for strict product liability usually runs like this: Software in most cases is distributed on data media regardless whether such software is individually developed or standardized. In both cases the actual computer program is nothing else but a certain physical property of the data medium. This medium can be magnetized. Thus the program is to be seen as a specific magnetized state created on the medium. It is just this special magnetized state - and not only the general ability of the medium to be magnetized - which forms the particular economical value of the medium.

Now if a computer is defective errors of the program are intrinsic to the special magnetized state of the medium. Therefore defects in programs are to be judged as defects of the data medium in a defined way. Data medium being undisputedly tangible things and therefore "products" one has to treat software defects as defects of the product data medium.

2. Testing and validating

2.1 Concepts

"Testing" means - reduced to a shorthand definition - finding aut and eliminating programming or documenting errors occured in the maintenance of the software.

"Validating" (or approving) software products, on the other hand, is to be understood as examining whether and to what extent certain software conforms in development and outcome with some predefined standards of software-engineering. Validating therefore is a fine example of what may be called more generally an examination of conformity with standards agreed upon in the community of developers. This examination necessarily has to be restricted to formally defined and empirically checked criteria of conformity. Therefore this examination does not extend to questions of practical applicability or the commercial success of the software tested. A typical instance of such formal procedures is the validation of computer language compilers (like those for ADA).

2.2 Security risks

It seems to be evident that defective **testing procedures** may create security risks in the application of the software to be tested. If testing procedures are ill-defined or testing tools developed incorrectly, using those procedures and tools may leave errors undetected in the code to be tested and can lead to personal and/or material damages. The primary causes of these damages are the defects in the testing procedures or devices. Example: A erroneous address command in the systems software may cause a head crash in the hard disk storage and, consequently, data losses or defective output of production machines controlled by computers.

The possible dangers of errors in **validating procedures** are not always clear at first glance. The risks depend on the criteria the validation is referring to.

Validation may cover only the syntax and vocabulary prescribed for a certain computer language. Even in this restricted domain incompatibilities of the actual language to be tested for conformity can arise that possibly cause inconsistencies and thus make the application of programs based upon this language unsafe. More immediate dangers arise e. g. from bad commands for formatting or securing files against overflow.

On the other hand errors may occur in the individual validation procedure caused by incorrect standards or the faulty (negligent) execution of the correctly defined procedure.

Therefore one has to distinguish between the defective development of standards and their faulty application. This distinction does lead to two different levels of risks and liability, a first one for designing, developing and testing validation criteria and procedures, and a second one for validating software on the basis of those criteria and procedures. Introducing different levels of risks and liability means to establish a hierarchy of duties to be complied with.

The development of standards for validation in some cases may have highest priority in liability because on this level special care is needed in defining concepts and procedure which are to be regarded as compulsatory.

3. The legal basis of product liability in EEC law

There are two liability regimes:

- **Legal product liability:**

Legal product liability in the European Community is based upon the EEC Product Liability Directive of July 25, 1985. The EEC Directive provides **strict liability** which not any more depends on proving faults of the product of goods. The Directive is to be transformed into national law of the member states of the EEC (in West Germany effective on January 1, 1990).

The EEC product liability comes to close to the US doctrine of strict liability in tort which also is based upon two requirements, the defect of a product and damages caused by just this defect.

- **Liability based on fault:**

The EEC does not set aside already existing national forms of liability based on (the proof of) fault. This liability is part of the general duty to maintain safety which comprises duties to produce safe products, to survey marketed products, to warn against errors detected or forseeable product misuse and to recall products if dangerous to persons. On this traditional basis the producer of a defective product still can exonerate himself from liability by proving "no fault".

Only products are subject to strict product liability. Services are covered by liability based on fault. Thus strict product liability applies if and to the extent testing or validation procedures are to be regarded as products. Otherwise there is, at least, the legal duty to maintain safety which has to be complied with.

Mere **testing** does not create products but serves to detect errors in already existing products. Printed descriptions or standards of testing procedures or testing devices like debuggers are products, however.

The same holds for **validation principles** or **procedures.** Defective methods or procedures of validating may establish liability based on fault. Printed and distributed collections of validating criteria, descriptions of validating procedures and validation software tools are products, on the other hand.

Thus one has to distinguish carefully between activities of testing and validating and products standardizing, prescribing or helping in testing, or validating.

4. Defects

If **testing** is part of developing software such testing belongs to the quality maintenance of software-engineering. Product liability therefore is not created by applying defective testing procedures or devices as such but by defects inherent to the distributed software remaining undiscovered because of those defective procedures or devices.

If testing is part of regular software maintenance faulty services may constitute breach of contract and, additionally, violation of the duty to maintain safety protecting also person who are not privy to the contract. If the maintenance contractor uses testing devices the producer of these devices may be subject to strict product liability.

Validations require a closer look at what is done in validating software. In case a public agency or a private federation or company makes compulsatory some validation standards - e. g. in connection with defining standards, placing orders or granting funds - these activities have to comply with the duty to maintain safety but do not fall under strict liability. Even under the less stringent fault-dependent liability regime making standards compulsatory may have relevant effects. This can exonerate all persons or corporations obliged to follow those standards if no deviating is allowed. No such exoneration takes place if everyone is free to meliorate. Thus compulsatory standardization can shift liabilities to the agency or company imposing these standards.

But of course one cannot blame standardization for each possible software defect making applications unsafe. Validation is, as noted before, a formal test for conformity. Only part of all standards to be tested against is related to safety.

Therefore validation is no genuine safety test.

Further more even if (and to the extent) safety is examined this test has to be a formal one. Testing does not allow to infer from testing results that the software tested, e. g. a compiler, is safe under all possible conditions of application. Validating software therefore does not exonerate from the obligation to design and do own tests and neither from full - even strict - liability for defects in the software products based on those standards. The standards themselves may have become obsolete and validating procedures normally cover only prototypes or samples, not each and every specimen of a series. Validation in most cases also does not comprise updates or new versions. The producers here take the risks of all deviations from validated versions and of defects hidden in validation procedures or undetected by testing.

5. Quality seals

Quality seals edited on a national or an European basis certify fitness for use according to typical criteria for adequate software applications. Some of these criteria may be related to the safety of the application (e. g. protection against bad commands or false input causing system crashes or protection against program viruses). But even in this case the examination has to be formalized thereby necessarily restricting the exonerative effect. Producers therefore continue to be obliges to examine all possible risks themselves and to accept the liability regimes.

For the reason stated above quality seals do not "summarize" the state of the art of developing software. Of course the examination includes a lot of items users are justified to expect. But the recent state of the developing art may already be one step further. Furthermore quality seals mainly are related to features of user interface, the "surface structure" of the software, not to the way of realizing these features in the hidden "deep structure" of the program itself. Only the quality of use is investigated, not the quality of the software engineering.

6. "State-of-the-art"-defense in the domain of software-engineering

Even under strict liability the producer may defend himself by proving that the defect could not be discovered at the time the product was put into circulation ("development risks").

This kind of defense presupposes that there is a certain "state-of-the-art" commonly agreed upon. Testing and validation procedures generally are not sufficiently agreed upon to be as "state-of-the-art" standard. Changing methods and fashions of software design do not indicate a successful process of standardization because until now a sonsistent, enduring and reliable standard cannot be shown. And without such a standard there is no binding "state-of-the-art" to be referred to in defending against liability claims. This also holds for agencies, federations or companies making compulsatory certain criteria and standards.

The "state-of-the-art"-defense therefore in most cases will not become relevant. If, on the other side, certain procedures are part of validating criteria the least the producer has to prove is that he complied with these criteria defining a kind of minimal standard.

7. Duty to reissue definitions of standards

Anyone who issues definitions of testing procedures and validation criteria has to comply with duties to maintain the safe applications of the definitions, criteria or software itself. If after issuing potential dangers or damages are reported the agency, federation or firm has to investigate whether and to what extent these dangers may become real and what to do about it. In case there is no other way, new definitions have to be issued and published. If necessary all developers and users have to be warned. Changing and reediting standards therefore can be part of the "classical" product liability based on fault. Developing new standards out of defective ones in this case cannot be done voluntarily but as an immediate response to reports and adequate to the potential dangers.

8. Documentation

Developing standards of validation and methods of testing must be documented. Such documentation is evidence. If sufficient documenting materials cannot be produced in court the whole case might be lost.

Documentations have to show what has been done to make standards and procedures safe. This entails testing of those standards and procedures and surveying their application in creating software.

9. US validations and the EEC

A lot of validation is done in the United States. US product liability is known to be very strict. Never the less at least printed versions of U.S. orginated criteria for validation are to be treated as "exotic goods", products from outside the EEC. EEC importers of these products are **liable** not **as** retailers or importers within the EEC but as **producers.** The importer therefore can defend himself only in some very restrictive cases (especially undiscoverable defect according to the "state-of-the-art"). If the importer does not make sure by contract to have access to all US documents needed for his defense there will be no defense.

US standards, on the other hand, may define what is to be regarded as "state-of-the-art". The description of this state cannot be confined to the bounderies of the EEC. Thus EEC producers (and developers of software and validation criteria) have to watch US standards. US standards therefore may establish EEC product liability in two ways: By defining consumer's expectations higher than in the realm of the EEC (in case the definitions are not complied with) and/or by defects on the definition of the expectations. So producers seem to live riskily with standards.

Approving Software Products
W. Ehrenberger (Editor)
Elsevier Science Publishers B.V. (North-Holland)

SOFTWARE QUALITY - SOME LEGAL ISSUES

Rosemary I WILSON and Ian J LLOYD

Law School
University of Strathclyde,
Glasgow, Scotland

This paper examines the major legal requirements which will be imposed upon software producers and considers the extent to which the introduction of a system of software certification will benefit producers and users. Specific reference is made to work conducted under the ESPRIT project SCOPE.

1. INTRODUCTION

By any criteria, the software industry constitutes a significant sector of modern economies. Quantitatively, annual software sales amount to billions of pounds whilst, qualitatively, software is increasingly involved in the control of life threatening activities. Despite these facts, the legal environment surrounding software sales and issues of liability for loss resulting from the improper operation of software resembles a primeval jungle in which the foot of man has barely trodden. Uncertainty is the natural consequence of this undeveloped legal state with even the most basic legal issues, including the categorisation of software as a species of goods or services admitting of no precise or certain answer.

In the short term, doubt as to parties' legal rights may offer advantages for software suppliers. As will be discussed, the attempt is frequently made to disclaim any measure of liability or responsibility in the event that software does not perform according to the customer's expectations. A customer who is uncertain as to their legal rights may decline to enter into what may prove expensive, prolonged and ultimately futile litigation.

Such a state of affairs may be considered inevitable within a new industry. With the onset of maturity different factors have to be considered and a determined effort made to place business relationships on a more secure and predictable footing. Three factors may be considered of particular significance. First, it is common commercial practice to seek insurance cover in respect of foreseeable risks. Although the extent of risk will obviously determine the cost of insurance, the insurer's prime demand will be that this should be susceptible of reasonable estimation. To this extent the precise allocation of responsibility between the various parties engaged in the production, supply and use of software is of limited significance. The vital requirement is that each party (or their insurer) should be clearly aware where their responsibilities begin and end.

A second factor to be taken into account is that the take up of new software products may be inhibited in the event that customers consider the legal protection and remedies offered to be inadequate. A final consideration relates to the prospect that, unless the industry puts its affairs in order, pressure for legislative intervention may develop. This may, of course provide a balanced and appropriate solution to the problems described above. The initial reaction of the UK legislature to a previous technical revolution, the development of the motor car provides a useful analogy and warning. Here the, so called Red Flag Act required that all motor vehicles be preceded by a man on horseback carrying a red flag to warn the public of the approach of the mechanical monster. The effect of the legislation was to limit the speed of the new form of transport to that attainable in a previous era. Hopefully, Parliament's appreciation of technology has increased, but the prospects of appropriate and valuable legislation will be enhanced if the legislature can build on developed and accepted practice as opposed to creating a new structure.

A second benefit which may flow from the establishment of firm legal foundations will lie in the assistance thereby offered to the operators of certification schemes. The act of certifying the attributes of any product carries with it a variety of legal obligations. This paper will consider the major legal consequences which will arise from the introduction of a system of software certification, a proposal being investigated in the ESPRIT project, SCOPE. In all cases, detailed references to legal authority will relate to provisions of English law. The principles under discussion and the problems identified, however, are common to all legal systems.

Under project SCOPE, the following legal tasks and objectives have been identified:

> The establishment and definition of those legal issues and requirements which might affect the development and application of uniform technical standards and certification procedures.

Particular reference is to be made to:

> the extent of the legal obligations - both contractual and non-contractual - imposed upon the producer and the supplier of software under the general laws of the participating states.
>
> the use of, and legal controls pertaining to, exclusion clauses to restrict, exclude or define liability in the event that software proves unsatisfactory from the

customer's standpoint.

national legal provisions relating to the certification of product standards and the liability of a certification agency.

This paper will discuss these issues with reference to preliminary conclusions which have been reached and to issues requiring further investigation.

2. CONTRACTUAL LIABILITY

The law of contract regulates obligations which have been voluntarily assumed. This contrasts with the delictual position where obligations are imposed by law. Traditionally, a contract has been defined as an agreement freely entered into by two parties possessing equal bargaining strength. In this event when their intention is clearly and unequivocally expressed rights and obligations arising under the agreement will normally be enforced by the courts. Two major problems may arise. In many cases it may not be certain what the parties have agreed. In particular, it may be difficult to ascertain the purpose for which the product has been sold or acquired. A second objection to the classical contractual model is that there may be an imbalance of bargaining power. In many cases, the customer's only option is to accept the supplier's terms and conditions or do without the goods or services involved. Much legal intervention has been designed to compensate for the inadequacies of the traditional contractual model. This paper will describe how provisions of the general law relating to product quality may be incorporated into a contract either to fill any omissions or ambiguities arising from the parties expressed intentions or to override these in the event that the second factor, inequality of bargaining power is deemed to be present. This paper will concentrate on the requirement that goods should be reasonably fit for the purpose for which they were supplied. A similar requirement is to be found in most legal systems.

At first glance, the requirement that a product should be fit for its purpose appears obvious. The question arises, however, what is the product's intended purpose? There may be a conflict of interests between buyer and seller in which the purpose for which the producer intends that the product be put is at variance with that intended by the user. In particular, the latter may have a special purpose in mind which may be unknown to the producer. Again, it is debatable how far the seller should be liable for the particular environment, in terms of a hardware/software combination, in which their product is required to operate.

These issues are not peculiar to software. A variety of factors may, however, make the application of the criteria of fitness for purpose more difficult in this context. With traditional products their purpose and limitations may be obvious. A vacuum cleaner, for example, is to be used for cleaning purposes, whilst no purchaser seeking an industrial cleaner should be under the misapprehension that a domestic vacuum cleaner would prove satisfactory. Save in the case where software is produced to the order of a particular customer, the supplier may have little knowledge of the use to which it will be put. Although the basic purpose of, eg, a word processing program can be identified, its suitability will be highly dependent upon the buyer's particular needs. Again, software does not exist in isolation. It must operate in conjunction with hardware and perhaps other items of software. Next, because the nature of the production process means that all copies of a particular piece of software should be identical, all defects are created at the design stage. This contrasts with more traditional products where most defects fall into the category of production defects which may affect one or a comparatively small number of the product. Although this does not affect the existence of liability, it is generally accepted that it is more difficult to establish the presence of a design than of a production defect.

A further problem which arises with software relates to the moment in time at which questions of fitness are to be determined. A recent English case, Saphena Computing v Allied Collection Agencies Ltd.[1] discussed this point. The parties had entered into two contracts under which the suppliers, Saphena, were to supply hardware and software to the purchasers, a debt collection agency. The first contract for the installation of a batch processing system was satisfactorily completed, the second envisaged its upgrading to enable on line operations. Installation of the system required a degree of modification to achieve compatibility with the existing system and the purchaser's modified specifications. In spite of attempts made to remedy the defects the system did not function satisfactorily and in the course of a telephone conversation the parties agreed to terminate their contractual relationship.

Following this conversation another programmer was contracted by the customer to work on the system. In the course of this work he copied the supplier's source code. They responded by instituting proceedings seeking remedies in relation to an alleged breach of copyright. Furthermore it was claimed that the customers had acted wrongfully in terminating the contract and that the suppliers were entitled to the price of the goods or services supplied under the contract. In a counterclaim for damages the customers alleged that the software supplied was not considered to be fit for its purpose.

It was held that there was an implied term as to the fitness for the purpose for which the software was required. It had to be reasonably fit for such purposes as had been notified to the suppliers before the orders were placed or were notified subsequently and accepted by them.

The court determined that, although at the moment of termination the software was usable, it was not entirely fit for the customer's purposes. There remained faults which required correction. However, at this time the customers were not entitled to terminate the contract on these grounds. With software contracts, it was recognised:

> (j)ust as no software developer can reasonably expect a buyer to tell him what is required without a process of feedback and reassessment, so no buyer should expect a supplier to get his program right first time.

rather a programme of testing and modification would be required. The customers, it was held, had not allowed the suppliers sufficient time to conclude these processes.

These arguments apply most strongly with regard to bespoke or to customised software. Even with standard software, however, although the customer will be supplied with a particular version in it's definitive form, there will invariably be provision for upgraded versions to be made available at a reduced price. To this extent, a continuing relationship between buyer and seller exists. In all cases, the critical question will be when a customer is entitled to take the view that software is not suitable for their needs. The eradication of defects may be a lengthy and painstaking process. In the absence of specific provisions relating to acceptance tests and procedures it is debatable as to how long the buyer must allow this process to continue.

3. EXCLUSION OR LIMITATION OF LIABILITY

Realising the liberal nature of the fitness requirement and the correlated potential liability incurred it is common practice for software producers to stipulate terms of exclusion in contractual provisions. A typical clause might provide:

> (the supplier's) .. liabilities hereunder shall be limited to death or direct physical injury caused by the negligence of (the supplier) who shall not be liable for any other direct or indirect loss or loss of profits howsoever caused and of whatsoever nature.
>
> This agreement is in lieu of and to the exclusion of all liabilities, obligations and warranties and conditions statutory or otherwise implied or expressed

The use of exclusion clauses raises the second issue identified above, the potential imbalance of bargaining power. In most legal systems, some controls now operate to restrict the use of exclusion clauses, typically to the situation where a court can be convinced that this is fair and reasonable in the circumstances of a particular case.

In the UK, such exclusion clauses will be held valid only insofar as they satisfy statutory criteria of reasonableness found in the Unfair Contract Terms Act 1977. Although few cases have been decided under this statute, it is suggested that many exclusion clauses used by software producers would be struck down by the courts as failing to meet the above criteria. More favourable treatment might be given to clauses which seek to limit rather than to exclude liability.

4. NON CONTRACTUAL LIABILITY

There may be instances where the person injured by a product has no contractual claim against the producer. Such a party must base a claim on provisions of non-contractual liability; traditionally under the law of tort or negligence, but with the prospect today of an action under the product liability provisions of the Consumer Protection Act. This statute, which seeks to give effect to the European Community Directive on Liability for Defective Products[2], introduces a system of strict liability for certain losses caused by a defective product.

a. Tortious Liability

For a successful claim in delict it must be established that a duty of care must be owed to the plaintiff by the defending party. There must be breach of that duty and that loss must result from that breach. The loss must not be too remote a consequence of the breach and the loss of must be of a nature acceptable as giving rise to a claim for compensation.

It is universally accepted that the manufacturer of a product owes a duty of care to anyone who is injured as a result of a defect in the product. Liability may additionally be incurred by other parties whose negligence resulted either in the appearance or perpetuation of the defect.

Not every act which causes loss to another will give rise to an action in delict. An element of fault must also be present. The concept of negligence can be defined as the failure to observe that standard of care which would be observed by a reasonable man in the position of the defender. The concept of the reasonable man requires adjustment to take account of the nature and circumstances in which an action occurred. In the vast majority of cases, compliance with accepted industry standards - the state of the art - will suffice to defeat a claim for negligence. Likewise, where the activities of a member of a profession are called into question the requisite standard will be that of the reasonable member of that profession. This may present difficulties in the software field where professional bodies have not acquired the recognition and status afforded to more traditional professions. In the US the doctrine of professional malpractice requires the observance of a higher duty of care by members of recognised professions. There are instances where the courts have refused to accept the concept of computer malpractice although in the most recent decision, _Diversified Graphics_ v. _Groves_[3], a Federal Court of Appeals upheld a finding of professional malpractice against a firm of accountants which, having accepted a commission to recommend a suitable computer system to clients, suggested a model which proved unsatisfactory for their purposes. The evidence of negligence in this case would appear to have been based on the accountant's failure to adhere to their own published standards of conduct.

b. Product Liability

The most recent innovation in the field of liability is the introduction of a system of product liability whereby a producer will be held strictly liable for damage caused by his product. Before discussing the extent of the liability the limitations of the Directive must be understood. Principally, damages are only recoverable in respect of death or personal injury and damage to property intended for private use. Additionally the cost of the damage must exceed £275.

For the purposes of the Directive a product is defined as:

> All moveables, with the exception of primary agricultural products and game, even though incorporated into another movable or immovable...

The EC Commission regard software as a product. However, this view is not shared by all Member States. In the case of the UK, the government have expressed the view that:

> Special problems arise with those industries dealing with products concerned with information such as books .. and computer software. it has been suggested that it would be absurd for printers .. to be held strictly liable for faithfully reproducing errors in the material provided to them which, by giving bad instructions .. indirectly causes injury. It does not appear that the Directive is intended to extend liability in such situations [4]

The question as to whether software is a product will be irrelevant where it is in an embedded form. For instance where a software programme controls an airplane navigation system. In the event of software malfunction and the plane crash the plane itself will be considered a defective product. The issue of the status of software will be significant where its purpose is to disseminate information or advice. Traditionally, considerable latitude has been extended to publishers and booksellers in respect of errors in books. In a number of recent American cases however, airline charts which contained errors were classed as products where the inclusion of inaccurate data caused accidents. In reaching this conclusion, the courts took account of the mass produced nature of the charts and the commercial aspects of distribution together with the fact that pilots were obliged to completely rely on their contents, the court concluding:

> ..although a sheet of paper might not be dangerous per se, it would be difficult indeed to conceive of a saleable commodity with more lethal potential than an aid to aircraft navigation that, contrary to its own design standards, fails to list the highest land mass immediately surrounding a landing site.[5]

Although speculative, it would seem that if the courts are willing to apply strict liability for defective charts they will do so in the case of defective computer software particularly those software packages upon which complete reliance is placed.

A product will be considered defective in the event that it fails to provide the level of safety which "persons generally" are entitled to expect. A variety of factors will be taken into account in determining the question of defectiveness including the intended or normal use of the product. In many cases the fact that a product is put to an unexpected use may rebut the presumption of defectiveness, however it may be insufficient to show that the use was unintended. For example should the pilot of a computer controlled airplane misuse the computer thereby causing an accident it might be argued that the software should have guarded against such conduct.

c. The Development Risk Defence

Undoubtedly the most controversial feature of the legislation is in the provision of the development risks defence. At the outset it should be noted that the Directive permits rather than requires, Member States to incorporate such a provision into their national legislation.

The onus is on the producer to establish the defence

> .. that the state of scientific and technical knowledge at the time when he put the product into circulation was not such as to enable the existence of the defect to be discovered.

This requires more than compliance with the state of the art. It encompasses theoretical as well as practical knowledge. Since the provisions came into force there has been no litigation and consequently interpretation of the defence remains uncertain. The significant issue for software will be the question whether the defence applies to defects which are undiscoverable or is limited to unforeseeable dangers. The distinction between unforeseeable and undiscoverable defects may be significant particularly in the software field where any producer will be aware that software has defects but where it is not practical to test the product in such an exhaustive fashion as to guarantee their discovery and eradication.

5. CERTIFICATION

Any discussion of product certification must commence with consideration of the legal aims and effects of this process. By granting a certificate, the certifier is to be taken as making some form of statement. As with all forms of statement a variety of legal consequences may follow from the initial act.

Certification can be regarded as the procedures which lead to the grant of a certificate. The word certificate is defined as consisting of:

> a written declaration, official or formal, of some fact: a statement of qualification or recognised professional status.

Three forms of certification can be identified each of which may result in various forms of legal liability. Self-certification occurs when a producer himself declares that his products conform with specified standards. In a second situation a particular buyer, frequently a governmental department, might require that products be submitted for certification by a specified body. Third party certification occurs when the certification process is carried out by a body independent of either the producer or the user. This paper will concentrate on the last of these activities.

In the vast majority of cases, certification constitutes a voluntary act on the part of producers and certifiers with no legal provisions requiring that a product be submitted to such scrutiny. In this event, considerable discretion is afforded to all concerned in defining the nature of the attributes which will be certified. The initial question to be addressed concerns the extent to which a system of certification should be based upon formal product standards or whether alternative criteria should be invoked.

To a considerable extent, the topics of standards and certification are inextricably linked and, indeed, the same bodies may be involved in both topics. The British Standards Institute (BSI) have commented that in devising a standard, the question of its suitability for certification should be considered. Thus:

> The wording of a specification for a product should enable compliance with its requirements to be verified equally by first party (supplier), second party (purchaser) or independent third party certifier.[6]

An attempt to create a certification scheme that is not based on clearly specified standards can have little value. At the very least, no claim could be made as to the repeatability of results. Nonetheless, the overlap between the two concepts is not total. The basic function of a standard is to describe the features which must be possessed by a product but these are described in the abstract. The purpose of certification is to state that a particular product (or a particular species of products) possesses specified features. Certification must, therefore, operate in respect of real products. Given that legal liabilities will result from the actions of a certification agency in ascribing conformity to a particular product, it might be a foolhardy agency who would look for no more than evidence of conformity with the standards upon which the certification scheme is based. To this extent, certification criteria may be more exacting than those applied in the formulation of product standards. An illustration of the relationship between standards and certification can be taken from the operations of the BSI in relation to the use of the "Kitemark" upon products. Any producer is entitled to claim that his wares conform with a specified British Standard. In order to qualify for the use of the Kitemark, the producer will be required to submit his activities to the scrutiny of the BSI. This involves examination not only of the product's conformity with standards but contains a requirement that the producer's processes should conform to the quality management requirements of BS 5750 (ISO 9,000). Thus the certification requirement does not simply demand that particular products conform to standards but that the production process should be of such a quality as to carry with it the likelihood that all products emanating from the producer concerned will comply with standards.

At present, few formal product standards exist in the software field. In the absence of these certification must relate to other formulations of product attributes. As has been discussed above, the major requirement imposed upon a producer is that goods should be reasonably fit for their purpose. The resolution of this issue requires consideration be given to the context of use. It must be accepted that a certification agency cannot possess knowledge of the specific purpose to which a particular user may put a product. Equally, however, the producer must produce with some market and some uses in mind. The attraction of certification for both producers and users would be much diminished unless it were to offer some assurance that certified products would be at least free from defects affecting safety or which would significantly impair its ability to perform its intended functions. For the certification agency two issues may arise. Should a certificate be granted and, if so, to what effect? These issues will be considered in the context of liabilities which may be incurred by certification agencies.

Many of the principles of contractual and delictual liability referred to above will be equally applicable in the situation where a product undergoes some form of certification process. It will almost always be the case that a contractual relationship will exist between the certification agency and the submitting producer. In respect of its duty to the producer, the agency will be required to perform its work with reasonable skill and care. Where terms are incorporated expressly or impliedly into a formal contract, two categories of obligation can be identified. Should unambiguous statements be made, relating, for example, to the tests which will be conducted or to the equipment which will be used, any failure to comply will constitute a breach of contract. The position is less clear with the qualitative aspects of the service. Clearly the price which is charged will influence the level of performance required but this will seldom be the determining factor. In this situation, the Common Law's most famous creation, the concept of the "reasonable man" will be called upon. Complaints may relate to two aspects of the certification agency's operations. Criticism may first be directed at the procedures which are adopted. The basis for comparison here might be with "good laboratory practice". The fact that one agency's procedures are different from those generally adopted cannot <u>per se</u> lead to the conclusion that they are unsatisfactory, but variance coupled with evidence of a faulty result, may set up a strong presumption of negligence.

A second aspect of the requirement that reasonable skill and care should be exercised concerns the manner in which any tests or examinations are conducted. In this regard, the legal fiction concerning the "reasonable man" assumes that this character is immune from the mistakes which any human being is capable of. A reasonable man would carry out tests exactly as prescribed in any organisational procedures and the fact that a deviation occurs will constitute evidence of fault. More difficult issues arise where the certification procedure requires the exercise of some form of discretion or interpretation. Where such subjective issues are involved, liability will arise only to the extent that it can be established that no reasonable person in that position and possessing the skill and expertise claimed by the certification agency, would have reached the same conclusion.

It may be the case that a decision whether to issue a certificate to a particular product or process will be influenced by or based on information supplied by a third party. Typically, testing work may be sub-contracted by the certification agency to a testing laboratory which possesses specialised equipment unavailable to the agency itself. Given EC trends towards mutual recognition there must be an increased prospect that certification decisions arrived at within the UK will be based on results supplied by an organisation located within another Member State. Two situations can be identified. In the first, the testing facilities are provided under contract to the certification agency. In such a situation, the certification agency will retain responsibility for the accuracy of the information supplied to it. In the event that these tests were negligently conducted, the certification agency will be liable on the same basis as if it had conducted the tests itself. A second scenario would see the results of tests previously conducted in relation to a product being submitted to the certification agency which is requested to issue a certificate on the basis of such details. It may well be that the certification agency is contractually bound to accept and to act on the basis of such data. In such an event, it would appear that the agency's responsibilities will be satisfied if it can be established that it acted reasonably in entering into the initial contract and, in particular, that it took reasonable steps to satisfy itself as to the repute and reliability of the other organisation. Even in the event that this can be established, liability may still follow if it can be established that the information supplied was implausible. In the event that the information is accepted on a more <u>ad hoc</u> basis, the requirement will again be that the agency acted reasonably in accepting the information and that there was nothing in the information itself which should reasonably have given cause for suspicion and further investigation.

The difficulty facing a claim for damages arising from the improper refusal of a certificate is that its possession will not normally be required by law in order for the product to be marketed. In determining whether damages should be awarded, evidence would need to be led as to the general practice in relation to products of a particular description. Much will depend on the nature of the certification process involved. If it seeks to certify the product's conformity with specified standards which are prescribed by law, the prospect of a claim for damages succeeding will be considerably greater than if it relates to standards devised by the certification agency itself or which operate on a voluntary basis. If it could be demonstrated that certification was normally regarded as essential by customers or should the agency be aware that certification is required as a prerequisite to the conclusion of a particular contract, damages might be awarded.

In the event that the presence of the defect can be traced to the failure of the certification agency, an action seeking recompense might be brought against them. Again, the major obstacle facing any claim for damages will lie in the fact that certification is not normally required for a product to be lawfully marketed. In effect, the certification agency are stating their opinion regarding the product's qualities. In the event that this is negligently given, they must accept some responsibilities but it is less clear whether they can be held liable for losses resulting from what is in fact the error of the producer. It may be that they should have detected the error, and as will be discussed in the following section, they may incur some delictual liability towards third parties but, as a general rule, there would appear little basis for such a contractual claim by the producer.

In the vast majority of cases, a contractual relationship will exist between the producer of a product and the certification agency to whom the product was submitted. As was discussed above, in the event that the certification agency performs its work in a negligent fashion, losses may be suffered by the producer. The present section will consider the legal consequences arising in the event that a certified product is put into operation only for its improper operation to result in losses to some third party.

Initially, the point may be reiterated that such a third party may possess contractual remedies in their own right. In the event that the product has been purchased, the provisions of the Sale of Goods Act will give a right against the seller. Other contractual rights and remedies may also be identified, the most relevant example might involve the situation where an employee is injured at work. Here, the contractual nature of the employment relationship will confer rights against the employer. In these cases, a chain of contractual rights and remedies may exist which will eventually lead to the party responsible for any defect. In other situations, however, an injured party may not have any contractual relationship with the party responsible for any loss which may have been suffered. An example might involve a pedestrian suffering injury in a motor accident caused by a failure of a car's computer controlled brakes. In such an event, the injured party's remedy will lie either in delict or under the product liability provisions of the Consumer Protection Act. Attention must now be paid to the possibility that such remedies may lie against the parties responsible for a product's certification. Given that it is an area susceptible of a near unequivocal resolution, attention will first be paid to the relevance of product liability legislation, before turning to consider the more significant provisions of the law of delict.

Under the provisions of the Consumer Protection Act, liability falls primarily on the producer of the product. As a certification agency cannot be regarded as a producer, no liability will be incurred under this statute.

Accepting that a certification agency owes a duty of care to third parties, the question arises as to its extent. Two issues will be particularly relevant here, the first concerning the establishment of the necessary link between the agency's negligence and the loss and the second relating to the forms of damage which may be compensated.

In a very few cases, product certification is required in order for goods to be placed on the market. In the event that the certification process is negligently performed so that a product which should have been rejected receives the necessary approval, there can be little doubt as to the agency's liability. In determining whether a sufficient link exists between negligent act and consequential loss, one of the major tests which is applied is the, so called, "but for" test. In the situation where certification is mandatory, but for the certification agency's negligence the product could not have been put on the market and, thereby, in a position to cause damage.

In the more common situation where products are submitted for certification on a voluntary basis, it will have to be established, first, that the product would not have been put on the market if certification had been refused, i.e. that the producer would have taken the product back for modification and improvement and, second, that the injury resulted, directly or indirectly, from reliance upon the certification agency. A simple example might be furnished in the situation where a customer could establish that he had looked for the certification agency's mark prior to buying or using the product.

The issues of liability discussed represent one aspect of the task of establishing the necessary link between breach of duty and damage. A second factor requires that the kind of damage suffered should be recognised at law. In the event that a defective product causes physical damage or injury compensation will, assuming negligence can be demonstrated, be payable. In the event, for example, that the injury resulted in the plaintiff being unable to work, a sum in respect of lost wages would be included in any award. The more difficult issues concern the extent to which damages might be claimed in delict for economic loss or in the situation where a defect is discovered prior to loss being suffered but with the result that the product cannot safely be put to its intended use.

6. CONCLUSION

In many respects, the law and the software industry make uneasy partners. The former is characterised by a respect for tradition, precedent and the search for stability whilst the latter thrives on innovation and change. As any builder is aware, new buildings require firm foundations if they are to possess a reasonable life expectancy. The location of software transactions within a solid legal structure is necessary to fulfil this task. If it is argued that the software industry should take more account of legal requirements, the same can be said of the law. Many legal provisions were framed in the years, or even centuries, before the computer was invented. Although, as this paper has argued, software can be brought within existing legal provisions, the special attributes of this product may call for more specific legal provisions. In any event, the development of an effective scheme of product certification holds the promise of improving customer confidence in the quality of any software which they may acquire.

References

1. Court of Appeal, 1989.

2. 85/374/EEC.

3. 1989 US Court of Appeals 868 F.2d. 293.

4. Implementation of EC Directive on Product Liability. DTI, 1985.

5. Fluor Corp. v. Jeppeson 170 Cal. App. 3d 468

6. BSO A Standard for Standards.

Approving Software Products
W. Ehrenberger (Editor)
Elsevier Science Publishers B.V. (North-Holland)
IFIP, 1990

Liability for unavoidable defects of computer software under German and EC law

by Dr. Benno Heussen, Rechtsanwalt

1. Legal definition of the term "unavoidability" of defects

a) Purpose of the definition

In the legal discussions in Germany and the EC member states on the question of the defectiveness of computer software reference is frequently made to the existence of "unavoidable" software defects. The impression is given that it is technically perfectly feasible to determine what a defect is and thus by means of a simple comparison with the state of the art to establish quite categorically whether a defect is avoidable or not.

This is the only explanation for the fact that lawyers regard the "unavoidability of defects" as technically indisputable and thus only concern themselves with the applicable <u>rules of liability</u>.

As we shall see in the following, a great many legal problems prove to be irrelevant if one merely carefully and precisely investigates the technical preconditions under which a defect is avoidable and those under which it is inevitable.

b) Areas of liability

German law differentiates between three areas of liability in which technical defects in computer software play a part, these being:

- Contractual liability in contracts for work and services and purchase, leasing and licensing agreements in accordance with the provisions of the German Civil Code [BGB] (Paras. 459, 633 and 537 BGB) introduced on 1.1.1900.

- Liability in tort pursuant to Para. 823, Clause 1 BGB

- Product liability under the Product Liability Act of 15.12.1989 (Bundesgesetzblatt 1989, Part I, p. 2198, enacted on 1.1.1990).

Contractual liability can only be enforced by the person who has concluded an agreement with the responsible party or is at least indirectly included in such agreement (e.g. via a "contract with protective effect for third parties").

Tort law offers (further) protection to persons who are unable to base their claims on a contract, but the protection only extends to certain legal objects (life, health or absolute rights) where the infringement was at least due to negligence (principle of fault).

Product liability does not require the existence of a contract, but relates rather to abstract risks arising from technically unsafe products which have (perhaps without intentional culpability) been introduced onto the market. This is where EC law comes in, since the German Product Liability Act became necessary when the EC Guideline on Product Liability (Guideline No. 85/374 of 25.7.1985, EC Official Journal L 210/85) compelled the member states to create a factual background for liability which is not based on fault. The regulation under tort law prevailing up to that time (Para. 823, Clause1 BGB) remains in full force in addition thereto.

To date, six other EC member states have translated the EC Guideline on Product Liability into national law:

- Greece: The Greek decree has been in force since 23.6.1988 following publication in the Greek Official Journal on 22.4.1988 (No. 230, Section 2).

- Italy: The Italian decree has been in force since 23.6.1988 and was published in Italian Official Journal No. 146 of 23.6.1988.

- United Kingdom: The UK Consumer Protection Act came into effect on 1.3.1988.

- Luxembourg: The Luxembourg law was passed on 9.3.1989 and has been in force since that date.

- Denmark: The Danish Product Liability Law came into force on 10.6.1989 (Law No. 371 of 7.6.1989).

- Portugal: The Portuguese decree No. 383 dates from 6.11.1989 (published in Portuguese Official Journal No. 255 p. 4880) and has been in force since 1.11.1989.

The other EC member states still have to convert the EC Guideline on Product Liability into national law. In such cases, an action may be brought before the European Court of Justice against the particular country by the EC Commission; the Commission does not assume the direct effectiveness of the EC Guideline on Product Liability in the individual countries.

c) The significance of technical standards in the definition of defects

The determination of the existence of a "defect" presupposes that one has a concrete technical idea of an object free of defects. Such a concept can be formed, for instance, if certain technical conditions are established by means of standards disseminated on a national and international basis. However, standards are only produced if a particular product is manufactured frequently, thus necessitating the definition of required standards. This does not apply above all in the case of "tailor-made" software packages intended to meet specific requirements. Thus, in order to determine what constitutes a "defect" in such cases it must be individually established in each particular instance how the service should have been provided under the contract or according to expectations of safety before any actual divergence therefrom can be defined. This often leads to the conclusion that certain defects must be expressly or tacitly accepted if one wishes to obtain a specific level of technical performance of the software. Thus in the final analysis the definition of a defect must also include a definition of the apportionment of risk.

If in the second stage of such investigation one addresses the question as to whether a defect was in fact avoidable, then again any existing standards are of significance in the same way as contractual agreements or safety expectations. This can be illustrated by an example from the medical field:

If computer tomography is used to analyse the effects of a cancer which can only be diagnosed with the aid of such equipment, any consequential damage caused by the actual operation is unavoidable if the operation was otherwise conducted in a technically correct manner. In this case the damage is only avoidable if the tests are not carried out at all. The definition of "unavoidability" thus also presupposes the creation of a relationship between means and ends which is individually adapted to the particular problem.

This adaptation is handled differently within the individual areas of liability, since the relationship between means and ends within the framework of contracts must be determined in a different manner than is the case under tort law or product liability law.

Whereas in contracts all legally permissible ends can be established individually and subjectively (from simple adherence to specific technical quality standards through to the assurance of concrete expectations of profit), both tort law and product liability regulations only offer protection in terms of consumer safety in the use of individual products.

However, the relative position of contract law to tort/product liability law is not one of greater or lesser import: on the one hand, a product may readily fulfil less stringent contractual agreements and (for that very reason) fail to offer the necessary consumer protection, while on the other hand individual contractual agreements may render a product defective in terms of contract law, despite the fact that it complies fully with "justified consumer expectations".

d) Individual prerequisites for the concept of faultiness

Up to now we have quite consciously referred exclusively to "defects" to indicate that we are concerned with a technical definition, the legal relevance of which in individual cases is still open to question.

If one attempts to arrive at a legal definition, it is suggested that the term "fault" be used, which again requires a quite different definition in the area of contractual liability than in the areas of tort/product liability.

aa) Definition of faultiness in contractual liability

In the area of German contractual liability the suggested definition is as follows:

An unavoidable fault in computer software exists if a technically unavoidable defect

- removes or diminishes the value or effectiveness of the performance (Para. 459, Clause 1 BGB)

- if it is not necessary to accept these shortcomings as insignificant in practice

- whereby the content of the performance is to be determined on the basis of the individual contractual agreement (subjective element)

- and the interpretation of the contract must be based on typical agreements in comparable cases (objective element).

bb) Definition of faultiness in tortious liability

German law in the area of tortious liability (Para. 823, Clause 1 BGB) prescribes in extract as follows:

"Anyone intentionally or negligently [and] unlawfully endangering the life, physical person or health ... [or violating] the property or any other right of another ..."

The difference in this case from the concept of faultiness in contractual liability resides in the fact that the term "unlawfully" relates only to those obligations which must be observed on grounds of consumer protection, whilst other quality criteria, which are of essential significance in the field of contractual liability, may be disregarded here.

In the case of a technically unavoidable defect there is

generally no <u>negligence</u> (which is a prerequisite in tortious liability), this being true for both unavoidable manufacturing defects and development defects (i.e. defects which are unavoidable according to the state of the art).

cc) Definition of faultiness in product liability law

As in the case of tortious liability, product liability law requires a definition of the concept of faultiness, since this again concerns consumer protection.

However, the <u>Product Liability Act</u> does not presuppose negligence, so that liability also applies to unavoidable manufacturing defects, whereas development defects are excluded from liability according to Para. 1, Clause 2, Sub-Clause 5 Product Liability Act. Moreover, in defining the relationship between consumer expectation and the expectation of the manufacturer as to how he anticipates his products to be used, Para. 3 of the Product Liability Act covers the same ground as Para. 823, Clause 1 BGB. According to this a product does not contain a defect if it (at least) offers the degree of safety which can be expected in consideration of all circumstances, in particular

- its presentation (particularly in advertising)
- the use which can reasonably be expected
- the time when it was introduced onto the market

whereby the fact that improvements are effected at a later date does not render defective a product which has been brought onto the market previously (Para. 3 Product Liability Act).

The obligations to be observed include in particular

- the obligation to base the product on existing technical standards
- the obligation to check throughout the manufacturing process
- checking of products from suppliers
- checking of instructions for use
- the obligation to warn of risks inherent in use
- the obligation to monitor use of the products in the market
- the obligation to recall defective products immediately.

dd) Overlapping of tort law and product liability law

Since they are intended to provide the same protection

(consumer safety) tort law and product liability law cover many identical aspects, although considered in detail they have different preconditions and legal consequences (e.g. in the area of time limitations), which may cause considerable difficulties, especially for foreign lawyers who are not so well acquainted with the German penchant for definitions.

It is generally expected that this will lead to an increase in "forum shopping" in order to avoid these difficulties foreseeable in the context of Germany.

2. Classification of unavoidable defects from legal aspects

Since the concept of faultiness in contractual, tortious and product liability overlaps to some extent, it is advisable to develop a system of defect classification which can be applied in all three areas, albeit to differing degrees. For example, if a defective set of operating instructions (breach of obligation to provide instructions) merely results in complete inability to operate a software program, this is undoubtedly a defect in quality, but not necessarily a breach of the consumer protection obligation, since a non-functioning program will in the majority of cases not cause any damage.

It has proved expedient to base the defect classification on the technical prerequisites for computer software production.

It is possible to differentiate between:

- planning defects / research & development defects
- concept defects / design defects
- programming defects / manufacturing defects
- defects in test procedures
- defects in instructions

Defects in the area of product monitoring or obligations to recall should be disregarded here, since they do not constitute technical defects in the narrower sense, although even they may be unavoidable; nor does the obligation in respect of product monitoring presuppose a perfect information system which could be required irrespective of the relationship between manufacturer's and consumer's expectations and the concomitant costs.

a) Planning defects / research & development defects

<u>Planning defects</u> can be broken down into

- analytical defects

and

- definition defects.

aa) Analytical defects

Analytical defects are those where the task has been incorrectly analysed. In this context the difference between standard and individual software, which will be discussed later, is of significance: with individual software the client is generally responsible for ensuring the correct definition of the problem to be solved with the aid of an individual software program, whereas with standard software the manufacturer himself analyses the technical problem and proposes certain solutions, which are then offered without amendment. In the case of individual software legal liability in this area will generally be precluded, since the liability does not fall within the scope of obligations of the software manufacturer. With standard software it will in most cases be difficult to prove that what the software manufacturer discerned as the problem did not comply with consumer expectations or the expectations of the other contractual party, since the standard software program already exists prior to its use and can thus be sufficiently investigated with regard to its capability to solve the problem.

bb) Definition defects

In the case of definition defects the correctly analysed requirements are incorrectly defined. This definition is in all cases the task of the software manufacturer and must therefore at all events conform to the state of the art. The characteristic feature of this group of defects is that, since they are embedded in the program, they often preclude the creation of a suitably functional product. However, in rarer cases a definition defect will remain hidden; liability will then depend on whether a correct definition (as is generally the case) was possible or not based on the state of the art.

b) Concept defects / design defects

In the case of concept / design defects it is necessary to differentiate between

- logical concept / design defects

and

- essential concept / design defects

aa) Logical concept defects

Logical concept defects occur in the logical organisation of the correctly analysed and defined program data of the concept to ensure that they can eventually be readily translated in programming terms (e.g. in the field of data flow plans). A typical example would be the definition of the interfaces between different software programs. Particularly in this area one should consider the limitations of the human capacity for conceptualisation which prevents even an approximate overview of such large, complex programs. Modern software production methods (linking of modules, rapid prototyping, quality assurance programs) offer a certain degree of control over these potential sources of problems. Nevertheless, it cannot be denied that the majority of unavoidable defects will occur in this area, since many problems can in fact only be simulated according to the "trial and error" principle on the basis of individual model procedures.

bb) Essential concept defects

The same applies in principle to essential concept defects, which concerns defects where, despite the fact that the task has been correctly analysed, defined and assessed in logical terms, the means to its solution contains essential defects. Such defects may affect the technical functioning of the program, for instance if a program (due to a restricted field length) rounds certain calculations up or down, which, repeated thousandfold, may result in considerable deviations in the overall calculation procedure. Such a defect is without doubt unavoidable in the narrower technical sense, but is not necessarily so in legal terms: rounding up or down after a minimum of three decimal places is acceptable for example in a book-keeping program (but not in a bank interest calculation program!), since the resultant errors in calculation are of no practical significance for the user. However, a quite different situation arises in the case of a medical program, which may require precision in calculation to many more decimal points before rounding off. This category of defects shows clearly that there cannot be an abstract definition of defects, but only one relating to the individual case in point.

The second area, which is almost of greater practical importance, is that of concept-related essential defects: these are defects where specific performance faults occur in the application of the program, as is the case particularly with expert systems. If a medical diagnostic system fails to take account of important diagnostical or therapeutical findings representing the state of the art, this constitutes an avoidable essential defect incorporated at the conceptual stage, for which the software manufacturer must assume liability.

c) Programming defects / manufacturing defects

In this respect one can differentiate between:

- contextual defects
- coding defects
- technical quality defects

Contextual defects are defects in the linking of individual

programming steps, coding defects incorrect manual inputs of individual program lines and technical quality defects the incorrect copying or faulty transfer of software.

Previous discussions have concentrated almost exclusively on this category of defects, stressing for instance the fact that even after using all standard test tools an average total of seven defects per thousand (manually input!) program lines remains, so that complex programs (of some 50,000 to 100,000 program lines) may contain 150-300 unavoidable coding defects.

The technical correctness of this view is irrefutable and this defect quota must presumably be regarded as the (current) state of the art. For example:

In a medical expert system a prescription is stated as 25 mg instead of 2.5 mg. This error in the placing of the decimal point may remain undiscovered despite all powerful debugging systems and result in a fatal dosage. In the absence of a test procedure which will reliably preclude such defects, such a defect will also have to be regarded as unavoidable in such cases.

Remarkably, the number of cases in which such defects have in fact resulted in actual damage appears to have been relatively low to date.

d) Defects in test procedures

The state of the art demands that test procedures be applied in software development. Interviews with manufacturers have shown that this has not been carried out with sufficient accuracy in many programs in commercial use. Software engineers with many years of experience in the USA repeatedly report that the proportion of really professionally produced software in Europe is not as high as in the USA. Should such a difference in quality indeed exist, this would still not represent an excuse for the software manufacturer.

However, the fact that test procedures (as software programs) are themselves potentially subject to unavoidable defects means that there is a limit to their effectiveness. This results in a reciprocal interdependence between the program under manufacture and the test program, which using Heisenbergian terminology can be referred to as a "relation of unclarity": unclarities in the program definition (which are technically unavoidable) may lead to unclarities in the test tools and the corollary of a (technically unperfected) test program may be a defective software product. As long as this inevitably remains the state of the art, no improvement will be possible.

e) Defects in instructions

The prime question in the case of defects in instructions is the level of experience of the user, since by no means all potential applications of a software program can be thought through in abstract from the outset and many defects (including operator errors) only prove to be relevant in practical use. This shows the broad scope of the interplay between the expectations of the manufacturer and the user, which are of significance not only in the field of product liability, but also in contractual liability. The main defects occur in:

- operator manuals
- instructions for use
- training materials
- individual operating instructions
- error messages which are either missing or open to misinterpretation
- printing errors, errors in content or translation errors in the documentation, in particular also in help programs.

3. Legal classification of software according to contract, tort and product liability law

Software programs have certain technical peculiarities which make it difficult to classify them into the normal system of liability within both contract law and tort/product liability.

a) Software within the system of standard contract types recognised in German law.

German law treats quality defects quite differently, depending on the particular type of contract in question:

- In the case of a sales contract the German system implicitly assumes that the product already exists and can thus be assessed in terms of quality prior to conclusion of the contract;
- in law relating to contracts for goods and services, where a product has yet to be produced, this is not possible and the quality of the product can only be assessed by means of an "acceptance test";
- in leasing agreement law the product does not finally pass to the lessee, but is merely made available to him for a specifically limited period.

These differences result in considerable discrepancies in the treatment of the legal consequences of quality defects:

- With sales contracts the purchaser of software programs can simply rescind the contract (rescission) or reduce the purchase price (diminution);

- Under the law on contracts for work and services the client must first give the software manufacturer the opportunity to rectify any defects detected in the acceptance test and is only then permitted to rescind the contract;

- Under leasing agreement law the software manufacturer is to a large extent liable for defects from the outset, including remote damage occasioned by the software.

However, these extensive legal consequences, which place a considerable onus upon the software manufacturer, only arise under sales contracts and contracts for goods and services if the defect occurs on handing over of the software (installation in the system of the purchasing party); if it only comes to light later, the manufacturer is only liable for a period of six months and is thereafter released from any liability, whereas under leasing agreement law he remains liable throughout the entire term of the agreement without such temporal limitation.

In many respects these variations appear arbitrary and legal discussions have only begun to deliberate on the question as to how an unreasonable outcome can be prevented in individual cases. In essence it can be stated that the fact that a defect was unavoidable only entitles the client to rescind the contract within six months of the installation of the software and liability thereafter is surprisingly restricted (due to the operation of the limitation period).

It would also appear unreasonable that by contrast a software lessor is liable without possibility of exemption throughout the entire term of the lease and to a disproportionate extent, even for remote damage occasioned by the software. The reason for this imbalance is presumably based on the consideration that it has proved difficult to integrate software with all its peculiarities as a contractual object in the previous contractual system of the German Civil Code. A significant part of scientific discussion has been concerned with the question as to how this imbalance can be avoided in practice. Jurisprudence has yet to produce a final solution to this problem.

Although German legal literature recognises the concept of the <u>licensing agreement</u> and it is even occasionally mentioned in judgements, it is not yet regulated by law. Since practically all foreign legal systems assume that software is sold on the basis of licensing agreements, this represents a major source of the problems of definition experienced between the German legal system and those of the individual EC member states.

Many authors have argued that software contracts should in general be subjected to the law governing sales contracts. However, this presents a plethora of obstacles in coming to grips with the copyright problems involved in the sale of software. In this context it will be necessary to await a fundamental ruling of the Bundesgerichtshof [BGH - Federal Court of Justice].

b) Tortious liability (Para. 823, Clause 1 BGB)

The question immediately arises in the area of tortious liability as to whether software is a "product" which engenders certain obligations in terms of consumer protection. The question is of some import, in that consumer protection obligations only arise for mass-produced industrial products, among which at all events individual software cannot be numbered. Most authors therefore adopt the view that only standard software can be considered for this liability. But even with standard software the question inevitably arises as to whether they are produced on an "industrial" basis. This is generally taken to mean a procedure where the manufacturing process is aimed at mass production. In the case of software, this may apply to the copying, but hardly to the planning and design of a software product. A ruling on this question is still awaited.

In tort law (Para. 823, Clause 1 BGB) in addition to proving that a defect exists in the product, the damaged party must further prove that

- the defect has arisen within the scope of responsibility of the manufacturer;

- the manufacturer has objectively breached an imposed obligation to prevent the damage;

- the life, physical intactness or integrity of an object has been violated;

- negligence has at least contributed to the creation of the defect in the product, although the burden of proof for absence of negligence resides with the manufacturer and not the injured party;

- the defect was causal to the arising damage.

c) Product liability law

In the field of product liability law, with the exception of negligence the same rules apply, with the difference that

- there is no possibility of excuse for unavoidable manufacturing defects

- but on the other hand there is no liability for development risks.

Liability under product liability law is linked to the fact, as expressly stated in the Product Liability Act, that the damage must have been caused by a "product", which can generally be taken to mean an "object" and not an "action", an "idea" or a "service". In fact, many foreign legal systems and in particular the system in the USA accept the difference between "product" and "service" and only apply product liability rules to "products" and not to "services". In this context software is regarded as a "hybrid" to which the product liability rules are applied if this is obviously required within the intended scope of consumer protection. A similar delineation will presumably also be adopted within the EC. However, the discussion in Germany is still addressing itself to the same questions of delineation as in German tort law (distinction between individual and industrial production).

4. Summary

The contention that software defects are unavoidable is too abstract. In fact, certain types of software defect are at all events avoidable, whereas others are unavoidable even given the highest technical standards. However, the latter category is extremely narrow and in view of rapid technological development must always be assessed in each individual case.

Such assessment is successful particularly if one defines specific categories of defects within which one can establish whether a defect can in general be avoided and to whom it is then to be ascribed. These categories of defects can be applied uniformly - albeit with a different scope of liability - both in contract law and in tort and product liability law.

LITERATURE

Belli/Fevzi, Modellierung von Software-Fehlern zur Bestimmung und Optimierung der Zuverlässigkeit in Gorny/Kilian S. 68-87 (ACM-Bericht)

Belli/Pfleger/Seifert (Hrsg.). Software Fehlertoleranz und -zuverlässigkeit, 1984

Deutsche Gesellschaft für Qualität, Software Qualitätssicherung, 1986

Gorny, Peter, Kategorien von Softwarefehlern, CR 1986, 673-677

Gorny/Kilian (Hrsg.) Computersoftware und Sachmängelhaftung Workshop des German Chapter of the ACM und der Gesellschaft für Rechts- und Verwaltungsinformatic e.V. 1985

Hausen/Müllerburg/Schmidt, Über das Prüfen, Messen und Bewerten von Software, Informatik Spektrum 1987, 123-144

Heussen, Technische und rechtliche Besonderheiten von Mängeln bei Computerleistungen CR 1988, 894/986

Kilian/Heussen, (Hrsg.) Computerrechtshandbuch, München, 1990

Krückeberg, Fritz, Prüfung von Software. CuR 1985, 47/113/175

Rombach/Basili, Quantitative Software Qualitätssicherung, Informatik Spektrum Nr. 10, 1987

Schmitz/Bons/von Megen, Software-Qualitätssicherung, 1983

Lee Sprague, Testverfahren für Software. IuR 1986, 248

Weigel, Qualitätssicherung bei komplexen Datenverarbeitungssystemen. CR 1989, 746

SESSION 7

METHODS

Approving Software Products
W. Ehrenberger (Editor)
Elsevier Science Publishers B.V. (North-Holland)

PROPOSALS FOR THE ORGANIZATION OF FINAL SOFTWARE BLACKBOX TESTS

Robert Lindermeier and Frank Siebert

Institute for Quality and Safety in Electronics
TÜV Bayern e.V.
München, West Germany

For several years international activities concerned with the field of software test have taken place. Today many of methods and tools are known, test centers for different purposes are established and standards have been published. Still many organizational problems which appear in most cases remain unanswered (e.g. coordination of several testers within the same test setting, ability to repeat tests, etc.). This paper discusses typical problems of blackbox software tests and refers to E DIN 66285. The standard E DIN 66285 deals with the quality of software products and their tests.

1. INTRODUCTION

During the last years an increasing number of issues concerning the topics software quality assurance and software test have been developed. On the one hand the everyday use of computers and electronic data processing explains, why programs have lost their status of infallibility and are more and more seen as "normal" products, which are subjected to the laws of market. On the other hand the complex form of computer programs increased the likelyhood of programming- and user-errors, which contradicts corresponding quality demands of a good product. Systematic software tests might therefore improve the quality of software production. Already in 1985 a beginning of software test standardization was made in West Germany with the standard DIN V 66285. A more advanced version is E DIN 66285, "Anwendersoftware - Gütebedingungen und Prüfbestimmungen" (Quality criteria and test regulations for application programs [1]). It was released at the end of 1989. Here, software quality criteria are defined as well as basic approaches for software tests. However, this basic approaches have to be transferred to a practical application. The main problems arising from this transfer of this standard will be discussed on the example of final blackbox software tests.

2. E DIN 66285

The purpose of E DIN 66285 is to define quality demands for software products describing suitable quality and their test criteria.

Quality criteria claim, that each software product according to E DIN 66285 exists at least of a product description, a documentation and the software itself (programs and data).

The product description has to cover some procedural and technical aspects to meet the quality criteria. Formally, the product description has to be named especially as such, plus the product has to be described clearly. The technical aspect emphasizes the purpose of application, functionality and characteristics of software products (e.g. legal restrictions, application limits, reliability and robustness, ease of use, maintainability and transferability, etc.). It also deals with presumed knowledge, form and extend of the delivery package as well as installation and assistance or maintainance service.

Following the quality criteria the documentation has to be complete and correct. Therefore it must comment on any necessary information for using, especially on installing the program. Furthermore the documentation of the product should be intelligible to the target group and must be clearly structured. If the documentation has not been edited already, the user should be able to print it out.

If according to the product description the manufacturer provides for the installation, it must be done with a hard- and software-setting which complies with the product description. If there is no installation assistance, the user should be able to install the software by himself following the installation guide and to prove wether installation was successful. Furthermore, the program functions should correspond to the product description and should be performed without errors. Besides that the hard- and software-system should never become uncontrollable or loose data (even in extreme situations). Also various demands are made concerning intelligibility, clarity and controllability. Next, consistency within and between product units is required.

According to the test regulations, tests have to be documented with a test plan, a test protocol and a test report. It should be possible to repeat the test procedure refering to test documentation (see Ch. 3.). The test report should sum up the test results. The report construction is defined by the standard. Before the test starts, a number of test requirements have to be considered.

Details going beyond this short summary can be found in the standard itself.

3. BASIC TEST POLICY

Besides the basic test regulations aquired by E DIN 66285, there are a number of general principles of software tests, which must be taken into account to guarantee a successful test procedure. We will focus here on a selection of main issues:

- The purpose of a software test is to detect errors and not to prove correctness.
- Basically a test always relies on certain specified requirements, whose fulfillment shall be examined. These requirements can be of special or universal nature. A test, therefore, will always examine already defined (and known) requirements a product should fulfill. Under no circumstances shall a test serve the investigation of unknown characteristics.
- The test procedure must be repeatable and must lead to the same results again. This will only happen if the test has been planned, and methods as well as results can be repeated following the test protocol. To ensure the test results are independent from certain test teams, the applied methods must be resistent to subjective influences.
- The applied methods plus the organizational setting, still following above claims, must allow an economically acceptable test performance.

A few other regulation are not considered here, as they play a subordinate role in the further discussion.

4. PARTICULAR IMPROVEMENTS ON SOFTWARE (BLACKBOX) TESTS

The examples in following chapter show some problems and possible solutions concerning the test of software. These practical problems were recorded by a software test center using above mentioned DIN standard. Especially when testing the final product these outlined problems came up. Meanwhile many elaborated solutions for this problems are known and applied successfully. In the following chapter we show some of the most important ones. As the tests could not be based on the source code, blackbox software test methods were applied. To simplify the transfer of the results to other related areas the problems are differentiated.

4.1. General Improvements

At this point improvements concerning the organization of software tests will be discussed.

4.1.1. Labour Estimation

The reliability of labour estimantion is necessary to deal economically with software tests. Therefore suitable analysis and forecast methods must be selected. Those should be able to provide precise statements under minimal labour. Especially, with blackbox tests people should consider, that mainly user documentation and user interface of the program are responsible for the forecast provided by selected methods.

Practice showed, that concerning application programs the following method is successful.

First of all some guidelines must be laid down:

Inputs and results are place holders for data. Hence, every input mask field represents for example an input. Each handed out value calculated by the program is a result.

Lower program functions are functions which demand only minimal computation efforts, e.g. saving, listing, deleting, etc.

Higher program functions normally require more computation efforts. These are functions like the combination of large data inventories, high standard calculations such as numerical procedures or image processing functions.

A number of inputs as well as the combination of suitable higher and lower program functions are necessary to carry out a sequence of operations, according to the practical use of the program by the user. This combination is called *complex program function.*

This classification can be seen only as a rough guideline. Its application demands a certain experience.

Following efforts for inputs, results or lower program functions can be estimated; the average values are based on experience:

- inputs/ results: 0.5 - 2.0 h (average: 1.0 h),
- lower program functions: 0.5 - 5.0 h (average: 3.0 h),
- higher program functions: 5.0 - 100.0 h (average: 10.0 h).

The effort for complex program functions equals the summed up efforts of its incredients neglecting the efforts for inputs and results. The total effort equals all summed up single efforts plus another approx. 25% for organization and supervision.

For PC-programs of average range one should allow 8 h for the labour estimation effort. It has been shown, though the method to evaluate the total effort is quite independent from the user, there can be still differences concerning the estimation of single efforts. The usage of this method requires familarity with the kind of the programs beeing examined.

4.1.2. Homogenity versus Flexibility of the Test

For an effective organizational performance, replication and supervision of tests it is advisable to provide a very detailed description of test methods, which allow standardized tests. Here a conflict exists, as tests can not totally be planned beforehand, also the tester should be allowed a range of possible decisions for efficient test performance.

This conflict can for example be solved when a formal framework (see Ch. 5.) is given. So, on one hand the organizational context and the structure of the test is given. On the other hand the framework guarantees the tester a free choice in detail conception and test performance. This approach needs experienced testers familiar with the formal framework.

4.1.3. Efficient Management of Test Performance and Results

The documentation of software tests can reach a magnitude of thousands of pages. To answer questions concerning,

- the latest status of a test,
- the latest results,
- the assignment of tasks to testers,
- the management of undetermined operations,
- etc.

an efficient management of the test documentation is necessary. Simpler and less demanding tests can be handled manually applying a well-contrived system. More elaborate tests, however, need support of a corresponding database. Chapter 5. introduces a hierarchical order of the formal framework, which leeds to an efficient manual management of the test performance. It is also suitable for a database supported implementation.

4.1.4. Test Quality

To guarantee the quality of software tests suitable quality criteria must be laid down. A few quality criteria of software test are a direct result of E DIN 66285 respectively of test principles (see Ch. 3.). Therefore part of the quality criteria are certainly the capability to replicate and thus to repeat the test procedure. Also the independence of results from subjective influences as well as the capability for adaptation and extension are important aspects. Among others further criteria are correctness, clarity, test consistency, standard conformity, efficiency, completeness and clearness. The formal framework described in chapter 5. can be helpful to avoid test errors in many of these characteristics. This way using appropiate denotiation rules, quality criteria such as the capability to replicate and repeat test procedures, clarity, completeness and consistency can be improved. Criteria like completeness, capability for adaption and extension will be supported by a thoroughly planning of the test. Those are already considered within the temporal and logical order of the formal framework. The organizational order of the formal framework backs up criteria like completeness, consistency, efficiency and independence of subjective influences. Through a cautious selection of test methods criteria such as correctness, independence of test results from subjective influences and efficiency can be supported.

Test error identification can be supported by the project leader, while and after the test ("check of check"). This can be archieved by applying reviews and audits. The checking includes content and formal aspects.

4.2. Improvements on Parallel Test Performance

Parallel activities of several persons cause always a number of problems. Some of them will be discussed in the following paragraph.

4.2.1. Term Definition and Methods

Today various different methods and concepts are employed for software test. The coordination of different testers needs definitely basic, common guidelines. These guidelines shall guarantee certain ways of performance and sufficient communication between all involved persons. Also, they have to be mediated to all testers. A standard vocabulary should be provided in a glossary containing term definitions and instructions for term usage. Furthermore a specified selection of methods has to be made available and to be obeyed. Glossary as well as method selection must be teached and improved constantly.

4.2.2. Coordination

A well known problem of parallel working is coordinaton. The total operation must be suitable to be split up in various units. These units must have defined interfaces and must be in temporal and logical accordance. So, the results of each unit can be combined easily to a homogenious total. Only if this is done efficiently the advantages of parallel working will be useful. There are various solutions proposed by project management guidelines. Examples can be found in [2]. A number of approaches suitable for software tests, trying to solve above problem are given within the formal framework in chapter 5.

4.2.3. Communication

A successful communication is a predisposition for a successful test coordination. The aspects of communication are related with the aspects of coordination. The communication effort increases overproportional according to the single units, which have to be coordinated. Groups with more than 10 people can exchange information sufficiently only in special cases. Alone, appropiate approaches by the project management provide a solution for the communication as well as the coordination problem. The formal framework introduced in chapter 5. deals with both and offers some instructions to solve them.

4.3. Improvements on Blackbox Tests

As the source code is not available for blackbox tests a number of specific aspects have to be considered.

4.3.1. Desired Preciseness and Overproportional Growth of Effort

Especially with blackbox tests, it can be found that test expenses grow overproportional with the desired preciseness of the test results. The reason is, that the number of needed test cases, to obtain appropriate test results increases overproportional by looking at the program in detail. In general it is not possible to find a solution for this problem, as these difficulties are a result of missing program information caused by the blackbox approach. As essential information about program structure and content is not available, only (partly competing) error hypothesis can be formulated. Each hypothesis then has to be backed up by corresponding test cases. Therefore one can not reduce the number of necessary test cases in general. At most they can be made more efficiently designed, administered and tested. Also there is hardly any possibility to compensate this disadvantage using suitable tools for test case generation, because these tools do not exist in a desirable size today.

4.3.2. Tools for Blackbox Tests

There are a number of tools, which support whitebox tests - i.e. software tests using the source code (see [3], [4]). For blackbox tests, on the other hand, hardly any tools exists, at most for the test administration. Especially, regarding overproportional growth of test cases corresponding to test preciseness, it would be desirable to have a large selection of appropriate tools. This problem might be solved by the development of tools. However, this needs a suitable market and organizations offering the right products. The test centres itselves are usually not interested in producing these tools. So they can only choose certain methods to reduce the test effort, to improve the organization, to use computers for test case administration and perhaps to lower the demands of a suitable software test. To get an idea of effort allocation during a test, figure 1 shows the relation between the different phases of a blackbox test and the efforts to be expected.

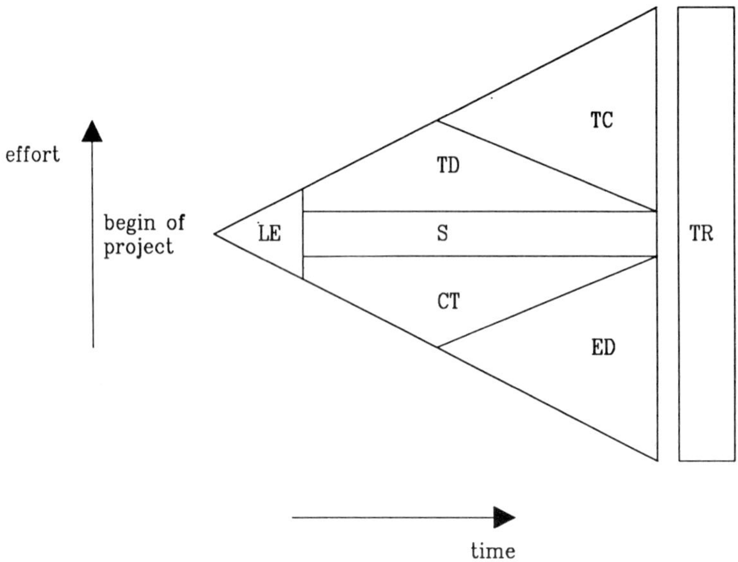

LE : labour estimation
S : supervision of formal frame regulations and technical aspects
TD : test of documentation
CT : creation and completion of test plan and test cases
TC : test of consistency
ED : execution and documentation of test
TR : test report

Figure 1: Relation between different phases and expected efforts

4.3.3. Effort Reduction versus Replication

The test documentation is even more important for blackbox tests than for whitebox tests. As the assumptions, leading to certain results can not be reconstructed via program, but solely via a detailed and effective documentation. On the other hand people should not underestimate the effort for such a test protocol and its administration. Especially the detailed description of error units of the software product requires more of an effort. A guideline for more effective and efficient test documentation is desirable. A part of a possible approache is the formal framework (see Ch. 5.). A computer supported administration of the tests can make the tests even more economical, too.

5. ORGANIZATION OF TESTS

Here, a concept for the organization of tests shall be introduced by giving a short description of its major elements.

The overall idea is equivalent to the formal framework already mentioned in chapter 4. On the one hand performance is guaranteed beeing as efficient as possible and easy to supervise. On the other hand there is left sufficient professional latitude for testers to be prepared for any situation. The concept of the formal framework has four basic ideas:

- a temporal order of the test,
- a logical order of the test,
- a hierarchical order of the test,
- a organizational order of the test.

The temporal order serves the division into phases. Each phase builds on its predecessor and shows defined interfaces as well as initial and final conditions. The concept of phases offers an unproblematic linear/ cyclical handling of the phases. The phases are: pre-test, main-test, error-reduction-test and follow-up-test. The pre-test covers only a part of the main-test and serves to assess whether the product is testable or not. The main-test includes the actual test of the whole software product. If the software product proved not to be correct in the main-test or in an earlier error-reduction-test, the actual error-reduction-test examines with the latest improved program release. A follow-up-test deals with the developements and changes of already well tested software products. Error-reduction-tests and follow-up-tests can appear cyclically.

The logical order is supposed to divide the software to be tested into related program functions, so-called blocks. For some standard software products (e.g. word-processing and database) there are already proposals for grouping the program functions into blocks. With word processing one can distinct, e.g. blocks like user control, data administration, interfaces, printing, etc. In case, such divisions do not exist, an analogous inference from existing groupings can be made. Each block is dealt by one tester or a test team, working together very closely. People choose the block grouping in a way, that the related program functions are in the same block. Thus, the interferences between different blocks are reduced. Normally there is still a rest of program functions, which refer to more than one block at the same time. As these cannot be classified under one block they have to be summed up in a so-called "block combined union". Additional to the block orientated tests, there exists the test of complex program functions, which concern the whole program and are related to a program application as usual. The logical test order makes coordinated, parallel working of more testers possible.

The hierarchical test order treats the test documentation. The highest element within this order of three levels is the test protocol. Here people can find entries, which document directly certain test functions, as well as entries for test functions for whose documentation people need to answer numerious, single questions. To guarantee a well organized test protocol these questions are laid down in a so-called "checklist" and not in the test protocol itself. In the protocol, then the appropriate checklist is mentioned. Therefore the checklists are the second level of the hierarchie. Certain questions in the checklist demand elaborate operations, which then have to be documented as well. Again, to guarantee clarity, these so-called "subordinate evaluations" must be done with the help of so-called "forms". These forms are the third and lowest level of the hierarchical order. In the affected checklist questions reference to the forms is made. The results of each hierarchical level and delayed points of operation, are transferred onto each higher level. Thus it is always possible to obtain the results and status of the whole test from the test protocol. The specified denotiations of each level are obligatory and in accordance with the different orders. The instructions and the denotations provided for the test protocol (protocol headings, test function headings, etc.) have to be obeyed by all testers. The formal framework contents further advises how to reduce the effort needed for the protocol (e.g. it will be shown how to design test cases, so that it is possible to use print-screens for the results documentation). Unfortunately these cannot be dealt here because of the demanded brevity.

The organizational order calls for a project leader who has to coordinate all testers employed for the test. Normally his duties are equivalent to a project manager ones. They include the planning and conception of the test, the delegation of tasks, the supervision of successful communication and the guarantee of test quality, plus others. Past software test projects have shown, that one project leader should supervise only one test project with ideally 3 - 5 testers. In regular time intervalls technical and organizational meetings must take place following defined aims (e.g. concerning the status of the test or actual difficulties). Definite "events" must be defined, which correspond to certain operations (e.g. the tester must inform the project leader, if he intents to diverge from the formal framework). To ensure the test quality all projects are controlled by a supervisor. It is also his duty to carry out adaptions to the formal framework.

Next to this solution, there are other possible approaches. One of these is the concept of permanently fixed test procedures, using programmed instructions. Because it is impossible to discuss this approach in this paper we refer to [5].

6. CONCLUSIONS

The approach described above has been developed by the software test center of TÜV Bayern e.V. It has been applied in various practical software test projects and has been permanently improved.

In an attempt to fulfill given limitations it is not possible to pursue the approach in detail. Therefore only a few principles could be explained.

Nevertheless the paper shows important possibilities how to improve various aspects of the organization of final software blackbox tests.

REFERENCES

[1] E DIN 66285, Anwendersoftware - Gütebedingungen und Prüfbestimmungen (Beuth, Berlin, Ausgabe 11. 1989)
[2] Gilb, T., Principles of Software Engineering Management (Addison-Wesley, New York, 1988)
[3] DeMillo, R.A., McCracken, W.M., Martin, R.J. and Passafiume, J.F., Software Test and Evaluation (The Benjamin Cummings, Menlo Park California, 1987)
[4] Myers, G.J., Methodisches Testen von Programmen (Oldenbourg, München, 1989)
[5] Schmidt, K., Rahmenprüfplan der GMD, Arbeitspapiere der GMD 312 (Gesellschaft für Mathematik und Datenverarbeitung mbH, St. Augustin, 1988)

Approving Software Products
W. Ehrenberger (Editor)
Elsevier Science Publishers B.V. (North-Holland)
IFIP, 1990

Can we afford formal third-party testing?

Eberhard Wegner

Gesellschaft für Mathematik und Datenverarbeitung mbH
(GMD, the National Research Center for Computer Science)
Schloss Birlinghoven
D-5205 Sankt Augustin 1, Federal Republic of Germany

Abstract

Formal third-party testing of software products against standards has been a technical success but, for many types of products, a commercial failure. The expenses and the company-internal cost for such external tests seem not to be recovered by the number of additional copies sold.

ISO/IEC Guide 2:1986 mentions a (manufacturer's) Declaration of Conformity. It is cheaper than a Certificate of Conformity because expenses for testing laboratories and certification bodies are saved.

If, for some type of software products, test software can be made available at a modest price, if such test software is usable with modest effort, and if customers insist on some evidence of conformity, then the Declaration of Conformity may be the solution to the problem.

Keywords

Software product, conformity, test method, test software, self-testing, declaration of conformity, certification system, certification scheme, testing laboratory, accreditation, third-party test, test report, certificate of conformity, mark of conformity

1. Organisations involved

The first conformity requirements for software were established by national government agencies (viz. in the USA for COBOL compilers), in particular for public procurement. Cooperation with national standards bodies followed.

Testing was initially done by government agencies themselves, later trusted to testing laboratories, and is now, in certain areas, subcontracted to commercial companies.

Formal testing requires some certification scheme describing the prerequisites for issuing a certificate of conformity (or a mark of conformity), including rules for the accreditation of testing laboratories. This accreditation may be done by government, by a standards body, by a certification body or by a particular accreditation body.

Many testing laboratories are affiliated with associations of manufacturers. However, testing laboratories affiliated with single manufacturers are also accredited provided that they are not subject to influence on the test results.

To avoid re-testing in other countries, bilateral contracts were concluded for mutual recognition of test results. There is also accreditation across national borders.

There is a Committee for Conformity Assessment CASCO (formerly CERTICO) in the International Organization for Standardization (ISO). However, I do not know of any activity of CASCO bearing on software.

ISO and the International Electrotechnical Commission (IEC) issue ISO/IEC Guides describing how to handle conformity testing, certification and related activities. A list can be found in the ISO Catalogue. ISO/IEC Guide 2 defines terms on standardisation, testing and certification [1].

The European Economic Community are creating the CE mark for products conforming to their regulations [2].

The European Committee for Standardisation (CEN) has adapted the contents of several ISO Guides into European Standards 45 001 to 45 004 and 45 011 to 45 014; they are promoting certification [2]. Members of CEN are the standards bodies of the twelve countries of the European Community (EC) and the six countries of the European Free Trade Association (EFTA).

In 1988, CEN Certification Committee 1 on Information Technology has adopted a certification scheme for IT, including Annexes for Pascal, the Graphical Kernel System, COBOL and FORTRAN. But CEN has not yet started it.

2. Some sad facts about conformity testing

For a general survey, see previous proceedings [3].

2.1 Compiler testing worldwide

Federal authorities in the USA began requiring certificates of conformity for COBOL (and later FORTRAN) compilers in the Seventies. Therefore vendors had to pay for tests provided by government agencies and their contractors. (Anti-trust legislation inhibits such a concerted action in public procurement here in the Federal Republic of Germany.) Later, it was left to the procuring authority whether they would require a certificate or not. GMD (the only testing laboratory for COBOL and FORTRAN in Germany F.R.) tests less than half a dozen compilers a year. This does not cover its expenses because offering a test service requires maintaining a center of expertise including at least two testers.

A stronger policy was implemented more recently for Ada compilers: Only certified compilers may be called Ada compilers, and of course public procurement in the USA requires certificates of conformity. If test services for Ada cover their cost, then this is due to this enforcement of conformity.

US authorities have recently dropped their test services for Minimal BASIC and Pascal processors.

British Standards Institution claim that their test service for Pascal processors is economically viable. They have worked hard to convince vendors.

GMD has dropped its test service for Pascal processors after having offered it for several years without a single order.

Many facts about conformity testing for the compilers mentioned can be found in the Introduction of the Validated Compiler List [4].

Years ago, GMD was asked by interested people to launch test services for APL and the process control language PEARL, but the number of compilers expected for testing is too small.

Test software for C compilers is being developed, based on the Draft International Standard 9899 for the C language.

2.2 Graphics software and devices

When the International Standard for the Graphical Kernel System (GKS, ISO 7942) appeared in 1985, large parts of the test software for GKS implementations were already written (partly financed by the Commission of the European Communities). All the GKS implementors informed themselves on the development of the standard and the test software. There was a race for the first certificates of conformity.

Copies of the GKS test software have been sold to about 40 companies (of these, 14 in 1989). 12 implementations were tested (2 in 1989), and certificates of conformity were issued for them. At the end of 1989, 4 certificates were valid. Business has suffered from the delay of the European certification scheme for information technology.

The levy on the software sales covers the cost of the continued development, and the tests cover the directly related expenses. Nevertheless there is a problem of motivation: The test service requires people able enough for difficult development, but most of the work is routine.

The Computer Graphics Metafile (CGM, ISO 8632-1 to 4) is a format for the storage and transfer of graphic images. A small US company developed and offers software for testing single metafiles. No certification scheme exists as yet.

The Computer Graphics Interface (CGI, ISO 9636-1 to 6) is a standardized format for data and control between a graphics device and the software controlling it. Test software for testing devices is being written.

2.3 Application software in the Federal Republic of Germany

In the early Eighties, two testing laboratories in the Federal Republic of Germany awarded test marks of their own to software products, without disclosing their quality requirements or test method. They attracted a considerable number of vendors because their generic name "TÜV" in the test marks was widely known from their obligatory bi-annual test of motor vehicles. Remarkably enough, this activity seemed a commercial success. After hard negotiations the two TÜV withdrew their marks in favour of the following mark.

In 1985 a Quality Mark for application software products ("Gütezeichen Software") was created. The quality requirements and testing directives were widely agreed and adopted as a national pre-standard DIN 66 285. (A slightly stronger version is going to appear as a standard with the same number.)

The knockout criteria are:
- documentation is incomplete,
- installation is impossible when following the instructions,
- minimal hardware configuration as indicated is insufficient,
- a documented function (or a part of it) is missing,
- a failure leads into a state which the user cannot control,
- a failure leads to loss or corruption of data,
- a failure leads to a wrong result,
- any regulation claimed to be satisfied is violated.

The present list of marked products contains 39 products only, most of them off-the-shelf software for personal computers originating from small enterprises, mostly business applications, craftsmen and engineering software, office communication, utilities. The number is so small because

- few of the products in the market comply with the quality requirements for the mark,
- testing is expensive,
- every new release with functional extension requires new testing, and
- software buyers hardly cared for the new quality mark (less than for the preceding TÜV marks).

A few more products have obtained the mark, but they originate from large hardware manufacturers which do not use it. Their company-internal testing laboratories (organisational units separate from software production units) have been accredited for these tests. This is established practice in other areas but new for software.

Quality marks tend to serve small and medium enterprises rather than big ones because the latter prefer to rely on their image rather than on marks. Big manufacturers contributed a lot to the development and administration but hardly helped to make the quality mark known.

In the early days of the Quality mark for application software, a representative of a multinational computer manufacturer sighed: If we do not promote this activity and it fails, we will be blamed, and if we offer our products with quality marks, we will be blamed for forcing the others to do the same.

2.4 Others

GMD offered conformity tests for system software with respect to magnetic tape file structure and labelling, with a single order within several years. People exchange tapes without labels (and thus with less security). A poll for the interest in a similar service for diskettes revealed only one company interested of about fifty asked.

The Physikalische-Technische Bundesanstalt in Braunschweig covers 5% of expenses for tests that are required by law.

I do not know enough to comment on the conformity testing scene in the areas OSI, OSF, UNIX, and X-open. It would seem that testing for telecommunication software pays its way. Reasons may be that admission to nets may be needed and that even otherwise nonconformities would inhibit interworking.

Certificates do seem attractive to people: ISO TC 159 on Ergonomics deals with a working draft for ISO 9241-11 "Visual Display Terminals (VDTs) used for office tasks -- Ergonomic requirements -- Usability statement". This part of ISO 9241 is intended to describe the form of a declaration on software products, but the properties to be stated are hardly defined.

ISO TC 176 on Quality Assurance is developing a guide to applying ISO 9001 "Quality systems -- Model for quality assurance in design/development, production, installation and servicing" (virtually only dealing with manufacturing) to software development. Institutions in the Netherlands and in the UK certify the production process for software. This acticity is supported by the CEC under the Conformance Testing Services programme.

Under the procedures required by EN 45 001 to 45 014 mentioned above, accreditation of a testing laboratory is expected to cost 15 000 ECU or more. Given the fact that most conformity testing services need subsidizing, these procedures may deter possible testing laboratories.

3. Aspects to be considered

3.1 The market is international

There are national variations like natural languages (putting requirements e.g. on documentation and keyboards), but I cannot see inherent (not administrative or legal) common particularities of the EC or of Western Europe (CEN covering EC and EFTA).

Given the importance of the US market, a purely European solution would be useless without mutual recognition with the USA, in particular the National Institute of Standards and Technology (NIST) [4]. In the USA, ISO work is gaining acceptance (however, I tried in vain to recommend the vocabulary of ISO/IEC Guide 2 to NIST). Unfortunately ISO work is neither fast nor not widely known.

It is difficult enough to organize consumers nationally. Internationally, there is little hope to establish consumer power.

3.2 Strengths and limitations of formal third-party tests

Advantages of third-party testing are:

- It does occasionally reveal errors that the manufacturer did not find even with the same test method (tools and procedures).
- Common test tools will be more mature than individual ones.
- Testing laboratories help manufacturers with their expertise.
- For the buyer it proves that thorough testing has really been done, and that quality requirements were not sacrificed to a deadline or to limits in budget.

Limitations:

- Even a certificate (or mark) of conformity cannot guarantee the absence of errors.
- No software product is delivered exactly as it was formally tested (said a representative of a major computer manufacturer). The vendor is responsible for the product anyhow.
- Testing laboratories and certification bodies do not warrant anything about products tested.

The second limitation is on purpose: A proposal that buyers may obtain copies of the tested version from testing laboratories was supported by nobody during the early preparation of the Ada compiler certification procedures in the European community, even though conformity was considered more important than for compilers for any other programming language. (I wonder whether software for admission to public nets or for safety-critical applications may be changed after approval; I have hints that it may.)

3.3 The essential question: Financing

First of all, test software is needed. Common test software to which many have contributed is cheaper (per copy) and better than if everyone devised tests of his own. However, it need be organised. Associations for promoting products conforming to a particular set of standards proved helpful.

Third-party testing is expensive for the manufacturer, in terms of both company-internal preparation and expenses. (Though preparation should be the same in case of a manufacturer's declaration of conformity -- probably it is not.)

Third-party testing is attractive for a manufacturer only if the additional cost pays

- by less internal testing cost ("cheap debugging service"),
- by an increased number of copies sold,
- by less hotline cost.

Customer satisfaction is important too but hard to quantify.

Compatibility pays if a manufacturer gains more clients than he loses. Such a gain need not be at the expense of other manufacturers because products become more attractive by compatibility so that greater numbers may be sold in total. (Would audio cassettes have succeeded if every manufacturer had sticked to his own form incompatible with others?)

Testing laboratories need subsidizing, at least for the initial development of the test software and for continued work in committees.

4. Value for Money: The Declaration of Conformity

Since responsibility for a product is with the vendor anyhow (never with the testing laboratory or the certification body) one should support and encourage manufacturers' "Declarations of Conformity" in the first place.

For this purpose, test tools should be made available at modest prices. They should be of a fair quality because otherwise implementors would too often have to find out whether an error is in the implementation or in the test software.

Users should ask for Declarations of Conformity.

Contributions of ideas and work to test tools may come from
- standards committees,
- research institutions,
- associations of many kinds (manufacturers, consultants, scientists, consumers and users),
- testing laboratories,
- unexpected corners such as insurance companies needing to have a software product assessed before insuring against liability.

References

[1] ISO/IEC Guide 2:1986 General terms and their definitions concerning standardization and related activities (* trilingual with the terms translated to five additional languages *). International Organization for Standardization, Case postale 56, CH-1211 Geneva 20, Switzerland.

[2] A global approach to certification and testing. COM(89)209 final - SYN 208. Official Journal of the European Communities, 19.10.1989, No. C 267, pp. 3-27.

[3] John L. Berg, Harald Schumny (ed): An analysis of the Information Technology Standardization Process. Proceedings of the International Symposium on Information Technology Standardization held in Braunschweig, F.R.G., 4.-7. July, 1989. Amsterdam and New York 1990: Elsevier. ISBN 0 444 87390 2. (Among others, sessions on conformity, certification, software quality. Many references.)

[4] Validated Compiler List (formerly Certified Compiler List). Issued quarterly by the U.S. National Institute of Standards an Technology, Software Standards Validation Group, Building 225, Room A266, Gaithersburg, MD 20899, USA. For Europe, copies can be obtained from the author's institution.

[5] ECTEL, EUROBIT: Conformity Testing for Information Technology Products (March 1990). Trilingual: German, English, French; 73 pages. To be obtained from EUROBIT Secretariat, c/o VDMA, Postfach 71 08 64, D-6000 Frankfurt (Main) 71, Tel. +49 -69 -6603 -530.

SESSION 8

TOOLS

Approving Software Products
W. Ehrenberger (Editor)
Elsevier Science Publishers B.V. (North-Holland)
IFIP, 1990

Experiences with Producing a Computerised Software Certification Tool

Bernard de Neumann and Alan Wingrove
Centre for Software Reliability
City University, London

Abstract: It seems evident from SCOPE that more than one certification model will be necessary: for example, different models may well be needed for each application domain, and that there may well be several levels of certification for each such domain. It will be assumed that each model will apply to an identified application domain and level of certification. A methodology will be considered whereby such models may be rapidly assembled from proven sub-models, or modules, in such a way that all modules presented for selection for the certification model are compatible, and furthermore any available data will also be compatible. Part of what is required for the process is a 'module-base' of proven sub-models (modules), all of which are compatible with at least some of the other modules. Another part of the requirement is for data. Essentially there are classes of Certification Models which may be constructed from the modules; some of these modules are not universally applicable, but there are sufficient in the module-base to build a model in each class catered for. This 'module-base' must be extendible so that new proven modules may be incorporated as they arise. Given the existence of such a library of modules, then in order to use it, it is necessary to both supervise it and aid the model-builder so that appropriate modules only are used in a particular construction. This library/'module-base' supervision/selection function may be handled by the (human) user, by (straight-forward) data-base type software, or by the application of an expert system. This enables the modeller to construct the most appropriate model, and ensures that modules used are compatible. Here the compatibility applies both to the modules and to the domain of application. In many circumstances the process may be automated, and then with the aid of a 'model-shell', (or 'model-skeleton', the basic structure into which the instructions for the component parts of the model are introduced, and which handles the interfaces) models may be automatically produced. The partition of models into 'modules' is a non-trivial task which requires a great deal of understanding of the processes.

The output of the modular Certification modeller is an appropriate procedure which may be used to certify software for application in a particular domain.. Of course it may well be possible to place this procedure, provided that it is in a computer language, under the control of a computer, and even to automate it entirely.

Approving Software Products
W. Ehrenberger (Editor)
Elsevier Science Publishers B.V. (North-Holland)

SUPPORTING SOFTWARE QUALITY ASSURANCE BY INTEGRATING DESIGN METRICS INTO A CASE TOOL

A. A. R. Riegg and R. J. Lauber

Institute for Control Engineering and Process Automation
University of Stuttgart
Pfaffenwaldring 47
D-7000 Stuttgart 80, Federal Republic of Germany

The technical aspects of approving software products are closely related to those of software quality assurance. The techniques of CASE (computer aided software engineering) tools as a constructive approach and those of software metrics as an analytic approach have been combined to form an improved method to achieve software of better quality during the development process. The integration of automated metrics analysis into a CASE tool allows to measure software design complexity at the place and time of its origin and reduces the effort to collect the various values. A classification model of design aspects which is related to a set of design metrics helps to interprete the results in order to support the design process on-line. Using an exemplary case study it is shown that design metrics can be used to identify possible weak parts in design and to distinguish between possible design alternatives.

1. INTRODUCTION

In the field of software quality assurance it is a well-known fact, that quality cannot be tested into software after its completion. Quality has to be built into the software during its whole life cycle. One solution to that problem is the use of CASE (computer aided software enginering) tools which support the software development process. They represent a constructive approach to improve software quality and cover one ore more phases in the software development process [1]. Another often proposed analytic approach to examine the achieved software quality is the use of metric techniques. In this field we have to distinguish between process metrics and product metrics [2]. In this paper we are refering to product metrics.

The practical application of such product metrics, first of all software complexity code metrics in practise is still very limited. That is due to:

- There exist no interpretation models with validated wheighting factors between the values measured and the quality to expect.

- Mostly used code complexity metrics are measurable late in the life cycle when the code or parts of it are available. In this phase the effort for necessary changes in design and code is very large.

- Tools for automated support of code complexity metrics and derivates are in use right now [3], tools for automated measuring of design metrics in earlier phases integrated into CASE tools are still missing.

However, recent publications [4,5] propose enforced steps in the direction of product measures applied in earlier life cycle phases called "design metrics". In pursuit of that direction, in this paper a method to combine (see Fig. 1) the advantages of CASE tools used in early design phases and design metrics techniques is described. A prototype implementation of this method in the shape of a design metrics tool system which avoids the problems mentioned above is explained.

Firstly, in the following section 2 is presented, how such design metrics have been adapted to the CASE tool EPOS [6]. Secondly, in the section 3 is shown, how the measured values of these metrics can be ordered and interpreted with the help of a classification model. Section 4 gives an example how this method has been used in practise.

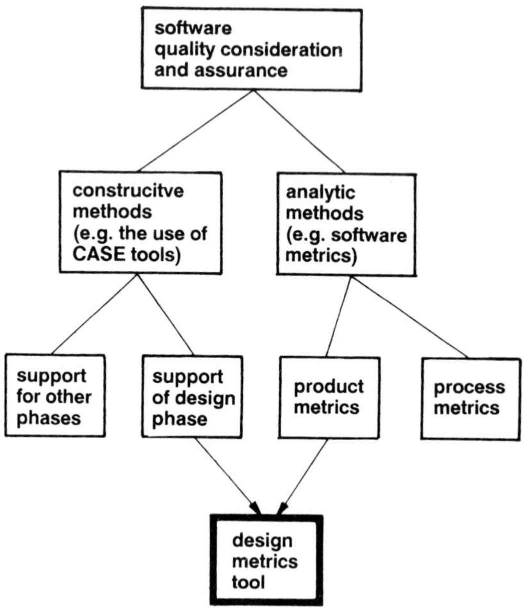

Fig. 1: The design metrics tool represents a combination of constructive tool support for the design phase and analytic

2. ADAPTING DESIGN METRICS TO THE CASE TOOL EPOS

2.1. The EPOS Design Model and Design Metrics

The EPOS tool, which is used in industry in over 800 installations all over the world, mainly in Europe but also in the U.S. is being used in all kinds of software projects up to more than 100,000 lines of code and covers all the phases of the software life cycle. As it is shown in Fig. 2, the EPOS tool provides three different specification languages:

- A requirements specification language (called EPOS-R).

- A system design specification language (called EPOS-S) to represent the design at different levels of abstraction. It includes seven design objects.

- A specification language (called EPOS-P) to describe project management information.

We achieved our goal to introduce software metrics in the design phase by taking the models and language of EPOS-S as the basis for metrics analysis. After entering the specified design informations using EPOS-S into the EPOS data base, they can be evaluated by a number of tool systems to support the software engineers. The design metrics tool system has been implemented on the same basis as all the other analysis tools thus being fully integrated in the CASE tool and thus strongly reducing the effort for its implementation.

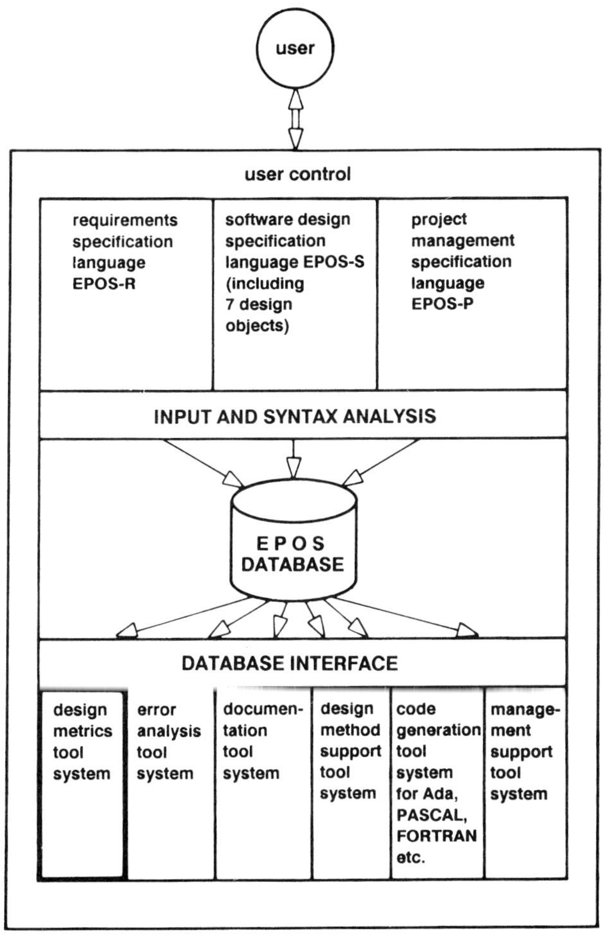

Fig. 2: Overview of the CASE environment EPOS for which the design metrics tool system has bees implemented as a prototype

To explain how the design metrics are working we have to give a short look at the EPOS-S design model. The platform of the system design using EPOS-S is shown in Fig. 3 which represents an excerpt of the EPOS-S design model. According to a top-down approach, all design information is transformed into the combination of seven distinct design objects. The boxes in Fig. 3 represent such objects, e.g. modules or actions. Among several existing design approaches of EPOS-S, this example forms the module-oriented approach. This approach is used for explanation at this point because the same approach has been used in the example described in section 4.

The upper levels of the design model (e.g. the modules and their interfaces) are defined during preliminary design, the lower levels (e.g. the calling hierarchy of the actions) are defined during detailed design.

The definition of these design objects takes place by invoking these objects, placing references between these objects (the lines and arrows in Fig. 3 mark such references) and by qualifying these objects with additional attributes. Our design metrics analyse and count these objects, references and attributes. A short explanation of exemplary design metrics will focus on the concepts presented in [7,8,9], although the details of these concepts won't be explained.

The design aspects to which these concepts are related to are modularity and hierarchy. The numerical evaluation of modularity uses the following references between design objects:

- module connections: the references between the design objects of type module, action and data using an import/export mechanism (e.g. see Fig. 3, the transformation of object data-a from module-a to module-b)

- module volume: the design objects of all types being part of a specific module (e.g. see Fig. 3, the objects action-a, -b, -c and -d being parts of module-b)

The numerical evaluation of hierarchy uses these references:

- decomposition hierarchy: the logical decomposition of modules into a hierarchy of submodules (e.g. see Fig. 3, the decomposition of module-0 into the submodules module-a, -b and -c)

- calling hierarchy: the calling references described by objects of type action starting at several entry points thus forming a calling hierarchy (e.g. see Fig. 3, the calling of action -e and -f from the entry point action-d)

2.2. The Integration of Metrics Analysis into the EPOS tool

The integration of design metrics analysis as described in the preceeding section into the EPOS tool has been realized as a prototype version on the basis of given internal interface layers. As shown in Fig. 4, the measuring algorithms within the design metrics tool system obtain their information using an existing retrieval layer. It is the same layer that is used by the error analysis tool system for example. That has the following advantages:

- the measuring algorithms work on pre-checked information. No additional checks concerning syntax errors (done by the input analysis) or simple errors concerning the formal specification language EPOS-S (handled by the error analysis tool system) are necessary.

- The measuring algorithms work on information, that has been transformed into a retrieval-optimized internal representation of the EPOS database. No extra text processing on the design specification described with the EPOS-S language is necessary.

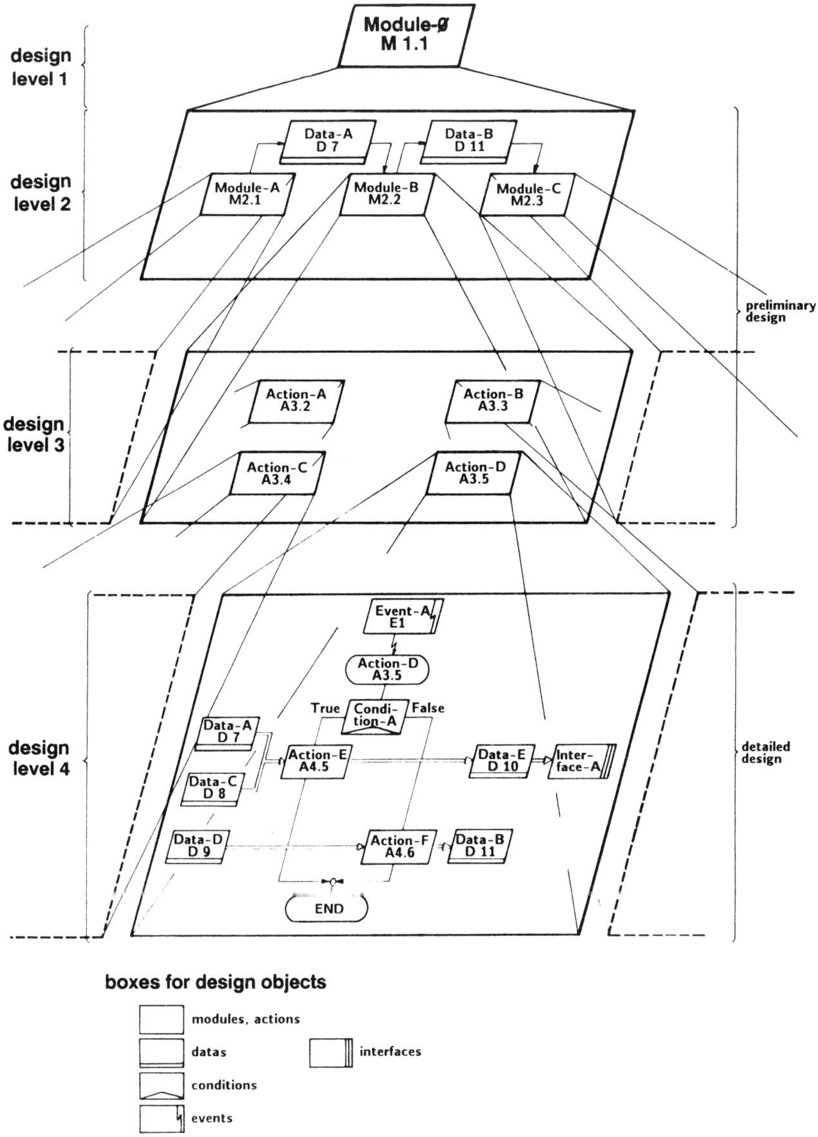

Fig. 3: The hierarchical model for a top-down design used by EPOS-S

The documentation of the measured values uses a special graphic output interface (Fig. 4) that is used by the management support tool system, too. No additional graphic processing algorithms to produce the various pictures are necessary. Examples of such graphics are given by Fig. 6 and 7. Finally, the whole design metrics tool system has been implemented in the same language as the other parts of the EPOS tool.

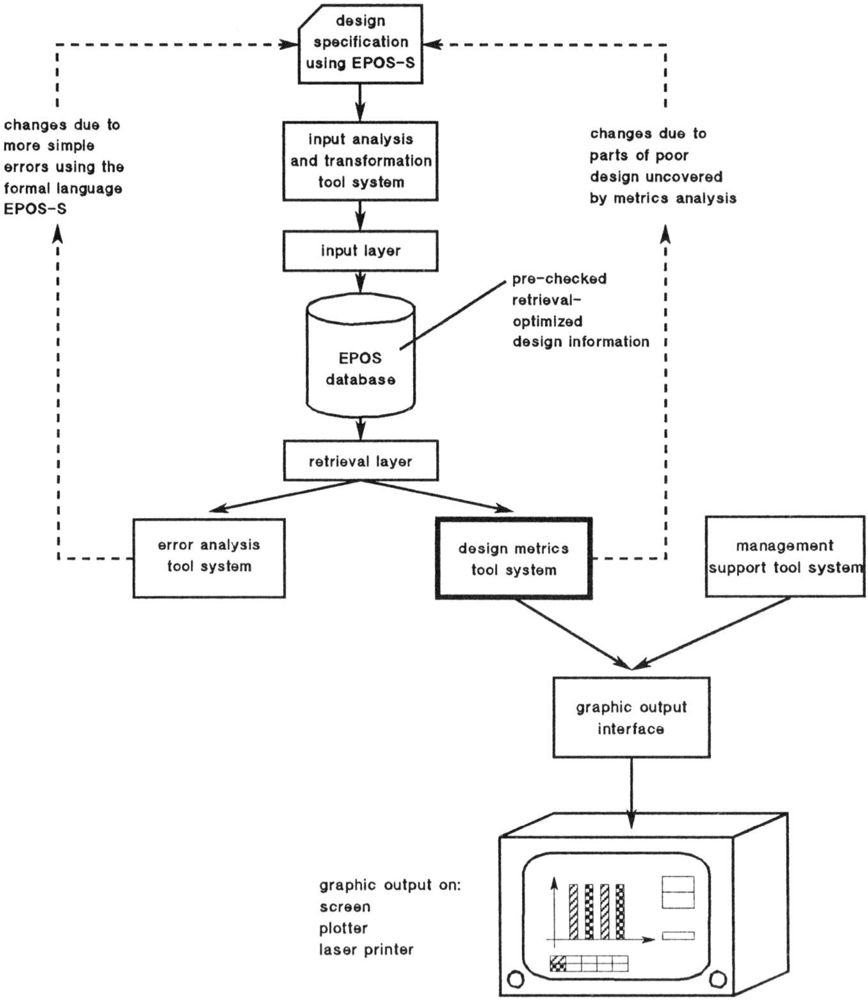

Fig. 4: The integration of the design metrics tool system into the EPOS environment

These integration strategies provide a design metrics tool system, that is:

- adapted to the design model of a CASE tool
- fully integrated into a wide spread CASE tool
- easy portable to other system tools
- provided with good performance

To obtain real benefits of design metrics, it is not enough to collect the metrics values automatcally. A framework that helps to analyse and interprete the measured values is necessary, too. The next section will describe the approach we made for such a model.

3. CLASSIFICATION MODEL OF DESIGN ASPECTS

Historically, work in software product metrics has been done mainly in the area of code complexity metrics. Early approaches [10,11] assumed, that one relative simple model could cover all the aspects of software quality. Further attempts to validate these theses showed, that there exist relationships between such single metrics and quality factors, but they showed also, that these metrics can't cover all the different aspects of software.

As a result of these investigations, new models came up trying to combine several aspects of software complexity by combining several code metrics. However, the method of calculating one metric value out of a set of several basic metrics proved to violate basic mathematic skaling principles [12] and showed no significant better validation results.

Additionally, the focus on program code as the unique representation for software metrics proved to be a too simple approach to handle all the aspects of software especially those, which have its origin much earlier in the life cycle than in the coding phase. The lack of this method, caused by too late measuring possibility cant't be compensated by using huge mathematic models derivated from intensive statistic analysis to separate the results.

Due to these reasons we found that a model consisting of a classification framework that covers all distinct design aspects which is dedicated to the design models of CASE tools and which is interrelated to a set of specific design metrics is an adequate approach to avoid the problems mentioned above.

This model has the shape of a hierarchical classification model (Fig. 5) for all software design aspects. It divides these aspects into twelve main groups:

- Coupling (manner and degree of interconnections between software modules)
- Data Representation (representation of data objects and their individual allocation)
- Information Flow (use of data objects and their flow)
- Control Flow (the intended sequence in which operations or actions are performed)

- Modularity (degree to which the system is composed of discrete objects)
- Hierarchy (structure in which the specification objects are ranked into levels of subordination)
- Timing and Parallelism (dynamical issues of the system, e.g. time constraints, parallel or distributed structures, real time issues)
- Synchronisation (influence on and control of system dynamic issues)
- Comprehensability (representation and description of the system)
- Programming Language (qualities, particularities, or peculiarities of the language to be chosen)
- Organisational Artifacts (type and degree of organisational and personal constraints influencing the development)
- Technical Items (system environment and technical constraints).

These main groups are subsequently refined into more than 100 subgroups (e.g. the hierarchy group into "refinement hierarchy of modules", "calling hierarchy of actions", "refinement hierarchy of data's" and more) [13].

All these subgroups are related to one specific design metric, aimed to characterize every subgroup by one quantitative entity. The whole model is used as a generic pattern which has to be instantiated for a specific project. In this process all design aspects are checked, whether they are considered in a specific software development project or not. In the most cases this results in a reduced classification model which is taylored to that distinct software development project.

This guarantees that all aspects considered in the design phase of that project are measured by a basic design metric and that all aspects not relevant in that distinct project are omitted, thus reducing the effort for the values collection.

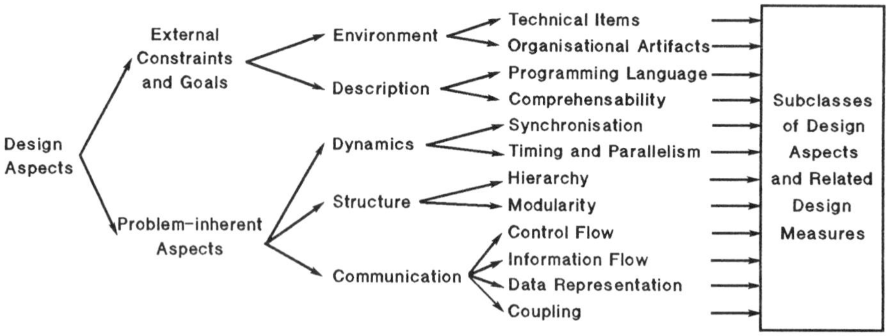

Fig. 5: Hierarchical classification model of design aspects

The analysis of the measured values uses these criteria:

- Direct checks if minimum and/or maximum bounds are violated
- Direct checks if given intervals are observed
- Statistic analysis to identify values lying far from the average
- Statistic analysis to discover high correlation between any measures

4. EXEMPLARY CASE STUDY

The design metrics tool system has been applied, as an example, during the development project of a control engineering software package. Involved in this project are about 10 engineering students. The estimated size of the project is about 20 KLOC. In this project the CASE tool EPOS has been firmly used in the requirements and design phase.

The instantiation of the generic design aspects model in this project leads to seven main groups with about 30 subgroups. The main groups are: Programming Language, Comprehensability, Hierarchy, Modularity, Control Flow, Information Flow and Coupling. For all the subgroups design metrics have been associated and implemented.

Fig. 6 and 7 give some examples of output protocols of these metrics:

- output protocol of modularity metrics (Fig. 6)
- output protocol of hierarchy metrics (Fig. 7)

The interpretation of the measured values was performed according to the criteria of section 3 and the used in the following ways:

- during preliminary design, the values were taken as additional indicators to distinguish between possible alternatives (e.g. the separation into submodules)
- during reviews at the end of the design phase, the results were taken as indicators to possible as weak points of the design (e.g. inadequate calling hierarchy, unsatisfying system description)

5. CONCLUSION

A method has been developed and implemented to apply software product metrics in the design phase of projects in combination with CASE tools. Based on an analysis of problems with product metrics up to now, our method consists of two parts:

- a classification model of design aspects that serves as a design metrics interpretation framework
- a strategy to integrate design metrics into a CASE tool for automatic support.

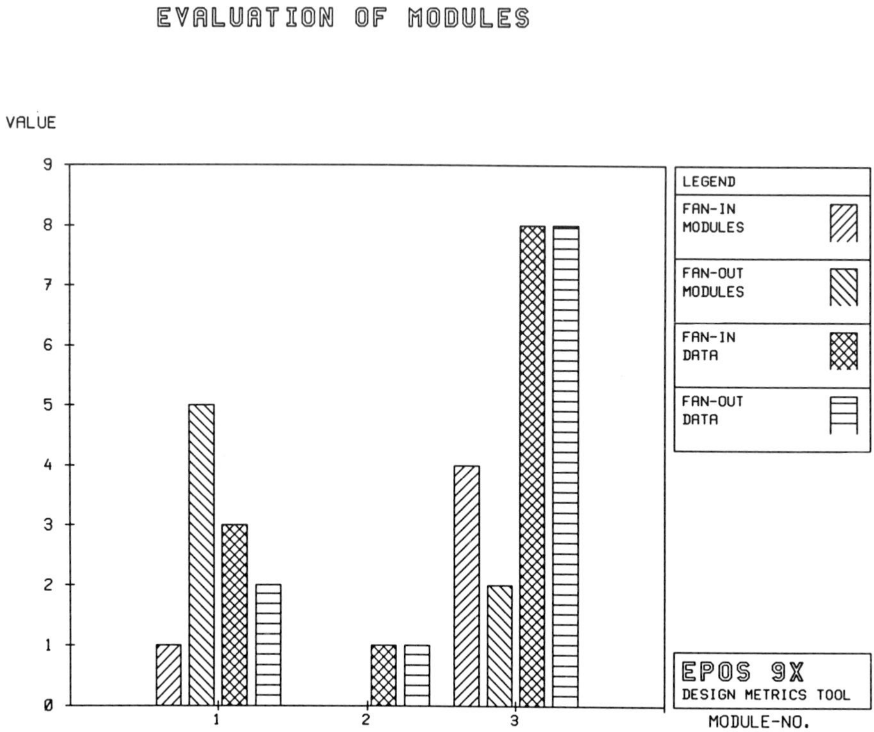

	1	0	4
	5	0	2
	3	1	8
	2	1	8
	MODULE-A	MODULE-B	MODULE-C

Fig. 6: Modularity measures (example for the output)

With reference to the goal of the conference we propose, that every approving mechanism of software products should comprise among other aspects, a consideration of the software development process. We are convinced that as a part of that consideration the real use of design metrics is one of the ways to improve this process. This consideration has to include the integration of tools, allowing easy automatic measurement, into a CASE tool. The engineers are thus prevented from additional work i.e. the measurement itself and the collection of the values taken. Additionally this consideration needs the provision of fundamental model based interpretation mechanisms for the values measured.

Exemplary use of the approach presented here showed, that these methods work in practise. However, future work is necessary and will focus on the relationships between the quality found in the application of the developed control software package and the design metrics interpretation mechanisms.

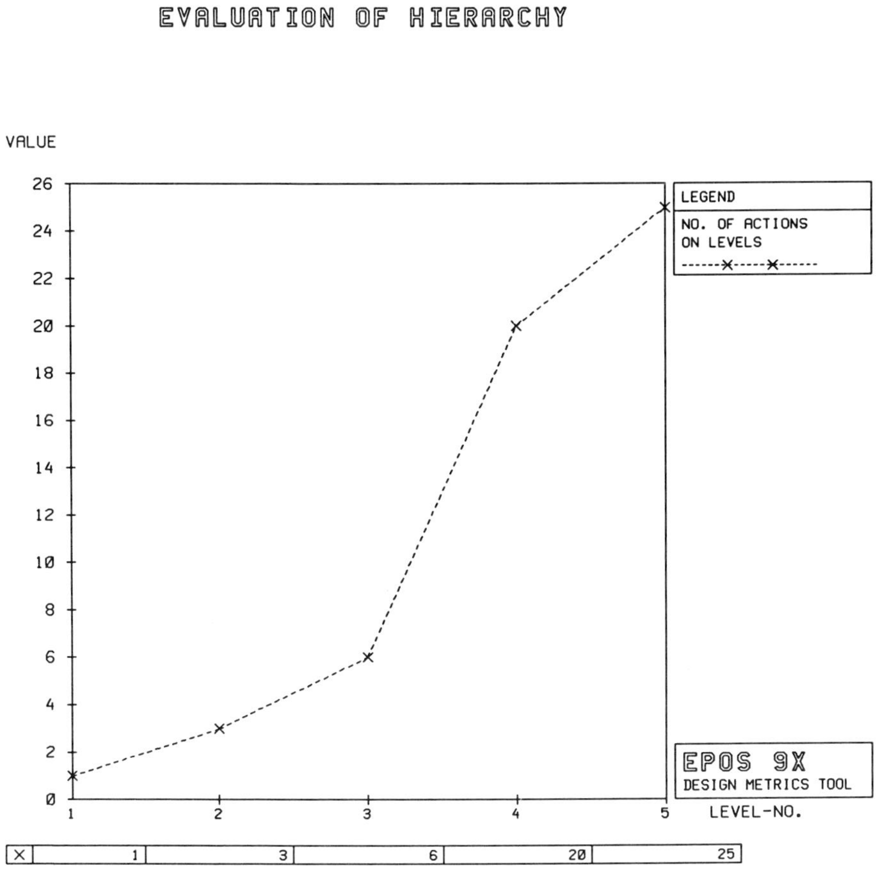

Fig. 7: Hierarchy measures (example for the output)

REFERENCES

[1] McClure, C., CASE is Software Automation (Prentice-Hall, Englewood Cliffs, 1989)

[2] Vincent, J., Waters, A., Sinclair, J., Software Quality Assurance (Prentice-Hall, Englewood Cliffs, 1988)

[3] Ward, W.T., Software Defect Prevention Using McCabe's Complexity Metric (Hewlett Packard Journal, April 1989) pp. 64-69

[4] Basili, V.R., Recent advances in Software Measurement (Proceedings of the 12. International Conference on Software Engineering 1990, IEEE Comp. Soc. Press, New York, NY, USA, 1990) pp. 44-49.

[5] Rombach, H.D., Design Measurement: Some Lessons Learned (IEEE Software, Vol. 7, No. 2, 1990) pp. 17-25

[6] Lauber, R. and Lempp, P., EPOS overview (available from GPP mbH, Kolpingring 18a, D-8024 Oberhaching, West Germany)

[7] Kitchenham, B.A. and Walker, J.G., A quantitative approach to monitoring software development (IEEE SE Journal Vol. 4, No. 1, January 89) pp 2-13.

[8] Yin, B.H. and Winchester, J.W., The establishment and use of measures to evaluate the quality of software designs (ACM software engineering notes, Vol.3 No.5, 1978) pp. 45-52.

[9] Blaschek, G., Statische Programmanalyse (Elektronische Rechenanlagen 27, Heft 2, 1985) pp 89-95.

[10] Halstead, M., Elements of software science (Elsevier North-Holland, New York 1977)

[11] McCabe, T.J.: A complexity measure (IEEE Transactions on software engineering, Vol. SE-2, No.4, Dec 1976) pp. 308-320.

[12] Zuse, H., Maßtheoretische Analyse von statischen Softwarekomplexitätsmaßen (Ph.D. thesis, Technische Universität Berlin, 1985)

[13] Ebert, Ch., Entwurf eines Modells zur Einbindung von Metriken in Entwurfsumgebungen (masters thesis at the institute of the authors, 1990).

Approving Software Products
W. Ehrenberger (Editor)
Elsevier Science Publishers B.V. (North-Holland)

Software Modification Assistance using Interaction Representation

Hiroyuki YAMADA* and Yoshikazu TEZUKA**

* Faculty of Engineering, Ehime University,
Matsuyama, Ehime 790, JAPAN

** Faculty of Engineering, Osaka University,
Suita, Osaka 565, JAPAN

Changing software costs much time and care owing to the side effect caused by the change (the interaction). This paper presents a Software Modification Support System (SMSS), which can assist the user by localizing the interaction in modifying a queuing simulation program. To accomplish assistance of the modification activity, our SMSS uses the information about interaction (Interaction Representation), which consists of the information about where the interaction occurs and how to deal with it. To represent such information, we introduce the Interaction Representation Language (IRL). Our IRL consists of high-level primitives corresponding to concepts relevant to management of the interaction. As a result, the IR has more readability than the information used in ordinary demon mechanism from a view point of description level. Furthermore, an example of modification of a ferry simulation program shows our system is prospective to make the modification easier.

1. Introduction

Software is often changed in order to debug it or to improve its performance and so on. However, it costs much time and care to change the software owing to a lot of non-creative operations caused by the change. In particular, a programmer must pay attention to side effect caused by the change. We call this kind of side effect interaction. That is, if he carelessly modify one part of software, some problems will be often introduced into the other parts. As a result, he must scrutinize the software for the interaction.

In order to modify software efficiently, the interaction need to be reduced. To accomplish this, the software need to have high modularity. So, the Object Oriented Programming Style (OOPS) has been introduced to elevate modularity [1]. However, software written in the OOPS is not free from the interaction perfectly, because several objects communicate with other objects to solve a given problem.

We have studied on an Software Modification Support System (SMSS) for a queuing simulation program [2,3,4] as one of the researches on the Software Maintenance Support Environment [5,6]. Our system can assist a user in

This work was supported in part by the Telecommunications Advancement Foundation.

modifying the software. That is, it gives him advice on how to deal with the interaction. In order to do so, our system uses the information about interaction, which consists of the information about where the interaction occurs and how to deal with it.

To represent such information, the data driven mechanism, "demon" [7] is usually used. The ordinary "demon" description is often represented in system description language. That is, it is represented by Lisp functions, for example. Thus, it is hard to understand the "demon" description. So, in order to have more readability than it, we have considered the Interaction Representation Language (IRL) [3,4]. This IRL consists of high-level primitives corresponding to concepts relevant to management for the interaction. As a result, the information written in the IRL has more readability than the ordinary "demon" description from a viewpoint of description level.

Firstly, we present interaction for software written in Object Oriented Language (OOL). Then, we present the overview of our IRL and how to represent information about interaction in this language. Secondly, this paper gives an outline of our system that can point out the interaction by means of the information represented in the IRL. Finally, this paper shows our approach is useful to make modification of software easier as an example of modification for a ferry simulation program.

2. Side effect caused by change

2.1 Interaction for software written in Object Oriented Language

An object consists of its internal data and procedures (methods) to deal with the data. Moreover, the method can only access to its own data. Therefore, the software written in OOL has high modularity. As a result, no influence on other objects occurs in modifying a method in the object. However, in actuality, the interaction will not be extinguished completely, because one object usually sends some messages to other objects in order to use functions in them. This paper supposes that when an object A uses a function in another object B, the object A is functionally related with the object B. Thus, several kinds of interaction will be left because of the functional relation between objects.

Moreover, This paper supposes that the interaction will occur in the following modification situations: change of an object (class) hierarchy, modification of methods and alteration of parameters. In case a new class is added to the class hierarchy, new methods to generate instances of the added class may be defined in other classes. Moreover, some methods in other classes may be modified in order to perform given tasks. In case a method is modified, in particular, a message pattern or a returned value of a method are altered, the methods calling the changed method must be modified. In case a parameter common to several methods is altered, all methods referring to it must be changed.

In order to suggest the where of the interaction occurring in these situations and how to deal with it, we have considered the Interaction Representation Language (IRL), which can represent the following information explicitly: (1) positions affected by interaction, (2) several kinds of information used to assist users in modifying the positions and (3) reasons for occurrence of the interaction.

2.2 Definition of Interaction Representation Language

The grammar of this language is defined with BNF terms as shown in Fig. 1. The superscript "*" means zero or more.

Each Interaction Representation (IR) describes the four relations we found to be important: class, method, parameter and resource. The class relation has information (<class interaction>) about the interaction caused by changing a class hierarchy. The method relation describes information (<method interaction>) about the interaction caused by changing a method. The

```
<Interaction Representation> ::=
    ((class_relation <class interaction>)
     (method_relation <method interaction>)
     (parameter_relation <parameter interaction>)
     (resource_relation <resource interaction>) )

<class interaction>::=
    (addition <method modification>*)
    (deletion <method modification>*)

<method interaction>::=
    (<message pattern> <method modification>*)*

<parameter interaction>::=
    (<parameter name> <method modification>*)*

<resource interaction>::=
    (addition <method modification>*)
    (deletion <method modification>*)
    (<resource name> <method modification>*)*

<method modification>::=
    ((condition <condition part>)
      (position (<message pattern (<class name>)))
      (reason <reason part>)
      (datum <data part>) )

<condition part>::= T ¦
    (<condition description>) ¦
    (<switch <condition part>) ¦
    <condition part>

<switch>::= and ¦ or ¦ not

<condition description>::= () ¦ (<string>)

<reason part>::= () ¦ (<explanation>)*

<data part>::= () ¦ (<data name> (<explanation>)*)*

<explanation>::= () ¦ <string>
```

Fig. 1. Grammar of Interaction Representation Language.

parameter relation has information (<parameter interaction>) about the interaction caused by changing a parameter's name or its type. The resource relation represents information (<resource interaction>) about the interaction caused by changing resources used in a queuing simulation program. This relation has task-specific information.

Moreover the information of resource relation can be represented by means of both the parameter relation and the class relation. However if both relations are used to represent the information about interaction for resources, the information is found here and there in IR. As a result, readability goes lower. Thus, the resource relation is introduced in order to elevate the readability.

The interaction information relevant to each relation is represented in a <method modification> in the relation. The <method modification> has several kinds of information about the interaction. It is used to assist a user in modifying software. It consists of four slots: condition, position, reason and datum. The condition slot has several conditions to determine that the <method modification> is applicable. When the all conditions in this slot are true, the <method modification> is applicable. Otherwise it is not applicable. If the condition slot has "T," the <method modification> is applicable unconditionally. The position slot has information about places influenced by interaction caused by changing object specified by the relation. That is, the place is represented by a pair of a <message pattern> and a <class name> including the method specified by the <message pattern>. The reason slot has why the interaction influences the place specified by the position slot. The content of this slot is shown in order to explain why the place needs modifying. The datum slot has the information about methods used to modify the place. The content of this slot is used to suggest the user what methods can be used. That is, both the reason slot and the datum slot are used to generate explanation about how to deal with the interaction. The explanation is generated from a template at present.

An example of IR is shown in Fig. 2. This is a part of the IR of the class SimulationObject in a queuing simulation program [2] mentioned in section 4. This IR has the class relation and the resource relation. If a class is defined newly, the "addition" part in the class relation is retrieved. Then, the condition part is checked. If the condition part is true, this information is applicable. As a result, we can find the interaction caused by adding a new class by the position slot in this information.

3. A Software Modification Support System

3.1 An outline of Our System

We have implemented an Software Modification Support System, which receives the information relevant to the change (the changed place and the operation done to change) from the user, and then points out the interaction. This system is composed of four modules (an interaction detector module, a user interface module, an explanation generator module and a modification module) and two files (an object-level software file and an interaction representation file) as shown in Fig. 3.

The user interactively gives the information relevant to change through the user interface module. The interaction detector module is a main part of our SMSS. When a program is changed, this module retrieves an appropriate IR from the interaction representation file, interprets it, then, points out where the interaction occurs. At this time, the user interface module can give suggestions for how to deal with interaction to him. The explanation generator module generates an explanation about how to treat the interaction and why the interaction occurs. The modification module is used to modify the positions effected by interaction. This module retrieves the method to be

```
(class_relation
   (addition
      ((condition (not (the class is an abstract class)))
       (position  (defineArrivalSchedule (FerrySimulation)))
       (reason ("new object must be scheduled to arrive at the simulation"))
       (datum (scheduleArrivalOf:accordingTo:startingAt:  ())
               (scheduleArrivalOf:accordingTo: ())
               (scheduleArrivalOf:at: ()) ) ) )
   (deletion
      ((condition (not ("the class is an abstract class")))
       (position (defineArrivalSchedule (FerrySimulation)))
       (reason ("instance generation part is removed"))
       (datum ()) ) ) )
(resource_relation
   (addition
      ((condition T)
       (position (defineResources (FerrySimulation)))
       (reason ("new resource must be defined before the use"))
       (datum (produce:of: ("static resource"))
                (coordinate: ("coordinated resource")) ) ) ) )
```

Fig. 2. A part of Interaction Representation of the class SimulationObject.

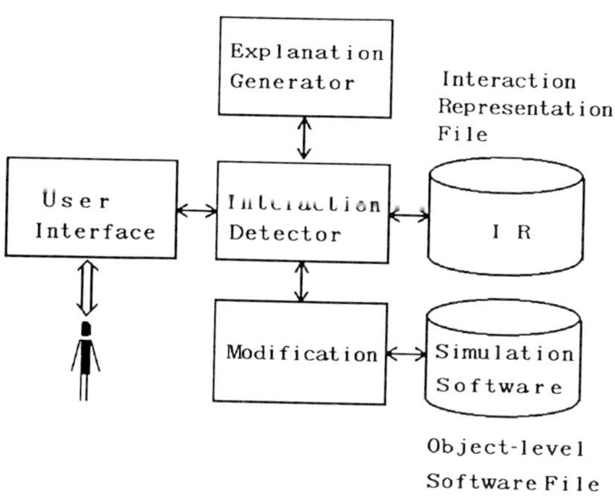

Fig. 3. System Organization.

modified from the object-level software file, then, puts it on an editor. The user modifies it himself.

The object-level software file has object-level software described in Object Oriented Lisp language that we have implemented [3]. This language is a kind of Frame Representation language including a message passing mechanism. The interaction representation file has information about interaction for the object-level software. The information about interaction is represented in IRL. In current system, all IRs are described by the expert programmer that developed the software.

All IRs relevant to one class are stored in one frame. We call this kind of frame a documentation class. Thus, each class always has one documentation class as shown in Fig. 4. Moreover, IRs common to several classes are stored in the documentation class of their super class. These IRs can be inherited from the super documentation class. As a result, redundancy of the information can be avoided.

3.2 Outline of our SMSS's behavior

In order to deal with interaction automatically, our system uses event (event to treat a class hierarchy and class definitions) driven mechanism. Our system works as follows.

When the object-level software is changed, the user inputs information relevant to the change. Then, the system retrieves IR relevant to the change through the class hierarchy. At first, IR is retrieved from the documentation class of the changed class. If an appropriate IR could not be found there, it is retrieved from the documentation class of the class's superclass. When the appropriate IR is found, the system interprets it, and then suggests where interaction may occur. After the user modifies the method pointed out by the system, he inputs the information about the change. Then, the system checks occurrence of new interaction caused by modifying the method. The system deals with the new interaction, if any.

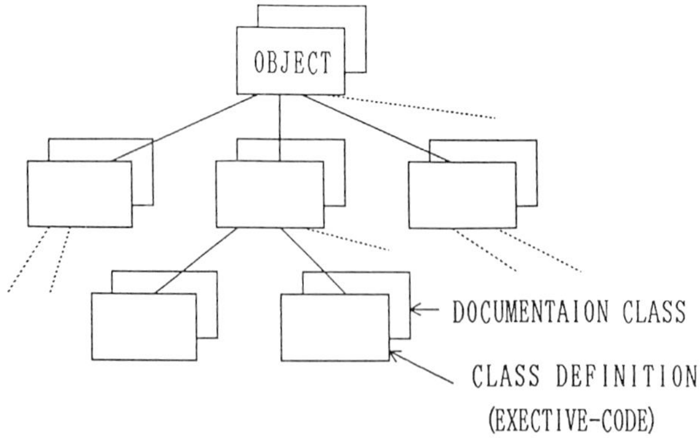

Fig. 4. Classes and documentation classes.

When no appropriate IR is found, the system asks the user whether the other interaction occurs. When an appropriate IR is not found and the user can not point out new interaction any more, the system finishes its work.

4. Software Modification Assistance

4.1 Object-level Software

The object-level software file has a queuing simulation program, which has been implemented according to [1]. This simulation is executed by event-driven style. An event is defined as an occurrence to move the internal state of simulated system.

This program consists of both fundamental classes and application classes. The former classes have fundamental parts of execution for queuing simulation. That is, they contain general methods common to the simulation program. Thus, these classes will be usually unmodified by the user, even if his simulation model is changed. The latter classes are defined according to an actual simulation model. These classes will be modified according to the change of user's specification. Thus, if the user wants to change the simulation model, he has only to redefine methods in application classes.

The model for Ferry simulation from [1] is considered here. This example is the simulation that a ferry shuttling between an island and a mainland carries vehicles. The ferry starts service at 7:00 a.m. and ends at 7:00 p.m. The ferry has a capacity of 6 cars. The ferry crosses from one side to the other if the capacity becomes full or no car waits at the landing place of the ferry. Moreover, the resting place for the evening is the mainland. A class hierarchy of this simulation program is shown in Fig. 5.

The methods describing the ferry simulation appear in the application classes, that is, subclasses of the class SimulationObject and a subclass of the class Simulation. The subclasses of the class SimulationObject (the class

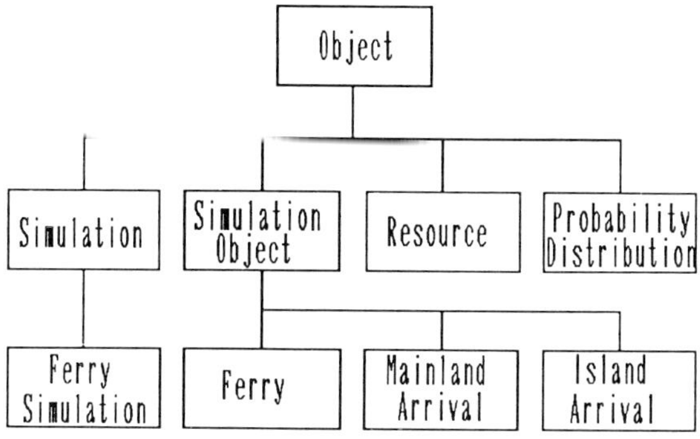

Fig. 5. A class hierarchy of the queuing simulation software for a ferry shuttling.

Ferry, the class MainlandArrival and the class IslandArrival) have methods for their tasks to be done while an object stays in the simulation. For example, generation of resources is defined in the class IslandArrival. In this simulation model, the resources corresponds to the vehicle arriving to the mainland or the island, that is, generation of the resources corresponds to the vehicles' arrival. Moreover, the subclass of the class Simulation (the class FerrySimulation) has methods for scheduling of arrival interval for each simulation object and the definition of resources used in the simulation.

4.2 An Example of assistance for modifying software

Suppose that the user tries to change the simulation model mentioned above into another. A new simulation model represents the simulation that the ferry carries a truck in addition to the cars and the truck goes from the mainland to get more supplies, and then goes to the island to deliver them. At this time, the ferry only crosses from one side to the other if it has the truck. The major changes are (1) to define a new class Truck so that the truck can pick up more supplies in the mainland, then it can deliver them in the island, (2) to change the class Ferry so that the ferry can load/unload the truck and (3) to synchronize the ferry's task with the truck's task. The following explains about the addition of the new class.

The user informs the system of adding a new class Truck. The system works the modification module to define the class. Then he defines it as shown in Fig. 6. In this case, it is added to the class SimulationObject. As a result, IR relevant to addition of the class will be retrieved from the documentation class of the class SimulationObject because the documentation class of the class Truck is not existed in the system.

Before using information of the addition part in the IR (see Fig. 2), the system asks the user if all conditions in the condition slot are true. In this case, the condition is true. Hence, the system can indicate that the method defineArrivalSchedule in the class FerrySimulation ought to be modified. Then, he modifies this method on the editor as shown in Fig. 7.

```
(Truck class
  (superclass (value (SimulationObject)))
  (class_variable ())
  (instance_variable ())
  (instance_method
   (tasks
     (while t
       (send self produceResource: 'TruckCrossing)
       (send self holdFor:
             (send (send Uniform from:to: 15 30) next))
       (send self produceResource: 'TruckCrossing)
       (send self holdFor:
             (send (send Uniform from:to: 30 45) next))))
 ))
```

Fig. 6. Definition of a new class Truck.

Since the method was modified, interaction may occur in other classes newly. Hence, IR relevant to modification of the method is retrieved from the documentation class of the class FerrySimulation. However, this IR is not applicable because condition in this IR is not true. Since there is no other appropriate IR and the user does not point out interaction newly, the system finishes its work relevant to adding the class Truck.

The behavior of our system is shown in Fig. 8. This example shows that adding a new class to existing software can be efficiently carried out by following the system's directions.

5. Conclusion

This paper discussed about software modification assistance using the interaction representation. Then, we presented the Software Modification Support System. Finally, this paper showed that the SMSS can help a user to modify software. The features of this system are shown as follows.

```
(defineArrivalSchedule ()
   (send self scheduleArrivalOf:accordingTo:startingAt:
              MainlandArrival
              (send Exponential parameter: 0.15)
              420.0)
   (send self scheduleArrivalOf:accordingTo:startingAt:
              IslandArrival
              (send Exponential parameter: 0.15)
              420.0)
   (send self scheduleArrivalOf:at:
              (send Ferry new) 420.0))
```

Before Modification.

```
(defineArrivalSchedule ()
   (send self scheduleArrivalOf:at: (send Truck new) 420.0)
   (send self scheduleArrivalOf:accordingTo:startingAt:
              MainlandArrival
              (send Exponential parameter: 0.15)
              420.0)
   (send self scheduleArrivalOf:accordingTo:startingAt:
              IslandArrival
              (send Exponential parameter: 0.15)
              420.0)
   (send self scheduleArrivalOf:at:
              (send Ferry new) 420.0))
```

After Modification.

Fig. 7. Modification of the method defineArrivalSchedule in class FerrySimulation.

1) To build up the knowledge base about the interaction, the information about how to deal with the interaction is explicitly represented in IRL we proposed. Our IRL consists of high-level primitives corresponding to concepts relevant to management of the interaction. As a result, the IR has more readability than information used in the ordinary demon mechanism from a view point of description level.

2) Our SMSS assists the programers by the localizing the interaction. As a result, modifying software can be efficiently carried out by following the SMSS's directions. Moreover, since the SMSS has information about the

```
What do you want to do?
Addition (A) ; Change (C) ; Deletion (D) ; Quit (Q) ? a
What do you want to add?
Class (C) ; Method (M) ; Resource (R) ; Parameter (P) ; Other (O) ? c
What is the class name?
Truck

New class Truck is defined.
OK ? (Y/N) y

         <Define new class "Truck">

The class Truck was defined.
Following condition is true (T) or not (F) ?

the class is an abstract class? f

By addition of the class Truck, interaction may occur in
method defineArrivalSchedule of the class FerrySimulation.

What do you want to do?
Modify (M) ; Explanation (E) ; Show the method (S) ; Cancel (C) ? e

Since a new object must be scheduled to arrive at the simulation,
you need modify the method defineArrivalSchedule.
You can use the methods as follows in modifying it.
1) scheduleArrivalOf:accordingTo:startingAt:
2) scheduleArrivalOf:accordingTo:
3) scheduleArrivalOf:at:

What do you want to do?
Modify (M) ; Explanation (E) ; Show the method (S) ; Cancel (C) ? m

      <Modify the method "defineArrivalSchedule">

Following condition is true (T) or not (F) ?

message pattern is changed? f

Is there any interaction caused by modification of the
method defineArrivalSchedule of the class FerrySimulation? (Y/N) n

Is there any interaction caused by addition of the
class Truck? (Y/N) n

Is there any change? (Y/N) y
```

Fig. 8. An example of our system's behavior.

interaction, the user has been released from the need to remember many details and to keep track of the many relations among these details.

3) Our approach will be applicable to other application programs described in Object Oriented Language because the IR represents functional relation between objects. Moreover, our approach is practical than the ordinary knowledge based programming systems because of acquiring knowledge about interaction from source codes directly.

In our current SMSS, an expert software developer must describe entire IR for target software. This will be an heavy burden on him. Therefore, as our future work, we will have to implement the mechanism to help the user describe IR.

Acknowledgment

We wish to acknowledge valuable discussions with Professor H. SANADA of Osaka University and Dr. T. YAMAGUCHI of Shizuoka University. We also thank Professor Y. TAKAMATSU, Professor T. AIBARA and Dr. K. MURAKAMI of Ehime University for their helpful contributions.

References

[1] Goldberg, A. and Robinson, D., "Smalltalk-80 The Language and Its Implementation", Addison-Wesley, 1983.
[2] Yamada, H., Yamaguchi, T., Sanada, H., Kakusho, O. and Tezuka, Y., "KNOWLEDGE BASED SOFTWARE DEVELOPMENT SUPPORT SYSTEM FOR QUEUEING NETWORK SIMULATION", Pacific Computer Communications Symposium, pp.348-350, OCT., 1985.
[3] Yamada, H., Yamaguchi, T., Sanada, H., Kakusho, O. and Tezuka, Y., "Simulation Software Development Support System Based on Knowledge Programming Approach", Proc. of Conference on Recent Advances in Simulation of Complex Systems JSST, pp.294-299, JULY, 1986.
[4] Yamada, H., Yamaguchi, T., Sanada, H., Kakusho, O. and Tezuka, Y., "High-Level User Interface Directed Language in Modifying Software ", Trans. IEICE Japan, Vol. J70-D, No. 11, pp. 2308-2313, NOV. 1987 (in Japanese).
[5] Wild, C. and Maly, K., "Towards a Software Maintenance Support Environment", Proc. of CSM-88, pp. 80-85, 1988.
[6] Waters,R.C., "The Programmer's Apprentice: Knowledge Based Program Editing", IEEE Trans. on Software Eng., vol. SE-8, pp.1-12, JAN., 1982.
[7] Rufflin, J. F., Derksen, J. A. and Waldinger, R. J., "QA4 : A procedural calculus for intuitive reasoning", Tech. Note, 73, SRI International, Palo Alto, Calif., NOV. 1972.
[8] Dhar, V. and Jarke, M., "Dependency Directed Reasoning and Learning in Systems Maintenance Support", IEEE Trans. on Software Eng., Vol. SE-14, pp. 211-227, FEB., 1988.

SESSION 9

CASE STUDIES

Approving Software Products
W. Ehrenberger (Editor)
Elsevier Science Publishers B.V. (North-Holland)

ASSESSING QUALITY FOR BUSINESS ORIENTED SOFTWARE : AN EXPERIENCE ON APPLICATION SUPPORTED BY RELATIONAL DATA BASE

G.Agostoni (*), P.Caliman (*), D.Di Ventura (**)

(*) Etnoteam SpA
via A.Bono Cairoli, 34
Milano, Italy
(**) Universita' di Milano
Dipartimento di Scienze dell'Informazione
Milano, Italy

1. Introduction.

In the last years, quality assurance has been, and ever more it will be, one of the most important tasks of software project management. Within the project development schema, it is possible to single out the main activities that should be performed in order to better software-product quality ([SCOPE]) :

. management
. development
. verification and validation
. measurement.

Each activity belongs to one or more steps of the most widespread software-life-cycle model [Boehm], that partition the life cycle into phases ranging from project requirements to project maintenance.
Third-generation-language quality assessment has basically evolved, using these concepts, from the easy and intuitive models to high-complexity evaluation schemata.
Many third-generation-language aspects have been taken into account to define possible evaluation techniques, for it is feasible to find many ways to classify these techniques. Here it is shown a classification that in some way matches the purposes of the developed work; in particular, the classification proposed belongs to the code-measuring phase of the quality-evaluation process :

. Lexical analysis (eg. Halstead Software Science [Halstead], size metrics, comment density, etc.) : metrics are defined on the basis of considerations regarding the code lexical structure; these metrics try to evaluate the code from statistical estimations concerning the use of language constructs.
. Structural analysis (eg. cyclomatic number [McCabe], etc.) : metrics are defined considering the logical structure of the program; the logical flow diagram (control flow graph) is analyzed in order to

obtain some measure of its complexity.

- Architectural analysis (eg. [Myers]) : metrics try to evaluate characteristics that belong to the program design, modularity, etc. . High level program structure is analyzed to obtain some measure of its architectural complexity and to test the effective use of high-level-program-management techniques.

To clarify the conditions and the goals of metrics in software development, it is worth recalling the reasons why it is important trying to evaluate software products :

- The most substantial one is that the achievement of computer potentiality depends deeply on the ability to create reliable software : it hence comes in a straightforward manner, that the role of metrics and models should be to help programmers in performing the software-development target.
- A correct use of this approach leads to a good software-development management : managers can employ measurement techniques to characterize and control essential features of software products and to predict development time.

It can now be clear the fundamental purpose in determining new metrics : helping managers and programmers in their own tasks. Plainly, most of quality evaluation techniques till now employed respect these conditions and they are useful tools for program development; nevertheless, it is essential to keep in mind these facts as basic constraints within the process of metrics definition.
For all these reasons, software metrics and models have been two of the most important components of software development in the last years.

On the other hand, we can observe that the programming-language market is now evolving towards new kind of products, the so-called fourth-generation languages (4GL). The creation of this kind of programming mean is due to precise trends observed within managers, developers and end users :

- the increasing need of user-friendly and easy-to-use languages, in order to augment the number of software producers;
- the possibility of developing software starting from higher-level product requirements, to obtain more reliable products spending less time;
- the need of obtaining higher-comprehensiveness products, in order to lower software-maintenance load.

The existence of such languages, the market expansion in this environment and the increasing presence of third-generation-language-oriented evaluation tools, result in a growing need of looking for new techniques specialized in 4GL evaluation.

2. General purposes.

The basic purpose of this work is the research of evaluation techniques for a particular 4GL. Partly, the achievement of 4GL potentiality derives from the ability to automatically navigate through a complex information structure. Within 4GLs exists a class, called

database languages, that group fourth-generation tools possessing this particular capability. In our opinion, the capability just described has a great importance and it will have a basic role in 4GLs market evolution.
For this reason too, in this research it has been analyzed SQL (Structured Query Language), a 4GL specialized in managing databases from the relational algebra model ([Codd]) point of view, that has ever more become a de-facto standard in the RDBMS (Relational Database Management System) world. Besides, SQL has been adopted as an official standard by ISO (International Standard Organization) and by ANSI (American National Standards Institute).
In a more specific way, the principal goal is to evaluate SQL language complexity and data integrity by mean of lexical analysis; this involves that attempts to rank SQL code from different kind of considerations (structural, architectural or even others) will not be investigated.
In order to experiment with the developed metrics, there has been the need to access to some quantity of SQL source code : for a commercial version of this language in a particular working environment has been chosen.
You can find a lot of SQL-based products that accomplish a SQL usable version; within this set, it has been selected SQL Oracle, trademark of Oracle Corporation. The reason of this choice is essentially the diffusion of this product at commercial level, also due to its availability on different hardware platforms.

3. SQL : a description.

SQL consists basically of a set of tools carried out to manage data inside a relational database (a relational database is from the logical point of view, a database that is perceived as a collection of tables, where a table is an unordered collection of rows). It is in fact a language that fulfills, in some practical form, some of the features of the abstract relational model.
SQL has been built around three main concepts regarding database management : definition, manipulation and control; it is in fact possible to group SQL instruction set in the following areas :

. DDL (Data Definition Language) includes instructions for the structure definition of a database; in practice it groups tools to exactly define the tables that will receive data. Almost always in a large database, this section requires the highest skill in order to optimize not only the data structure, but also to minimize the load that most employed functions will need; hence this task is performed by a specialized group headed by the database administrator (DBA).

. DML (Data Manipulation Language) includes instructions to query and update a database. It is probably the most utilized section : its statements allow most part of the tasks over a database that can be performed by less-skilled users. The general consequence of these instructions is the modification of data stored in the tables.

. DCL (Data Control Language) includes instructions to manage two substantial items : data security and data sharing. One of the basic goal of RDBMS is to physically record data only once (this obviously implies the impossibility to give each user a duplication of needed data), in order to guarantee information integrity. This gives rise to a clearer situation, not allowing self-contradictory data; on the other hand this cause the exigency to share data between different users or applications. Sharing in turn determine security problems :

which users or applications are allowed to access certain data? From these considerations derive the concepts of DBA, user's identification, authorization, password, privilege, etc. that are all applied in this section.

Another useful concept is the work session; we can define it as the number of events that happen between the time a user connects to SQL and the time he or she disconnects. Events are in general statements taken from the three sections above.

It will now be given an overview of SQL strengths and weaknesses (see [Date] for more details); among SQL strongpoints are :

. simple data structure,
. powerful operators,
. short learning period,
. integrated data definition and data manipulation;

among the weakpoints :

. lack of orthogonality [Date] (a language is orthogonal if independent concepts are kept independent and are not mixed together),
. aspects of the relational model not supported.

In the end, it is worth noting that SQL is a database language, for it is not a complete programming language : a typical application will involve not only SQL statements, but also statements in some host language (usually a third generation language) adding features not present within the specialized environment. To allow this kind of behavior, standardization committees included a set of appendixes defining embedded SQL versions for some third generation languages.

4. SQL code evaluation methodology.

4.1. What exactly to evaluate.

As we said above, the research main aim is to evaluate reliability and integrity (we will define them as quality attributes). Trying to focus in a more practical way these concepts, it is essential to pay attention to the following : in general it is very difficult to straight observe them and it is nearly impossible to measure them; therefore it is almost primary to find indirect ways for their evaluation. For this purpose we believe useful to point out some ideas and clarifications from the related literature.
Generally, product evaluation refer to a quality model in order to allow the use of a coherent method. After the identification of the quality attributes that are to be assessed (in our research, reliability and integrity), the following step is to redefine each one by mean of observable quality criteria. Various theories try to solve this problem defining functions that relate quality attributes to quality criteria, for example Arthur's ([Arthur]), McCall's ([McCall]), Boehm's ([Boehm1]), etc. .
Complying with these ideas, we will in a following section give some quality criteria for the two quality attributes we chose.

4.2. Basic considerations over database languages.

Within database-language world, it is possible to focus some fundamental considerations which are correct from an intuitive point of view, and for that can be useful in defining new evaluation criteria.
In advance, it is necessary the definition of two concepts that will be used in the following :

. By structural complexity of a database is meant the number of tables (included the number of columns of each table) together with the relationships existing between the tables; in other words it is meant the logical complexity of data organization.
. By database extension is meant the quantity of information (i.e. data) present in a database; that is concretely speaking, the number of rows inserted into a specific data structure.

It is now possible to explain the considerations anticipated above :

. The greater is the extension of a database, the lower is the user's control level when performing an operation : it can increase the phenomenon of user's bad perception of operation cost and consequences.
. The more complex is the data structure, the lower is the user's understanding level when performing an operation : it will be more difficult to interact with the system.
. The more complex is the kind of operation involved, the less will be self-evident the actual congruence of system answers.

It is remarkable that the last point has gained importance with 4GL use : in general 4GLs own higher-semantic-level constructions than third generation languages, where higher semantic level means the presence of instructions that put away the user from the lowest coding levels. This feature yield user's higher concentration on substantial goals, but it can cause a phenomenon called by Martin semantic disintegrity ([Martin]) : user can misunderstand operation complexity because the statements are apparently easy, determining even greater incongruity and finally making worse system user-friendlyness.

4.3. Some considerations over SQL.

Taking into account the structure of SQL, it is possible to stress some useful considerations.
SQL division into DDL, DML and DCL can bring the idea to use different evaluation schema for each section : considering the different targets of every section, we can give specific weights connected with relative importances we attribute to each class or we can evaluate specific language aspects. More in detail, we will try to evaluate structural complexity from data definition section, operational complexity from data manipulation section and data integrity from data control section.
Analyzing SQL statements it is observable that the data manipulation section is the most complex, and in particular that exist a trouble in language comprehensiveness due to a specific DML statement : the query (Select) one. In fact while it is quite a simple task to understand a generic SQL statement, the interpretation of certain queries that can be

written in SQL is not so obvious ([Ceri,Got]) : therefore it will be worth keeping the attention on this SQL peculiarity, trying to measure it.

4.4. The quality criteria.

Given all these considerations and following the concepts of the previous sections, we will now try to use them to define quality criteria for the quality attributes we chose :

- Reliability : this quality attribute is function of the following quality criteria : complexity, consistency, fault tolerance, modularity. Within the purposes of this research we decided to point our efforts to evaluate the complexity criterion. In order to assess it we have taken into account metrics deduced from Halstead's Software Science ([Halstead]), applying them following operand and operator SQL definitions; besides we defined a new Software-Science-derived metric (we called it 'readability') that seek an evaluation of users' (programmers, analysts, etc.) effort to understand SQL statements. Referring to Halstead's elementary metrics ([Halstead]), we defined readability (R) as :

$$\text{Readability } R = \frac{\text{Effort}}{\text{Instr\_Compl}}$$

- Integrity : this quality attribute is function of the following quality criteria : auditability, instrumentation, security. The easiest way SQL allow you to measure this attribute is evaluating security criterion. To assess this quality criterion we can evaluate SQL instructions belonging to DCL section.

5. Research project realization.

The research has been realized by the use of different tools running on two systems.

The starting step has been the fulfillment of a SQL parser; it is worth noting that it has been considered a specific version of SQL-Oracle : version 5.1 released in 1988 ([Oracle]). The parser has been realized on a workstation SUN 3/60 with operating system UNIX BSD 4.3 . The reason of this choice has been the availability under this operating system of a sophisticated environment for the development of language processors. This environment consists essentially of two software tools : YACC (Yet Another Compiler Compiler) and LEX (LEXical analyzer). LEX is a tool that reads a particular specification file and generates the corresponding lexical analyzer; moreover the lexical analyzer generated is in essence a C program that, when compiled, behaves as defined in the LEX specification file. In the same way, YACC generates a C program that recognize a grammar detailed in another specification file. Using these tools, we carried out the SQL parser.

Then, we performed the porting on a MicroVAX system with VMS (Virtual Machine System) operating system. This step was possible because the output of YACC and LEX is a C program, so we merely performed text file porting : when recompiled in the new system we obtained a SQL parser running on MicroVAX. In this system exists a software quality analysis tool called Logiscope produced by Verilog that facilitate software evaluation; in particular it allows metrics representation by mean of different kind of graphs. Hence, we fulfilled a communication interface between SQL parser and this product, in order to obtain clear representations of the metrics applied to SQL.

6. Experimenting with SQL.

6.1. General approach.

According to the SQL definition given, the experimentation focus on specific analysis of each SQL area (i.e. the sublanguages DDL, DML and DCL). We considered as uncompounded component the single SQL instructions; hence we evaluated a number of metrics for each statement body.
We grouped the measured data in two ways :

- by the SQL sublanguage to whom each instruction belongs, so to obtain a total measure inside each SQL section;
- by kind of instruction (i.e. all 'select' instructions, all 'insert' instructions, all 'delete' instructions, etc.); hence we obtained a specific-meaning evaluation of each instruction kind.

6.2. Each instruction evaluation.

We gathered the metrics computed for each instruction according to the above principles. In this way we found different ranges for both sublanguage and instruction kind criterion, confirming our expectations : the different goals achieved by each group result in not-uniform-value classes. In fact these results didn't allow meaningful indications from a statistical point of view, and led us to wide the SQL code experimentation; further this drove us to enlarge the initial methodology.

6.2.1. The experts point of view.

We decided to look for estimations allowing an instruction-complexity evaluation coming from programmers' experience and unbiased in respect with software measurement concepts. In order to obtain such results we referred to a group of skilled SQL programmers with an average experience of four years, but without a specific knowledge of evaluation methodology. This allowed the acquirement of a set of judgements measuring the perceived complexity by specialized users about a number of SQL instructions; therefore we asked the staff to fill in a form for each instruction, with marks ranging from 1 to 10, directly proportional to the analyzed aspect estimation.
This work gave us a way to understand the meaningfulness of the SQL code examined in respect with a standard use of the language. Moreover, it gave us a way to compare the judgement criteria of high-skilled personnel with evaluation criteria contained in Halstead's Software Science.

6.2.2. A practical approach.

Carrying out these ideas, we realized the importance of the following : programmer-complexity evaluation measures both semantic of the instruction and trouble for its perception, while standard lexical metrics

are not able to weigh this characteristic. It is hence normal to find some differences between the two points of view.
In spite of that, we tried to find a method to bring the new evaluation technique near to users' complexity perception. Inside of Halstead's metrics we believe the nearest one to this concept is the effort metric (E); hence we defined a compound metric that includes both R and E, and we called it 'inst_compl' (i.e. Instruction Complexity or IC) :

$$\text{Instr\_Compl} \quad IC = \frac{\text{Nb\_Stmt}}{\text{Eta1} + \text{Eta2}}$$

The statistical correlation arising from the set of programmers' marks and the set of computed IC is quite good, and it shows a linear direct correlation between these data. Moreover, this correlation is confirmed by each sublanguage measurement and by each kind of instruction.
In the following picture, is shown an example related to some DML 'select' instructions together with the computed values and the marks given :

INSTRUCTION	E	R	IC	Mark
SELECT16	963.25	0.34	2833.09	5.5
....	......	...	....	...
SELECT20	255.78	0.23	1112.09	4.5
SELECT21	262.50	0.20	1312.50	4.5
....	......	...	....	...
SELECT28	1486.74	0.23	6464.09	7.5
SELECT29	**2598.51**	**0.17**	**15285.35**	**8**
....	......	...	....	...
....	......	...	....	...

As more detailed example here we examine a specific select instruction (the one identified by 'select29'). In the pictures below are reported the whole instruction body and the Kiviat's graphical representation of Halstead's metrics - together with the new defined metrics R and IC - provided by Logiscope :

```
Select deptno, min(sal), max(sal)
   from employee  /* select from the table called employee */
   where deptno in (
                    select   dept.deptno  /* a nested select statement */
                           from dept, employee
                           where dept.deptno = employee.deptno
                              and loc in ('dallas', 'chicago') )
    group by  deptno  /* output format option */
    having min (sal) > ( select avg (sal)
                            from employee)
    order by deptno;
```

AXIS	LOWER	UPPER	VALUE
NB_STMT	4	10	11
NB_COM	0	5	3
ETA2	4	20	21
N2	2	10	7
ETA1	5	25	44
N1	2	15	7
P_LENGTH	10	30	65
V_SIZE	5	20	14
P_SIZE	10.20	55.45	39.30
P_VOLUME	20.50	131.20	247.47
INT_CONT	14.30	21.90	23.56
NB_ERROR	0.00	0.03	0.06
P_LEVEL	0.00	0.60	0.09
DIFFICUL	2.50	6.80	10.49
EFFORT	45.00	1020.00	2598.51
P_TIME	11.00	44.00	144.36
L_LEVEL	2.09	6.43	2.24
D_COMM	0.00	1.00	0.27
D_LING	2.00	6.00	5.90
READ	0.17	0.50	0.16

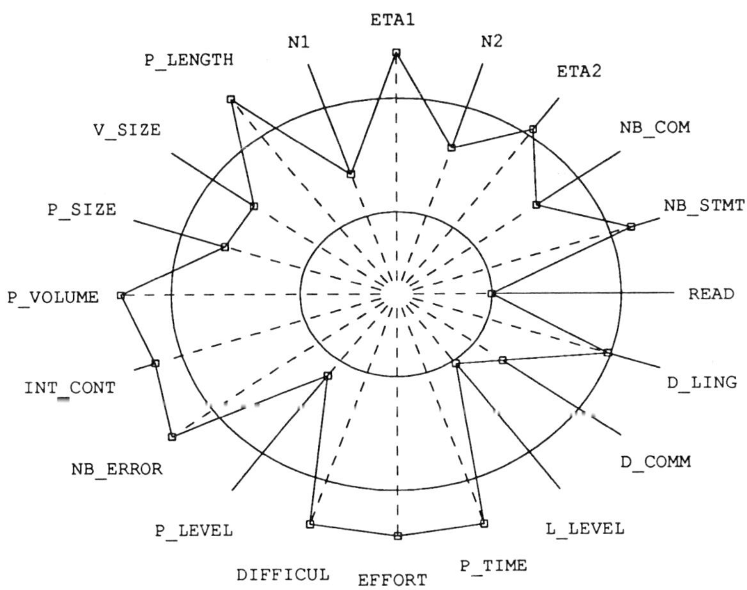

Application: SOURCE | Kiviat diagram | Language: SQL

Module: SELECT29 | Level: Module

6.3. The comparison between sections.

The different purposes of each sublanguage allow a meaningful grouping inside each area. Moreover it is possible and reasonable to look for and detect certain kind of relationships among areas.
We found the most meaningful statistical correlation between DDL and DML sections. This relation is from a logical point of view twofold. As said above, the project of a database structure must be performed by a high-skilled staff in order to take into account various tasks ranging from structure clearness to performance efficiency. While database structure complexity affects the effort required to manipulate data by mean of DML, a high overload in manipulating informations can unveil a structure not well suited with the needed purposes. In other words, a high DML complexity means in general an inadequate DDL organization, and a high DDL complexity is adequate as far as an intense DML load is detected.
To make clear these ideas, we built a table containing - for each possible combination of high and low complexity levels of DDL and DML - some related considerations :

DDL / DML	HIGH	LOW
HIGH	In spite of a high-complexity structure, the DML load is too high.	The DML load, in general too high, and the low DDL level display a bad project structure.
LOW	The database structure is well suited to the DML requirements. This is the best situation.	The database structure, even easy, is suitable for the required DML use.

As a final consideration, we are trying to define an index to point out 'query functional complexity' (QFC) considering together the effort of the query instruction itself and the related data structure definition; plainly, as part of this index we have to include the human factor (i.e. user ability). Practically, we defined QFC as a function of the 'select' effort, the global DDL effort and a scalar value representing human influence that varies relating to users' skill, experience, etc. :

Query Functional Complexity $QFC = F(E(query), E(DDL), HF)$

The select effort is Halstead's measure limited to the instruction itself and the global DDL effort is the Halstead's measure over the whole DDL instruction set.

Acknowledgments.

The authors thank the Etnoteam database staff and in particular B.Guarneri and A.Sciessere for their contributions, F.Vignola and M.Pravettoni for their useful comments about SQL, P.Ferrara for his help in the parser development, R.Lancellotti for his suggestions.

References.

[Arthur] : J.Arthur
Software quality measurement
Datamation, Dec 1984.

[Boehm] : B.W.Boehm
Software Engineering Economics
Prentice-Hall, New York, 1981.

[Boehm1] : B.W.Boehm, H.Kaspar, M.Lipow, G.J.MacLeod, M.J.Merrit
Characteristics of software quality
North-Holland, 1978.

[Ceri,Got]: S.Ceri, G.Gottlob
Translating SQL into relational algebra : optimization, semantics and equivalence of SQL queries
IEEE Transactions on Software Engineering
vol.SE-11, no.4, April 1985.

[Codd] : E.F.Codd
A relational model for large shared data banks
Communications of the ACM
vol.13, No.6, June 1970.

[Date] : C.J.Date
A guide to SQL standard
Addison-Wesley, June 1987.

[Halstead]: M.H.Halstead
Elements of Software Science
Elsevier 1977, North Holland.

[Martin] : J.Martin
Fourth-generation languages, vol.1
Prentice-Hall, 1985.

[McCabe] : T.J.McCabe
A Complexity Measure
IEEE Transactions on Software Engineering
December 1976, pp.308-320.

[McCall] : J.A.McCall, P.K.Richards, G.F.Walters
Factors in software quality, vol.1-2-3
US Rome Air Development Center Reports, 1977.

[Myers] : G.J.Myers
Reliable Software through Composite Design
Van Nostrand Reinhold Company, New York, 1975.

[Oracle] : Oracle corporation
SQL language reference manual, version 5.1
September 1988.

[SCOPE] : SCOPE
Software Certification : State of the Art
CEC, September 1989.

Approving Software Products
W. Ehrenberger (Editor)
Elsevier Science Publishers B.V. (North-Holland)

Experiences of Automated Data Collection from Software Development Projects

K B Kirkwood, R B Hunter and A K Rae
University of Strathclyde

Abstract

Collection of process and product data from software projects can be expensive and unreliable. Automating the collection process should increase confidence in data accuracy and lower the cost of collection. This paper discusses some of the issues involved in collecting software data from various software tools, and recounts experience of automated data collection gained within the context of the ESPRIT II project SCOPE. The views expressed are those of the authors and are not necessarily held by the SCOPE consortium.

1. Introduction

A pre-requisite for the assessment and improvement of software processes and products is the availability of valid data on which to base analysis. Measures and associated models appeal to software engineering academics and industrialists alike as a potential means of quantifying the process of software development in terms of quality, schedule and cost. Successful quantification is necessary for accurate prediction and control of both process and product and is a basis for process enhancement, cost modelling, software experimentation and quality assurance.

To date, paper-based data capture techniques have been favoured by data collectors. In practice, development personnel are interviewed and/or issued with forms to be completed at appropriate stages of development. One of the first projects to employ this technique was the Alvey-funded Software Data Library (SWDL) project [1], set up to produce a library of software engineering data. Data collection was also an important element of contemporary ESPRIT I projects in the domain of software quality and reliability, such as MUSE Q/R, REQUEST and TRUST. Indeed, such was the overlap between SWDL and REQUEST [2], the two were able to profitably collaborate. Data collection also features in current ESPRIT II projects, particularly those concerned directly with metrics, such as: COSMOS (Cost Management with Metrics of Specification), MERMAID (A Metrication, Estimation and Resource Modelling Aid), METKIT (Metrics Educational Toolkit), and SCOPE (Software CertificatiOn Programme in Europe).

In the USA, paper data collection forms have been used by the Software Engineering Laboratory (SEL) [3] to record data on flight dynamics projects. The SEL have also contributed software development data to DACS (Data Analysis Centre for Software), an American organisation whose function is to maintain a computer database of empirical data collected on the development and maintenance of software, for dissemination to software researchers. A similar record is maintained at Purdue University, Indiana, [4] as input to a Software Metrics Data Collection (SMDC) system which supports statistical and graphical analysis and is intended to facilitate research into applications for metrics.

These initiatives have helped identify a number of problems with paper based data capture. Firstly, the method is heavily dependent on *individuals* who ultimately can not be relied upon to complete forms either accurately or at the appropriate time. Secondly, the method is obtrusive, insofar as it can be perceived as a chore by development staff and an overhead by project management. Thirdly, the method necessitates repeated transcription of original data thereby introducing additional room for error.

Ideally, data collection would be immediate, systematic and unobtrusive. To avoid dependency on human memory and ensure the capture of transient data, collection should occur as soon as possible after data becomes available. In addition, prompt data collection facilitates some validation and analysis during a project's lifespan, affording the opportunity to correct erroneous collection procedures and if necessary [5] secure management cooperation by offering immediate returns on data collection. Collection has to be planned. Clearly, some data collection activities should focus on management whilst others should concentrate on programmers throughout. But at all times, data should be collected by data cognisant staff, otherwise there is a risk of introducing errors due to ignorance of the data itself. Staff and management are most likely to comply with requirements if inconvenience is minimised. Making the activity as subliminal as possible also helps counter the so called Hawthorne effect [6] which holds that the behaviour of individuals is influenced by the presence of observers. Similarly, to obtain cooperation and unbiased data, it may be necessary to reassure staff that data collected will not be used to assess individual performance.

Automated data collection is inherently systematic, immediate and unobtrusive. Manual methods of data collection may yet have a role to play in the collection of subjective data where the environment prevents the use of on-line electronic forms tools. However, in all cases automatic methods of data capture are preferable having the advantages of: speed, automatic data validation, reliability, reducing labour overheads and eliminating the human element from data transcription and conversion. Potential sources of process data include Computer Aided Software Engineering (CASE) tools, project planning tools, resource management tools and configuration management tools. Similarly, product data may be sourced from static and dynamic analysis tools.

Ideally, we would want to integrate collection within the development environment, and this approach is discussed in a paper by Kitchenham and McDermid [7], which addresses the issue of designing IPSEs with a view to automatic data collection. A paper by Rombach [8] surveys five current SEEs (Software Engineering Environment, aka. IPSEs) (viz. ARCADIA, DAPSE, GENESIS, ISTAR and TAME) with particular emphasis on TAME (Tailoring a Measurement Environment) [9] under development at the University of Maryland, USA. Researchers on the TAME project have learned the importance of automated support [10] arguing that the volume of data accumulated during a measurement based approach to software development simply can not be managed manually. Also, without automated support, results can not be relayed to interested parties in time to support project decisions.

This paper describes work aimed at gathering data from development, management and assessment tools with a minimum of manual effort. The work was carried out as part of the ESPRIT II SCOPE (Software CertificatiOn Programme in Europe) project, therefore the primary concern was certification-related data, some of which was obtained from static analysis tools and all of which was destined for storage in a database. Nevertheless, we believe the experience gained to be of general applicability, particularly as databases and the various interfacing requirements they impose on data collection are in widespread use.

The next section discusses how data may be collected 'automatically' from a number of software tools, while section 3 describes how these ideas were applied in a software development case study monitored by the University of Strathclyde as part of the SCOPE project. Section 4 describes experiences of collecting data from various static analysis tools. Finally, section 5 draws some conclusions from our experiences.

Before proceeding further we ought to explain the meanings of some of the terms which we use in this paper in connection with data collection.

- Data collection is the identification and capture of relevant (process or product) data for analysis or transfer to a suitable repository.

- Data transfer is the movement of collected data from the collection site to a suitable repository.

- Automatic data collection is used to refer to a data collection process which does not require human intervention.
- Automated data collection refers to a data collection process which is mainly automatic but may require some human guidance.

2 Automated Data Collection

2.1 Aims and potential

The basic aim of data collection is to obtain data for purposes such as statistical analysis or report generation. Irrespective of the purpose of collection, it will generally be necessary to store the data in a repository. This might be a database; a spreadsheet; statistical analysis package; or simply a file, depending on the complexity of the data (in terms of structure) and desired analysis. We note that :

- required data is often held by tools rendering manual collection redundant.
- the repository is almost always hosted on a computer.

As the data source and destination are often both computer-based, it is sensible to explore the possibility of automating the process of collection and transfer so that a minimum of human guidance is required. This automation has several attendant advantages, for example increased confidence in accuracy and reduced cost.

Software tools are commonly used to support the software production process and assess its products. Many of these tools are potential sources of process and product data. Several approaches may be taken to the collection of such data for example, recording on paper followed by entry into electronic forms. A better method would automate the collection, perhaps by means of a collection tool which interfaced with the existing tool, to produce output in the required form. As far as data collection is concerned, the ideal situation would be that development tools are hosted in a Software Engineering Environment (S.E.E.) as this has mechanisms and an an interface suitable for automated collection. However, the state-of-the-practice is that Environments are not widely used, many developers use a loosely-coupled set of tools based around a conventional operating system (in Alvey terms, a first generation IPSE). For the time being, at least, there is therefore a necessity to pursue the automation of data capture from independent tools.

We repeat that the goal of automation can be considered as minimisation of the human guidance required for collection of the required data and provision of it in a form suitable for input to a 'repository'.

2.2 Classification of tools

Any approach to automation is driven by the tools which hold the required data. For example, where the source code for a tool is available it is often a good idea to make alterations to produce output in the required form. However, source code for commercial tools is seldom available for data-collectors to 'tinker' with so it is usually necessary to interface a 'collection tool' to the data-holding tool.

Some examples of tools which hold relevant and potentially collectable data are :

CASE tools	e.g. design metrics, change data
Operating systems	e.g. resource data
Version Control systems	e.g. change data
Configuration Management systems	e.g. configuration information

Static and dynamic analysis systems	e.g. code metrics, coverage measures
Test-case tools	e.g. test metrics

A collection tool, and its interface, are strongly dependent on the corresponding data-holding tool. Three classes of these tools can be identified:

1) Tools which have a 'program' interface by means of which a collection tool can interface directly with the tool while it executes. These generally have been designed with inter-operability in mind and are well-suited to automated collection.

e.g. The CASE tool TEAMWORK which supports specification and design
The version control tool DEC CMS,
SEE-based tools

2) Tools which produce output files from which data can be extracted with little or no difficulty, usually in an off-line fashion. There form a broad spectrum - in general, collection is possible but can be complex.

e.g. The static analysis system LOGISCOPE [11],
The version control system RCS (UNIX)

3) Tools which have output which is difficult to capture (e.g. graphs, histograms) or which have output files the format of which is unknown or difficult to process. Typically, these tools produce graphical output using a windowing system (such as X-Windows) making capture of data infeasible.

e.g. An early version of the static analyser QUALMS [12]

Note that these classes are not mutually exclusive. For example, DEC CMS belongs to both the first and second category since collection can be based around its program interface or its output reports. LOGISCOPE fits into the second and third since metrics can be output to a file, but call-graph information is only available graphically.

2.2.1 Tools which produce output files

Many common tools fit into the second category making it worthwhile to concentrate on these. Output can be in one or more files or may only appear on the user's terminal and is pretty-printed or unformatted.

Automated collection is greatly simplified if tool output is to a file so that where output usually appears on a terminal it should be captured somehow. Tools which do not use windowing systems will generally produce terminal output by means of a mechanism provided by the host operating system. Many operating systems have the facility to 'redirect' this type of output to a file rather than a terminal; this is a candidate capture mechanism. Where tools use windowing systems, capture of output is sometimes possible, but it is generally in the form of a pixel-dump from which collection would be difficult.

Once tool output has been obtained in a file, the required data must be extracted. This may not be trivial because it is quite common to find output containing textual labels, messages, separators, and tables constructed from characters such as | and =. Such extraneous characters must be separated from the useful data, this problem can often be solved by employing a parser-generator (such as YACC [13]) and/or lexical analyser generator (such as LEX [13]). YACC uses a syntax specification (in a language similar to BNF) to automatically generate C code which recognises a sequence of matching tokens. The syntax specification can have C language statements embedded so that particular actions are carried out when certain parts of the input have been read. A YACC-based collection tool would therefore consist of a specification of the syntax of the input file (that is, the output from the data-holding tool) together with code to process the input as it is recognised and produce appropriate output. Some advantages of using YACC in the construction of collection tools are:

- Automatic code generation means that (providing the syntax specification is correct) parts of the code require less testing and take less effort to produce.
- The syntax specification is easily checked against the file format so validation is simplified.
- Changes in file format are easily accommodated by means of alteration of the syntax specification.

LEX provides support to YACC by processing character strings and converting them into tokens according to programmer-defined rules. LEX has a language for expressing regular expressions and has advantages similar to those of YACC. Depending on the file format, either LEX may be adequate or both YACC and LEX may be needed.

2.3 Output from the collection process

It is of considerable importance when devising a collection scheme to keep in mind the destination of the collected data as it determines the output from the collection process. Where this destination is a database, it may seem useful to interface the collection tool to the database directly - this is the method adopted by some previous collection schemes. However, this is undesirable for reasons which include the following:

- It prevents collection from tools hosted on a machine remote from the database. This is a severe restriction since analysis is often performed at a different installation from development.
- A consequence is that the collection tool is specific to a particular database management system and data model. Changes to the model would require change to the collection tool. This should not be necessary since the data items collected by the tool will not usually change.

Our experience suggests that a collection interface can be defined, based on text files without any implied structure which have been called 'flat-files'. These have the advantages of being easily transferred and processed by simple tools. Maximum independence is achieved if the format relates to the data collected from the tool rather than the database.

2.4 Tool usage

When considering data collection from tools, it is prudent to consider the context of tool use. For example, where collection is from a version control system, an investigation into the usage of the system should be performed. Different organisations and personnel use version-control systems in different ways; each usage leading to different data. One usage might involve a configuration-item being checked-in after each change, however minor. Another usage might only check-in items after a number of changes had been effected. In each case, the same type of data is collected, however the interpretation given to it must be different if a proper analysis is to be effected.

2.5 Naming conventions

There are several reasons why establishment of naming conventions is a prerequisite to effective automated collection. Firstly, an entity must be uniquely identifiable so that it can be distinguished from other entities of the same type. This is obviously necessary if the results of analysis are to be related to the original data source. For example, if data analysis leads to the conclusion that a particular source module is unduly complex and requires inspection then the naming convention for that module must be such that it can be located. This is only possible if modules are uniquely identifiable and it is preferable if an identifier relates to the module name.

In general, data collected relates to some object or to a relationship between objects. For example, the cyclomatic number metric relates to the object *program procedure* (or function) whereas test coverage is an attribute of the relationship between a set of test data and a module. Where two or more tools collect data relating to the same entity (i.e. data which are attributes of that entity) or relationship then it must be ensured that the names used to identify the entity/relationship can be harmonised. For example, a static analyser may provide data relating to 'module' entities, where a module may be a procedure or function in the language concerned. The tool will have some convention for module identification, perhaps the module name. If another analyser, or some other tool, collects data pertaining to a module, it will be useful to relate the results to that of the analyser. The association of the results of one analyser with those of another tool can only be achieved if the module identification used by both can be linked. This is best done by devising a naming convention for all entities and ensuring that all collection tools use it.

Here we will detail an example of a possible naming convention for program procedures or functions. Many programming languages do not require components such as procedures or functions to have a unique name; a *path name* would be required in order to identify each component uniquely. For example, consider a Pascal program with two procedures named *setup,* one declared within a procedure *date* and one within a procedure *time,* where *date* and *time* are declared at the outermost level. The strings *date.setup* and *time.setup* could be used to identify the two procedures uniquely. To summarize, where a Pascal procedure or function is declared within another, a path name containing the names of each enclosing procedure or function is required for unique identification. This scheme serves to identify a module within a source file but requires extension to allow identification of a module within a system comprising multiple programs.

A naming convention is language-dependent and to be useful, must be adopted throughout the collection. A convention such as that detailed above can lead to long component names, for example, the names required to identify Ada procedures are likely to be particularly long since procedure names can be overloaded, so that the parameter types have to be included in the path names.

3 Strathclyde Case Study

3.1 Case-study

As part of a contribution to the ESPRIT II SCOPE project, the University of Strathclyde has been collecting data from a software development hosted by an (external) industrial organisation. A collection scheme was devised and implemented to enable collection and transfer of data from this "case-study" to a database.

The software project monitored is from the data-processing domain and is of medium size with a total effort of over 10 man-years and code size in excess of 50 thousand lines. The Language used is C and the target machine is a DEC VAX running VMS.

There were three main factors which encouraged an emphasis on automated collection from the case-study. Firstly, the development was sizeable and so manual collection would have been expensive both in terms of the overhead imposed on the host organisation and in terms of the effort required to manage the data. The second factor was that at the time of starting collection, the development had progressed to the system test stage. Much of the data of interest was available but was 'locked' in the tools used by the developers. Thirdly, the extent of tool support to the development process suggested that an automated approach would be fruitful. Automated collection centered around (but was not limited to) the following tools:

• A Configuration Management System	: change information for code & documents
• A resource management tool	: project tasks, schedule dates, effort data
• The static analysis system LOGISCOPE	: source code metrics, e.g. Halstead metrics
• The static analyser QUALMS	: flowgraph metrics, e.g. VINAP
• The document analyser STYLE	: document readability, word distributions

In the fourth section of this paper, we will concentrate on detailing experience of collection from the last three tools, which we classify as static analysers.

3.2 Confidentiality

An issue which influenced our data collection was confidentiality. Although this is more of a political issue than a technical issue, it did nevertheless significantly influence the cost and feasibility of the collection. For example, many commercial organisations, including the host of our case-study, are unwilling to allow a third-party to have possession of source code relating to a software project. This can constrain the collection effort since source code must be analysed at the development site and therefore analysis tools must be available for the development hardware.

4 Experience of data collection from static analysis tools

4.1 Applying static analysers

Static analysis tools process source code without executing it, examples are QUALIGRAPH [14], QUALMS [12], LINT [13], LOGISCOPE[11], MALPAS[15], SPADE[15] and TESTBED[16]. Some of these tools may provide support for other activities such as development or testing though here we are not concerned with this. The purpose of static analysis can be to analyse the code (for conformance to standards, anomaly detection) or to present abstractions of the code (e.g. flowgraph, call-tree) or to calculate code-based metrics (e.g. McCabe's cyclomatic number).

This section details the authors' experience of data collection from certain static analysis tools which evaluate complexity and other source code metrics, in addition the document analyser STYLE is considered. It should be emphasised that the experience has been mostly gained as a result of applying the static analysers to the industrial case-study mentioned earlier rather than in a research context.

Typical features of static analysis tools are :

- a language-dependent "front end" for analysing the source code and a language-independent "back end" for evaluation and output of the metrics.
- a complex menu system for interactive use.
- graphical output.

The front-end/back-end paradigm allows source code analysis and metric evaluation to take place at different sites - a useful feature if, for confidentiality reasons, the source code cannot be taken from the development site. An added complexity however, is that metric values may originate from the front-end of the analyser as well as the back-end. The case-study monitored by University of Strathclyde was subject to normal commercial confidentiality constraints meaning that source code could not be removed from the host company's jurisdiction. It was therefore necessary to do all source code analysis at the development installation. This was achieved by using the front-end of the tools at the development site and transferring the intermediate files to the analysis site for processing by the back-end.

The use of a menu system is not consistent with ensuring a particular output from an analysis tool. Most static analysis, and other, tools are intended for interactive use and expect the user to supply information; select from options; and respond to prompts. An example option is the production of output files (which may be used as input to a data-collection process). To ensure that a tool is operated in an appropriate way it is best to devise operating instructions. Alternatively, the human operator can be replaced by a program employed to activate the tool and supply input as necessary. An operating system command language program (such as a UNIX shell-script) can be used for this 'Usage Management'. In addition to ensuring that the static analyser is used in a 'standard' way this should also help to make the metric collection process efficient.

We have already noted that graphical output is not conducive to data collection.

Next, we will detail our experiences with applying the tools LOGISCOPE, QUALMS and STYLE, concentrating some of the issues already identified : Usage management, Naming conventions and Data collection.

4.2 LOGISCOPE

LOGISCOPE [11] is a static and dynamic analysis system developed and marketed by VERILOG of Toulouse, France. Collection of dynamic analysis results is beyond the scope of this paper and shall not be addressed further.

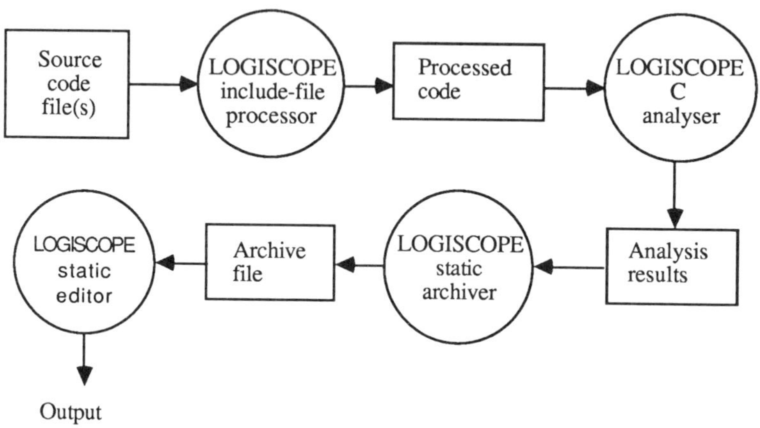

Figure 1. Architecture of C LOGISCOPE

As can be seen from the above diagram, usage of the LOGISCOPE static analysis system is not trivial. There are several components, each of which must be activated separately with options selected in response to menus and prompts. This presents the user with a significant problem, especially when analysing a large system.

The code pertaining to the case-study monitored consisted of over 300 files. To perform analysis, an operator would need to activate the appropriate LOGISCOPE components over

300 times and supply a total of more that 2500 options/responses. Such an approach would have been error-prone and was therefore not attempted.

To ease this difficulty, a tool was developed to act as an executive, controlling the execution of the LOGISCOPE components and supplying input automatically, as required. This "Usage manager" presents a high-level interface to the user, requiring supply of a list of files for processing.

LOGISCOPE produces data relating to two entity-types : the 'module' and the 'application'. For the case of the language Pascal a module is considered to be a procedure, or function, or the program body itself, while in C, a module is a function. An application is, roughly speaking, the whole program although it can in fact be any collection of modules having a non-trivial non-disjoint call-graph. Note that a software project may produce a system, which can consist of several complete programs and therefore can have several 'application' entities.

For each module, LOGISCOPE calculates source code metrics such as Halstead's software science measures and McCabe's cyclomatic number. For each application, call-graph metrics such as Structural Complexity and Testability and Control Entropy are calculated. A full list can be found in [17].

The naming convention used by LOGISCOPE results in unique identification of a module or application within a single program. The basis for the module identifier is the actual procedure or function name, however, since some languages do not require a module name to be unique, a language-dependent convention is used to obtain a program-unique module identifier. The LOGISCOPE convention does not however address the issue of unique identification of a module within a system comprising several programs. The naming convention therefore had to be modified to take account of the possibility of several modules from different programs within the same system having the same name. This can be done by including a subsystem identifier in the module identifier.

LOGISCOPE has a facility which allows a metrics file containing the values of a number of metrics to be generated. A collection tool was built to extract metric values from this file and output them in a form suitable for input to a database. This tool was built using both LEX and YACC.

4.3 QUALMS

QUALMS [12] is a static analyser developed at South Bank Polytechnic to calculate a number of metrics from a module's flowgraph. The external architecture of the QUALMS system is shown in the diagram below:

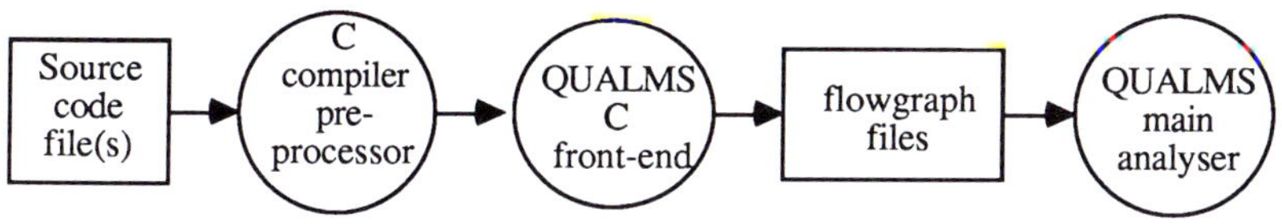

Figure 2. Architecture of QUALMS

QUALMS produces data relating to program modules where a module is for example, a procedure or function. For a full list of the metrics see [17]. The naming convention of the C front-end version 1.3 is the same as that of LOGISCOPE.

The original QUALMS main analyser displayed results (flowgraph, decomposition tree, metric values) using the X-windows windowing system. This made collection practically impossible. The approach taken for the SCOPE project was to have the source code for the QUALMS main analyser changed so that metrics were available in an output file. Additional alterations have eased the problem of usage management by means of a 'batch' option whereby many flowgraph files are automatically analysed to produce a metrics file.

4.4 STYLE

STYLE [18] is a UNIX-based analyser for English natural language. It computes a number of readability and other measures as well as giving counts of sentence and word types.

Figure 3 - Architecture of STYLE

STYLE is depicted above, there is one input file, an English natural language document. STYLE takes account of the formatting commands used by certain word processors. The output from STYLE is usually displayed on the user's terminal, it consists of text interspersed with metric values. As there is no run-time interaction required, management of the tool is straightforward. There is usually a single parameter, the filename of the document file.

The STYLE tool processes documentation. The unit presented for analysis can be from a single sentence to several concatenated documents although usually, complete documents would be separately analysed. The first line of the STYLE report identifies the document analysed; the file-name of the input file is taken to be the document identifier.

The output from STYLE is a textual report containing metric values : Part of such a report appears below :

```
sentence info:
        no. sent 92 no. wds 1631
        av sent lent 17.7 av word leng 5.48
        no. questions 2 no. imperatives 0
```

A collection tool was constructed using LEX to extract the required data from the STYLE report and output it in a form suitable for input to a database.

5 Conclusions

We have attempted to describe some of the issues involved in collecting software data from existing construction and analysis tools. (Clearly the situation would be different, and hopefully simpler, in the context of a SEE which provided appropriate tool interfaces.) As it is, a number of issues have to be considered if the data collected is to be reliable and comparable with data collected from other sources. These include

- controlled use of analysis tools
- adoption of component naming conventions

- analysis of file output
- design of suitable file interfaces

The solution to these issues will normally depend on an understanding of how the tools are used and the entities which they handle. In addition an understanding of the various outputs of the tools will be required.

We hope to have demonstrated that if the above issues are properly addressed, data collection from a variety of software tools can be achieved in an efficient and practical manner.

References

[1] Comer, P. and Bradley, P. and Ross, N., Software Data Collection Manual - Issue 1, (SWDL Deliverable No. 4), Consortium: GEC, ICL, Logica, NCC, STC, Systems Designers PLC., UKAEA.

[2] Ross, N., REQUEST : High-level Data Model Design Ref : REQUEST/STL-nfr/111/S3/DC-RP/01.1 (June 1989). Consortium: STC Technology Ltd., Cisi Ingénerie, Esacontrol, Elektronikcentralen, UKAEA-NCSR, Gesellschaft für Reaktorsicherheit, Thomson-CSF/DSE.

[3] Heller, G., Data Collection Procedures for the Rehosted SEL Database, Software Engineering Laboratory Series (Ref : SEL-87-008, Systems Development Branch, Code 552, Goddard Space Flight Center, Greenbelt, Maryland 20771, USA, October 1987).

[4] Yu, T. J.; Nejmeh, B. A.; Dunsmore, H. E.; Shen, V. Y., SMDC: An Interactive Software Metrics, Data Collection and Analysis System, The Journal of Systems and Software 8, pp. 39-46 (1988).

[5] Ross, N., The Collection and Use of Data for Monitoring Software Projects, Measurement for Software Control and Assurance (Elsevier Science, 1989), pp. 125-154.

[6] Brown, J., The Social Psychology of Industry (Penguin, 1954).

[7] Kitchenham, B. A. & McDermid, J. A., Software metrics and integrated project support environments. Software Engineering Journal,Vol. 1, No.1, (Jan '86) pp. 58-64 .

[8] Rombach, H. D., The rôle of measurement in ISEEs in: Ghezzi & McDermid (eds.), Proceedings of ESEC '89, Lecture Notes in Computer Science 387, (Springer-Verlag, 1989), pp. 65-85.

[9] Basili, V. R. & Rombach, D., The TAME Project: Towards Improvement-Oriented Software Environments IEEE Transactions on Software Engineering, Vol. 14 (1988).

[10] Rombach, H. D., Design Measurement : Some Lessons Learned. IEEE Software (Mar '90) pp. 17-25.

[11] VERILOG S.A., Toulouse, LOGISCOPE general presentation, VERILOG, 1989.

[12] Bache, R.M. & Leelasena, L., QUALMS - A Tool for Control Flow Analysis and Measurement (Department of Mathematics, Glasgow College, 11th July 1989).

[13] A.T. & T., Unix Programmers Guide (Prentice Hall, 1989).

[14] Computer Research and Innovation Center, Budapest, QUALIGRAPH user's manual.

[15] NCC, The STARTS Guide, Vol 2 (NCC, Manchester, 2nd Edition 1989).

[16] Program Analysers Ltd, TESTBED Technical Description (1989).

[17] AEA technology and Strathclyde University, SCOPE project deliverable report R1.3.1, Database Definition : Data & Data Issues Report (SCOPE project, Feb 1990).

[18] Cherry , L.L. and Vesterman, W., Writing Tools - the STYLE and DICTION programs, UNIX Time-sharing system : Programmer's Manual (Bell Laboratories, Murray Hill, New Jersey 07974, 1987).

Approving Software Products
W. Ehrenberger (Editor)
Elsevier Science Publishers B.V. (North-Holland)

VALIDATING TECHNOLOGIES FOR CERTIFYING SOFTWARE

Richard M. BACHE and Martin D. NEIL

Software Engineering Research Group,
Department of Mathematics,
Glasgow College,
Glasgow, UK

An important part of software certification will be the assessment of maintainability and testability by static analysis. Statistical techniques are discussed for establishing independent pass/fail criteria to be used when certifying products for maintainability and testability using structure and size metrics. This is realised by comparing and contrasting data collected from two software projects.

1. INTRODUCTION

Software certification will use a number of different certification technologies such as static analysis, testing, reliability modelling and inspection to assess the quality of software products. Although these methods are currently used in software development, it has yet to be established how they would be applied by an independent certification laboratory to arrive at a pass/fail decision.

A key task in setting up a certification system is establishing pass/fail criteria based on the data obtained by certification techniques. We show how pass/fail criteria can be derived for static measures to assess maintainability and testability. This is done by analysing structural and size metrics derived from two software products. We use statistical techniques to explore the measurable differences between two software products. From these exploratory results more objective pass/fail criteria can then be derived. This work is as part of the ESPRIT II Project 2151 SCOPE (Software CertificatiOn Programme in Europe) [1].

The metrics assessed in this paper are based on structure of control flow at the procedure or module level. However the proposed methods of analysis and derivation of pass/fail criteria are generally applicable to other types of measures and other certifiable attributes of software.

2. ASSESSING MAINTAINABILITY AND TESTABILITY

We define maintainability as the effort required to make changes to software after release. These changes may be bug fixes but in many cases will enhance or adapt the system or prepare the software for future maintenance [2]. Testability is the effort required to execute a chosen test strategy. Clearly testability relates closely to maintainability since after any maintenance change, the software may be re-tested.

Software certification will be applied to both bespoke software and off-the-shelf software. Bespoke products are supplied to a small number of customers (usually one) and are charged often on a 'cost plus' basis. The customer is thus required to pay for maintenance through the life of the product and this may, in the long term, exceed the original cost of development. In this situation, the customer will clearly be interested in the maintainability, and thus the testability, of the software since the quality costs in this area (costs incurred through lack of quality) will be borne by him.

When certifying bespoke products, it will be important to assess the maintainability of the delivered code. Of course it is not possible to predict the maintenance effort after release since this will depend on how the software is used and how the requirements and environment alter through the life-cycle. However, it is possible to determine if the properties which contribute to ease of maintenance are present. We show that these properties can be characterised in an objective and measurable way.

We propose that the maintainability and testability of software will depend on:

• The structure of the implementation (module size, structured programming),

• The level of self-documentation of the implementation (Eg module headers describing what a module does),

• The presence and quality of documentation (design documents, specs etc).

The last two of these may be implemented by means of structured checklists which determine the presence or absence of a particular feature. However in this paper we will concentrate on the first of these, structural measurement.

3. METRICS OF STRUCTURE

It is now widely recognised that the quality of software is strongly influenced by its structural properties [3, 4, 5]. In order to assess the structural properties of a software product, in an objective and repeatable way, we use metrics which characterise particular aspects of the structure. We do not propose that there is one single measure which will tell you everything, but rather identify a number of measures, each capturing a different structural property. In his paper we are concentrating on measurement based on two attributes: the control flow structure and size at the module level.

The measures were derived automatically from the source code using a research tools QUALMS [6] (QUality AnaLysis and Metrication Software). This is a research tools produced by South Bank Polytechnic. It derives flowgraphs and calculated metrics based on the Fenton-Whitty [7] theory. It produces 18 control flow metrics of which some are described below. The results are stored in a file which can be read by commercial statistics packages such as Statgraphics ™ and Statview 512+ ™.

We considered the following measures. Definitions are given in the literature, here we informally summarise what they seek to measure.

• Number of Nodes of the control flowgraph (NODES) - This measures the size of a module in terms of the number of imperative statements (ignoring declarations). It determines the size of a module in a way better defined than lines of code,

• McCabe's Cyclomatic Number [8] (MCCABE) - This measures the number of decisions in the program plus one. It has been proposed as a measure of complexity. We do not accept that it captures all the factors which would contribute to complexity. Nevertheless it is a useful measure of decisions,

• Is D-structured - [9] This is a two valued measure yielding 1 if the program uses only simple control structures (IF-THEN, IF-THEN_ELSE, WHILE-DO etc). Otherwise it yields zero. A value of zero would generally indicate the presence of GOTOs

• Biggest Prime (BIGGEST) - [9] control flow prime is an indecomposable element of the control flow. If this metric is high it indicates the presence of spaghetti code. Note that these measures are derived from the control flow graph rather than directly from the syntax, we can thus distinguish between the structured and unstructured use of GOTOs,

• Product VINAP metric (PVINAP)- [10] This is a composite measure which attempts to capture all the features of control flow structure and is based on a set of axioms,

• Branch Testability metric [11] (BRANCH) - It estimates the minimum number of executions necessary for branch coverage assuming that any path through the program is possible. It is one of a family of testability measures.

4. DETERMINING PASS/FAIL CRITERIA

4.1 Properties that Pass/Fail Criteria should possess

To be meaningful and lasting pass/fail criteria for certifying software should ideally be:

- derived from real software project data sets,
- based on large, representative sample sizes,
- objective, scientific and reproducible,
- constructed for only those metrics and techniques which have been demonstrated to have a predictive and pragmatic capability in certifying software,
- updated to include evidence gathered from new software products/projects and from recent research,
- independent of other pass/fail criteria.

Satisfaction of these conditions will result in pass/fail criteria which are dependable and applicable to many software products.

4.2 Strategies for Deriving Pass/Fail Criteria

The following is a list of the possible strategies for deriving pass/fail criteria.

• Single Expert's Judgement

The subjective judgement of a recognised expert is used to arrive at boundary values for criteria. Thus criteria chosen are totally dependent on the experts opinions, motivation, experience and knowledge.

• Expert Panel Judgement,

Selection of pass/fail criteria is made based on a group of experts. A disciplined technique such as the Delphi technique [12] as used in other disciplines could be applied.

• Internal Comparison,

This approach would derive pass/fail criteria by analysing the data from the product or process currently being certified. Analysis of the components of a software process/product is performed with the aim of deriving the criteria from the same product or process and then comparing the metrics against these pass/fail criteria.

Statistical methods such as outlier analysis and box-plots [13] could be used to detect those components which deviated from the 'norm' value for the whole product. In essence variation in quality is examined 'within' the software product or process to arrive at pass/fail criteria locally for one product.

• External Comparison

This approach would rely on the assessment of products or processes which have been analysed. This historical product/process data is used with the aim of obtaining pass/fail criteria. Statistical methods such as regression and discriminant analysis could be used to derive pass/fail criteria from the data derived from past products. Use of this approach will, in general, result in pass/fail criteria which are externally valid and dependable. Products which are to be certified are then assessed against these past products which are well understood. Here variation in quality is examined between past products/processes to arrive at pass/fail criteria for the future for all products.

• Composite Approach

The composite approach is a synthesis of expert judgement and statistical derivation. Essentially any of the above approaches can be used within this composite approach but the dangers of allocating too much power to the subjectivity should be realised. Use of the composite approach should be restricted to special cases where data is sufficient to warrant the use of statistical techniques but where the results of applying these techniques is not conclusive.

The fact that trade-offs' exist between quality attributes means that there is a danger that pass/fail criteria may not be independent. Trade-offs' exist in natural and social phenomenon and are not peculiar to software engineering. Pass/fail criteria may be dependent simply because the metrics used may measure similar attributes in the product. An example of this would be when using the same metrics to certify for different quality factors. The inclusion of many correlated metrics in a certification framework is undesirable because the cost of collecting dependent metrics may outweigh the benefit of the information. By minimising these trade-offs' we will minimise the cost of certifying software.

The predictive capability of metrics must be determined in order to demonstrate whether they really are related to actual software quality. Software certification may only apply those metrics which satisfy this requirement. A metric's correlation with a quality factor will indicate its predictive capability. Thus empirically validated metrics will be accorded the most power in the certification process.

4.3 External comparison of two projects

We have analysed data from two projects with the aim of demonstrating that the derivation of pass/fail criteria by external comparison is useful. The benefit of using external comparison is that by comparing the product to be certified with historical products which are reasonably well understood we can arrive at a pass/fail decision based on experience and hindsight. We consider pass/fail criteria derived from historical experience more likely to be representative and objective.

5. DATA ANALYSED

We used as the subject of our study, two software projects. Project A was an industrial project which performed mathematical calculations to monitor an industrial plant. It was produced by 9 people and reused code from previous software products including a bought-in numerical calculations package. It was estimated to have taken 60 person months. The languages of implementation were CORAL 66 and FORTRAN 77. The numerical package was written in FORTRAN77.

Project B was a research tool produced by research staff in an academic institution. It took about 20 person months to produce. It was written by three people and no code was reused from old systems. The project was implemented in C.

The relative sizes of the products are summarised in Table 1 below:

Table 1: Summary Statistics for Projects A and B

Project	Effort	Number of Modules	Size (nodes)	Mean Module Size
A	60	73	5942	81.4
B	20	163	2498	15.3

Effort is estimated in person-months.

It should be noted that the metrics being applied are language independent and are based on the structure of the software. Of course this does not mean that there are not significant differences in the metrics between different languages because of the way they are used.

6. STATISTICAL TECHNIQUES AND ANALYSIS

6.1 Descriptive

The first stage of analysis was to display the data in the form of histograms, box and whisker plots and pie charts. We include here only the histograms and a pie chart. Insight and understanding can be gained by looking at the graphs and this would provide useful information for managers who may wish to use this type of information to direct the development process. We do not propose that these graphical methods should be used for certification because interpretation is subjective. They are useful in that they indicate where to employ more elaborate statistical techniques.

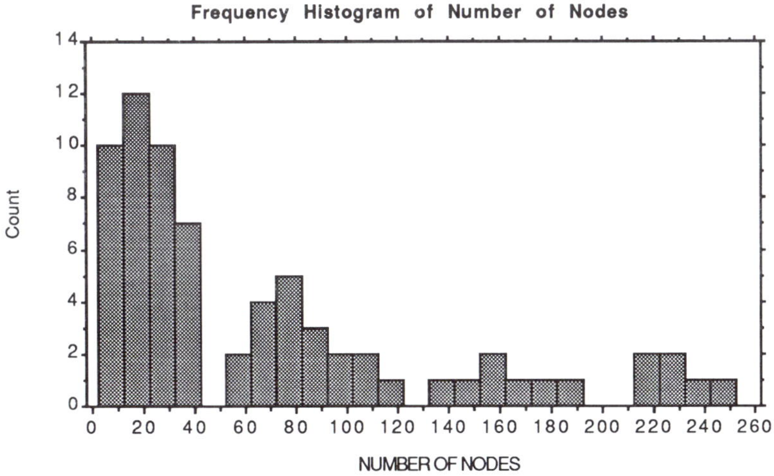

Figure 1: Frequency Distribution of Number of Nodes from Project A

Figures 1 and 2 show the number of nodes in each module. Clearly the mean in project A is much higher, but also, in Project A, there seem to be several clusters of modules. We believe this is due to different programmers preferring different module sizes. One module which had 859 nodes is not displayed here. A study by Dunsmore [14] showed that software which was reasonably modularised was easier to maintain than software which is over or under modularised. We would therefore want the distibution of module sizes to have a small variance around some ideal mean. In project B, most modules a have 12 nodes or less. This too could indicate a lack of maintainability by being over-modular.

For other metrics, three modules from project A have been excluded from the analysis because there were technical problems in calculating metrics.

Figure 3 and 4 show the depth of nesting for the two projects. The mode in both cases is 1. This means that in most modules the control constructs go only to one level (zero nesting is a sequential module with no branching). Very high levels of nesting will make the module difficult to understand (as thus to maintain). The outliers in project A may characterise such difficult modules.

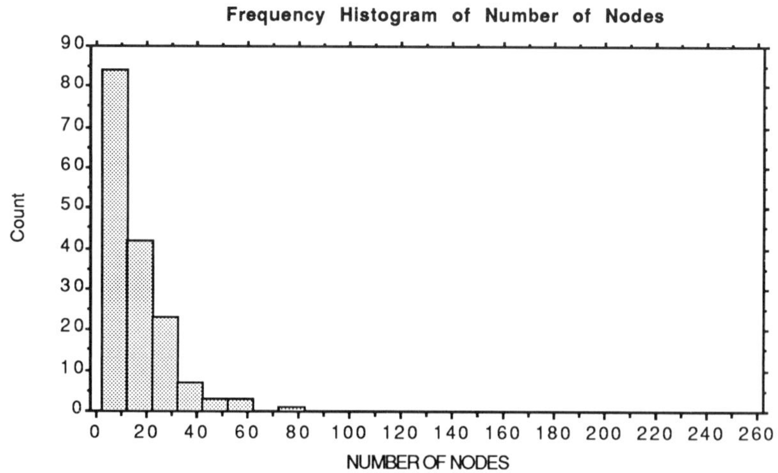

Figure 2: Frequency Distribution of Number of Nodes from Project B

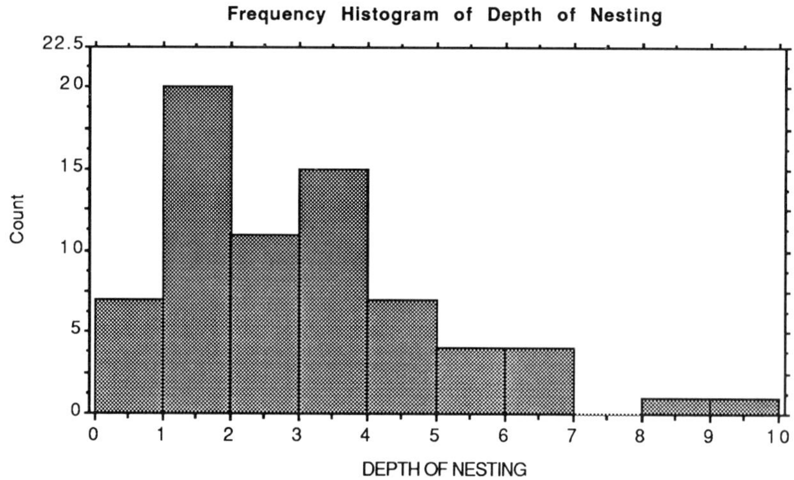

Figure 3: Depth of Nesting in Project A

The pie charts in figure 5 show that many of the modules in project A did not conform to the rules of structured programming. Most of the unstructured modules were in FORTRAN and a large number of those were from the bought-in package. This contrasts with project B where only one module was unstructured. To determine the degree of unstructuredness, we look at the biggest prime metric shown in figures 6 and 7. Primes of size 4 or less are well structured (WHILE and IF-THEN score 3, IF-THEN-ELSE scores 4). Primes up to around 8 in node size represent minor deviations from structured programming. Higher values indicate progressively more unstructured code. It has been argued by Dijskra and is now widely accepted [15] that these unstructured constructs lead to unmaintainable code.

Project A has a number of outliers with primes of around 40, this again would indicate spaghetti-like code which may be difficult to maintain. It should be noted that these were from the bought-in package. The only module in Project B which does not follow structured programming has a size of 6. It is unlikely that this would present a maintainer with a serious problem.

The McCabe's metric and the Product VINAP metric showed that project A had higher values which were unevenly distributed but in Project B the values were much lower with less variation. This concurred with the results of the number of nodes. These are not shown for reasons of space. The distribution branch testability metric was similar for both projects except that project A showed outliers which represent modules that are difficult to test. (Note that testability can only be calculated for structured modules).

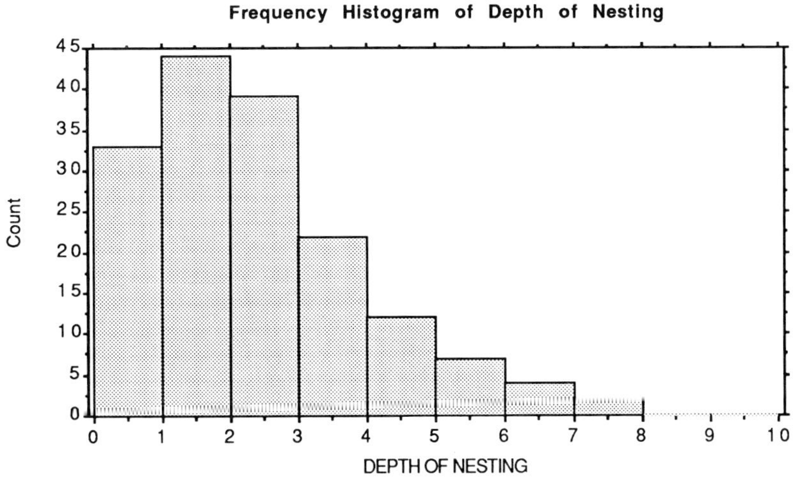

Figure 4: Depth of Nesting in Project B

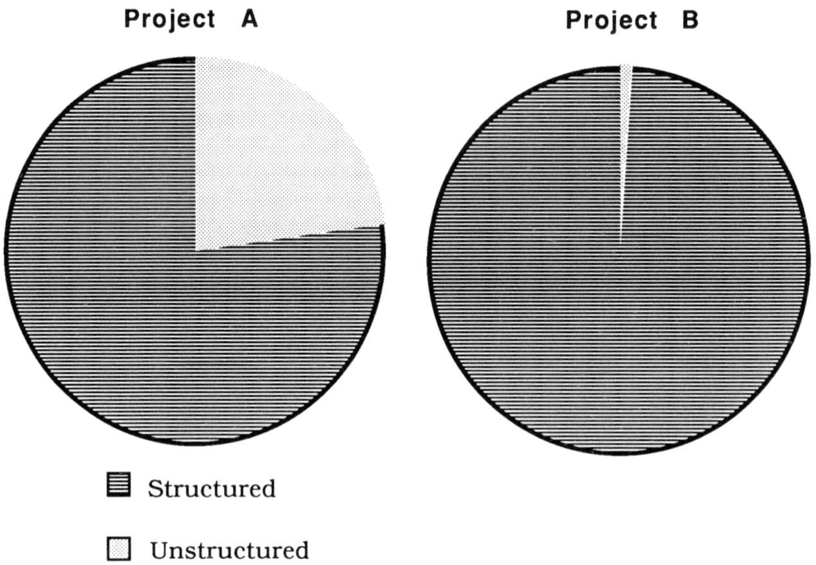

Figure 5: Use of structured programming in Projects A and B

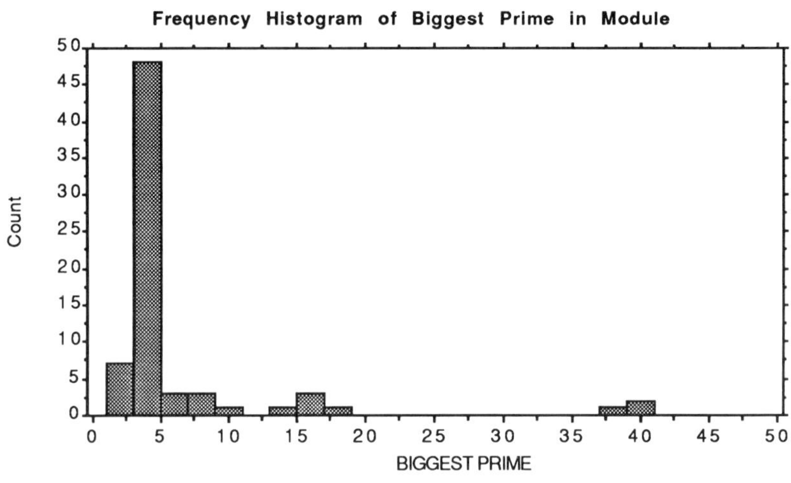

Figure 6: Biggest Prime per Module in Project A

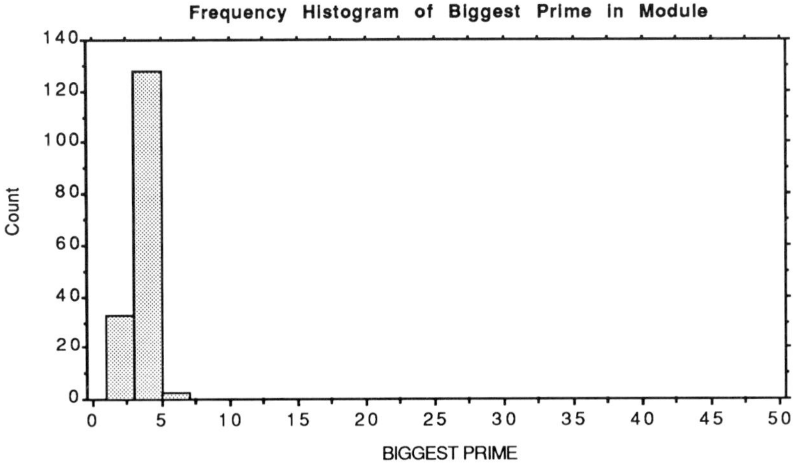

Figure 7: Biggest Prime per Module in Project B

6.2 Median Comparisons

Since all procedures from both projects have been statically analysed a direct comparison of median values can be performed. The advantage of using static analysers has meant that all procedures in a software product can be analysed cheaply without the need to take samples. This of course means that no sampling error is introduced and that median values can be directly compared.

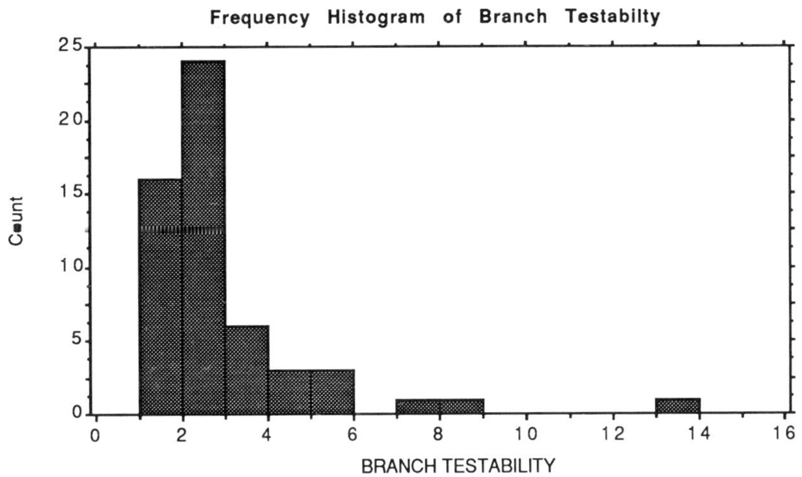

Figure 8: Branch Testability in Project A

Table 2 shows the median values and also the minimum and maximum for Number of Nodes, McCabe's metric, Biggest PRIME, Product VINAP, and Branch testability for Project A and B.

The differences in median values are most pronounced for NODES, MCCABE, BIGGEST and PVINAP. From this it can be concluded that in general people on Project A have a different module design style than those in Project B. This is further emphasised by the high degree of variability in the data for Project A when compared to Project B. The maximum values for all metrics in Project A are much significantly higher than the maximum values for Project B. Special note should be attached to the maximum value for PVINAP in Project A. This very large number indicates the existence of some very unstructured procedures. Both Projects are very similar in the distribution of values for NESTING and BRANCH although this is deceptive because BRANCH is only defined for structured code. A few unstructured procedures from Project A do not have BRANCH values. This suggests that these procedures will be more difficult to test.

Table 2: Summary Statistics for Projects A and B

	Project A			Project B		
	med.	min.	max.	med.	min.	max.
NODES	37	2	859*	11	2	76
MCCABE	8	1	56	3	1	23
BIGGEST	4	1	40	3	1	6
PVINAP	40.5	1	×	12	1	109
NESTING	2	0	9	2	0	7
BRANCH	2	1	13	2	1	6

* The data point with this value was evaluated for NODES only,

× 6291670

6.3 Factor Analysis

Factor analysis (FA) [16] is used to examine the interrelationships between metrics. This is useful when we want to find those metrics which are statistically independent. In this section statistical independence is restricted to mean the degree of correlation between metrics not the degree of correlation between metrics and observed behaviour. The use of statistically independent metrics will imply independent pass/fail criteria. Certifying software products using independent pass/fail criteria will mean applying the minimum number of metrics necessary to capture the largest amount of information. We therefore undertook to empirically examine the relationship between the structural and size metrics from both projects in order to find the 'best' size and structure measures.

It should be noted that this use of FA in no way proves the validity of these metrics in indicating or predicting actual maintainability or testability. Other more suitable statistical techniques would determine these relationships.

Initial investigation using FA showed that most metrics correlated highly with size as measured by the number of nodes. This showed that size was an attribute captured by the structure measures in the majority of cases. For procedures with high values for the structural measures the correlation with number of nodes was considerably lower. This leads to the conclusion that the structural measures were appropriate for detecting structural outliers and that they measured size only for structured code. It was therefore necessary to remove the size component contained within the structure measures. To this end McCabe's metric and the Product VINAP metric were 'normalised' by dividing them both by the number of nodes. These normalised versions were named NPVINAP and NMCCABE. Figure 9 shows the plot of the metrics along the two factors axes after outliers were removed.

Factor Analysis Plot of Metrics from Projects A and B

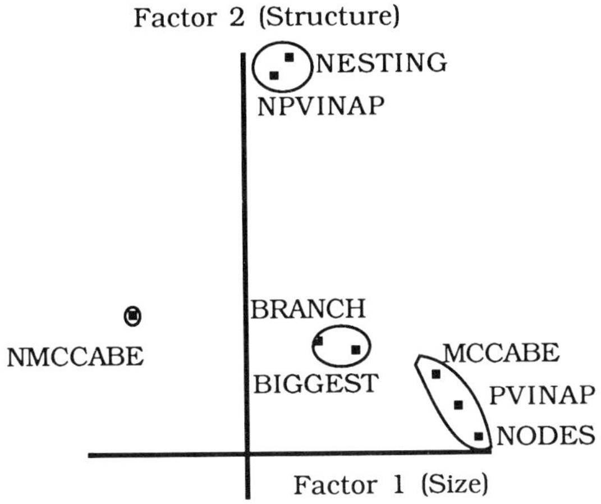

Figure 9: Factor Plot of Metrics from Projects A and B

The factors axes are labelled size and structure because these attributes are intuitively indicated by the metrics. From Figure 9 it can be seen that PVINAP, MCCABE and NODES are all grouped along the size factor axis thus suggesting common explanation of variance. The normalised structure metric NPVINAP and NESTING lie near the structure factor axis suggesting that they measure structure rather than size. BIGGEST PRIME and BRANCH testability metrics neither lie near the structure factors axis or the size factor axis and so appear to measure neither structure or size. The NMCCABE metric is not grouped with any other metrics and seems contrasted with size but not with structure. Perhaps NMCCABE is indicating some other structural attribute not present on the graph.

These results suggest that certification should apply NPVINAP or NESTING to measure structure and NODES to measure size. BRANCH seems independent of the other metrics and so does not measure structure or size.

7. CONCLUSIONS

We have shown that we can compare objective measures between two or more projects to characterise maintainability and testability. Of course this approach can be generalised to measures from other static analysers such as Logiscope™, which we are currently using, as well as other measures which capture quite different quality factors. This method of externally comparing software projects will lead to the derivation of pass/fail criteria which are objective and which are based on experience and hindsight.

To use this approach we would need a set of previously analysed projects which had been assigned pass or fail for a particular attribute. So for, say, maintainability some of the projects have been passed and other have failed. Given a new project to be certified, we compare its metrics with the metrics of the previous projects. By applying a discriminatory procedure [16] we can decide if it falls into the pass set, or else it falls into the fail set. Thus we can base certification on objective and measurable properties.

At present we do not have a set of previously certified software projects, and so at the current time we cannot arrive at a decision about the maintainability and testability of projects A or B. We can only identify the similarities and differences in the data. However the SCOPE project will have about 20 case studies of software products (of which project A is one) and this will provide a satisfactory basis for certifying software.

We have also shown that the complex interrelationships between metrics can be analysed and that this analysis can reduce a set of dependent metrics to a smaller set of independent metrics. From case study data SCOPE will determine independent pass/fail criteria and the absolute minimum number of metrics to apply when certifying software.

REFERENCES

[1] SCOPE Technical Annexe - ESPRIT Project 2151 , SCOPE Consortium, 1989.
[2] Roger S. Pressman. Software Engineering: A Practitioner's Approach.
[3] Fenton NE, Kaposi AA, 'An engineering theory of structure and measurement,' CSR conference, September 1987.
[4] Stockman SG, A constructive approach to software quality assurance, Proc 1st European Conference on Software Quality, European Organisation for Quality Control (EOQC), 1988.
[5] Conte SD, Dunsmore HE and Shen VY, Software Engineering Metrics and Models, Benjamin/Cummings Publishing Company, Inc. 1986.
[6] Lasitha Leelasena, QUALMS and CASSANDRA user manuals, CSSE, South Bank Polytechnic,1989
[7] Fenton NE, Kaposi AA, 'Metrics and Software Structure,' Information and Software technology, 29(60; 301-320, July/August 1987.
[8] McCabe TJ, 'A complexity measure,' IEEE trans Software Eng. SE2, 308-320, 1976
[9] Bache RM, Classification of Flowgraph Metrics, CSSE report CSSE015, South Bank Poly., 1988.
[10] Bache R,'Metricating A-KINDRA,' BT project 610287, Document W021, South bank 1987.
[11] Bache RM and Muellerberg M, Measures of Testability as a basis for Quality Assurance, Software Engineering Journal, March 1990.
[12] Boehm B. W. Software Engineering Economics, Prentice Hall, 1981.
[13] Kitchenham B. 'Software Quality Modelling, Measurement and Prediction: Quality Factors, Quality Criteria and Quality Metrics'. ESPRIT REQUEST (ESP/300).
[14] Dunsmore HE. The effect of comments, mnemonic names and modularity: some university experimental results. Proceedings of Second Symposium on Empirical Foundations of Information and Software Sciences, (1985).
[15] E. Dijkstra, 'GOTO considered Harmful,' Comm ACM, 11, p147-148 1968.
[16] W.R. Dillan and M. Goldstein. Multivariate Analysis, Methods and Applications. John E Wiley & Sons ,1984.

ADDITIONAL CONTRIBUTIONS

Approving Software Products
W. Ehrenberger (Editor)
Elsevier Science Publishers B.V. (North-Holland)
IFIP, 1990

Cost Management with Metrics of Specification: The COSMOS Project*

Norbert Fuchs
Alcatel Austria-ELIN
Ruthnergasse 1-7, A-1210 Vienna, Austria

Ka Lun Tse
Nijenrode, The Netherlands School of Business
Straatweg 25, 3621 BG Breukelen, The Netherlands

Robin Whitty,
South Bank Polytechnic,
Borough Road, London SE1 0AA, UK

Abstract

COSMOS (ESPRIT Project 2686) represents a new approach to obtaining objective information about the evolution of software products during the early stages of the life cycle. Non-trivial information about product structure is captured from formal specifications and designs. As these formal documents undergo elaboration, the information is continually presented to designers and managers using simple uni-variate and bi-variate plots in an attempt to identify trends and outliers from trends. This in turn aids decisions regarding rescheduling or future allocation of resources within a development team.

Consistent use of the COSMOS tools should ideally lead to firm hypotheses about the behaviour of various product metrics within a particular environment, or for particular specification or design methods.

*Research supported by the CEC under ESPRIT II Project 2686 COSMOS. This is COSMOS document COSMOS/GC/WP5/REP/18.1

1. The COSMOS Philosophy

This paper outlines an important theme in development management, which is the subject of a four year investigation under the ESPRIT II programme, as project 2686: *Cost Management with Metrics of Specification (COSMOS)* [COSMOS88]. The philosophy of COSMOS is complementary to the more traditional approaches to cost modelling [ALBREC83, BOEHM81, BOEHM88]; cost modelling allows the software product developer to predict and then to monitor resource expenditure, to set and then to adjust budgets; COSMOS looks for ways to discover how a software product will evolve and to monitor this evolution. Objective information of this type has hitherto been almost entirely lacking in software development; yet it is the most important *engineering* information that the developer can have; and it is the first line of information for cost management: first the developer detects technical problems with the product; after that, if the problems are not corrected, they will be detected in budget overruns and missed deadlines [TSE90].

There are two main elements to the strategy which COSMOS has adopted to fulfil the project philosophy: firstly, a mature theory of structural product metrics is applied to software products in the early life-cycle. Secondly, a strong management interpretation emphasis is placed on how these metrics are presented to development managers. Some progress on these two elements are described in more detail in the next section. In the last section future plans for the project are discussed.

2. Technical Aspects of the COSMOS Approach

The first phase of the COSMOS project is concerned with demonstrating that metrics for specifications and a usable management user interface can be brought together in a prototype management tool. In the second phase of the project the tool will go into use at a number of industrial sites during observation studies designed to assess the impact of the COSMOS strategy. Integrating the strategy with the wider issues in cost modelling and management will become all-important in the observation studies.

Much of the theoretical metrics background for the COSMOS project comes from a UK Alvey project (SE069) which made an in-depth study of attributes relating to structure. The project is documented in [FENTON90]. One of the main achievements of SE069 was the incorporation of many metrics of product structure within a theory of flowgraphs, allowing attributes such as structuredness, amount (depth and breadth) of nesting, size and variety of structural primitives and amount of decision making could all be expressed in the same form, within the theory. The theory of flowgraph metrics is implemented in the QUALMS tool [BACHE89] which generates a wide range of structural metrics from flowgraph representations of programs and specifications in several languages and notations. The metrics are documented in [WHITTY90].

Much progress has been made in building a metrics 'engine' the *Core Metrics Tool*, based on the QUALMS tool, for incorporation into the COSMOS tool. This work has been spearheaded by British Telecom Research Labs. Indeed, the theoretical metrics material and background as a whole has been complemented by the practical experience of metrics and tools available in the industrial partners, particularly Alcatel Austria-ELIN and British Telecom Research Labs.

As well as identifying a well-established theory of product measurement, the COSMOS project needed to consider what is involved in using measurement early in the software life-cycle, that is using so-called 'front-end' metrics for specification and design documents. In practice, it is of equal importance for the project to work with notations that are in actual use, and that are supported by tools to the extent that specifications or designs are stored electronically.

The COSMOS product metrics are the result of a programme of work to adapt the axiomatic flowgraph metrics to obtain front-end metrics. Thus far, greatest progress has been achieved in the work of Alcatel on the LOTOS notation [FUCHS89]. Typical of the technical problems which have been addressed include: how to capture recursion using flowgraphs; whether nestedness should be measured in the same way as for source code languages; and what implications for existing metrics lie in the sparsity of structural primitives in LOTOS. Work is currently in progress with SDL [ROCK82] and Z [SPIVEY89]. We can also draw on the work of another UK Alvey project (SE075) which studied the use of functional language metrics in cost estimation [SAMSON88].

The COSMOS metrics provide well-defined, theoretically sound information about the structure of an evolving product. Intuitively, this information has great potential for monitoring development progress: a well-structured interface can relay relevant parts of this information to the development manager to allow recognition of relationships in the metrics data, with sufficient confidence for these relationships to help in decision making.

COSMOS is adopting an approach to designing the management interface which has been advocated by the Software Data Library project [ROSS89], and by others, notably Kitchenham, as exemplified in [KITCH90]. This approach is to identify trends in product metrics using scatter plots and then to make decisions on the basis of outliers from these trends ('rogue modules'). In some cases, measurement of a single variable may be sufficient to yield outliers, using box plots, for instance. A general rule to be followed is: if a manager cannot see something useful in a single-variable or bi-variate plot, then probably it is not worth using more complex statistical methods to generate information automatically. The COSMOS interface is designed to help the manager 'home in' quickly on those plots which will be useful. Other design decisions were made to minimise training time and usage overheads: a few well-chose plots should quickly become the defaults, so that a manager merely has to glance at these on a daily basis and act accordingly. Modern windowing systems lend themselves well to this type of interface; a nice example is the PERFIDE reliability tool [MAIN90]. Demanding minimal overheads for training and use dictates that the maximum number of windows and menus open at one time should probably be quite small: perhaps two or three. The work on the management interface has been carried out jointly by TechForce and Telefonica Sistemas.

4. Future Directions in the COSMOS Project

The key to success in the second phase of the COSMOS project will be the identification of observation study sites at which specifications or designs are being used on real projects and stored electronically, allowing automatic measurement and data collection. Only when the COSMOS tool is in daily use by managers in genuine development situations can we expect feedback on how useful are the various metrics when used in conjunction with the COSMOS interface.

Designing a mechanism whereby feedback from three or four simultaneous projects can be coordinated is not a trivial task. This is particularly the case because we cannot expect much similarity between the different observation study sites or projects. Luckily, all the industrial partners are principally involved in real-time software production which adds some degree of coherence. The COSMOS strategy recognises the crucial distinction between *experiments*, set up to confirm or refute some hypothesis, and *observation studies*, whose aim is to allow a greater level of understanding. The COSMOS team recognise that software metrics is not as yet ready to support scientific investigation by controlled experiment. If, as a result of the COSMOS project, development managers feel that they have better understood the influence of product attributes on their budgets and schedules, this will be significant progress in the field of software metrics.

Acknowledgement

The work described in this paper has benefited from too many people to mention individually. Particular mention is due to Fred Hirdes and his team at TechForce BV, Sieglinde Stainer of Alcatel Austria-ELIN, Alan Todd, Alan Pengelly and Conrad Simons of British Telecom Research Laboratories, Bob Lockhart of Goldsmiths' College University of London, Frans Donders of The Netherlands Business School, Fernando Medina and Gonzalo Sanchez of Telefonica Sistemas, the COSMOS Project Officer at the CEC, K. C. Varghese, and the COSMOS project reviewers, Hugh Browton and Roland Carn.

References

[ALBREC83] Albrecht, A. J. and Gaffney, J. E., Software function, source lines of code and development effort prediction: a software science validation, *IEEE Trans. Software Eng.*, vol. SE-9, no. 6, pp 639-648, 1983.

[BACHE 89] Bache, R. and Leelasena, L., QUALMS: a tool for the analysis and measurement of software structure, Glasgow College, Cowcaddens Road, Glasgow G7, UK.

[BOEHM81] Boehm, B. W., *Software Engineering Economics*, Prentice Hall, 1981.

[BOEHM88] Boehm, B. W. and Papaccio, P. N., Understanding and controlling software costs, *IEEE Trans. Software Eng.*, vol. SE-14, no. 10, pp 1462-1477, 1988.

[COSMOS88] *Cost Management with Metrics of Specification*, ESPRIT Project 2686, Technical Annex, TechForce BV, Niels Bohrweg 11, 2333 CA Leiden, The Netherlands, 1988.

[FENTON90] Fenton, N. E., Software metrics: theory, tools and validation, *Software Engineering Journal*, vol. 5, no. 1, pp. 65-78, 1990.

[FUCHS89] Fuchs, N. and Stainer, S., Subtask 1.3.2: Assessing feasibility of formal specification language and model - extension of the flowgraph model. *ESPRIT project 2686 COSMOS, Report COSMOS/AI/WP1/TEC/89011.2*, Alcatel Austria-ELIN, Ruthnergasse 1-7, A-1210 Wien, Austria, 1989.

[ISO86] ISO/TC 97/SG 21/ WG1 -FDT/SG-C, *LOTOS, a Temporal Ordering Specification*, December 1986.

[KITCH90] Kitchenham, B. A., Pickard, L. M. and Linkman, S. J., An evaluation of some design metrics, *Software Engineering Journal*, vol. 5, no. 1, pp. 50-58, 1990.

[MAIN90] Mainini. M. T. and Billot, L., PERFIDE: an environment for evaluation and monitoring of software reliability metrics during the test phase, *Software Engineering Journal*, vol. 5, no. 1, pp. 27-32, 1990.

[ROCK82] Rockstroem, A. and Sorocco, R., CCITT-SDL specification and description language, *IEEE Trans. Commun.*, vol. COMM-30, 1982.

[ROSS89] Ross, N., The collection and use of data for monitoring software projects, in *Measurement for Software Control and Assurance* (Kitchenham, B. A. and Littlewood, B., eds.), Elsevier Applied Science, 1989.

[SAMSON88] Samson, W. B., Dugard, P. I., Nevill, D. G., Oldfield, P. E., Smith, A. W. and Titterington, G, Predictive software metrics based on a formal specification, *Alvey Project SE075, Final Report vol. 1*, Dundee Institute of Technology, Bell Street, Dundee DD1, 1HG, UK, 1988.

[SPIVEY89] Spivey, J. M., *The Z Notation, A Reference Manual*, Prentice Hall International (UK) Ltd, 1989.

[TSE90] Tse, K. L. and Whitty, R. W., Cost modelling decision support by monitoring product evolution, in *Proc. European COCOMO Users' Group Meeting*, 65 Terrington Hill, Marlow, Buckinghamshire SL7 2RE, UK, 1990.

[WHITTY90] Whitty, R. W. and Lockhart, R., Structural Metrics, *ESPRIT project 2686 COSMOS, Report COSMOS/GC/WP1/REP/7.3*, Goldsmiths' College, New Cross, London SE14 6NW, UK, 1990.

Approving Software Products
W. Ehrenberger (Editor)
Elsevier Science Publishers B.V. (North-Holland)
IFIP, 1990

INTERACTION OF MAN AND TOOLS DURING STATIC ANALYSIS

Manfred Kersken

Gesellschaft für Reaktorsicherheit (GRS) mbH
Forschungsgelände
D-8046 Garching, FRG

ABSTRACT

Static software analysis can be used for the detection of faults and anomalies, for the preparation of test cases and it is shown that it can even be applied to demonstrate the compliance of implemented functions with specified ones. It can also serve as a means for the collection of software metrics which may be used for the quantitative description of quality attributes.
The steps which are taken to perform static analysis are usually supported by tools. A large amount of work, however, has to be performed by the human brain. In view of the assessment of this human performance within static analysis some analogies are shown between tasks performed for measuring human problem solving performance in fault diagnosis and static analysis tasks.

1. INTRODUCTION

Often licensing bodies and associated companies receive software for certification only after it is already coded, these institutions can participate in V&V via assessing the V&V procedures of the producer, which is said to be passive V&V here. Passive V&V can assess fault-avoidance and fault-removal. If, however, an assessor likes to take part actively in V&V he is left with the analytical techniques of fault-removal only. The main analytical techniques are static analysis and testing. For an independent assessor it is often impossible to establish test cases for software which was developed by others - in spite of the fact that good software should be designed to be testable. Static analysis is remaining as a flexible and powerful means for fault-removal, but also for the preperation of tests and for demonstrating that specific program features (functions) are well established in the code.

In practice analysis is performed by an interaction between human and computerized tools. The power of the method of static analysis is dependent on the performance of this man-tool interation. This performance should be measured.

2. STATIC ANALYSIS

There are four possible objectives for applying static analysis to software, i.e. (1) to collect product metrics, (2) to prepare test cases, (3) to identify faults and anomalies and (4) to demonstrate the compliance or non-compliance of actually implemented functions with the specified ones. Product metrics, as e.g. number of lines of codes, number of loops, number of distinct operands/operators are collected with the aim to determine high level software quality attributes like maintainability, enhancability, reliability, usability /1,2/. This objective is not considered here, instead the contribution concentrates on (4) which more or less also implies (2) and (3) as will be seen in an example.

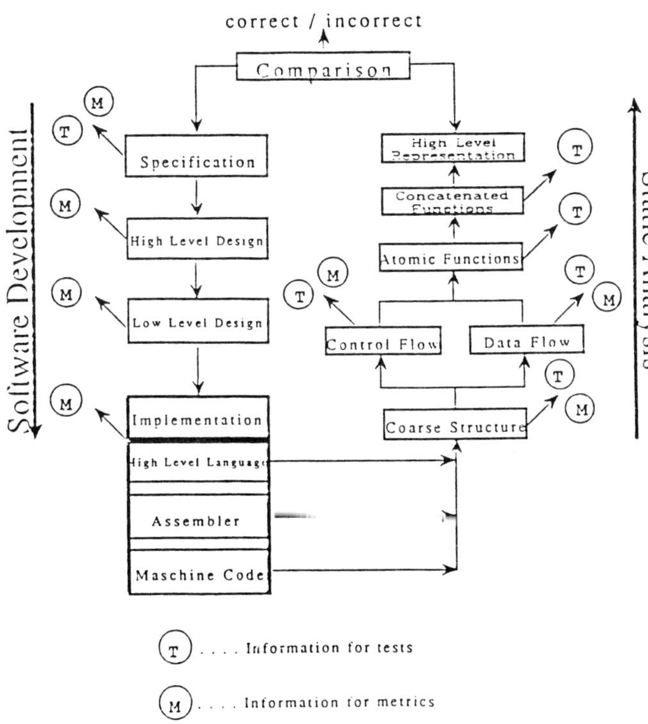

Fig. 1.: Software development and static analysis

Fig. 1 shows some possible levels of program development and static analysis. The software may be implemented as a high level language, assembler language, or machine code. Some highly safety critical applications require start of analysis from machine code as the ultimate form of a program. This is to avoid a rigid verification and validation of complex software like a compiler. In a first step the coarse structure (e.g. calling hierarchy) is identified, afterwards the more detailed structure in terms of control flow and data flow. Up until this level static analysis is well supported by computerized tools. The next step is based on a common view of control flow and data flow, i.e. what happens with the data when a distinct path or set of paths is traversed. This is the identification of "atomic functions" which are (not well defined) small actions, e.g. read an array, perform some linear operations on it and write the result in another array. These functions are then concatenated to bigger ones, etc. until all the program functions are represented in a way which allows comparison with the specified functions. If e.g. the specification contains logic diagrams, then the high level representation derived by static analysis should also be a logic diagram.

Within this process of static analysis two major sources of human errors can be seen. The first ones are errors during the non-computerized task of identifying atomic actions and concatenating them, the second ones occur when applying the computerized tools for the extraction of control flow and data flow, including misinterpretation of their output.

The following example which is taken from a core protection system shows how static analysis of a piece of assembler code is performed in a purely mental way. This example is meant to give an impression about the variety of errors that may occur in the course of this procedure. In this procedure the source code is converted instruction by instruction into a graphical representation called the Control Flow and Data Flow Diagram CDD (Fig. 2), clearly illustrating control and data flow. The source code is split into sequential parts SP´s starting either at the entry point of the module or at a label or after a branch.

In Fig. 2 the symbol SPi, i = Ø,...,22, denotes the SP´s of the module and the lines between the SP´s represent the control flow. On the right hand side of the SP´s columns are reserved for the register of the computer GØ,...,G7, for the constants K used in the module, and for the input and output area E and A respectively.

The data flow is recorded in this part, i.e. the right hand side of the SP´s whereby the symbols denote:

X read access

O write access

ⵀ write access, where the previous content of the register/storage location is relevant, e.g. arithmetic or logic instructions.

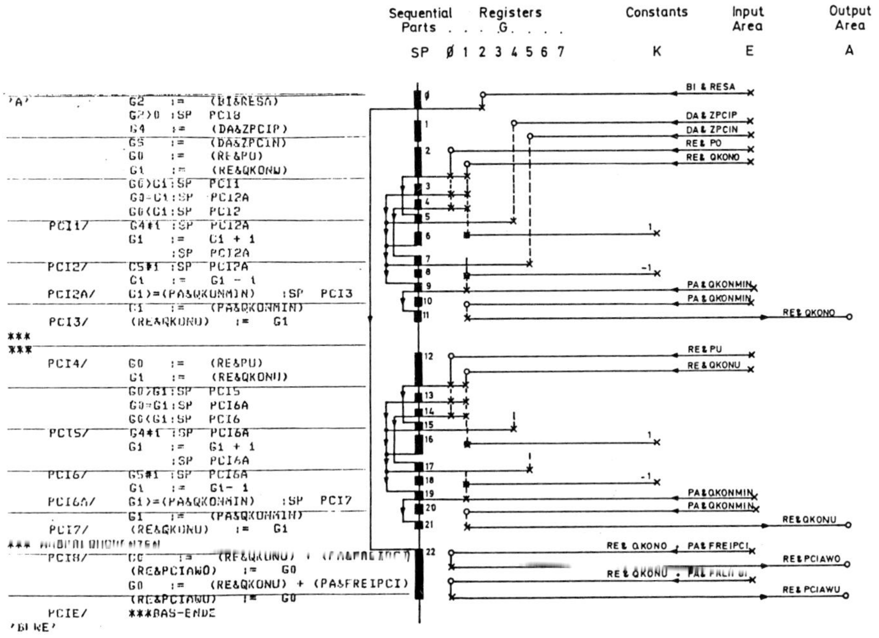

Fig. 2: Code example with control flow and data flow diagram CDD

Fig. 3 shows the control flow in a manner more suitable for path analysis. Without detailed evidence it can be stated that the number of paths in SPØ,22 is 14x14+1=197. The code, however, reveals some of them as not logical (shown in brackets), i.e. they are never used due to the branching conditions. The branching conditions in SP2,3,4 are GØ > G1,GØ = G1 and GØ < G1; thus, a jump is identified, within SP2,SP3 or SP4 and a transition SP4→SP5 is impossible. It is also noted that SP1,11 and SP11,21 reveal the same structure. This is explained by the same computations performed for the upper and lower part of the reactor core.

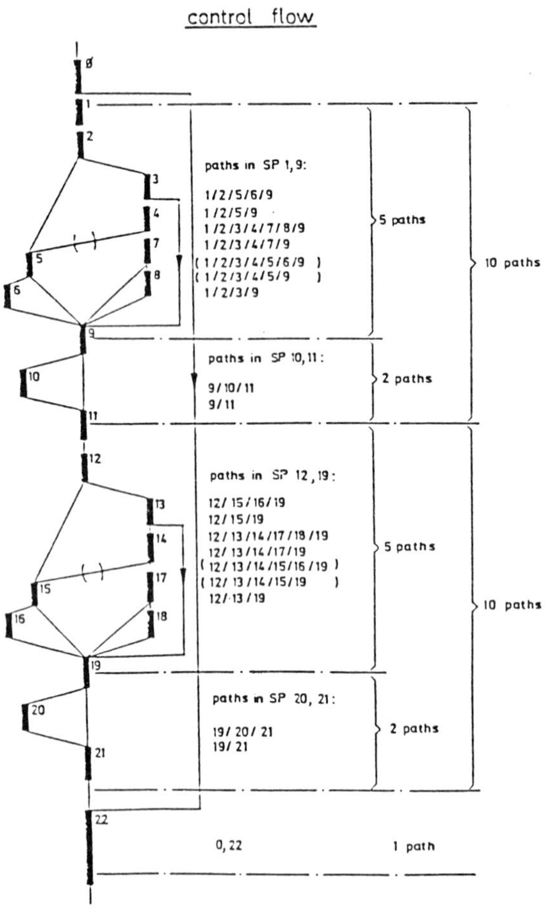

Fig. 3: Control flow for path analysis

On behalf of the information from path analysis the number of test cases for checking the whole structure of SPØ, 22 may be reduced to:

10 test cases for SP1,11
10 test cases for SP11,21
1 test case for path SPØ SP22

i.e. 21 test cases remaining.

Obviously all 197 paths could easily be tested as concerns this example. The intention of this example was only to demonstrate that by simple path analysis based on CDD the number of test cases can be reduced considerably.

Based on the knowledge about control and data flow from CDD and some additional information from the code, test cases may be specified for the module under consideration which allow testing of the structure and the functional properties as well. The basic testing criteria refer to the functional properties of the module. Additional tests with a path coverage growing with increasing importance of the module - with respects to the contribution to overall software reliability - should be performed.

The table in Fig. 4 lists the 21 test cases stated above for the example module. The operands indicated in the head of the table have to be chosen in such a way that the operators OP in the branching conditions receive the logical values ($>, \leq, \geq, =, \neq$) of the table entries. After successful execution of the individual path, the result given in the column "action" must appear.

	path - no.	path	SPø RESA OP ø	SP2,3,4 PO OP QKONO$_{old}$	SP5 ZPCIP OP 1	SP7 ZPCIN OP 1	SP 9 QKONO$_{new}$ OP QKONMIN	Action	
	ø	S ø / 22	>					<QKONU°>$_{new}$ = <QKONU°>$_{old}$	
upper part of core	1	S 1 / 2 / 5 / 9 / 11	<	>	≠		>	<QKONO>$_{new}$ = <QKONO>$_{old}$	
	2	S 1 / 2 / 3 / 9 / 11	<	=			>	" = "	
	3	S 1 / 2 / 3 / 4 / 7 / 9 / 11	<	<		≠	≥	" = "	
	4	S 1 / 2 / 5 / 6 / 9 / 11	<	>	=		≥	" = <QKONO>$_{old}$ + 1	<PCIAWO> =
	5 = 2	S 1 / 2 / 3 / 9 / 11	<	=			≥	" = <QKONO>$_{old}$	
	6	S 1 / 2 / 3 / 4 / 7 / 8 / 9 / 11	<	<		=	≥	" = <QKONO>$_{old}$ - 1	=<QKONO>$_{new}$ + <FREIPCI>
	7	S 1 / 2 / 5 / 9 / 10 / 11	<	>	≠		<	" = <QKONMIN>	
	8	S 1 / 2 / 3 / 9 / 10 / 11	<	=			<	" = "	
	9	S 1 / 2 / 3 / 4 / 7 / 9 / 10 / 11	<	<		≠	<	" = "	
	10	S 1 / 2 / 5 / 6 / 9 / 10 / 11	<	>	=		<	" = "	
	11 = 8	S 1 / 2 / 3 / 9 / 10 / 11	<	=			<	" = "	
	12	S 1 / 2 / 3 / 4 / 7 / 8 / 9 / 10 / 11	<	<		=	<	" = "	

	path - no.	path	SPø RESA OP ø	SP 12,13,14 PU OP QKONU$_{old}$	SP 15 ZPCIP OP 1	SP17 ZPCIN OP 1	SP 19 QKONU$_{new}$ OP QKONMIN	Action	
lower part of core	13	S 11 / 12 / 15 / 19 / 21	<	>	≠		>	<OKONU>$_{new}$ = <OKONU>$_{old}$	
	14	S 11 / 12 / 13 / 19 / 21	<	=			>	" = "	
	15	S 11 / 12 / 13 / 14 / 17 / 19 / 21	<	<		≠	≥	" = "	
	16	S 11 / 12 / 15 / 16 / 19 / 21	<	>	=		>	" = <QKONU>$_{old}$ + 1	<PCIAWU> =
	17 = 14	S 11 / 12 / 13 / 19 / 21	<	=			≥	" = <QKONU>$_{old}$	
	18	S 11 / 12 / 13 / 14 / 17 / 18 / 19 / 21	<	<		=	≥	" = <QKONU>$_{old}$ - 1	=<OKONU>$_{new}$ + <FREIPCI>
	19	S 11 / 12 / 15 / 19 / 20 / 21	<	>	≠		<	" = <QKONMIN>	
	20	S 11 / 12 / 13 / 19 / 20 / 21	<	=			<	" = "	
	21	S 11 / 12 / 13 / 14 / 17 / 19 / 20 / 21	<	<		≠	<	" = "	
	22	S 11 / 12 / 15 / 16 / 19 / 20 / 21	<	>	=		<	" = "	
	23 = 20	S 11 / 12 / 13 / 19 / 20 / 21	<	=			<	" = "	
	24	S 11 / 12 / 13 / 14 / 17 / 18 / 19 / 20 / 21	<	<		=	<	" = "	

Fig. 4: Table for testing the example module

Summarizing this static analysis procedure the following two objectives can be identified:

- Detection of faults and demonstration that the code corresponds to the program specification. Control flow faults are detected, as well as data flow faults (e.g. use of wrong registers).
  Theoretically a detection of specification faults is not possible, because the result of the static analysis is compared with the specification, implying that the specification has to be checked separately. Nevertheless some specification faults can be found as well. This may be explained by the detailed knowledge of the program attained from the procedure of static analysis. For example unsymmetries in control flow or a conspicuous treatment of variables suggest a possible inconsistency of specification. Cooperation with the producer of the specification may reveal whether there is a fault or not.

- Specification of test cases: The information on the structure and functional properties of the software attained from the static analysis procedure is used to specify test cases.

As already mentioned the process of static analysis can be based on tools up until the step exhibiting control flow and data flow. Some tools provide for more than control flow and data flow but in most cases these additional features are only applicable under servere restrictions of the code. The control flow is represented by many tools similar as shown in Fig. 3, as they use a graph-theoretic approach to break down the source code to be analyzed. Thus the sequential parts of Fig. 3 are represented as nodes of a graph and the lines between the sequential parts become directed arcs of a graph. An example of a control flow representation of a static analysis tool is shown in Fig. 5.

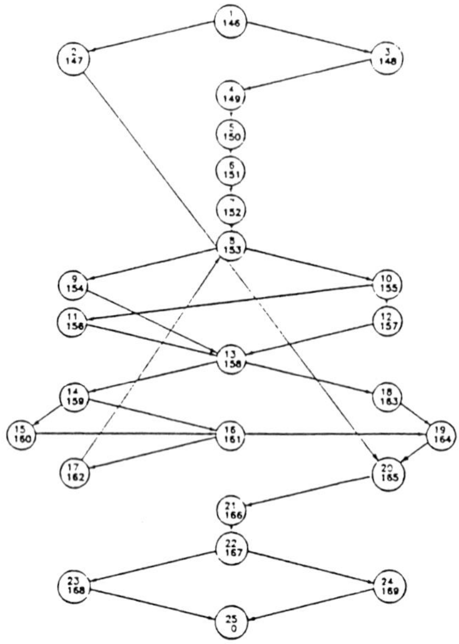

Fig. 5: A control flow graph representation

Data flow is represented in many cases in a similar manner with nodes and arrows, but using a tree structure to show which variables contribute to the generation of a new one.

3. HUMAN PERFORMANCE IN STATIC ANALYSIS

At a first glance the involvement of human and computerized tools in static analysis suggests to discuss the human error in this man-machine system in terms of man-computer interaction. Most of the static analysis tools, however, are applied only a few times to the source code to be analyzed - in the extreme case only once. Thus there is no real interaction of man and computer, but a very intensive interaction between man and computer output in the form of lists and graphical representations as shown e.g. in Fig. 2, 3 and 5. Of course in practice these lists and graphics are much more voluminous than in the figures. According to the classification scheme of Lee et al., /4/, human error performance in this task falls into the class of fault diagnosis and quality inspection. Clearly the tasks performed during static analysis aim in detecting, diagnosing and removing faults. Models of human problem solving performance in fault diagnosis are already proposed /5,6,7/.

The experiments which were performed within this work are of particular interest for the assessment of human performance during static analysis. Within these experiments two computerized troubleshooting simulators were applied.

One of them, TASK = Troubleshooting by Application of Structural Knowledge, requires the subjects to find faulty nodes responsible for unacceptable network outputs. This is a context-free problem solving environment.

The other one, FAULT = Framework for Aiding the Understanding of Logical Troubleshooting, uses functional block diagrams of systems, where a fairly general failure symptom serves as a starting point, and subjects gather information by checking components in this system and performing tests, etc. This is a context-specific environment.

Both activities performed in TASK and FAULT are related to activities which happen during static analysis. Control flow representations in form of networks (see Fig. 2, 3, 5) are used in static analysis to identify code parts where a fault is situated which leads to a failure in the output of a program. These structures are also used to prepare white-box (structured) tests and to determine which percentage of the whole control flow has been covered during tests (test coverage measures).

The logical troubleshooting approach of FAULTS can be compared with the reverse development of atomic functions and their concatenation towards a high level representation as shown in Fig. 1 and explained in the example of chapter 2. Information is gathered from control flow and data flow to reveal functions and their logical and temporal connections. This scheme is then used to reveal and diagnose faults and to prepare black-box (functional) tests.

4. MEASURES OF PERFORMANCE

Cognitive style, aptitude, and human ability may be referred to as high level attributes of human problem solving performance. Cognitive style describes the personal route of a human to learn or to solve a task, aptitude describes the skill necessary for a job, and ability refers to intellectual capability. To determine useful and obtainable metrics from the process of static program analysis we would like to restrict ourselves to aptitude and cognitive style.

The latter one may be determined by counting the number of times an analyst uses certain documents like control flow diagram, data flow diagram, CDD (see Fig. 2), program listing, etc. and the amount of time he uses to look at these documents. The most direct metrics, however, should be those dealing with aptitude.

In the case of static program analysis these could be

- amount of faults identified
- time (costs) consumed per fault identification
- number of lines of code changed to remove a fault
- amount of (predefined) atomic functions identified
- time (costs) consumed per identification of an atomic function

an similar ones.

There is again a close correlation to the descriptive measures of performance used in the TASK and FAULT experiments /5, 6, 7/.

5. CONCLUSION

The comparative investigation of the human-process interaction during static program analysis and experimental methods used to measure human problem solving performance revealed a variety of similar actions involved in both. This investigation has been performed to suggest a possible route of assessment of human analysts who apply static analysis as a part of the verification and validation process for safety critical software. It is suggested to restrict data collection to the measure of human aptitude.

6. REFERENCES

/1/ Boehm, B.W., et al.,
Characteristics of Software Quality,
North Holland, 1978

/2/ McCall, J.A., Richards, P.K., Walters, G.F.,
Factors in Software Quality, Volume I, II, III,
RADC reports NTIS AD/A-049, 014, 015 and 055, 1977

/3/ Maertz, J., Dhodapkar, S.D.,
Data Flow Analysis of Common Assembly Language Programs
by Means of Static Analysis Tool STAN,
Hardware and Software for Real Time Process Control,
J. Zalewski and W. Ehrenberger (Eds.),
Elsevier Science Publ. (North Holland), 1989

/4/ Lee, K.W., Tillman, F.A., Higgins, J.J.,
A Literature Survey of the Human Reliability Component
in a Man-Machine System,
IEEE Trans. on Reliability, Vol. 37, No. 1, April 1988

/5/ Henneman, R. L., Rouse, W.B.,
Measures of Human Problem Solving Performance in
Fault Diagnosis Tasks,
IEEE Trans. on Systems, Man and Cybernetics,
Vol. SMC-14, No. 1, January/February 1984

/6/ Rouse, S.H., Rouse, W.B.,
Cognitive Style as a Correlate of Human Problem
Solving Performance in Fault Diagnosis Tasks,
IEEE Trans. on Systems, Man and Cybernetics,
Vol. SMC-12, No. 5, September/Oktober 1982

/7/ Hunt, R.M., Rouse, W.B.,
A Fuzzy Rule-Based Model of Human Problem Solving,
IEEE Trans. on Systems, Man, and Cybernetics,
Vol. SMC-14, No. 1, January/February 1984

Approving Software Products
W. Ehrenberger (Editor)
Elsevier Science Publishers B.V. (North-Holland)
IFIP, 1990

Defining a Method for Software Certification

Hans-Ludwig Hausen — Ndombe Cacutalua
GMD, Schloss Birlinghoven, D-5205 St.Augustin 1
e-mail: hausen@dbngmd21.bitnet
e-mail: ndombe@gmdzi

June 1990

1 Introduction

A certification framework has to be based on a certification model and certification methods. [1]

A certification model defines the notions used in a certification process(e.g a certification of software product by followed software quality or characteristic: *correcteness, reliability* and *efficiency*). The certification model is composed of a software product model, a software process model, a software quality and productivity model or a software characteristics model, a software tools and methods model and a measurement model.

A certification method identifies the software product, which is to be certified. It identifies in particular the software product parts and the relevant elements of the respective development process(e.g: source code, user's manual or software quality assurance plan used for the development of the product). The information of a certification method framework is needed from the certifier to classify available data. For the identification task in the certification framework a software product model is provided. Moreover the goal of software product model is to characterize or classify a software product before the product should be certified. The aim is not to identify all the elements present in a software product but only those that may be useful in the certification process.

A certification method specifies a software quality and productivity to be assessed. This selection is based on examination of the product description. The examination process is to be instrumented by methods and tools invocation system, which is to be provided by a methods and tools model. Additionally a software process model is provided. The software process model has to identify items of the process that may be useful to facilitate product measurement or assessement.

A certification method specifies also a choice and an application of measurement and assessement methods. The choice depends on the operational definition of the quality and productivity attributes (e.g correctness) to be assessed or achieved.

The certification process uses information from the software product model, from the software process model and from the software quality and productivity model.

The present text therefore is divided into the following main sections. The next section introduces a software product model. In that section a basic concept, by which a software product should be characterized, is defined. A framework by which elements of a software development process should be specified is also defined in that section; e.g elements of testing workplan. The third section describes a generic software process model. Activities, objects and their relations are described by a set of matrices, each of which can be used independently. The model might be implemented in a entity-relationship data base or by a plain file system. The model of describing software characterisitcs, i.e. quality and productivity attribute, is provided in section four. An acyclic graph describes the relations between factors, charcateristics and metrics. A procedure to compute a value for the characteristics is also described. The fifth section introduces a generic certification method for software products. Rules are used to define product model, process model characteristics model and their interrelations. This constitutes a certification model which precisely defines the notions applicable to certify a software product.

[1] The work presented has been founded by the Esprit Project SCOPE 2151

2 Software Product Model

An economic representation of software product might obey the following principles

- **Abstraction** of non-relevant details.
  An abstraction serves an identification of maximun exactness in each stage of development of a software product.

- **Orthogonality** of description.
  An orthogonality of a description avoids that the same problem aspect has to be described multiply and in different ways.

- **Minimality** of representation.
  A minimality of the representation reduces the set of internal dependencies to the absolutely necessary extent.

To be able to express a software product model, which is representing a software product, in a powerful manner, we have defined a set of basic concepts. Elements of the set of basic concept are able to identify the software product parts, which are useful in the certification process, and are able to identify elements of development process of software product.

2.1 Basic Concept

The software product model provides basic concept for defining the following kinds of elements:

- Software product parts

- Elements of software product development

The set of basic concept of software product model consist of following main elements:

- **Product type.** A product type is describing a class of software product, which is to be certified. For an example the product is from the class of *software production environment.*

- **Product component.** A product component is describing a class of items, which are taking part in the product type. For an example a document management system or a configuration management system as part of software production environment.

- **Is-comp-of.** A "Is-comp-of" relates a product components to a specific product type.

A software product development task consist of following main stage

- **Requirement or Application.** A requirement stage defines and specify <u>what</u> is needed for achieving a goal for which the software product is to be developped.

- **Design or Specification.** A design stage specify <u>how</u> the required framework should be realised or implemented.

- **Implementation or Code.** An implementation stage realises the designed framework.

For defining any stage of software product development process the software product model provides a class

- **Layer.** A class layer describes a stage of software product development process.

The relationship **is-layer-of** relates a class "product type" with a class "layer".

For identifying elements of the software process in each stage the software product model provides also the following elements:

- **Activities.** An activity is describing the transformation of one or more objects at a particular stage.

- **Objects.** An object is capturing information about a specific activity at a certain stage. An object could contained anothers objects as subobject.
- **States.** A state is relating activities with specified objects.

The relationship **is-activity-in** relates an "activity" with a specific software product development "layer".

The relationship **is-object-of** relates a object with a specific software product development "layers"

3 Software Process Model

A process models describes objects consumed or produced as well as activities applied to construct, examine, measure, or assess a software artifact. Currently one will find a number of types of process models frequently used in practice. For a detailed evaluation a precise definition of the models is needed, but in most cases there is no such definition.

3.1 Types of Process Models

These process models can be characterized as:

- Sequence process models
  In terms of such a model, layers are ordered in sequences on a time axis. For each layer a sequence or even an unstructured set of activities is defined. Usually nothing is said about the relationships between activities within a single layer. The relationships between objects are also not defined very precisely. Such models describe whether an object has passed a certain layer and its status (e.g. tested) at the end of each layer. In other words, the layers are queued on a time axis and the objects are pipelined through the sequences of development activities.
- Loop process model or Waterfall model
  Models of this type are improved sequence models. Layers are viewed as groups of encapsulated activities producing a certain type of output. Normally the activities within a layer are ordered on the basis of a special method of working (e.g. design method). Feedback to previous layers can also be modelled. Incomplete objects will be identified in succeeding layers and returned to the preceding ones. If the loss of information during layer performance or at the transition to a next layer is modelled, a model is called a '(cascaded) waterfall model'.
- Axes process model
  Construction activities are often separated from validation tasks. Then for each area a sequence model or a loop model can be used. The two models have a junction point on the code or program level of the objects. The model looks like a V where the left axis represents the software construction model and the right axis represents the validation model. In an improved axes model the left axis and right axis are divided into levels where objects of a certain type (requirements, specifications, programs, executable code or document text) are handled. If so the relationship between construction activities and validation activities can be defined level-internal and level-to-level.
- View process model
  Software development is a process involving, amongst others programmers, documenters, and customers or users. Each of them plays a specific role because their tasks are more or less different. Since their duties differ, their views on the software system to be developed differ. A model concerning such different views - in terms of activities to be performed and objects to be relevant to each role - is called a view model. It provides means for grouping and ordering activities and objects according to a given number of roles. An 'interlacing view model' is given, if all views are intermixed activity-wise and object-wise.

A system development process is defined by two dimensions:

- by the layers as the set of the attributes of an object under consideration,

- by the views as the interpretations which different individuals and groups involved may hold about this object.

The essential development process is defined by several layers of activities. Every layer aims at answering certain substantial questions. This is done by refining the different models belonging to the layers in an appropriate way. The process will show a change of design and validation activities.

3.2 The Generic Process Matrix Model

The software development and analysis model is given as a representation schema for activities and views within a development strategy. Following the ideas of data abstraction, the objects of development are defined by the functions (activities) which can be applied to data. These objects of development and the appropriate functions are related to the different views of the development process. Here we would suggest distinguishing at three views or aspects – that of software construction (Con), that of software validation (Val) (incorporating the aspect of (e)valuation), and that of management, organization, and planning i.e. administration (Adm). Thus we can derive a number of state matrices, each representing the state of objects with respect to the different views at a given point of the development timescale.

```
Views on the Objects (state matrix)

                  | Adm | Con | Val |
             -----+-----+-----+-----+------
             0.1  |     |     |     |
             -----+-----+-----+-----+------
             0.2  |     |     | sm.n|
             -----+-----+-----+-----+------
                  .
                  .
             -----+-----+-----+-----+------
             0.n  |     |     |     |
```

While it is possible to choose any time slot dt as the distance between state matrices (according to the scope of concern), it seems to be useful to have at least four cuts, in order to represent the different states of the four main phases of the development process (s.a.). The specific elements of a state matrix SM may indicate the type or name of an activity (A), target information (T), source information (S), and a weighting of the relevance (R) for the appropriate view. That leads to the state quadruple:

$$sm.n := (A , S , T , R)$$

As everyone assumes, it is possible to create for each type of entry a separate matrix out of this state matrix, i.e. for A, S, T or R a specific state matrix might be created. This will be appropriate in an instrumentation of this matrix by a data base or the likewise. While the state matrices give a fair overview of objects, activities, and views, they are not sufficient to represent the interdependence of objects and activities with respect to the different views. To enable a representation of this relation, we suggest a set of incidence matrices as refinements of each state matrix, one for each view. Given a cut t.n, a view XYZ, and the appropriate state matrix SM in a specific stage of the system development process, the incidence matrix belonging to this state would have the following structure:

```
            Object-Object Incidence Matrices (O-O-IM)

      Val  | 0.1 |           | 0.7|        | 0.n
           |     |           |    |        |
      -----+-----+...........+----+........+------
       0.1 |     |           |    |        |
      -----+-----+...........+----+........+------
           .     .           .    .        .
```

```
         Con  | O.1 |           | O.7 |        | O.n
              |     |           |     |        |
         -----+-----+...........+-----+........+------
          O.1 |     |           |     |        |
         -----+-----+...........+-----+........+------
              .     .           .     .        .

Adm  | O.1 |           | O.7|        | O.n
     |     |           |    |        |
-----+-----+...........+----+........+------
 O.1 | A.1 |           | R.7|        |
-----+-----+...........+----+........+------
     .     .           .    .        .
     .     .           .    .        .
-----+-----+...........+----+........+------
 O.n |     |           |    |        |
     |     |           |    |        |
```

In this object-object incidence matrix the <Oi,Oi> element denotes the activity (or set of activities) Ai to be performed on object Oi. All other elements of row i describe the relations R between Oi and all objects needed as source or target of information for Ai. Thus the incidence matrix may lead to a partial order of activities for a specific view in a given state (situation) of the system development process. In addition to the O-O-IM one will also get an activity-activity incidence matrix as follows:

```
     Activity-Activity Incidence Matrix (A-A-IM)

      | A.1 |           | A.7|        | A.n
      |     |           |    |        |
 -----+-----+...........+----+........+------
  A.1 | O.1 |           | S.7|        |
 -----+-----+...........+----+........+------
      .     .           .    .        .
      .     .           .    .        .
      .     .           .    .        .
      .     .           .    .        .
 -----+-----+...........+----+........+------
 ,A.n |     |           |    |        |
      |     |           |    |        |
```

In this incidence matrix the <Ai,Ai> element denotes the object (or set of objects) Oi dealt with in activity Ai. The other elements of row i describe the relations Si between activity Ai and the other activities performed at the current development stage. The above matrices describe the situation of the objects, the status of the activities and the involvement of the different view-holders at a certain point in time. The question now is, how can one interrelate these state matrices with state matrices at another point in time. If this is possible, one will ask whether it is possible to relate all state matrices to each other or not. It seems to be obvious that this is a need, because the ability to govern a large software development project requires at least the description and control of the relations and interactions between different development stages.

By way of explanation, we will take the following names to denote, like classical lcm's, a couple of different states during the life time of a software development project or the life time of the software system itself.

```
ips-ra:  Information - Processing - System - Requirements - Analysis
ips-de:  Information - Processing - System - Definition
```

sws-ra: Software - System - Requirements - Analysis
sws-ds: Software - System - Design and Specification
swp-dc: Software - Program - Development and Coding
sws-ih: Software - System - Installation and Handing Over
sws-ap: Software - System - Application
sws-ma: Software - System - Maintenance

Our approach to solving the questions of interrelation of states is to use matrices again. But here the matrices describe the relations between objects, activities and views at different situations. First, as in the SM above, we can interrelate the entries of the pure state matrices. This will lead to the state interrelation matrix SIM as follows:

State Interrelation Matrix (SIM)

	ips-ra	ips-de	sws-ra	sws-ds	swp-dc	sws-ih	sws-ap	sws-ma
Adm								
Con								
Val				sim.n				

As in the SM an SIM entry provides information on objects dealt with at the stage n. So sim.n denotes the objects under construction at state n (here: SWS-RAS) The primary objective here is the state-state relationship. We would therefore like to express the dependencies of the objects located at different development stages. This leads us to the state-state incidence matrix S-S-IM in the following form:

State-State Incidence Matrix (S-S-IM)

	ips-ra	ips-de	sws-ra	sws-ds	swp-dc	sws-ih	sws-ap	sws-ma
ips-ra	OS.1							
ips-de		OS.2	ssim.N					
sws-ra		ssim.n	OS.3					
sws-ds				OS.4				
sws-dc					OS.5			
sws-ih						OS.6		
sws-ap							OS.7	
sws-ma								OS.8

In the S-S-IM an OSi entry denotes the Set of Objects under construction within the state i. The entry ssim.N shows the objects which will be used in stage n and which therefore have to be completed at least at stage n-1. The objects which will be worked out completely or for which work will be finished at stage n will be denoted by the entry ssim.n. This matrix provides us with a partial ordering on the objects in accordance whith the stages in which they will be produced. From the matrices given above we can derive the next matrix showing the relationships between objects and stages directly.

```
          Object-State  Matrices (O-S-M)

    Val
       |ips-ra |ips-de |sws-ra |sws-ds |swp-dc |sws-ih |sws-ap |sws-ma
    ---+-------+-------+-------+-------+-------+-------+-------+-------
    O.1|       |       |       |       |       |       |       |
    ---+-------+-------+-------+-------+-------+-------+-------+-------
    O.2|       |       |       |       | osm.n |       |       |
    ---+-------+-------+-------+-------+-------+-------+-------+-------
       :       :       :       :       :       :

  Con
     |ips-ra |ips-de |sws-ra |sws-ds |swp-dc |sws-ih |sws-ap |sws-ma
  ---+-------+-------+-------+-------+-------+-------+-------+-------
  O.1|       |       |       |       |       |       |       |
  ---+-------+-------+-------+-------+-------+-------+-------+-------
  O.2|       |       |       |       | osm.n |       |       |
  ---+-------+-------+-------+-------+-------+-------+-------+-------
     :       :       :       :       :       :

Adm
   |ips-ra |ips-de |sws-ra |sws-ds |swp-dc |sws-ih |sws-ap |sws-ma
---+-------+-------+-------+-------+-------+-------+-------+-------
O.1|       |       |       |       |       |       |       |
---+-------+-------+-------+-------+-------+-------+-------+-------
O.2|       |       |       |       | osm.n |       |       |
---+-------+-------+-------+-------+-------+-------+-------+-------
   :       :       :       :       :       :
   :       :       :       :       :       :
---+-------+-------+-------+-------+-------+-------+-------+-------
O.n|       |       |       |       |       |       |       |
```

Here an entry osm.n denotes whether the object Oi is under construction, is involved in validation or is subject to an administration activity, or whether the object will be completed or is not tackled at a certain stage.

Given all the matrices mentioned above, we will have the ability to describe completely the process of using and developing a software system. Moreover we are able to define and analyse the work performed in certain steps as well as the relationships between individual work activities at different steps. This way of defining the software development process allows for different ways of development: top-down, bottom-up, inside-out, etc. Having all the matrices at the several stages we are also able to look at the system under development in accordance with a specific view. If we do so we will get something like a cut through the set of state descriptions. Each line cutting a state description, where a view represents or denotes the objects belonging to that specific view within the particular development stage.

3.3 Representations and Implementations

As discussed above items of interest and their relationship will be represented by matrices. These reflect in a first approach the aspects of software development and analysis at a certain point in time. They may be viewed as cuts through the concurrent views as defined by pragmatics, semantics and construction aspects. In a second approach we would also like to handle the relationships between different points in time. We would like to apply the same method, thereby obtaining a representation consisting of matrices of matrices. For some purposes, it is interesting to know about starting and termination of activities. To organize construction and analysis as parallel tasks, it is necessary to know the activities of construction which have to be finished before an analytic activity can be started. Similar things are true of objects. It has to be known which objects are in status, because there is in general no coincidence between finishing a task and completing an object or transforming an object into a required temporary status. In order to have a uniform and simple representation structure we propose the use of matrices to show relationships between different stages of a software development and analysis process. The whole model consists of a set of matrices. In modern data base systems one will also find matrices, but there they are called relations or entities. As matter of fact the abstract process model can be implemented by an entity-relationship data base. In this implementation the data model developed in phase one can beused to describe any particular processmodel as needed for a particular case study. On the other hand having the abstract model Scope has a elementary, simple scheme to define an implementable process model. Thirdly, the certification process, which also handles activities and objects, can be defined and implemented in any relational data base. In case there is no relational data base available the abstract process model can be implemented on a plain file system, as has been done by GMD.

4 Software Quality Model

The evaluation schema presented here is based on a hierarchy of the factors of software quality. The two-level hierarchy shown allows each quality factor to be represented by its relationsship to evaluation factors, obtainable by means of commonly applied software measuring procedures. A method of evaluating software based on this hierarchy is then given, which computes quality values of two levels. The first level quality value is computed on the basis of the measured evaluation factors. Quality factors, described in terms of evaluation factors, are used for the computation of system values of level two. The overall system quality then is computed by comparing quality values of both levels with user- defined required values for quality. A quality computation procedure is outlined which shows how the proposed method can be applied.

4.1 Representation of Characteristics

The value of a software system may be represented as a tree. Each leaf of the tree represents an evaluation factor. Evaluation factors are those which cannot or should not be subdivided. The evaluation factors may be obtained by appli- cation of measurement procedures, such as those for calculating complexity measures. Other values may be defined by the user or owner of a software system. A set of evaluation factors constitutes a system-value of level 0. On the basis of these evaluation factors quality factors may be defined. For each evaluation factor a weighting factor determines to what degree it contributes to a quality factor. By this procedure a system value on level 1 is defined. For the calulation of the system values it is necessary to define a basis for the computation of the difference between the quality characteristics of the the actual software system and the quality characteristics of the required software system. For the actual software system all the evaluation factors can be computed by measurement procedures. Many such procedures are given by so called complexity measures, e.g. cyclomatic number computing. Others may be defined by the users needs.

The factors for the ideal or required system could be obtained by definition of this system, i.e. an effort has to be made to define the system requirements in terms of required evaluation factors and in terms of required quality factors. This definition of requirements then constitutes a so-called set of required evaluation factors and required quality factors. Both kinds of factors, actual and required ones, may be represented by n-ary vectors in order to make use of correlation functions defined for vectorial descriptions of systems. These correlation functions serve here as means for computing the relationship between an actual software system and the required system.

```
                              The Value Tree

Actual                                   asqv
System Quality Value                      |
                         +---------+----+--------------+
                         |         |                   |
Actual                   o         o                   o
Quality Factor         aqf.1     aqf.2               aqf.n.1
(Level 1)                |         |                   |
```

```
                                |         ...                |
                          +---+-+-----+              +---+-+-----+
Actual                    |   |       |              |   |       |
Evaluation Factor o   o       o              o   o       o
(Level 0)       aef.1 aef.2 ... aef.n.2          aef.1 aef.2 ... aef.n.2

                          |   |       |              |   |       |

Required         ref.1 ref.2 ...ref.n.2          ref.1 ref.2 ... ref.n.2
Evaluation Factor o   o       o              o   o       o
(Level 0)                 |   |       |              |   |       |
                          +---+-+-----+              +---+-+-----+
                                |         ...                |
                                |           |                |
Required                    rqf.1       rqf.2            rqf.n.1
Quality-Factor                o           o  ..............  o
(Level 1)                     |           |                  |
                              +-----------+----+-------------+
Required                                       |
System-Quality-Value                          rsqv
```

4.2 Definitions

a. actual evaluation factors
aefv = (aef.1,aef.2,aef.3,...,aef.n.1)
where aef.n : denotes value of a measurement (e.g cyclomatic number)
b. actual quality factors
aqfv = (aqf.1,aqf.2,aqf.3,...,aqf.n.2)
where aqf.n : denotes quality factor n
aqf.n := (a.n,1<op>aef.1,a.n,2<op>aef.2,...,a.n,n.1<op>aef.n.1)
where a.n,n : weighting factor
a.n,n : denotes the contribution of aef.n to aqf.n
0.0 leq a.n,n leq 1.0 or
a.n,n elem <(0,1)> for boolean expresions
c. required evaluation factors
refv = (ref.1,ref.2,ref.3,...,ref.n.1)
where ref.n : denotes value of the ideal or required value for ef.n
d. required quality factors
rqfv = (rqf.1,rqf,2,rqf.3,...,rqf.n.2)
where rqf.n : denotes value of the ideal or required value for qf.n
or alternatively the computed set of required quality factors
rqfv = (rqf.1,rqf.2,rqf.3,...,rqf.n.2)
where rqf.n : denotes quality factor n
rqf.n := (a.n,1<op>ref.1,a.n,2<op>ref.2,...,a.n.n.1<op>ref.n.1)
where a.n,.n : weighting factor
a.n,.n : denotes the contribution of ref.n to rqf.n
0.0 leq a.n,.n leq 1.0 or
a.n,.n elem <(0,1)> for boolean expresions

4.3 Evaluation and Quality Factors

4.3.1 The Objects of Measurement

Object to be measured: specification Form of description or representation of the object to be measured:

```
    -  specification text (i.e. the string of specification)
    -  static structure of the specification expression  (i.e.
       the structure of the specification functions) (i.e. the
       functional structure of the speci- fication)
    -  static structure of the specification expression  (i.e.
       the structure of the specification functions)
    -  ---
Object to be measured: imperative program
Form of description or representation of the object to be measured:
    -  Program text
    -  Control flow graph
    -  Data flow graph
    -  Storage space usage
    -  Execution time consumtion
    -  ---
Observeable attribute: Programm-Text
-> atomic attributes:
   number of chars
   number of chars
   number of words
   number of sentences
   number of chapters
   number of varibales and types
   number of operators and control structures
   frequency varibales and types
   frequency operators and control structures
-> non-atomic attributes:
Observeable attribute: Graph
-> atomic attributes:
   edges
   nodes
-> non-atomic attributes:
   subgraphs
   connected subgraphs
   strong connected subgraphs
   maximal connected subgraphs
   nesting of subgraphs
   .... of subgraphs
```

4.4 List of Quality Factors and Metrics

4.4.1 Quality Factors

A relvant set of software characteristics might comprise factors as:

- Correctness
  A software system is correct if it has been proved strictly that the system accomplishes the required tasks fully, not more and not less.

- Efficiency
  The evaluation of system performance mainly comprises the consideration of the measurable indicators for throughput, response time, availability and utilisation of resources.

- Reliability
  A system which is able to handle unexpected events in execution under allowable conditions without assuming undefined states is considered to be reliable.

- Robustness
  If a system is able to process expected or unexpected events in execution under unallowable conditions without assuming undefined states, it is considered to be robust.

- User Benefit
  The extent to which the requirements are met indicates the benefit to the user. Even this incomplete list of criteria clearly shows that a strict sepa- ration is actually not possible. For emphasising individual aspects of examination and evaluation of software such a division is however required.

4.4.2 Selected Metrics

The set of candidate metrics might comprise:

Author	Name
Balzert	Total Complexity Measure
Card et al.	Keystroke-Level Model
Chen	Maximal Intersection Number
Dale/Chall	Readability Index
DeYoung/Kampen	Readability Measure
Flesch/Kincaid	Readability Formula
Gilb	Logical Complexity Measure
Gilb	Portability Measure
Gilb	Structural Complexity Measure
Gong/Schmidt	Complexity Measure Based on Selection and Nesting
Gordon	Program Clarity Measure
Gunning	Fog Index
Halstead	Measure E
Hansen	2-tuple Complexity Measure
Hecht	Numerical Reliability Index
Hellerman	Measure of Computational Work
Joergensen	Readability Measure
Keutgen	Modularity Metric U
Langer et al.	Hamburg Comprehensibility Concept
Littlewood	Measure of Availability
Maekawa	Measure of Extensibility
Maier	Measure of User Friendliness
McCabe	Cyclomatic Number
McCall et al.	Accuracy Metric
McCall et al.	Completeness Metric
McCall et al.	Generality Metric
McCall et al.	Machine Independence Metric
McCall et al.	Software System Independence Metric
McClure	Complexity Measure
Mohanty/Adamowicz	Test Measures
Musa	Execution Time Measure
Myers	Interval Complexity Measure
Myers	Module Independence Measure
Nelson	Reliability Measure
Ottenstein	Error Prediction Measure
Oviedo	Program Complexity Measure
Paige	Test Effort Measure
Pearson	Measure of Computer User Satisfaction
Pimont/Rault	Test Effectiveness Measure
Remus/Zilles	Model of the Defect Removal Process

Schick/Wolverton	Probabilistic Measure of Reliability
Steiwer	Readability Formulas
Svanks	Integrity Metrics
Thayer et al.	Logic Complexity Measure
Woodward et al.	Knot Count Complexity Measure
Woodward et al.	Test Effectiveness Metrics
Yau/Collofello	Logical Stability Measure
Yin	Independence Metric I
Yin/Winchester	Measure for Software Design Quality
Zolnowski/Simmons	Complexity Measure

4.5 Method of Evaluating System Quality

Assessment can be a comparison of actual and required characteristics. Assessment can be a comparison of actual and required values. Evalutions/computations lead to values on different scales, comparisons can de done on values of the same scale, evalution values can be compared pairwise, quality factor values can be compared pairwise.

In this approach to software evaluation the user is required to put his view into the procedure. A first step occurs when the user defines his beliefs in certain measures by defining the ideals for the evaluation factors. The second step is given by the user-made definition of the degree of contribution of a measure to a quality factor. Therefore, this kind of procedure for software evaluation then defines some sort of a software metric which rests on user deci- sion as to the value of certain measurable evaluation values and on a user-made definition of the relationship between evaluation values and quality factors.

```
                              The System Values
     The Computation of the Level-0-System-Value (sv0)
actual system value vector
asvv0 = (asv0.1,asv0.2,...,asv0.n.1)
where asv0.n = c.n(aef.n,ref.n)
     where c.n : correlation (distance) function
required system value vector
rsvv0 = (rsv0.1,rsv0.2,...,rsv0.n.1)
where rsv0.n : denotes the ideal or required value for sv0.n
level-0 system value
                              sv0 = c(asvv0,rsvv0)

     where c : correlation function (distance function)
     The Computation of the Level-1-System-Value (sv1)
actual system value vector
asvv1 = (asv1.1,asv1.2,...,asv1.n.2)
where asv1.n = c.n(aqf.n,rqf.n)
     where c.n : correlation (distance) function
required system value vector
rsvv1 = (rsv1.1,rsv1.2,...,rsv1.n.2)
where rsv1.n : denotes the ideal or required value for sv1.n
level-1 system value
                              sv1 = c(asvv1,rsvv1)
     where c : correlation function (distance function)
     The Computation of the System Quality Value
System Quality Value
====================
                         sqv = c((sv0,sv1),(rsv0,rsv1))
                         ==============================
     where c : correlation function (distance function)
```

```
sv0, svv1 : as defined above
rsv0, rsvv1 : the respective ideal or required values
```

A very simple procedure is given which computes a system quality value on the basis of measurable evaluation values. It is assumed that different users have different views on what is relevant to a certain quality factor and how a measurable value belongs to such a quality factor. Therefore the proposed procedure gives freedom to each user to define his or her own quality factors in terms of measurable evaluation factors. The computation procedure outlined above shows that the determination of a system's quality is as complex as a program with a number of for-loops, nested up to the level one. For business appli- cations the proposed procedure has to be transformed into a small DB application wherein all the standardizable factors have to handled.

The proposed procedure works for vectorial representations of system character- istics. This is a simple representation schema but it is able to describe all of the currently proposed quality models. The principles of the schema are adopted form an evaluation method for adaptive information retrieval systems [?], where it has been proven that evaluation based on such elementary schema are often more effective than highly complex procedures. A procedure similar to the system quality determination method discussed can be used for the evalutation of software tools or software tool systems, such as software engineering environments.

5 Rule Based Certification Method

Since there is no theory of assessing software we need to have a knowledge based approach to define a certification method. Means to handle models for products, processes, and characteristics have to be offered in order to allow a certifier to define and operate an appropriate method.

In order to build-up a knowledge-based system concerning model selection knowledge about model has to be represented. Knowledge about models is represented by rules. Generally, a rule consists of a condition-part and an action-part:

IF	condition part
THEN	action part

Rules are well suited for representing heuristic knowledge and experiences, a fact which is important in nearly all aspects of software engineering. Generally, rule systems are not deterministic. In our case, nondeterminism is required because there is no general applicable model for the problem domains and therfore a model has to be instantiated for the product to be certified, the processes that produced the product, the product characteristics to be examined and the supporting instruments.

Model rules are of following general form:

IF	sub-model.1, sub-model.2, ..., sub-model.n	*is specified*
THEN	model M	*is defined*

A rule is a 'formalization' of the devide an conquer principle, because an IF-part refines the THEN-part. As shown [Neus86a] rules can be to structure and represent software engineering tasks and objects.

For the product model one will get

IF	requirements model, specification model, program model *is specified*
THEN	product model M *is defined*

The process model might be described by rules like

IF **or** **or** **or**	sequence model, waterfall model, axis model, role model, *is specified*
THEN	process model M *is defined*

Characteristics might br represented as follwos:

IF	sequence charactersitics,
or	waterfall charactersitics,
or	axis charactersitics,
or	role charactersitics,
	are specified
THEN	process charactersitics *are defined*

for process attributes. For product attributes one might get

IF	requirements charactersitics,
	specification charactersitics,
	program charactersitics
	is specified
THEN	product charactersitic M *is defined*

In order to represent the methods and tools to be applied to obtain real values for a set of characteristics one has also to define the corresponding rule sets.

IF	method predicate
THEN	method predicate

and

IF	tool predicate
THEN	tool predicate

Often a method is to complex to be instrumented directly by a tool or a set of tools. In those cases a complex task first has to be decomposed into subtasks which then might be instrumentable. Those decompositions are not part of a method and therfore a separate rule set is used to define them. As a consequence we get the following interrelation rules:

IF	interrelate predicate
THEN	method predicate **OR** interrelate predicate

For the interrelations between the characteristics and the methods we get the interrealtion rules:

IF	interrelate predicate
THEN	characteristics predicate
	OR interrelate predicate

In case a mapping can be done straight forward a characteristics, methods and tools are interrelated by:

IF	method predicate
THEN	characteristics predicate
together	with
IF	tool predicate
THEN	method predicate

Since there is no chance to develop the one and the only approach (or set of approaches) some flexibility is required for a rule system to be able to handle different application constraints. In general one will have a set of rules which are applicable in every area and smaller sets which are useful for selected domains only. In order to reduce the amount of rules to be maintained it is necessary to identify the range of a rule by parameters. A second form of flexibility is given by weights, which can be used to rank the sub-rules to be visited. We get rules of the form:

IF	condition part	**RANK**	weight part
THEN	action part	**ENVIRONMENT**	parameter part

To be able to instantiate a certfication method one has to select models for each sub-domain. A selection might depend on a special certification task and therefore knowledge about the applicability of those models has to be incorporated into the knowledge base. As a consequence both the knowledge about models as well as the knowledge on their interdependence is to be represented by rules.

A certification method now is to be defined by relating the models by rules, thereby instantiating each model according to the selected certification goals and objectives. We now get:

(IF	product model A		
and	process model K		
and	characteristics model R		
RANK	...some weight...)		
XOR			
...			
XOR			
(IF	product model B		
and	process model N		
and	characteristics model T		
RANK	...some weight...)		
THEN	certification method B	**ENVIRONMENT**	application domain X

By this rule a certification method B is defined for the application area X, e.g. operating systems. The body of the rule comprise a set of alternative instantiations, each of which leading to a particular instatiation of the process model, the product model and the model of the characteristics. The later is, as defined above, interconnected with the method and tool rules, which imediately lead to the instrumentation of the certification process.

6 Conclusions

Examination, measurement and assessment of software artifacts and the software process are represented by respective models. Complementary we have a model for the software characteristics, each of which connected to a method (or a set of methods) defining the procedure of how to obtain a value it. The methods are implemented in terms of tools which execute the respective method.

We are using rules to define the certification method, which is to be implemented by a set of rules. The type of rules proposed are easily to implement on either a data base, a expert system shell or just using pure Prolog.

References

[Basi78] Basili, V.R.; Ely, E.H.; Young, D. *Executive Summary of the Second Life Cycle Management Workshop* In *Proceedings of the Second Life Cycle Management Workshop* IEEE; Atlanta, Georgia 1978

[Beni83] Benington, H. D.; *Production of Large Programs* in: Anals of the History of Computing, Volume 5, Number 4 Oktober 1983

[Crow79] Crowley, J.D. *The Application Development Process: What's Wrong with It?* In *Proceedings of the Application Development Symposium* Monterey, Cal., Oct.1979, p.41-55 Share Inc.; 1979

[Dows86] Dowson, M.; *Iteration in the Software Process: Review of the 3rd International Software Process Workshop* In: *Proc. 9th International Conference on Software Engineering* IEEE; Monterey, March 1986

[Floy81] Floyd, C. *A Process-Oriented Approach to Software Development* In *Proceedings of the 6th ACM European Regional Conference on Systems Architecture* ICS 81, S.285-294 1981

[Floy87] Floyd, C. *Cooperation and Gestalt Formation in Software Development* In: Shackel, B; Bullinger, H.-J.; *Proceedings of the 2nd IFIP Conference on Human-Computer Interaction* INTERACT'87, Stuttgart 1987

[Hans81] Hansson, H.U. *On the Problem of Different Knowledge and Languages During the Systems Development Process* In: Pentti Kerola; Erkki Koskela (eds.), Report of the Fourth Scandinavian Research Seminar on Systemeering, pp. 96 - 110 University of Oulu; Oulu 1981

[Haus84] Hausen, H.L. *Software Validation* Proceedings of the Symposium on Software-Validation, North-Holland, Oct. 1984, 375 pages

[Haus87] Hausen, H.L.; Müllerburg, M.; Schmidt, M. *Examination, Measurement and Assessment of Software Products and Projects.* in: Proceedings EOQC'87, Munich, June 3.-5., 1987

[Iiva83] Ivari, J. *Contributions to the theoretical Foundations of Systemeering Research and the PIOCO Model* Acta Universitatis Ouluensis, Scientiae Rerum Naturalium No 150, University of Oulu, 1983

[Kero80] Pentti Kerola *On Infological Research into the Systemeering Process* In: Lucas; Land; Lincoln; Supper (Eds.) *The Information Systems Environment*; IFIP, pp. 199 - 217 North-Holland Publishing Company; 1980

[Kero81] Pentti Kerola *On the Comparison of the Highest Level Problem Solving Approaches in Information Systems Development* In: Pentti Kerola; Erkki Koskela (eds.), Report of the Fourth Scandinavian Research Seminar on Systemeering, pp. 132 - 140 University of Oulu; Oulu 1981

[Lehm87] Lehman, M. *Comments to the Software Development Process* in: Proceedings ICSE9, IEEE, Monterey, 1987

[Lund79] Lundeberg, M. *An approach for involving the users in the specification of information systems* In *H.-J. Schneider (ed.), Formal Models and Practical Tools for Information Systems Design* IFIP TC-8 Working Conference, pp. 195 - 217 North Holland; Amsterdam 1979

[Sten86] Stenning, V.; *On the Rols of an Environment* In: *Proc. 9th International Conference on Software Engineering* IEEE; Monterey, March 1986

[Thom81] J.C. Thomas; J.M. Carroll *Human factors in communication* In: IBM Systems Journal, Vol. 20, No.2, 1981, pp. 237 - 263

[Buch85] Bruce G. Buchanan *Expert Systems and the Research Literature*. Stanford Univeristy,, Report No. STAN-CS-86-1094 also KSL-85-37

[Cloc81] W. Clocksin, C. Mellish *Programming in Prolog* Springer, Berlin-Heidelberg-New York, 1981

[Drap84] W. Draper *The Nature of Expertise in Unix* Proceedings of INTERACT '84, FIRST IFIP Conference on Human-Computer Interaction, Elsevier Science Publishers, Amsterdam, Vol. 2, 182–186,(1984)

[Haus84a] H.L. Hausen (Editor) *Software Validation* Proceedings of the Symposium on Software-Validation, North-Holland, Oct. 1984, 375 pages

[Haus84b] H.L. Hausen *Comments on Practical Constraints of Software Validation Techniques* in: H.L. Hausen (ed), Software Validation, Proceedings of the Symposium on Software-Validation, North-Holland, Oct. 1984, 12 pages

[Haus84c] H.L. Hausen, M. Müllerburg *An Introduction to Quality Assurance and Control of Software* in: H.L. Hausen (ed), Software Validation, Proceedings of the Symposium on Software-Validation, North-Holland, Oct. 1984, 6 pages

[Haus85a] H.L. Hausen *Systematics of Means for Software Validation* in: H.J. Scheibl, Nationales Symposium Software-Entwicklungssysteme und -Werkzeuge, Technische Akademie Esslingen, 3.-5. September 1985, 13 S., ISBN 3-924813-04-3

[Haus85b] H.L. Hausen *Effektive Software-Qualitätssicherung durch integrierte Techniken der Software-Validation ?* R.Lauber (Ed.), Technische Zuverlässigkeit, Generalthema: Softwarequalität und Systemzuverlässigkeit, VDE-Verlag, Berlin, ISBN 3-8007-1416-7, S. 63-78

[Haus87b] H.L. Hausen, M. Müllerburg, M. Schmidt *Über das Prüfen, Messen und Bewerten von Software — Methoden und Techniken der analytischen Software-Qualitätssicherung* — erscheint in: Informatik Spektrum, 1987, Heft ?, Band ?

[Kers86] L. Kerschberg *Expert Data Base Systems* The Benjamin/Cummings Publishing Company, Inc. Menlo Park.

[Neus87] H. J. Neußer, U. Schwamborn *Wissensbasierte Software-Validation unter Unix* Diplomarbeit, Bonn, 1987

[Neus86a] H.J. Neußer *Ein Ansatz zur regelgesteuerten Softwarevalidation mit Unix-Werkzeugen* Zweite Sitzung des Arbeitskreises Software Engineering und Künstliche Intelligenz der Gesellschaft für Informatik 6. Oktober 1986, Berlin

[Norm81] D. A. Norman *The Trouble with Unix* DATAMATION, nov 1981, 139–150 (1981)

[PCS84] PCS *Munix-documentation* München, 1984

[SUN86] SUN *System V.2 Documentation* Mountain View , CA, 1986

[DEC86] DEC *System V Documentation*

[APOLLO86] APOLLO *System V Documentation*

[APOLLO86] APOLLO *Aegis Documentation*

[AT&T86] AT&T *System V Documentation*

Approving Software Products
W. Ehrenberger (Editor)
Elsevier Science Publishers B.V. (North-Holland)

CASE STUDY "WHISKY" - AN EXPERIMENT OF A CERTIFICATION PROCESS

Alexander BORS, Manfred KERSKEN

Gesellschaft für Reaktorsicherheit (GRS) mbH
Forschungsgelände
8046 Garching, F.R.G.

This paper describes an experiment of the Certification Process: the Case Study "WHISKY" which was performed within the SCOPE-Project since april 1989 till august 1990. This Case Study has been monitored by the GRS and is one of several Case Studies which were performed during the same time period. Each of these Case Studies proposes an approach for definition and implementation of possible certification techniques. The output of the Case Studies should support to establish the European Certification Model Definition. The Case Study has not been finished yet, thus this paper does not provide definitive statements, however, it gives insight into the problems involved with the Case Study.

1. INTRODUCTION

The Case Study "WHISKY" applied candidate assessment procedures and methods to a selected real life software product. The benefits and also the practical limitations of methods applied were determined. In preparation of a (future) investigation of the relationships between high level quality attributes and program metrics, product based metrics obtained during the Case Study will be provided to the Project Central Data Base.

2. PRODUCT DESCRIPTION

The software system on which the case study WHISKY is based is an operator information system (OPINF). It is written in FORTRAN 77 with a size of approximately 10.000 lines of code (incl. comments). OPINF is embedded in a system, which condenses a large amount of information without any loss. Therefore, the actual state of the technical process on which OPINF is used must be taken into account when selecting and synthesizing the required information. This is achieved by means of alarm reduction, disturbance analysis as well as post-trip analysis /Fel87/.

The most important part of OPINF is an on-line interpretation task. It performs the information synthesis and generates the actions. This is done on the basis of signals arriving from the process and a stored knowledge base.

2.1 The Task of Disturbance Analysis

A typical technical process control application of this kind must deal with a signal processing capability of several thousands of binary signals and analog measuring values. Parameters important for safety must be kept within predefined limits. The problem is to present this flood of data in an elaborated form on the operator monitor. The operator must be able to recognize the status of the process quickly, i.e. a compressed form of the information which is important for a specific situation must be prepared. In spite of this no information must be lost. In OPINF this is achieved by analysing the actual relevance of the distinct signals w.r.t. the whole process state. Adequate information which is fitted to the specific need is thus provided.

2.2 The Task of Alarm Reduction

If the process is in a faulty state a vast amount of messages will be brought to the attention of the operator. Most of them are of no importance at the moment and are suppressed. The messages actually shown, should be only few and should contain aids for diagnosis in time-critical situations.

2.3 The Task of Post-Trip Analysis

In time-critical situations sometimes actions on the process are automatically prompted. At the same time subsequent annunciations (belonging to primary ones) are suppressed. In this situation post-trip analysis is performed on the (logical and temporal) sequence of events (running in the background). Possible faults are immediately recorded to the operator.

2.4 Knowledge Base

The knowledge base contains procedural data which are stored in the form of data models. The data models are stored in the form of graphs. Their nodes represent the related functions; the edges represent logical and chronological connections. These data models are typed in off-line by means of a syntax-driven editor, in order to prevent syntactical wrong inputs at the earliest possible stage. The input syntax is represented by a formal grammar; its rules are the procedural descriptions (process procedures!).

2.5 Interpretation Task

All events, i.e. changes of binary and analog values of process signals are stored in a ring buffer RSP1 (see Fig. 1). When the interpretation task is called, it processes all elements in RSP1 sequentially. For each element a check is performed whether the knowledge base contains a corresponding start node. If this is not the case the RSP1-element is copied to another ring buffer RSP2.

If there is a start node in the data model corresponding to the event, then the event is propagated through the data model. This is done as long as the values of successor nodes are changing. If a final node is reached, the semantic actions associated with this final node are executed. Either a readable output (protocol) is generated, or logical derivations (status vectors, blocking criteria, ...) of the original RSP1-signal are entered after its copy in RSP2.

3. CERTIFICATION APPROACH

Within the case study the feasibility and efficiency of a mentally performed, but tool supported approach for the reverse development of software, starting from the code level and leading back to some high level representation which is comparable to the specifications is to be evaluated.

The reverse development process which aims in the demonstration of correctness uses some well known analysis techniques. We call this approach conventional testing, inspite of it contains also static elements as inspections, walkthroughs and static analysis. But these are used in a simulative way to understand the dynamic behaviour of the program.

The means of demonstrating the so called functional correctness is the comparison of the functional specification with the product. This assumes a complete and correct specification of the functional requirements. If there is no specification there is no definition of correctness. Hence there is nothing to verify!

3.1 Methods to Ensure Functional Correctness - General aspects

On principle there are three methods to verify the functional correctness of a software product:

The first and most powerful verification method is the program proof. There are several program proof methods of which the most common one is the method of inductive assertions of Floyd and Hoare. The goal is the development of a set of theorems about the considered program. The proof of these theorems guarantees the absence of errors in this program. The method requires the statement of assertions describing the programs input conditions and correct results. These assertions are expressed symbolically in a formal logic system, usually in the first-order predicate calculus. Then the program has to be partitioned into a fixed number of fixed-length paths. For each path, the input assertion is taken, moved along the path using the program semantics and if the end of the path is reached, a derived assertion is obtained (a so called post-assertion). Then a theorem is written, stating that the original assertion implies the derived assertion, and attempts are made to prove the theorem. If the theorems can be proved, the statement is made that the program is error free (i.e. meets its input and output assertions) provided that the program terminates. A separate proof is necessary to show that the program will always terminate!

Program proving is an exciting idea, but not without problems. The greatest problem is that it requires an enormous amount of intellectual effort. As a result no large programs could be proven yet, nor have proofs been applied to commercial production programs. There were of course (with some success) attempts [King] to automate a great deal of this process: automatic proof of the (human made) pre- and post-assertions as well as automatic generation of such assertions. It may have profound influences on software verification (and development) in the future.

Another approach is the compliance analysis which uses semantic analysis and aims in comparing automatically program properties and specification. In this case it is necessary that the specification is written in a special formal language.

In both cases mentioned, however, it is absolute necessary that the programming language used is one with formal semantics.

The second verification method is the method of symbolic testing. It is a compromise between a proof of correctness and conventional testing (for conventional testing see later). Hereby the subject program is executed, but it is executed symbolically, i.e. all inputs get symbolic values (similar to the proof of correctness). Because it is impossible with symbolic values to decide which branch of an condition statement should be traversed, a complete execution tree will be created with algebraic expressions which relate initial and final states of variables for distinct paths.

There were also attempts to automate this method (semantic analysers /Car84, Bra87/). Like with program proofs there are also great restrictions in applying this method to real-world programs. Normally the algebraic expressions become very lengthy and although they can be reduced by means of an algebraic simplifier, it remains a difficult task for the analyst to interpret them.

The third and most applicable method is the conventional testing. The difference with this and the other methods is that one can almost never test with all possible input data. Hence it is necessary to build equivalence classes for test cases from which always some representants will be chosen. The consequence is that one can never be sure of a program being perfectly free of errors.

Within the limits of conventional testing the following can be done:

- static analysis
- dynamic analysis (white box and black box tests)
- inspections and walkthroughs

3.2 Static Analysis

The static analysis includes the analysis of source code.

The objectives for applying the static analysis are:

- collect product metrics
- prepare test cases
- identify faults
- indentify functions

Static analysis (and conventional testing at all) as against program development is performed bottom-up, i.e. from the smallest functions which are then concatenated to bigger ones etc. until all the program functions are represented in a way which allows comparison with the specified ones. Some highly safety critical applications require to start the analysis from machine code as the ultimate form of a program (in this case the V&V of the compiler can be avoided). But normally if the program has been written in a high level language, the smallest units observed will most probably be the procedures, functions or subroutines on the level of this language (one has to believe of course that the compiler works correctly).

In the first step of static analysis the coarse structure (e.g. calling hierarchy) is identified, afterwards the more detailed structure in terms of control flow and data flow. The next step is based on a common view of control flow and data flow, i.e. what happens with the data when a distinct path/set of paths is traversed.

3.3 Dynamic Analysis

In dynamic analysis the program is executed. First a so called black box test (or functional test) can be done. The test cases for it are derived merely from the functional specification of the software product. Secondly so called white box tests (or structural test) are performed. The test cases for these are created with the knowledge of the source code structure. In both cases (black box test and white box test) the aim is the comparison between the expected and the obtained results. The best method of course is the application of both the black box test and the white box test, as their effects are supplementary.

3.4 Inspection Methods

Experience reported with inspections and walkthroughs has shown that they are effective in finding from 30% to 70% of the (found) logic design and coding errors in typical programs. They are, however, not effective in detecting "high-level" design errors, such as errors made in the requirements-analysis process.It was shown that the human processes tends to be more effective than the computer-based testing processes in finding certain types of errors, while the opposite is true for other types of errors. The implication is that inspections/walkthroughs and computer-based testing are complementary; error-detection efficiency will suffer if one or the other is not present.

4. TOOLS APPLIED

4.1 RXVP80

RXVP80 is a set of tools to validate FORTRAN programs.
Its components are

- static analysis
- program documentation
- execution coverage analysis

4.1.1 Static Analysis by RXVP80

The static analysis component performs an analysis of the source code. Its output is a source listing.which is commented with warnings and errors.

Typical errors that can be detected by this component are:

- mode inconsistencies in expressions and assignments
- mode inconsistencies between formal and actual parameters in subroutines and functions
- variables that are referenced without being set, and set but never referenced
- possible infinite loops and unreachable code

4.1.2 Program Documentation

This component also works on the source code. The results are extended cross-reference reports, calling trees and a statement profile report which characterizes each module in terms of the number and type of statements it contains.

4.1.3 Execution Coverage Analysis

This component measures the path coverage during the structural tests. It produces coverage reports, including the paths which are taken through the program, along with which paths are not taken and also the frequency of each path. The path analyser reports contain the individual test case reports followed by a cumulative summary report for all test cases. RXVP80 does not supply test data for the tested program.

4.2 QUALMS

QUALMS /Bac89/ is a static analyzer which uses mathematical theory to split up and analyze the basic components of control flow of a program. Each flowgraph can be splitted in subflowgraphs, which are subgraphs with only one entry (startnode) and one exit (stopnode). A trivial subflowgraph is one which represents the program or procedure with one statement. If a flowgraph has no proper subflowgraphs except trivial ones, it is called a prime. The key part of the theory on which QUALMS is based is a theorem [Fenton-Whitty] which states that any flowgraph may be uniquely decomposed into a hierarchy of primes. The input to the main QUALMS system is language independent. So the first stage is to pass the software through a front end which produces details of the control flow. The flow graph is presented on the screen. Then the system identifies the primes and so called decomposition tree where the primes are nodes and edges can be drawn. Finally up to 17 metrics are calculated from the decompositon tree.

4.3 FANAL

The FORTRAN-analyzer FANAL /Puh89/ is used for the analysis of control flow and data flow.

FANAL provides possibilities for an interactive traversal of the control flow graph to show the reachability of nodes (forward, backward, both direction) for chosen parts of the graph. Concerning data flow, the tool enables the representation of data dependencies. A typical question is: What variables are used to generate the value of a distinct variable?

4.4 VAX/VMS-Debugger

The VAX/VMS-Debugger is an interactive tool which allows to observe and manipulate a running program. Setting of breakpoints at any points desired, stepwise execution, changing and observing of variable data values, etc. are possible.

5. RESULTS

5.1 Results obtained by static analyser tools

As shown above only some special kinds of errors can be detected by static analysers.

5.1.1 RXVP80 /RXV85/

5.1.1.1 RXVP80-Static analyser component

The output of the first RXVP80-component concerning OPINF contains 440 pages. There were no errors but several warnings highlighted:

There were 3 warnings which indicated either unreachable code or an endless loop.

By reading through the source code it was found out that all these 3 cases do not come true. So this is a fault with the tool.

Furthermore RXVP80 issued 216 warnings in mode checking. All these warnings come true except one. This exception concerns the character*1 mode, which is obviously incorrectly interpreted by the tool.

All of these warnings concern mode inconsistencies in assignments. With FORTRAN especially, this kind of programming is widely applied and usually intended by the programmer. With regard to software safety, however, this should be avoided. In modern programming languages this is rejected as an error by the compiler.

Finally there were 11 warnings in set/use checking concerning variables which are set but their values are never used. In 9 cases these were parts of functions which were not implemented later. In 2 cases there are relicts of changed program parts. Such variables can eventually lead to errors if the same variable names are used later.

5.1.1.2 RXVP80-Program documentation component

The output of the second RXVP80-component concerning OPINF contains 483 pages (source code not included). For each module a symbol table was presented, a cross reference list and a table of calls of the module itself and from the module to other moduls outside.

As a result several subroutines which were never encountered had been detected. They were removed from OPINF.

The tables obtained enable a quick overview for the analyst. They are followed by the statement profile of the analysed program. The source code is divided into declaration-, execution-, decision- and documentation statements. The percentage of each statement class to the whole code is determined. With this a first indication is given whether the code is sufficiently documented. From the statement profile the balance of the usage of structured constructs (IF THEN ELSE) and unstructured constructs (GOTO) can be seen.

The statement profile can also be used for the surveillance of programming standards and enables some statements about the compliance with quality requirements.

A large part of RXVP80-program documentation, however, is only useful for software verification when using it for focusing on problem areas which may contain faults and inconsistencies detected during testing.

Concerning the RXVP80-program documentation, it can be said that the modularity of OPINF is quite good. It consists of 55 subroutines and 15 function modules. A percentage of comments of 58.63% (from the volume) indicates a sufficient amount of code documentation. The IF THEN ELSE statement is used 284 times, as against the GOTO statement which is used 136 times. The amount of GOTO statements is fairly high. Special care shall be taken of a routine containing 49 GOTOs.

5.1.1.3 RXVP80-Path analyser

RXVP80-Path analyser was used to support structural tests (see 5.2).

5.1.2 FANAL

The control flow graphs of FANAL output were compared to calling trees and path instrumentation obtained by RXVP80. Both were used as a support for creation of test data for structural tests (see 5.2).

5.1.3 QUALMS

QUALMS was used for the collection of product metrics. OPINF was propagated through the FORTRAN front-end and its results were sent to the Glasgow College. These results will be evaluated later.

5.2 Results obtained by manual testing

The functional specification delivered with the tested program is not very complete and in many cases it was difficult to extract the functionalities of certain program parts. Other program documentation was not delivered.

During the work it was shown - as expected - that testing tools are only suitable as a support for the tester during the validation. The experience of the tester during this process cannot be renounced - the tester has to become acquainted with the tested program to the minutest detail. This is the reason why we do not believe in a fully automized verification procedure in the future.

If the program documentation (functional specification etc.) is not very detailed (as it was in our case) it means a hard job for the tester to familiarize himself with the program. The effort of this, beside others, is dependent on the size, modularity, structuredness, etc. of the system to be tested.

A big support for the tester would be some kind of test support implemented by the system developers and delivered with the system to be tested (for instance a testbed, test cases and test data).

There was no test support delivered with our system and so it took several month of time to work ourselves in the details of OPINF. Special care shall be taken of the circumstance that the biggest problem was not the understanding of the program actions but the understanding of the mapping on bulky global data structures and the manipulation on it.

As it was our intention to provide profound tests, a detailed understanding of these data structures was necessary, as the most OPINF-subroutines operate on these structures.

Of course it is possible to imagine several levels of testing - on some low level it would not be necessary for the tester to become acquainted with the program internals - perhaps if some functional tests would be sufficient.
In such cases the functional specification has to offer an adequate support. Testing is facilitated in such a case if the effects of the tested program are obvious in an easy manner (for instance only output parameters and no global data are affected).

Some quality assurance mechanisms which would be set up to control testing could qualify what level of testing is required and what should be carried out.

5.2.1 General aspects of testing OPINF

In general the first important step within a testing process is to assign a functionality to the tested components. The reason is that the tester has to decide what output data (respectively what affecting of global data) is expected as a response to the entered input data.

The functional specification we obtained was not systematic enough, thus concerning some subroutines a profound understanding of their functionality was not possible till reading the source code and the comments included.

With respect to testing of OPINF there was an additional complication as compared to "conventional" programs. With OPINF there are not simply "output data" as a reaction on "input data" because a knowledge base is comprised as a fixed component of the program installation, which intervenes besides the program code into the object run. It determines together with the input data the output of the run. This means: a changed knowledge base with the same input data produce different output data.

To make it easier to the tester to understand what happens during an OPINF-run only a small knowledge base was used during the tests. Of course it is desirable that OPINF works correctly together with all possible knowledge bases. It was however not the aim of this case study to show this. Clearly the tests with all possible knowledge bases (which build the vocabulary of a LALR-grammar) cannot be done. We performed our tests with an OPINF-installation possessing a fixed knowledge base. (If OPINF is used in a real plant, only one fixed OPINF-installation is delivered as well; the knowledge base represents the actual process engineering state of this environment). Of course it has to be declared then, that only this special OPINF-installation has been tested.

The comparisons of expected data with the obtained data is often supported by the testbed. As we had none, the comparisons had to be made manually.

5.2.2 Single module tests

At first tests of single subroutines were performed, functional as well as structural tests.

For subroutine tests it is not only necessary to supply them with input parameters but in general to provide for a complete environment consisting of global data and called subroutines (existing at least as stubs). If a testbed was delivered with the program such an environment is a part of it. If there is no testbed it would be of advantage (if enough time available) to write a simple testing environment for the tested program.

A lot of subroutines within OPINF produce no output at all, they only deal with global data, for instance with the knowledge base. Therefore it was necessary during the tests to have a look at a lot of global data including the knowledge base. Herewith a good support was the so called "DEBUG-Level" implemented within OPINF. If the DEBUG-level was set, several global data contents including the knowledge base were typed out on a line printer.

Because of lack of time we did not write a test environment yet (we still intend to do it), but took the following approach:
We executed the whole linked system under the VAX/VMS-Debugger and set a breakpoint where the tested subroutine was called. At such a place there was already a complete environment available for the called subroutine (OPINF is completely implemented). Then the considered values were assigned to the subroutine parameters. Afterwards it was possible to view the effect of the subroutine run to the environment (output parameters, global data), for instance by setting a breakpoint behind the subroutine run.

In this way only the subroutines which are reachable by the control flow were testable. On the other side it should be said that subroutines in a system which are never called (dead code) do not really belong to the system, and so it would make little sense to test them. Anyway these are found during static analysis.

The important part of a program documentation should be the description of allowed parameter areas. In the absence of such a description the tester will possibly detect errors which are due to values which were not considered by the system implementor. Such subroutines can be marked as not robust enough, not abnormal. A robust kind of programming, of course, is preferable. It means each subroutine should accept all reasonable parameter values and bad values should be rejected - they should not cause a damage. If a subroutine which is not robust enough would be used later in another context (maybe by another developer) an abnormal condition could be established.

Test data for functional tests are prepared exclusively with the help of the functional specification and without knowledge of the program implementation. The success hereby is largely dependent on the subtle feeling of the tester. If there is a bad specification however, the best tester cannot provide meaningful test cases.

For structural tests, test data is prepared more systematically on the basis of the flow graph. The tester uses generally heuristic techniques. An initial set of test data is proposed and then refined using the experience and judgement of the tester. A path analyser (which measures path coverage) can indicate which parts of the program have been executed, thus guiding the tester in selecting further test cases. However it should be stressed that the aim of structural testing is not to test all possible path combinations but to ensure that test data are selected so that all possible paths are traversed at least once.

Using metrics as the path coverage can be dangerous as it may give an impression that the program has been thoroughly tested whereas all that can be said is that some percentage (perhaps 100%) of the independent paths in a program have been executed. It should not be forgotten that the aim of testing is the comparison of data obtained with data expected - the path coverage describes only some depth of the test.

During structural tests we used the RXVP80-path analyser tool for path coverage measuring. First the original FORTRAN code was instrumented by RXVP80. Hereby a total amount of 1238 disjunctive paths was determined. Then the instrumented FORTRAN code was compiled with the DEBUG-option.

To reach selected program paths during the structural tests it was necessary to prepare a special knowledge base and to select input data matching certain graph nodes of the knowledge base at the same time.

As all tests were made on a VAX/VMS environment, some subroutines of OPINF which were foreseen for other environments could not be tested.

5.2.3 Compound tests

As a next step after the single module tests, usually bigger components (subsystems etc.) are tested. One possible way herewith is to put only a few subroutines together first and to test these parts. Thus it is possible to build up the whole system stepwise.

If some system partitions (subsystems or other parts) are foreseen in the functional specification and the functionalities of such parts are exactly described, it is a good way to put exactly these components together and test them.

The compound tests are important, as the interaction of system parts is tested. Experience has shown that the most common problems which arise in large software systems are interface mismatches. The stepwise procedure should provide a help for an easy localisation of interface errors.

In our case study emphasis was put on interface testing. The reason for this is that OPINF is written in FORTRAN. In FORTRAN the parameter interfaces are not checked by the compiler. From this it can be seen that the way of testing should be language specific. If we had another programming language (where parameter interfaces are checked by the compiler) we could have saved a lot of testing work.

With OPINF there is no other partition foreseen in the functional specification than subroutines and functions. With a deeper knowledge of the system it can be said that a further partition would not be sensible.

5.3 Inspection methods

Inspection methods (inspections, walkthroughs) with the developers were used with the main objective to provide a better understanding of the program internals as it was not the main intention to correct the errors found and then to make further regression tests on corrected versions - as it is the case during program development. Our trials were made on a frozen system version.

6. CONCLUSIONS

The tests have not been finished yet. More particulars will be treated in the final evaluation report.

REFERENCES

/Fel87/ L. Felkel, F. Schild
Ein intelligentes System zur Aufbereitung situationsgerechter Prozeßinformation
Kerntechnik 50 (1987), No. 2

/Car84/ B. Carre
Lecture Notes on Program Validation
University of Southampton, June 1984

/Bra87/ B.D. Bramson
Tools for the Specification, Design, Analysis and Verification of Software,
Royal Signals and Radar Establishment, Malvern
Report No. 87005, July 1987

/RXV85/ General Research Corporation
RXVP80, User Manual, Version 4.2,
Santa Barbara, USA, 1985

/Bac89/ R. Bache, L. Leelasena
Qualms - A Tool for Control Flow Analysis and Measurement,
Glasgow College, 1989

/Puh89/ P. Puhr-Westerheide
Interner Bericht, FANAL
GRS, 1989

Approving Software Products
W. Ehrenberger (Editor)
Elsevier Science Publishers B.V. (North-Holland)
IFIP, 1990

EXPERIENCES WITH PRODUCING A COMPUTERISED SCHEME FOR PRODUCING CERTIFICATION MODELS

Bernard de Neumann
The City University
London, U.K.

Aim: To discuss a general means of producing appropriate and trustedmodels, generally relevant to particularised application domains, with special emphasis on Certification models. Thus we will begin with a paradigm for constructing trusted models in general, which relies upon a metamodelling concept.

Introduction: It seems evident from the State of the Art survey conducted by SCOPE (ref 1) that more than one certification model will be required: for example, different models may well be needed for each application domain, and that there may well be several levels of certification for each such domain. It will be assumed herein that each model will apply to an identified application domain and level of certification. A methodology will be discussed whereby such models may be rapidly assembled from proven sub-models, or modules (bricks), in such a way that all modules presented for selection for the certification model are compatible, and furthermore any available data will also be compatible. In what follows we use the term module (brick) to refer to an implemented sub-model.

The Scheme: The following represents a general method of producing trusted models which may be useful to the certification modelling task. Part of what is required for the process is a 'module-base' of proven sub-models (modules), all of which are compatible with at least some of the other modules. These modules may, perhaps, be formally specified in some formal specification language, and implemented using the formal methods and practices of Software Engineering. (It is not practical to go into further details of this "meta-modelling paradigm" here, and so this will be fully dealt with in a future paper, ref 2.). Another part of the requirement is for data, but since this can be treated in much the same way as the modules, we, for simplicity, will not treat it in the initial discussion below.

Essentially there are classes of Models which may be constructed from the modules; some of these modules are not universally applicable, but there are sufficient in the module-base to build a model in each class catered for. This 'module-base' must be extendible so that new proven modules may be incorporated as they arise. Given the existence of such a library of modules, then in order to use it, it is necessary to both supervise it and aid the model-builder so that appropriate modules only are used in a particular construction. This library/'module-base' supervision/selection function may be handled by the (human) user, by (straight-forward) data-base type software, or by the application of an expert system. This enables the modeller to construct the most appropriate model, and ensures that modules used are compatible. Here the compatibility applies both to the modules and to the domain of application. In many circumstances the process may be automated, and then with the aid of a 'model-shell', (or 'model-skeleton', the basic structure into which the instructions for the component parts of the model are introduced, and which handles the interfaces) models may be automatically produced.

As regards the implementation of this paradigm towards software certification, it is perhaps worth remarking that software cannot on its own cause loss or damage, and thereby create a liability, it is through its actor, the system in which it resides, that real risks can arise. Thus software certification cannot, and should not, take place without proper attention being paid to the encapsulating system's intended domain of application. Furthermore Certification can only take place when the attributes to be certified are fully specified. Thus, for example, it is possible to certify that a particular development methodology has been used, that particular individuals were in the development team, that some fraction of a specified set of Quality techniques has been applied, or that some metric has been exceeded; many other things could in principle be certified. Again the certification is not necessarily a positive statement that the software is of sufficient standard for a particular use; it could also be a negative statement that the software must not be used for particular applications; or a mixture of the two. Once the certification attributes are known it should be possible, given a knowledge of the domain of application of the software to be certified, to determine the certification model. The production of the model will not generally be in the control of the certifier; most likely it will be in the control of a national or international body responsible for the overseeing of certification procedures. This body will probably employ model architects to oversee the production of certification models, and, indeed, the activities of the meta modeller, considered below. The model will be a procedure which has to be applied under the control of the certifier to the software under consideration.

Figure 1, below, depicts the use of the Modular certification modeller (MCM), or meta-modeller. Of course its use places rigorous constraints upon the boundaries of the modules, and each module has to be well specified. Furthermore the partition of models into 'modules' is a non-trivial task which requires a great deal of understanding of the processes. For example it may be necessary to partition various program structural analysis techniques such as control flow analysis, into separate modules to avoid repetition in the final model.

It is likely that several attempts will be necessary before a viably extendible 'core' module-base is forthcoming. This is because the partitioning is not unique, but we require a minimum partition. However such redesign of the modules will not effect the architecture of the modular Certification modeller. It follows that the development of the 'meta' software for the modular Certification modeller (or meta-modeller) can proceed independently of, and in parallel with, the development of the module-base and data-base.

The output of the modular Certification modeller is an appropriate procedure which may be used to certify software for application in a particular domain.. Of course it may well be possible to place this procedure, provided that it is in a computer language, under the control of a computer, and even to automate it entirely. It may be that some proprietry techniques are deemed essential to some particular certification schemas, and that the owners are not willing for anyone to partition their product, in which case it may be necessary to resort to embedding it in some concealing software, perhaps running it in a virtual machine for example, so that the gory details are obscured to the certifier. This is somewhat analogous to giving it a plain brown paper wrapper.

In figure 1, a requirement for a new model is set. With the assistance of the module-base/library supervisor, the model architect can select the most appropriate modules from the library, and in the case where some modules don't yet exist, may initiate the construction of new modules for later inclusion in the library. The library supervisor function may be automated and its function may further be enhanced with the aid of an expert system which can also aid in the choice of the most appropriate module. The modules selected form an integrated model - in the case where the whole process is automated, and a model-shell is available, the result is an integrated computerised model. The resulting model is monitored in use, and, if necessary, new modules are specified, or maintenance of existing ones carried out.

Figure 2 depicts a fully automated schema for producing certification models.

In view of the international nature of the SCOPE project it may well be worth also introducing a 'dialogue-base' so that in computerised generation of models the dialogue between the model architect and the computer, and the user (not necessarily the certifier) and the computer can take place in the user's native tongue. Figures 3 and 4 depict a means by which (natural) language dependent certification models may be built and utilised.

Examples of the content of potential modules, possibly with major modifications to the original products, are Logiscope, Spade, Malpas, etc, Test generation methods, test coverage metrics, random test generation, Littlewood Reliability model, Albrecht function point technique, various checklist methods, various metrication techniques.

Hypothetical Examples: Suppose we wish to certify the software of three robots. (I) One which carries products between destinations in a person-free factory (ie an automated truck). (II) One which does welding in a car construction factory (ie a six degrees of freedom robot arm, fixed at one end, and with an electric arc welder at the other). And (III), one which loads and unloads fuel rods in a nuclear reactor (ie an automatic vehicle which carries a robot arm). Simplistically these all are in the robotics application domain. Yet they each, whilst having some commonality, seem to need different certification models. This is due to differing application domains and differing criticalities.

In (I) the functionality is relatively low, and the application not safety critical. All the system needs to do is: upon instruction move from point A to point B, along well defined routes (say marked out by coloured lines), halting when and while the path is blocked, and waiting for a further instruction at point B. Provided the truck halts at any obstruction there is no real risk other than possible pecuniary risk. Moreover the system can be safely aided by humans. Thus for the software it may be necessary to verify that the software complies with the specification, do a logiscope-type static analysis and examine the control flow and data flow, do a fault tree analysis and a failure modes effects and criticality analysis (both including system characteristics), generate to a limited extent test data for test coverage purposes. It may not be necessary to estimate reliability.

In (II) the functionality is higher than for (I). Furthermore there is potential for the system to cause loss of life or serious injury to humans and itself through self-mutilation. However there is also the opportunity for human intervention to help recover the system in the event of it failing or going berserk. All of the techniques mentioned for (I) could be utilised for certification, but they will be handling a much bigger problem. Furthermore it will be necessary to estimate the probabilities of (rare) safety critical hazardous events, which may well be facilitated by knowledge of the control flow of the software, thus indicating the desirability of producing a 'control-flow' module.

In (III) the functionality is much the same as for (II). Furthermore there is potential for the system to cause devastation on a geographic, if not global scale, major loss of life and serious injury on a wide scale, and further to cause major pecuniary loss, and environmental, economic and social destabilisation. There is no opportunity for human intervention since the environment of the robot is life annihilating. In these circumstances a very deep analysis will be required using the methods suggested for (II), amongst others. However it may be that the capabilities of existing techniques will not be stringent enough. This is certainly true of the presently existing software reliability models. It is ironic, if not downright perverse, that it is in precisely those safety-critical certification areas for which highly accurate reliability assessments are required that they, at present at least, cannot be done. That is, it is possible to determine the reliability of low reliability software fairly readily, whilst it is beyond present methodology for (anticipated) very highly reliable software.

Thus at least two certification models will be necessary, and possibly three or more. These are needed to take account of the varieties of application domain. It is not possible to divorce the certification of software from its domain of application.

Research Considerations: The scheme outlined herein requires the solution of a number of problems in order to produce a workable example of a modularised certification modeller. Amongst the problems are: interface specifications for the modules, and the shell; partition of the techniques which are deemed to be desirable for certification purposes; security and integrity of the modularised certification modeller; integrity of the overall certification process; production of new 'trusted' certification models; construction of module-base, dialogue-base, and data-base supervisors; application of expert system techniques to the supervisor and constructor function; establishment of a secure certified software-base in which copies of all certified software are available for comparison purposes. The resolution of just some of these problems will lead to a lasting contribution to certification modelling, whilst the resolution of more will lead to a major step forward, with influence lasting well beyond the end of the SCOPE project.

Conclusions: The Modularised Certification Modelling Scheme allows for several realisations ranging from a manual scheme to a fully automated certification scheme which communicates in the certifier's native language. Amongst the possibilities are:

(i) Manually generated certification scheme, manually applied.
(ii) Automated generation of certification scheme, manually applied.
(iii) Automated generation using AI of certification scheme, manually applied.
(iv) (ii) with construction dialogue.
(v) (iii) with construction dialogue.

(vi) (v) but with computer control of certification process and 'native tongue' dialogue with certifier.

Since there are many potential certification models, and, no doubt, more will occur in the future, the scheme outlined here offers a means by which trusted bases of modules, and data, may be built up, so that new trusted certification models can be constructed rapidly, economically and safely.

References

1 SCOPE State of the Art Report. SCOPE consortium. 1989.

2 Meta-Modeller for the production of Trusted Models. Bernard de Neumann. To be published.

3 Software Reliability Handbook. P. Rook. Elsevier, 1990.

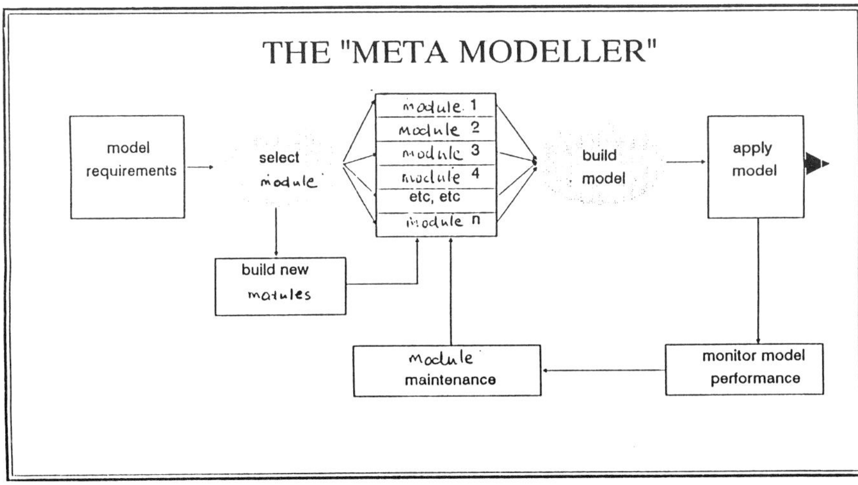
THE "META MODELLER"
model requirements
select module
module 1
module 2
module 3
module 4
etc, etc
module n
build model
apply model
build new modules
module maintenance
monitor model performance

Fig. 1

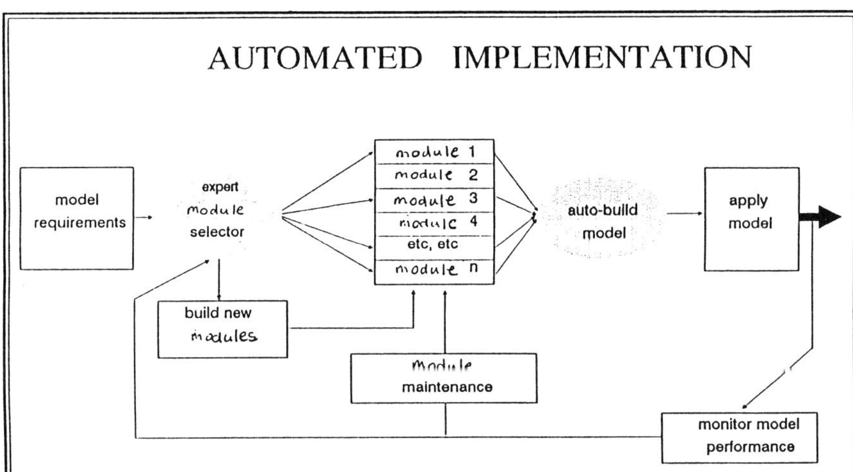
AUTOMATED IMPLEMENTATION
model requirements
expert module selector
module 1
module 2
module 3
module 4
etc, etc
module n
auto-build model
apply model
build new modules
module maintenance
monitor model performance

Fig. 2

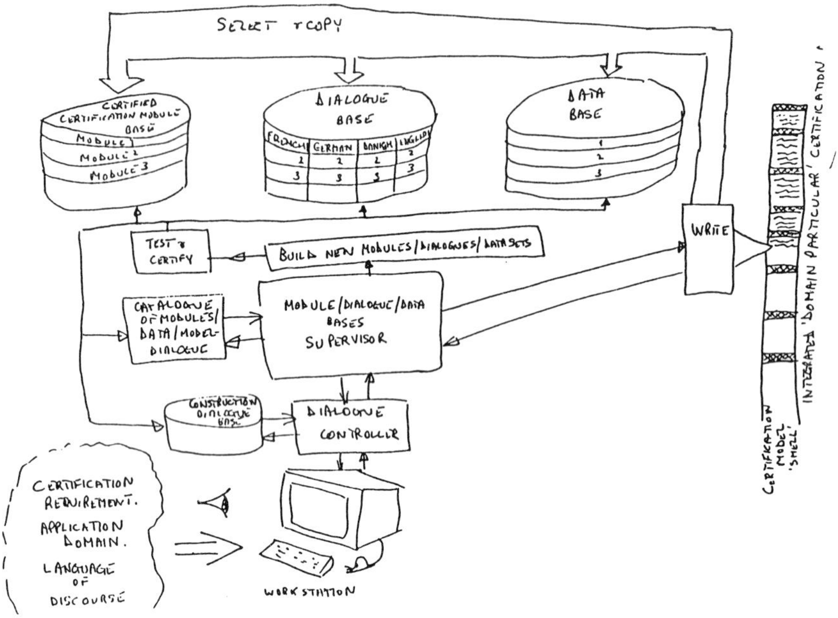
SELECT + COPY
CERTIFIED CERTIFICATION MODULE BASE
MODULE 1
MODULE 2
MODULE 3
DIALOGUE BASE
FRENCH
GERMAN
DANISH
ENGLISH
DATA BASE
TEST & CERTIFY
BUILD NEW MODULES/DIALOGUES/DATA SETS
WRITE
CATALOGUE OF MODULES/ DATA/MODEL-DIALOGUE
MODULE/DIALOGUE/DATA BASES SUPERVISOR
CONSTRUCTION DIALOGUE BASE
DIALOGUE CONTROLLER
CERTIFICATION REQUIREMENT.
APPLICATION DOMAIN.
LANGUAGE OF DISCOURSE
WORK STATION
CERTIFICATION MODEL 'SHELL'
INTEGRATED 'DOMAIN PARTICULAR' CERTIFICATION

Fig. 3

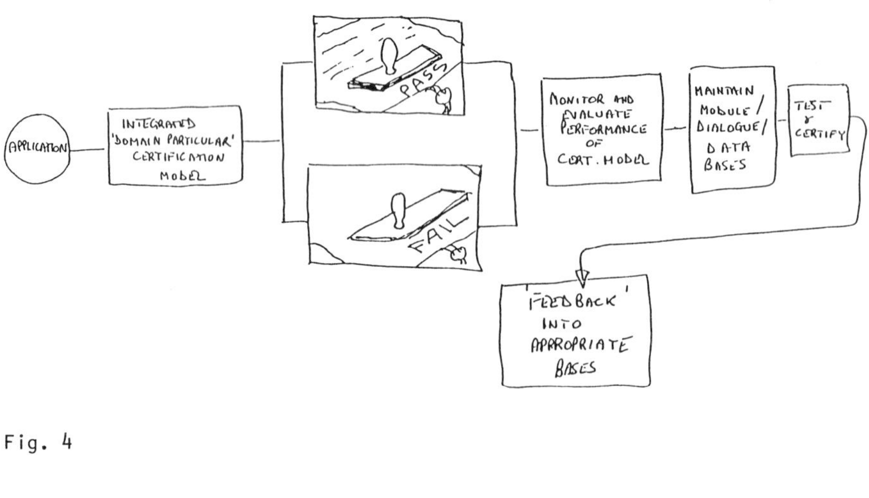
APPLICATION
INTEGRATED 'DOMAIN PARTICULAR' CERTIFICATION MODEL
PASS
FAIL
MONITOR AND EVALUATE PERFORMANCE OF CERT. MODEL
MAINTAIN MODULE / DIALOGUE/ DATA BASES
TEST & CERTIFY
'FEEDBACK' INTO APPROPRIATE BASES

Fig. 4

Approving Software Products
W. Ehrenberger (Editor)
Elsevier Science Publishers B.V. (North-Holland)
IFIP, 1990

SOFTWARE CERTIFICATION BY DEMAND: AN EXPERIENCE FROM A THIRD-PARTY LABORATORY

A. BERTOLINO, C. CARLESI, M. FUSANI, V. LAMI

Istituto di Elaborazione dell'Informazione, CNR, Pisa, Italy

ABSTRACT

There is still a sort of ambiguity surrounding the expression "software certification". The dated, common-sense IEEE definition [IEEE/729] "a written guarantee that a system or computer program complies with its specified requirements" does not provide useful guidance for organizing an effective certification service. Besides, a certificate issued according to this interpretation is inevitably mistaken for a "guarantee" of product adequacy, that which can definitely not be risked on at the state of the art.

As an independent laboratory which has been offering this kind of service for some years, on request from Public Administrations, users and producers, we have been becoming more and more aware of this. Thus, we have conceived and applied a process in which a defined set of characteristics of both software product and developing project undergo a defined Validation Suite. This process ends with a formal declaration illustrating the actions performed and their results.

This is what we mean by software certification.

The Validation Suite must be designed for a class of product criticality and may be adjusted for each application field.

In practice, our laboratory had to perform both the tasks of putting together Validation Suites for a number of cases and of carrying out the certification processes. If we would refer our work to some proposed certification schemes (like the European Community's), this would not be exactly the role of a *certification body*, which is not supposed to work directly in definition of standards. However, lack of established, commonly agreed rules, along with pressure from the demand side, convinced the laboratory to take on both aspects of the job.

The paper describes some critical aspects faced by the laboratory during the preparation and application of the Validation Suite to actual software products certification.

In particular, the concept of certifiability (that determines the feasibility of applying a Validation Suite leading to a positive certificate) is added to the yet conspicuous set of -ilities qualifying a product.

Techniques used in the Validation Suite are picked up from defined standards and recommendations for designing "good" software, and provide a way to deal with imperfect user specifications. Such techniques include inspection, testing and tracing specifications to code and vice-versa.

Problems rising from the peculiar experience of independent certification, such as dealing with manufacturer's privacy and interfacing software products to external inspectors, are also presented and a trace for their solution is proposed.

1. BASIC CONCEPTS

1.1. Foreword

In this paper we refer to the problem of approving general purpose software products, i. e., those for which it is not possible to devise functional standards.

When functional standards can be produced (compilers, communication protocols, graphic kernels), then it becomes possible to derive standard test suites which enable an external organization to approve or not approve the products, independent of the development process.

When general purpose applications are to be examined, we claim instead that the development process must be considered in conjunction with the final product in order to be able to express any evaluation (see [Copigneaux88] for a slightly different view). Thus, throughout the paper, relevant distinction between software products and their development process is seldom made.

1.2. Definitions

Nowadays, terms such as "Verification and Validation" (V&V) and "Certification" are largely used within the software industry, in spite of scarce understanding (or rather, wide misunderstanding) about their meaning.

In this paper, by touching on some of the related concepts, we do not pretend to enlighten people about them (basically, there is little to understand: it is a matter of achieving common agreement on the concepts); we only think it is useful to discuss some of our experiences.

According to an authoritative source such as ANSI/IEEE standard [IEEE/729], software certification is "a written guarantee that a system or computer program complies with its specified requirements".

Let us comment shortly this definition. First of all, a statement like "... complies with ..." looks somewhat drastic, a sort of all-or-nothing declaration, useful for, perhaps, some well defined technologies that depend on Nature's immutable laws. So far, software does not seem to have reached such a level of universality. Thus, we suggest replacing the expression with an ambiguous (why not? it fits the idea) "how well". Or, if we are not too afraid to be committed to a search for quantifiable concepts, we could better say "how much" and leave other details to further work in metrics.

If we continue to explore the above definition, we find another critical point: validation must be conducted against "specified requirements". What one would naturally argue is that a system is always created in order to satisfy a set of "user's needs". Thus, validating the user's needs would sound more reasonable and understandable. Only, this would not help in establishing a validation policy. In fact, the user's needs are hardly known by the user himself when a project starts, and will not be much better known when the product is shipped, (granting that it will be). So, the quoted expression "specified requirements" fits better from the operating point of view. Unfortunately, the open question of whether the specified requirements reflect the user's needs remains.

When the process of V&V is conducted by [IEEE/729] "an organization that is both technically and managerially separate from the organization responsible for developing the product", then we speak of IV&V. Thus, the remaining part of the paper will chiefly concern IV&V.

1.3. The demand for IV&V

In spite of the fact that people do not exactly agree on what software validation is, there is a considerable demand for it.
The following comments do not pretend to be an analytical survey of this demand, but directly result from the experience of our IV&V Unit (this will be described in the next section).

Our experience tells us that demand derives chiefly from the user's world, where certification is mistaken for a kind of guarantee. Thus, what is requested is just the end product of the validation, that is a **certificate** declaring (hopefully) that "the product complies with the user's needs". If this opinion is shared by others, as we assume, it is small wonder that some organizations refuse to issue certificates regarding software products.

Manufacturers may also be willing to have their software validated, at least for a couple of reasons:

1) To add value to the product. In fact, products accompanied by a validation statement (here, certificate) would make better sellers than those with no certificate at all.

2) To add value to the process. Obviously, manufacturers could take great advantage by submitting their production apparatus to analyses and tests performed by an independent organization.

However, we expect manufacturers are aware of the limits outlined above in validating user's needs, so they could ask for taking more realistically the "specified requirements" as the comparing object.

On the other hand, manufacturers are concerned with the extra-cost implied by an independent validation. Thus, many of them (unfortunately, the bigger companies, which mostly influence the market) fiercely resist any external attempt of performing validation or suggesting methods for validation, because the proposed actions would not be in harmony with their internal development processes, in which money and efforts are invested. Apart from this, some claim that formal documentation requested by external organizations unavoidably introduces undesired, awkward bureaucracy.

Some requests for IV&V comes from Public Administration. It is a known fact, for example, that the U.S. Department Of Defense (DOD) asks for formal IV&V declarations. Such declarations may in fact be conceived and executed according to the definition given in Section 6, where the validation procedure is requested to follow a defined standard that may be, for instance, the [DOD/2167].

We are also aware of a request for IV&V from the Italian Administration, as we have been involved for some years in the job: that is the history of the so-called "Fiscal Meters" certification [Bertolino87]. The initial request from the Ministry of Finances in 1984 was just for validating reliability and integrity of the fiscal software functions and issuing a certificate for them. The job could not be done, at that time (nor now, in a sense), but we took the challenge to come up with an answer. We are still working at it. Sections 4, 5, 6 are intended to illustrate how this answer is being formed (while evolving, the approach has been (had to be) applied to many real cases).

Another, more vague, source of demand is simply the expressed will to "know more about" or "to be very interested in", that we could detect in almost any environment where technical, administrative or commercial activities are performed.

Finally, we have observed that a good deal of demand is not explicitly expressed, but results directly from the fact that software is embedded in a vast range of products of various technologies, for which certification is requested (this was exactly the case of the Fiscal Meters).

In front of this wide spectrum of requests, devising a feasible, practical solution for software IV&V can absolutely not be postponed to when the art is settled. In the immediate future, certificates stating something about properties of products (medical equipment, for instance) that also depend on the behaviour of a program will have to be able to circulate through Europe. Among many questions that may arise, let us choose three:

1) Will such certificates explicitly include the software component?

2) How is this component to be approved?

3) Who is going to give the approval?

Two quick answers. Point 1): Yes, of course. Point 3): The European Certification Scheme, with its (to be) accredited Certification Bodies and Testing Laboratories [M-IT 03] would well provide the "approvers".

Point 2) takes a little longer. Our proposal will be presented in Sections 4, 5 and 6.

2. AN INDEPENDENT V&V UNIT

2.1. Profile of our IV&V Unit

Our IV&V Unit comes from a joint venture between a *Public* research & service Institute working in IT, and an Independent *private* Testing Laboratory (Figure 2.1).

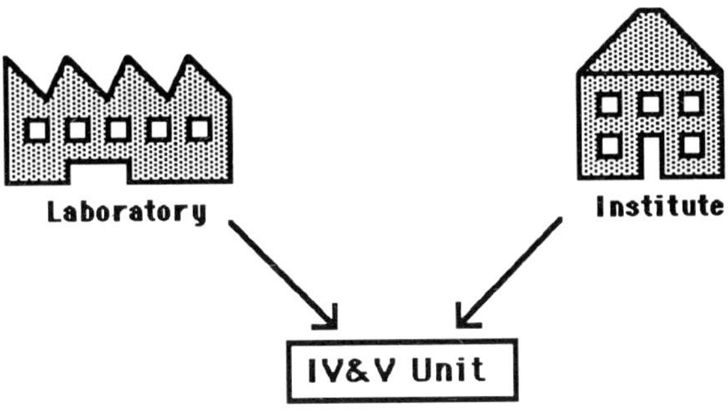

Figure 2.1 - IV&V Unit

Including a public-financed entity seems to have some advantages:

ADV:
- financial stability (the Institute can also choose other private laboratories as partners);
- larger inventory of tools;
- easier access to confidential project information;
- technical-scientific updating

and some disadvantages:

DISADV:
- complex organization;
- lack of flexibility;
- lack of efficiency due to a non business-oriented organization.

Our aim is to manage to get benefits from both types of organization. From the laboratory, we have:

ADV:
- flexible organization;
- sensibility to time schedule;
- business oriented staff.

2.2. The job of an IV&V Unit

In [Deutch88] the activity of an IV&V organization is naturally presented as not just monitoring ("reading", we would say) the developing process, but also interacting with it and influencing it in some way. Actually, at first we were rather concerned about the fact that an independent organization might, in a sense, approve or not what is also a consequence of its own activity. But the processes of reading and modifying are so intricated that it is impossible to play just one role. Therefore, we tolerate the fact that we are driven by demand, and articulate our job in the following actions:

- Assisting the user to prepare the Software Requirement Specifications.
- Monitoring software development activity during the entire life-cycle;
- Assisting the software developer during the entire software life-cycle;
- Preparing system test plans and integration test plans;
- Performing system tests;
- Reporting to the customer.

Each time we are called for a validation, we tailor these specific actions to the particular request.

As far as regards the criteria to be adopted for each point, our efforts are aimed to select and integrate from various sources:

1) State-of-the-art in software engineering.

2) Current standards, recommendations and guidelines, especially those likely to be referred to in the EEC environment.

3) Self-developed strategies, when sources 1) and 2) are not sufficient.

One of the methods of our Unit is to use the standard Forms for inspection, described in Section 4.

3. PROBLEMS WITH IV&V

Problems particular to IV&V are not easy to find in literature regarding the subject. Are there intrinsic differences between IV&V and Manufacturer's V&V (MV&V)? In our experience some critical, mutually related aspects can be pointed out:

- cost;
- lack of documentation;
- excess of documentation;

- difficulty in using automated testing tools;
- privacy of process and product information;
- manufacturer's resistance;
- certification.

Cost is probably the reason why IV&V is only recommended for critical software [Deutsch88]. However, we have observed that any software product, brand new from the developing phase, always contains defects. Therefore, it should be considered as a critical product. Perhaps it is not always risky, but it is worth spending some extra money in inspections and testing: why not by an Independent Unit? Of course, we agree that getting acquainted with someone else's project is more expensive.

Documentation is the main way we have for examining the process. Unfortunately enough, all the documents we were given during our activity interfaced very badly to external reviewers. Either the documentation is scarce, or, being richer, it is not easily accessible: in the latter case, one has to first review all of it to define the way of establishing an easier search for definite subjects.This enormously increases the cost of external validation.

It is for this reason that we have been investigating a low-cost method of extracting information about a process and are now experimenting standard Forms.

The use of automated test tools seems the practical solution to take the burden of effectively testing software products. Yet, in the case of IV&V, the independent organization must be prepared to accept products implemented in a variety of languages and dialects for a variety of hosts and operating systems. Therefore, each time, a new testing environment must be decided. Again, IV&V costs raise, in comparison with MV&V, in which testing must be reasonably equipped once and for all.

This paper cannot deal with all of the problems outlined above. However, employing standard Forms (Section 4) and a tailored Validation Suite (Section 5) can help, in our opinion, with more than one of these problems at a time.

4. STANDARD FORMS

The Forms are formatted documents designed by the IV&V Unit and filled up by the manufacturer's staff. They are an evolution of a previous approach of using ad-hoc questionnaires [Bertolino87] to allow an external organization to get acquainted with a project: they collect information about aspects of both the phases of the developing process and the final product, as well. This information is represented in a standard way, in order to help the independent reviewers to perform inspections.

Basically, a Form contains one or more questions about a specific function, part, structure, developing strategy, along with alternatives, where possible, or places for the answers. Besides, this contains spaces in which to put references to manufacturer (standard) documents. Figure 4.1 shows the general layout of a Form.

The underlying idea is to let the manufacturer explain the process/product: this should reduce the cost of external inspection, in that the manufacturer is obviously better better acquainted with what he has done. The references for the documentation are necessary in order to check whether the answers are correct and the Form is not a fake. We rely on the belief that the cost of a fake is comparable to that of documenting the real thing, so the manufacturer is encouraged to fill the Forms truthfully.

We distinguish two classes of Forms:

Process Forms: conceived to look for usability, traceability, consistency of process documentation;

Product Forms: conceived to look for critical points in the application (they are application dependent).

In order to cope with the problems presented in Section 3, the Forms should have the following characteristics:

- standard;
- synoptical;
- easy to manage;
- traceable.

In particular, traceability implies both the ability to reach inner details of the process/product, and the existence of a structure in the Forms system, so that a function or part of a product may be "pointed to" by a hierarchy of Forms.

5. THE VALIDATION SUITE

In order to choose the actions to be performed to validate a software product, we have devised a general scheme which includes a sequence of possible actions, and we denoted it as Validation Suite (VS). Basically, we apply inspection on a required subset of documentation, possibly supported by adequately filled forms, and testing on the executable product, possibly supported by automated testing tools. This implies that:

1) adequate documentation is available;

2) the product is testable.

Among all the possible scenarios, there is the case of the manufacturer performing his own validation (MV&V) (this matches with our experience). In such case, the best thing an IV&V Unit can do is to simply perform a validation over the MV&V documented (possibly with Forms) activity. This would keep the cost even lower for IV&V, and would prevent (through not involving deeper traceability) private process/product information from being disclosed.

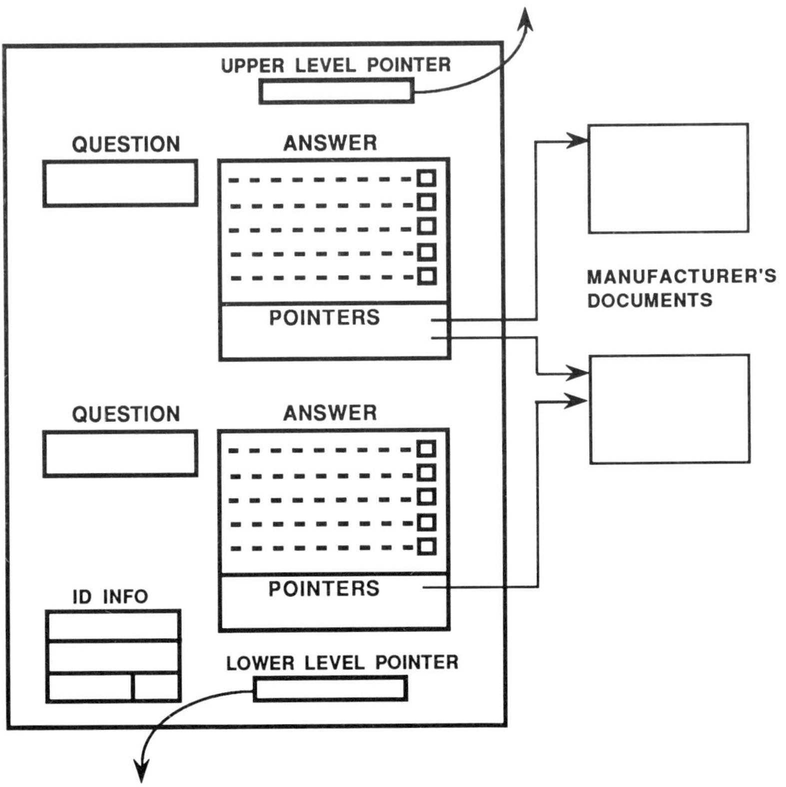

Fig. 4.1 - Form layout

The validation activity is divided into two phases: in the first one, to keep costs low, a preliminary short analysis of the documents submitted is performed, to check whether or not a more thorough validation can be carried out in the second phase. In case of insufficient documentation, the validation process is stopped and will be resumed when the manufacturer complies with the request for more information. We use the term "certifiability" to express the ability of a product to pass this first acceptance analysis.

Let us briefly comment on the concept of certifiability just introduced. Unfortunately, as it already happens for many others of the -ilities qualifying a product, also for certifiability it is difficult to give an objective definition, least of all a measurable one. Once again, the leading criterion is "cost": in a sense, we state that a product is "certifiable" if we judge that the cost for its IV&V, i.e. the time and effort we must invest, is "reasonably" adequate on the basis of our "good-sense" and of product criticity.

Once we accept starting a validation process, we also use this first phase to become acquainted with the product/process under examination and to tailor specific forms.

In the second phase of our validation activity, inspections, analyses and tests selected from the VS can be monitored or executed, depending on the degree of confidence we want to get with the process/product, and on the budget at disposal for the particular validation process.

Hereafter we report a synopsis of the VS:

1 Request for software product

- 1.1 Documents probably existing
  - 1.1.1 Functional specifications
  - 1.1.2 Design schemata and flow graphs
  - 1.1.3 Source code listings
  - 1.1.4 Documents describing the developing environment of the product to be validated: Hardware, Operating System, Applications, Approaches, Tools.
  - 1.1.5 Documents describing the actions performed during product development and testing
  - 1.1.6 Reference standards for 1.1.1, 1.1.2, 1.1.3, 1.1.4, 1.1.5 documents
- 1.2 Documents to be prepared
  - 1.2.1 Missing documents from point 1.1
  - 1.2.2 Filled Forms
- 1.3 Product instance
  - 1.3.1 On a support suitable for available host hardware
  - 1.3.2 With its target hardware

2 Acceptance analysis (Certifiability)

- 2.1 Adequacy criterion
- 2.2 Completeness criterion

3 Inspections

3.1 Document inspection, supported by Forms

3.1.1 Check lists for documents (various levels)

3.1.2 Forms (various levels)

3.2 Code inspection

3.2.1 Check lists for code

4 Tests (planning/execution)

4.1 Functional tests

4.1.1 Unit, Integration, Subsystem tests
4.1.2 System tests

4.2 Structural tests

4.2.1 Branch Coverage

The Validation Suite would involve a great deal of work if applied as a whole. In practice, it represents all of the possible actions, of which only some are reasonably worth performing in a single case of IV&V. The point is to devise the best subset to exercise each time, depending on product criticality, availability of documentation, cost constraints.

6. THE CERTIFICATE

Our validation process finishes with the issue of a "certificate". According to the position taken throughout the paper, in it we do not "guarantee" any property for the system validated. Instead, our certificate is a plain and exhaustive documentation of the validation process.

Thus, we certify that the product has passed the acceptance analysis, which is also described into the certificate. Then, we document the subset of the VS which has been performed, together with analysis results and evaluations.

The certificate presents a standard, formatted report, consisting of eight pages expressly designed to enhance self-descriptiveness and completeness of its contents.

In brief, the certificate statement can be summarized as follows:
"the product P and the accompanying documentation d1, ..., dn were submitted to the actions a1, ..., an of the VS. Results and evaluations are reported at the points r1, ..., rn of this certificate".

REFERENCES

[Bertolino87] Bertolino, A., Fusani, M., "Software Validation: A Government-imposed Challenge to the State-of-the-Art in Certification", *Computers & Standards*, Vol. 6, 1987, pp. 433-436.

[Copigneaux88] F. Copigneaux, "Software Process and Product Certification", in *CSR Software Certification Workshop*, Gatwick, 13th-16th September 1988.

[Deutsch88] Deutsch, M. S., Willis, R. R., *Software Quality Engineering: A Total Technical and Management Approach*, Prentice Hall, 1988.

[DOD/2167] DOD-STD-2167, Defense System Software Development, 1985.

[IEEE/729] ANSI/IEEE Std 729-1983, IEEE Standard Glossary of Software Engineering Terminology.

[M-IT-03/87] CEN, CENELEC, CEPT, Memorandum M-IT-03 on Certification of Information Technology Products, 1987.

Approving Software Products
W. Ehrenberger (Editor)
Elsevier Science Publishers B.V. (North-Holland)

SOFTWARE FOR FARMERS IN THE UNITED KINGDOM

John Nixon

School of Business
Royal Agricultural College
Cirencester, Gloucestershire GL7 6JS

ABSTRACT

This paper looks at the problem of developing appropriate software for agricultural applications. In this area, the gulf between the user and the writer of the software is potentially very great, with the practical farmer usually having no background in information technology and the systems designers and programmers typically unclear about what the users need and what level of IT background can be assumed. The main emphasis of this paper is the possibilities that exist for overcoming the gulf by participation of users in the decision making concerning what software needs to be developed, and the actual design process.

This theme will be developed both from the standpoint of the commercial software firm and the farmer. Firstly, the paper gives a brief background into the market for commercial packages for the farmer in the UK. Secondly, it turns to the supply side of this market looking at the life cycle of a software product. To make this life cycle more concrete we will look at the development process within the major firm producing agricultural software in the UK, Farmplan. This section will emphasise the efforts made by Farmplan to involve farmers in the process, especially during the specification and testing stages. Thirdly, it looks at the demand side. It looks at the experiences of farmers with microcomputers using various studies, mainly in the UK. Fourthly, it summarises our conclusions. It discusses the possibility of regulation of this market, but suggests that the arguments for regulation are hardly overwhelming and that the free market provision of software products as it exists may prove to be an acceptable solution.

1 INTRODUCTION

The use of computers "on" the farm began with the arrival of microcomputers, principally 8 bit machines with DOS operating systems, in the late 1970's. Previously, farmers had made use of mainframes and used the services of computer bureaux on an occasional basis, but this was a relatively expensive business, as it meant entrusting the farm's data to an outside agency and paying for the storage of the data on a permanent basis. Micros brought the possibility of a local, personal control over the farm's data, and with this the possibility of being instantly able to update, amend and retrieve relevant data to help in the day to day control of the farm.

In order to use the micro, relevant software had to be developed and the first generation of agricultural software was born. There was an urgent need for accounting/financial packages suitable for farming. The demand for such programmes came more from the consultants working with the farmers than the farmers themselves. The standard accounting packages had not been found easy to adapt to farm businesses which were different to normal trading firms. On farms each enterprise had to be treated as an individual sector, and the assets, because of the biological nature of the business, are constantly changing in value, animals are born and die, crops grow. So one of the first sectors to be explored was the financial programme area especially to enable innovating farmers and consultants to produce enterprise reports mainly through the use of spreadsheets. At the same time there was pressure for better financial recording from the banks and from the Ministry of Agriculture in order to monitor the activities of farmers in receipt of EC grants.

Thus for eighty per cent of farmers using computers for business purposes the first application was in using financial programmes. The other main area for early development was husbandry software especially for dairy herds.

After the initial phase of development feedback from the farmers began to be received by the software firms. One major complaint was that the programmes were much too sophisticated and complex for farmers' needs. The software was designed primarily for the specialist consultants and not for the ordinary farmer. For example, an early programme could generate 155 different financial reports and it was very difficult for the non specialist to sort through all the available options. The tendency, for Farmplan at least, has been to simplify and to produce a product which does a basic job rather than incorporate all the sophistications which the specialist accountant and financial consultant would like.

Another development in agricultural software has been driven by developments in the agricultural industry. In the 1970's and early 1980's the emphasis was on increasing efficiency. This focused attention on the cash flow situation with the result that the production of cash flow information became a dominant consideration. Producers with the biggest gross margins tended to make money. The current situation is for a much greater emphasis on financial structure rather than production. For example, it is possible to be a highly efficient dairy producer, but to be overcapitalised, having to pay high interest rates and to be financially insolvent. The thrust of current financial packages is to place much greater emphasis on the balance sheet and the structure of assets rather than gross margins.

Farmplan have slowly come to realise that what is important to the user is not just the purchase of a one off piece of software, but a whole service package. The package includes not only the hardware and software but also:

1 The initial training with the software, which gives the user confidence to sit down and work with the programmes;

2 Crucially, the advice hotline which is open for the user to ring up and get information on how to do the things he/she needs to do. Often these questions are not of a specialist computer nature, but are rather book-keeping or accounting queries;

3 An updating service, so that improvements in software can be incorporated into the user's system, without their having to alter their data disks. If the changes in software are significant the new version will be explained by the trainers who will work the users through the new procedures;

4 A problem solving service, so that if any hardware problems arise replacement parts or whole components of the system can be installed within forty eight hours. If software problems occur or the user's data is corrupted, replacement of the software or a restoration of the data disk can be normally achieved within two days.

For many farmers what is important is a stable long term relationship with the software supplier. This is a difficulty within the industry. Many of the products are the brain children of people within the industry, farmers, advisers or academics, who have a good idea, perhaps about beef rearing, and produce a good programme in this area. With the enthusiasm inspired by their ideas and the knowledge that this programme is good they sell this programme to farmers, often in a narrow geographical area. Because they are prepared to work long hours promoting their own programmes they are able to market them at comparatively low prices. However, many such firms have found long term survival a problem. Working a hundred hours a week doesn't seem to be an attractive long term proposition. If these small firms then leave the industry, the farmers who have bought their programmes then find themselves without any backup or possibility of enhancing their products. However, there is large turnover in the industry because of an absence of barriers to entry, so new firms are continually trying their luck. Entry tends to keep the price of software low and not only software, but maintenance as well. For example, a small firm may guarantee to maintain its programmes for as little as sixty pounds per year. The problem is just how much service can be expected for such a low fee and how valid this promise of service can be when the firm cannot be earning enough to adequately compensate the owners for their own labour.

Much of the software in the United Kingdom originated when a farmer had an idea that by using a computer he or she could save time, have more accurate or a greater amount of information. The farmer if he had sufficient capital, invested money in developing his idea and produced a professional piece of software through employing specialist analysts and programmers. This is how the Farmplan organisation originated. On the other hand if the farmer did not have the capital he either tried to teach himself how to produce a programme or took his idea to an adviser or academic institution where a programme could be produced at virtually no cost. Developments such as these seldom made the commercial market, whereas the former developments where professional help was purchased have provided the basis of the UK farmers' library of software. The underlying reasons for commercial success in most instances had more to do with the quality of the back-up services than either the standard or the content of the programmes. Many badly written programmes have been used and have had a useful working life, while other programmes which have been beautifully and professionally constructed have been practically useless because they have not produced the desired output.

2 THE LIFE CYCLE OF A PRODUCT

2.1 Germination

At the present time problems such as these are being overcome by feedback that identifies the farmers' requirements. Feedback in the Farmplan organisation comes from several sources:

The Sales Department are aware of what competitive products are able to achieve and what deficiencies potential customers are pointing out in existing products. The Sales Team might be having problems selling because of competition from other products which can perform certain functions that the firm's own software cannot. Usually, the sales force comes from an agricultural background and is able to speak the same language as the farmers. The Department tries to avoid a philosophy of making a quick sale and then never seeing the customer again. The approach is rather to establish a long term relationship with the customer.

Customer services are dealing with dozens of telephone enquiries per day. These phone calls are analysed and the programme enhancements and suggestions are noted. The on-line advisers are the people in the firm who are closest to the consumers. They ring the users after they have been working with a new product for a few weeks to find out how they are getting on with it and encourage the users to ring in with their questions. These advisers are all from farming backgrounds, mostly farm secretaries and mainly with some previous experience of using the software they are dealing with. The queries are of a very diverse nature. Many of them are about the accounting and book-keeping programmes and are questions about the correct book-keeping procedure to follow. The users of the programmes come from different backgrounds, even though they are all involved in the agricultural industry - they include farmers, farmers' wives, secretaries, farm managers (who are sometimes reluctant users of computers), agents, accountants and advisers. The problem of appealing to all these constituencies in specifying a package is not readily soluble.

The trainers who help users get to know the products also provide feedback on the difficulties they encountered and what the users actually want to be able to do. Outside Contractors are used as trainers. They tend to be farm secretaries using the programmes. Seminars are organised throughout the country to familiarise the trainers with new products, enhancements and developments. They provide opportunities for feedback on the software. People working on software development have the chance to get out in the field and receive comments from the farmers about how they use the programmes and what they would like to be able to do. Also they learn about the way the farming industry is moving which gives ideas about future computer applications.

These Departments are involved not only in the early stages of a product. When the programme is actually being written and tested thought will also be going into how it will be sold, how it will be supported and what training needs to be provided.

2.2 Feasibility Study

The first stage in the life cycle is to sift all these sources of information about consumers' demands to see if it is economically viable to satisfy these demands with a software package. The market for such a product and the associated costs need to be estimated.

2.3 Analysis

Perhaps the feasibility study involved some market research. This also identifies potential customers for a new product and these are the sort of people who would benefit from the product and are thus likely to cooperate in its development. These potential users would then be approached and interviewed to find out what sort of output they want from a programme.

If user requirements are standard then the analyst can put together a specification for a package, if they are very diverse then any end product would be confusing for everyone. A software package cannot do everything for everyone, and in this event the project would have to be abandoned.

The end product of the analysis stage could be thought of as the Agricultural Specification. This includes:

All screen menus;
Displays and report printouts required;
All capacities and calculation requirements.

It is this information that the analysis is designed to extract. This analysis process would often involve several phases. First interviewing potential users to obtain a general idea of the output required and the data that needed to be stored; then producing a written specification and returning to the users for a discussions of this specification in detail, after the users have had time to study it. Time spent on getting this Agricultural Specification right is normally reckoned to be well spent. It is easier and less costly to put things right at this stage rather than later in the cycle or when the product has been released.

2.4 Development

It is necessary to turn the Agricultural Specification into something the programmer can work with. A technical specification needs to be produced which defines which modules need to be written and what file structures are required. The programmes then need to be written and tested.

2.5 Testing

A problem that small firms have is of adequately testing their products. The only programmes widely used within the agricultural industry which are tested externally to the firm are the payroll programmes which undergo standard testing procedures by the National Computing Council. These testing procedures built up together with the Inland Revenue and the Department of Health and Social Security ensure that all payroll programmes should produce the correct wage slips for a wide variety of cases. (Though even here agriculture has problems because of widespread use of casual labour and unusual payment in kind). Apart from this, all initial testing must be conducted internally to the firm.

It is impossible to test all the possible combinations of input messages that a programme may be subject to and some users will always be able to press the keys in such a way that the programme will be stalled. Nevertheless, software firms try to subject their products to a great range of testing procedures. In the initial specification there will be test specifications, perhaps a sample set of reports for an accounting package with a base set of data. At a later stage a number of widely different sets of data will be used with the programmes. The packages will be put through as many cycles as possible. For example, with an accounting package any new developments will be tested by running a full year's data through to see if the correct output, which is of course already known, emerges.

Each module of a programme will be tested by the programmers separately and then together with the other modules. One problem, common to all software testing, is that when a change is made to get one part of the programme working, this will have unforeseen repercussions which upset the working of the programme somewhere else. So that modules which have been successfully tested need to be constantly retested. There are aids to this process of repetitive testing. The exact keystrokes previously used in a test can be recorded and replayed so that the process of testing can be to some extent automated via testing programmes. In these testing programmes, for example, a correct version of the required output on the screen at various stages can be recorded. The testing programme can compare the current output with this correct version to see whether the changes have created further errors.

The final testing procedures are when the product is released to a few farmers before general release. This is often done in a limited geographical area local to the firm so that the farmers' experience and problems can be closely monitored. These are typically users with a long term relationship with the firm. Often they are enthusiastic computer users anxious to get the new product or the enhancement a little sooner, willing and even keen to take part in the testing process. They will be asked if they are willing to run the new version alongside the old version of the programme of the manual system, to test the new product on a live situation.

Every farmer uses the programmes in slightly different ways so there can be situations which have been overlooked by the software developers. Even after several years in operation an unusual transaction or situation will arise which the programme cannot deal with. Hence the programmes need MAINTENANCE which involves respecification of part of the software and the consequent amendments to the programmes and documentation.

2.6 General Characteristics of the Software

The Farmplan programme which is the end result of this process will tend to have the following characteristics:

1 Be menu driven. At each stage the user is faced with a screen which tells him exactly what is expected of him. A number of different choices are presented to the user and depending on his selection the appropriate processing is carried out.

2 Data entry and report generation. These are separated into different modules, so that if a manager is only interested in seeing a result he can skip through to that section.

3 Error spotting. When data is inputted the software tries to trap errors. This involves understanding the underlying agricultural logic, so that errors such as harvesting a crop which has never been sown can be eliminated.

4 Routines. All routines such as copying disks, formatting disks, erasing files etc. have been simplified on a set up disk so that the user is always operating in a familiar environment, selecting options from a menu, just as in a application programme, so that no knowledge of the operating system is required. (Normally a user is linked directly to the operating system and would be required to know the appropriate commands and how to use them with the correct syntax).

5 Page linking. This is a facility which connects the programme you are working with to the appropriate page in the manual where the user can get help and explanation about what is on the screen at the moment.

6 Help. On screen help so that pressing a function key brings up onto the screen a summary of the documentation. Programmes have reached a stage where they know precisely where the cursor is on the screen and are able to present a page or pages of help that is directly relevant to that point. More up-to-date software provides this facility and a line of help along the bottom of the screen. The ultimate intention is to replace all the documentation with on screen information. It is doubtful if many users read the manuals associated with the programmes much, if at all. Normally, it is quite a task to find your way through a manual. The less documentation required to understand a programme the better the software is.

3 THE FARMERS' DEMAND FOR COMPUTER SYSTEMS. A REVIEW

This section looks at the demand side of the market to see what information we have about the farmers' experiences with computers. There have been a number of surveys carried out on UK farmers using computers. Corbett and Perrott [1] interviewed thirty computer owning farmers in 1984. (This was as a follow up to a large scale survey of 1000 farmers about computer ownership. Incidentally this survey revealed that only five per cent of the sample farms had computers for business purposes). Overall satisfaction amongst these thirty farmers was high. Only three were dissatisfied because they felt, in retrospect, that they had bought the wrong system. The overall impression was that the benefits of the computer systems was not so much in cost or even time saving, but rather creating greater confidence that the businesses were being run efficiently because more information was readily available. Two conclusions emerged from these farmers which are especially interesting: Firstly, the software package was thought to be much more significant than differences in hardware. Especially important was a knowledge of what the software could not do. Secondly, they felt that the choice of suppliers was vital. There was a trade-off here because the farmers wanted both a local presence and the security that the firm was financially stable and not likely to go out of business. A local presence meant that problems with hardware and software would probably be solved more quickly. The farmers wanted typically a 24 or at most a 48 hour response time. However, they were also worried about long term backup from the suppliers in terms of developing new packages, enhancing existing programmes, advice, training and maintenance. They stressed that maintenance contracts were essential.

A second survey of farmers' experiences was carried out by the Agricultural Computing Team of MAFF [2]. They interviewed one hundred and seventy four farmers using computers. These farms tended to be large, with three quarters of them having four or more full time staff. When considering buying a system the main criteria mentioned by farmers were the overall suitability of the output for the farms' requirements, its clarity and style, the level of service and support offered by the suppliers and their general impression of the supplying companies. One complaint which arose commonly before purchase, was that the companies were less keen to find out the farms' actual requirements than to sell their own package.

Some problems arose during the introduction of the computer systems onto the farms. Twenty six per cent had to have a complete change in their systems of enterprise recording. A major complaint was that the systems were too complex and took a long time to set up. The manuals were often regarded as giving no help. There were complaints about lack of training in the new systems from the suppliers. There were also some staff problems experienced with seven per cent of the farms reporting that staff left because they did not like the new systems. However, after the introduction there was a "reasonable" level of satisfaction with the systems. Two thirds of the sample were happy that the software had met their expectations. The main benefit perceived from the systems was that more and more detailed information was available to help in management decisions.

Some indication of US farmers' attitudes towards microcomputers emerges from a survey of Extension Service users conducted by Novak and Stegelin [3]. Ninety three per cent of respondents expressed themselves satisfied with their systems. Among the seven per cent who were dissatisfied the two main causes of this dissatisfaction were an inability to find the software that met their needs and inadequate software documentation.

Heinrichs [4] looked in detail at one particular application of agricultural software - dairy herd management and ration formulation software, numerically the second most important application of agricultural software, after accounting and financial packages. Twenty five different dairy programmes were evaluated by three testers with dairy farming backgrounds. The criteria for evaluating the programmes were:

a) Ease of data entry;
b) Usefulness of output;
c) Ease of error handling;
d) Documentation.

The second stage in the evaluation was to build up a checklist of items that it would be beneficial to have in the dairy package. The idea to produce a type of consumer guide to programmes, listing exactly what each package is capable of, what input data it can handle and the output data it provides.

Some general conclusions can be tentatively drawn from the information we have available about farmers' demands in this market. We must remember always that current farm computer users are not representative of the main body of farmers who do not use computers at all. They tend to be from larger farms and possibly those who have a personal interest in modern technology.

For the computer users price was not a major consideration in their choice of system, but for the non users, price - a feeling that systems were still too expensive for them - played a major role in their decision not to buy.

The major objective for users was to obtain software which would produce useful output for decision making on the farm. Just what this useful output is, however, varies from user to user. Some users of agricultural software are specialist advisers and consultants. They would like highly sophisticated programmes to be able to analyse the businesses of their clients in detail. Most farmers require much simpler output and reports, often just to keep basic track of farm accounts. A software package can never satisfy all users unlike tailor made systems. It is for this reason we must be doubtful of such approaches to evaluating software packages as that of Heinrichs, where a long checklist of possible items the programme might record or report on is produced. Presumably the programme which is able to include the most items on the list is judged to be the best. But for the majority of farmers i.e those who don't use any existing computer system, the best might well be a very basic, easily understandable programme that produced the handful of items which were most important to them.

A very important objective for farmers is the maintainability of the system once it has been purchased. It is important that hardware and software problems can be quickly rectified by the supplier, that advice and training are available. This desire is nothing to do with the software per se, but the other services provided by the computing firm. The software might be perfect, but without the long term backup provided by a reliable firm the farmer might find himself in a difficult position in a short space of time, especially in view of the rapidly changing nature of the computer industry. For example, many farmers bought Apple Computers in the early 1980's. Now, in a world dominated by IBM and IBM compatible PC's, Farmplan maintains all those systems based on Apples for farmers it has a long term relationship with, updating their programmes and ensuring that the new software can run on the old machines.

Thus meeting the objectives of users of agricultural software inevitably involves some trade-off. The desire for a secure long term backup is incompatible with buying from the cheapest source. Small companies are able to offer low prices partly because they do not have the large training, maintenance and advice departments of the larger established companies. Similarly in the software itself the desire for a complete perfect product to satisfy all users, including the most sophisticated, is in conflict with keeping the product simple and transparent.

4 CONCLUSIONS

The problem of "approving software products" can be seen as part of an old debate in economics about consumer protection. Many economists and politicians have argued in a wide number of markets that suppliers will take advantage of the consumers' lack of specialist knowledge and sell them inappropriate, overpriced or inferior goods. Therefore, it is necessary to intervene in the market and regulate it in some way to protect the consumer.

Rehman and Esslemont [5] discussed the problem of approving agricultural software products. They suggested that concerned advisory bodies and pressure groups such as the Agricultural Development and Advisory Service of the Ministry of Agriculture, the Milk Marketing Board and the National Union of Farmers combine to perform a testing and evaluation service for the users. There are some problems with this proposal apart from the practical ones of setting up the testing organisation. External testing might delay the introduction of new products and innovations. Secondly, as suggested previously, there are problems in testing how well a product meets users' needs. Users are very different in their level of expertise and expectation. The testers are likely to be experts and might be expected to prefer the perfect "all singing, all dancing" programme rather than a simple product which satisfies most farmers' needs.

A market system tends to give rise to other mechanisms which help the consumer to make his choice amongst a welter of competing goods. Firms have an interest in building up their brand names. As we have argued, Farmplan, the company used as an example, sees it in its own long term good to build up a reputation as a reliable supplier of products which the farmer really wants. This reputation is possibly one of its main assets enabling it to charge higher prices than smaller less well known firms.

From our brief look at agricultural software packages the market seems to be functioning well. Most consumers expressed themselves as satisfied with the products they have purchased. There are no high barriers to entry in the industry so that there is a continuous entry of new firms, products and ideas. The market has a dominant firm, Farmplan, but there is no danger of it exercising monopoly power because of the ease of entry not only of new firms, but of imported products and other software firms which do not currently produce agricultural software. Farmplan has made great efforts to provide the products that consumers want because it is in its own long term interest to do so.

REFERENCES

[1] Corbett and Perrott. "The Computer as a Farm Management Tool". British Institute of Management. Centre of Management in Agriculture. 1984.

[2] Agricultural Computing Team. Ministry of Agriculture, Fisheries and Food. ADAS. "Computing on the Farm". 1985.

[3] Novak J L and Stegelin F R. "US Farmers' Attitudes Towards Microcomputer Uses". Computers and Electronics in Agriculture, No. 3, 1989.

[4] Heinrichs A J. "Evaluating Dairy Herd Management and Ration Formulation Microcomputer Software in the United States". Computers and Electronics in Agriculture, No. 3, 1989.

[5] Rehman T and Esslemont R J. "Computers in Farming". Department of Agriculture and Horticulture. University of Reading. 1981.